THE CANADIAN FEDERAL ELECTION OF 2021

MCGILL-QUEEN'S/BRIAN MULRONEY INSTITUTE OF GOVERNMENT STUDIES IN LEADERSHIP, PUBLIC POLICY, AND GOVERNANCE

Series editor: Donald E. Abelson

Titles in this series address critical issues facing Canada at home and abroad and the efforts policymakers at all levels of government have made to address a host of complex and multifaceted policy concerns. Books in this series receive financial support from the Brian Mulroney Institute of Government at St Francis Xavier University; in keeping with the institute's mandate, these studies explore how leaders involved in key policy initiatives arrived at their decisions and what lessons can be learned. Combining rigorous academic analysis with thoughtful recommendations, this series compels readers to think more critically about how and why elected officials make certain policy choices, and how, in concert with other stakeholders, they can better navigate an increasingly complicated and crowded marketplace of ideas.

1 Braver Canada
Shaping Our Destiny in a Precarious World
Derek H. Burney and Fen Osler Hampson

2 The Canadian Federal Election of 2019
Edited by Jon H. Pammett and Christopher Dornan

3 Keeping Canada Running
Infrastructure and the Future of Governance in a Pandemic World
Edited by G. Bruce Doern, Christopher Stoney, and Robert Hilton

4 The Age of Consequence
The Ordeals of Public Policy in Canada
Charles McMillan

5 Government
Have Presidents and Prime Ministers Misdiagnosed the Patient?
Donald J. Savoie

6 Cyber-Threats to Canadian Democracy
Edited by Holly Ann Garnett and Michael Pal

7 The Canadian Federal Election of 2021
Edited by Jon H. Pammett and Christopher Dornan

The Canadian Federal Election of 2021

EDITED BY JON H. PAMMETT
AND CHRISTOPHER DORNAN

McGill-Queen's University Press
Montreal & Kingston • London • Chicago

ISBN 978-0-2280-1381-5 (cloth)
ISBN 978-0-2280-1382-2 (paper)
ISBN 978-0-2280-1383-9 (ePDF)
ISBN 978-0-2280-1384-6 (ePUB)

Legal deposit third quarter 2022
Bibliothèque nationale du Québec

This book has been published with the help of a grant from the Faculty of Public Affairs, Carleton University.

Funded by the Government of Canada | Financé par le gouvernement du Canada | Canada

Canada Council for the Arts | Conseil des arts du Canada

We acknowledge the support of the Canada Council for the Arts.
Nous remercions le Conseil des arts du Canada de son soutien.

Library and Archives Canada Cataloguing in Publication

Title: The Canadian federal election of 2021 / edited by Jon H. Pammett and Christopher Dornan.
Names: Pammett, Jon H., 1944– editor. | Dornan, Chris, editor.
Series: McGill-Queen's/Brian Mulroney Institute of Government studies in leadership, public policy, and governance ; 7.
Description: Series statement: McGill-Queen's/Brian Mulroney Institute of Government studies in leadership, public policy, and governance ; 7 | Includes bibliographical references and index.
Identifiers: Canadiana (print) 20220219958 | Canadiana (ebook) 20220220107 | ISBN 9780228013815 (cloth) | ISBN 9780228013822 (paper) | ISBN 9780228013839 (ePDF) | ISBN 9780228013846 (ePUB)
Subjects: LCSH: Canada. Parliament—Elections, 2021. | LCSH: Elections—Canada—History—21st century. | LCSH: Voting—Canada.
Classification: LCC JL193.C3588 2022 | DDC 324.97107/4—dc23

This book was typeset in 10.5/13 Sabon.

Contents

Tables and Figures | vii

Preface | xi

1 An Election Waiting to Happen | 3
Christopher Dornan

2 The Out-of-Control Election and the Frustrated Liberals | 14
Brooke Jeffrey

3 The Conservative Campaign:
Erin O'Toole and the Conservative Dilemma | 36
Faron Ellis

4 Jagmeet Versus Justin:
Leadership and the NDP's Political Marketing | 60
David McGrane

5 The Bloc Québécois as a Safe Bet | 84
Éric Montigny

6 A Climate of Chaos: How the Election Unfolded for the Environment and the Greens | 105
Sarah Everts and Susan Harada

7 Polling in the 2021 Federal Election | 127
Éric Grenier

8 The Media: The Narratives that
Defined the Mainstream Election Coverage | 148
Brett Popplewell

9 Regionalized Campaign Communication:
Facebook Advertising in the 2021 Federal Election | 171
Andrew J.A. Mattan and Tamara A. Small

10 Still Not There: Diversity and Inclusion
in the 2021 Canadian Election Campaign | 192
Erin Tolley, Aneurin Bosley, and Nana aba Duncan

11 Progress or the Status Quo?
Indigenous Peoples, Participation, and Representation | 220
Chadwick Cowie and Liam Midzain-Gobin

12 Immigrant Voting in the 2021 Canadian Federal Election | 246
Stephen White

13 Not Kids Anymore: Millennials and the 2021 Election | 270
David Coletto

14 Canada Votes in a COVID Election | 295
Harold D. Clarke, Thomas J. Scotto, and Marianne C. Stewart

15 The Elusive Liberal Dynasty and the
Continuation of Minority Government | 322
Lawrence LeDuc and Jon H. Pammett

Appendix: Results of the 2021 Canadian Federal Election | 343

Contributors | 345

Tables and Figures

TABLES

4.1 Percentage coverage of themes in federal NDP press releases by week | 76
4.2 NDP electoral results in 1962–2008, 2011, 2015, 2019, and 2021 | 79
7.1 Final surveys of all national polling firms by total error | 138
7.2 Average overestimation (+) and underestimation (–) of each party's support in the final polls of the campaign | 139
9.1 Number of Facebook ads by party | 179
9.2 Aggregated region summary of Facebook ads by party | 180
9.3 Number of regionally dominated Facebook ads by party | 181
9.4 Number and percentage of pan-national ads by party | 185
10.1 Candidate race and indigeneity, 2008–21 | 195
10.2 Candidate gender, 2008–21 | 196
10.3 Candidate gender, race, and indigeneity, 2021 | 198
12.1 Vote by birthplace, 2021 (%) | 248
12.2 Most important issues by birthplace, 2021 (%) | 249
12.3 Leader evaluations by birthplace, 2021 (%) | 250
12.4 Party preference by country of origin, 2013 (%) | 258
12.5 Estimating the impact of the immigrant vote on seats won, 2021 | 262
13.1 Millennial vote from 2011 to 2019 | 275
13.2 Economic impact of the COVID-19 pandemic | 278
13.3 Emotional impact of the COVID-19 pandemic | 278
13.4 Federal party leader image: millennials vs. other Canadians | 288
13.5 Vote choice in 2021: millennials vs. other voters | 291

14.1 Changes in probability of voting for various political parties associated with changes in statistically significant predictors | 308
14.2 The flow of the vote, 2019–21 | 314
15.1 Percentages of total vote in four elections | 326

FIGURES

4.1 Percentage coverage of themes in NDP English TV ads (2021 election) | 73
4.2 Percentage coverage of themes in NDP French TV ads (2021 election) | 74
4.3 Percentage coverage of themes in Singh's TikTok (2021 election) | 75
5.1 Léger polls, Quebec only (2021 election) | 86
5.2 Party election promises in areas of constitutional jurisdiction, 2021 | 93
7.1 Polling by Léger during the 2021 federal election | 140
7.2 Polling by EKOS Research during the 2021 federal election | 141
9.1 Example of 2021 Facebook ad and summary data | 175
9.2 Example of a regionally dominated Facebook ad | 182
10.1 Candidate diversity by party and district competitiveness, 2021 | 201
10.2 Proportion of MPs by race, indigeneity, and gender, 2008–21 | 202
10.3 Proportion of MPs from each party by race, indigeneity, and gender, 2021 | 203
12.1 Liberal Party vote by birthplace, 1965–2021 | 252
12.2 Ratio of Liberal Party support, immigrants vs. born in Canada | 253
12.3 Percentage of immigrant arrivals from ALA countries, quarterly data, 1955–2013 | 255
12.4 Estimated Liberal vote share by the immigrant population in electoral districts, 2021 | 263
13.1 Millennial generation share of the electorate and share of voters since 2004 | 273

13.2 Millennials: estimated voter turnout and number of electors since 2004 | 274
13.3 Federal government approval rating among millennials | 279
13.4 Top policy priorities for Canadian millennials (June 2021) | 280
13.5 Net federal government approval on specific policy areas (June 2021) | 281
13.6 Top two issues impacting vote choice at the start of the 2021 election campaign | 284
13.7 Millennial vote intention during the 2021 Canadian federal election | 290
14.1 Evaluations of the state of the Canadian economy, 2011–21 | 297
14.2 Most important issues facing the country, 2021 | 298
14.3 Party best able to handle all most important issues, 2021 | 298
14.4 Party best able to handle five most frequently mentioned important issues, 2021 | 300
14.5 Feelings about party leaders in 2015, 2019, and 2021 | 302
14.6 Party leader traits: Justin Trudeau, Erin O'Toole, and Jagmeet Singh, 2021 | 303
14.7 Federal party identification, 2011–21 | 305
14.8 Parties' vote shares in the 2019 and 2021 federal elections | 313
14.9 How switching from the PPC to the CPC would have affected parties' seat shares in the 2021 federal election | 316
15.1 Feelings towards Justin Trudeau and the Liberal Party | 323
15.2 Turnout (%) in Canadian federal elections, 1965–2021 | 330
15.3 Estimated voting by age groups in the 2019 and 2021 federal elections | 331
15.4 Impressions of Justin Trudeau, 2021 | 336
15.5 Best performing leader in the election campaign | 337
15.6 Preferred prime minister | 338

Preface

The editors first and foremost thank our contributing authors, not only for agreeing to write their respective chapters but for the speed with which they did so, and for their good cheer and patience in handling the editors' queries.

On behalf of all the contributors to this work, the editors would like to thank Prof. Jonathan Malloy, The Hon. Dick and Ruth Bell Chair for the Study of Canadian Parliamentary Democracy at Carleton University, and the Department of Political Science which hosts the chair, for financial support in bringing this volume to press. We would also like to thank the Department of Political Science Research Assistance Fund for support that allowed us to secure the editorial services of Micaal Ahmed, without whom we could not have assembled and processed the manuscript with such dispatch. We are especially indebted to Micaal for his conscientious work, much of which was conducted while he was subject to the incessant blaring of truck horns as protestors occupied the parliamentary precinct and downtown core of Ottawa, and Erin O'Toole was ousted as leader of the Conservative Party by his caucus colleagues. David Coletto, of Abacus Data, kindly allowed access to a postelection survey for several chapters in this book, and substantially contributed to our ability to thoroughly analyse the results.

We also thank the three anonymous reviewers who took the time to read the manuscript over the Christmas holidays and delivered helpful criticism and comments so swiftly. The completed book is that much stronger for their insights and suggestions.

We are most grateful to our editor at McGill-Queen's University Press, Emily Andrew, and the rest of the team at the press, for giving this work their professional attention and enthusiastic support, and for making its publication a priority. Thanks to Neil Erickson and Louise Piper for their excellent work in compiling and copyediting the manuscript.

Finally, we would like to pay tribute to Harold Clarke, who died suddenly as this book was nearing completion. With substantial research awards from the Social Sciences and Humanities Research Council of Canada, from the Economic and Social Research Council UK, from the National Science Foundation US, and from other sponsors; with twenty-one books with Cambridge University Press, Oxford University Press, and other publishers; and with multiple articles in many major journals, Harold was a major figure in election analysis. He wrote about the contingent nature of public support in a representative democracy, and of elections and the performance-based evaluations that many people bring to their electoral choices in America, Britain, Canada, and Taiwan, and other democracies. And, with research methodology expertise and extraordinary teaching skills, Harold Clarke significantly helped students to learn and to use multilevel modeling, survey research methodology, structural equation modeling, and time series analysis to address interesting and important research questions. We will miss him enormously.

Jon H. Pammett and Christopher Dornan
Ottawa, February 2022

THE CANADIAN FEDERAL ELECTION OF 2021

1

An Election Waiting to Happen

Christopher Dornan

The theme of the 2021 Canadian election, it was universally agreed, was why have an election at all?

The Liberal government, although a minority in the House, was in no immediate danger of being toppled. While the administration of vaccines against the COVID-19 virus was proceeding apace (at the time the election was called, 78.6 per cent of Canadians aged twelve or older had received at least one dose[1]), the country was still in the grip of the pandemic, which had deformed public life and placed inordinate strain on the economy, healthcare systems, public services, and the mental health and well-being of the entire population. And the pandemic notwithstanding, the election was called in the doldrums of late summer, when traditionally the electorate is at its least politically attentive.

Since the election was held at the instigation of the governing Liberals, it fell to them to justify what amounted to a further imposition on the civic responsibilities of a public that for eighteen months had been soldiering through mask mandates, school closures, travel restrictions, capacity limits on indoor gathering, periodically shuttered gyms, bars, restaurants, churches, theatres, concert halls, sports arenas, and other venues of social interaction. For a year and a half they had been told that congregation was the enemy of the public good. Now they were being told that a mass exercise in collective deliberation – a form of political congregation – was essential to the national interest, so much so that it outweighed the burdens, risks, and costs of forcing the vote.

In the months preceding the election, the Conservatives had been doing their best to frustrate the minority government's agenda, stalling passage of bills that would ban so-called conversion therapy, reform the *Broadcasting Act*, and set targets for the reduction of greenhouse gas emissions. In June, Liberal House leader Pablo Rodriguez accused the Conservatives of resorting to "complex procedural tricks" to obstruct the work of the House.[2] Finance Minister Chrystia Freeland said the "COVID consensus" that united the parties at the outset of the pandemic had collapsed, and that it was "increasingly just not possible to get the business of the country done."[3] For his part, the prime minister talked of a dysfunctional "level of obstructionism and toxicity in the House."[4]

But even if the Conservatives were using procedural measures to thwart the will of the government, that is the role of the official opposition – to oppose policies with which they disagree. For the government to trigger an election on the grounds that it is being prevented from getting its way smacks of petulance, if not a political tantrum. And the fact that most Canadians were satisfied with the way the federal government had so far managed the pandemic response indicated that the public did not share the Liberal Party's exasperation. People had gotten on with their jobs and made the best of things for a year and a half under the most trying circumstances; surely their political leaders could be expected to do the same?

So, the Liberals pitched the necessity of the election on what they proclaimed was their need for a mandate to continue management of the pandemic and to implement economic recovery measures – a slender reed, at best. It amounted to asking for authorization to keep doing what the government was already doing. The failure, or inability, of the Liberals to provide a persuasive justification for the election was not just a messaging miscue. It became the absence through which the election was publicly received and by which it would be remembered. Like the insidious blanket pardon given to Milady de Winter by Richelieu in *The Three Musketeers* ("By my order and for the good of the state, the bearer has done what has been done"), the warrant for the election was the election itself. And without a compelling argument for why an election at this moment was in the public interest, the Liberals invited charges of opportunism: that it was in their interests – the interests of a political faction, not the interests of the nation as a whole – to send the country to the polls. They called the election for no other reason than that they liked their chances of winning a majority.

United in their determination to prevent that from happening, if in nothing else, their opponents opened the campaign with the complaint that the election was unnecessary, especially so given the pandemic, and closed with the same complaint. It was, they said, a cynical ploy on the part of the Liberals to capitalize on whatever political goodwill the government had garnered through its pandemic management in order to gain unchecked power. As Brett Popplewell points out in chapter 8, this also became the master narrative of the news media, shared alike by left-leaning and right-wing outlets that would have agreed on little else: the election was presumptuous, self-serving, and even as a gambit ill-considered (the latter especially so when Liberal fortunes appeared to wane in the first two weeks of the campaign while momentum apparently shifted to the Conservatives). Since the news media are the major means by which the public is politically informed, these were the terms by which the public was invited to apprehend the 2021 election. This is not to say that the news media dictated or determined public understanding. It is part of the job of journalists to register and record the mood of the moment, and they certainly take their cues from the greater public. But the fact of the election as an exercise in political ambition over the public good was affirmed and reaffirmed in a feedback loop between the media and their audiences. As Éric Grenier points out in chapter 7, on public opinion surveying during the election, a Léger poll conducted after the election found that 80 per cent of Canadians – including 60 per cent of those who voted for the party that had called it – thought the election was a waste of time and money and should never have been held.

It was a verdict seemingly only confirmed by the final tally, in which little changed. The Liberals won three more seats than in the 2019 election, for a total of 160, and were once again returned as a minority government. The Conservatives lost two seats for a total of 119. The Bloc Québécois (BQ) were unchanged at thirty-two seats. The New Democratic Party (NDP) won a single additional seat for a total of twenty-five, while the Greens lost a seat for a total of two. As Chantal Hébert, political columnist for the *Toronto Star* and *L'acualité*, quipped on CBC TV on election night as the results became known, this was an election that "nobody wanted, and nobody got what they wanted."

In some quarters, the fact that next to nothing changed in the seating arrangements of the House was taken as evidence that the election was not only unnecessary but that it did not matter. Some went further, charging that the election put needless strain on the political union, exacerbating division and inflaming animosities (it provided a platform for the People's Party to normalize its extremism; it stirred up conflict between Quebec and English Canada), as though an election is an inherently hazardous thing, to be used sparingly and handled gingerly, rather than a mechanism necessary to liberal democracy for the expression and contestation of political difference.

But of course, as every thoughtful commentator recognized, all elections matter. As for the accusation that this one was a cynical ploy on the part of the Liberals, it was certainly a ploy, but that does not make it cynical. All partisan politics is a series of ploys and counter-ploys, manoeuvres contrived to best one's opponents; and if the Liberals' goal in calling this election was to consolidate their hold on power, all partisan politics is conducted with the aim of seizing and exercising power (or frustrating the will of those who are in power). Just because opposition parties do not want an election does not mean the decision to call one is underhanded or illegitimate.

So, for all that the news media framed the election as uncalled-for, this was not the mindset of partisan insiders, whatever their political stripe. To them, a minority government is just an election waiting to happen. By late spring and early summer 2021, in the estimation of party strategists, an election was clearly on its way. Their opponents sized up the circumstances and recognized that it would be altogether surprising if the Liberals were not to call an election. The government was riding a wave of popularity that surely could not be sustained – some scandal or unforeseen development, or just the onset of winter, would bring those polling numbers down. The vaccine rollout was going well. From the one-shot spring heading into the two-dose summer, people were feeling less anxious. And although collective nerves were still frayed by the pandemic, summer weather was a salve. People could have backyard barbecues and socialize on outdoor patios of restaurants and bars. Softball leagues had resumed. Parents could take their kids to the lake and the beach, to swimming pools and splash pads.

Calling an early election might have been a gamble, and a risky one at that, but both the Liberals and the opposition parties well knew that, for the Liberals, it was better to control the timing of the vote than allow the opposition parties to engineer the fall of the minority government. That was the thing for the Liberals to guard against. In the calculus of the Liberal strategists, therefore, an election at this time was most decidedly called-for, if only for reasons of expediency. Because in the theatre of partisan politics, expediency is not a pejorative, it is an imperative. So, those in the election preparedness and planning echelons of the major parties – and even the minor parties – knew this election was coming. To the best of their abilities, they had worked on their fundraising and put their electoral apparatus in place. It would have been incompetent not to.

The other parties claimed to be shocked, shocked at the calculated arrogance of the Liberals in calling the election, but this was a posture and a countergambit. Nobody in any of the opposition party campaign engine rooms was caught by surprise. They would have preferred to manage the timing of the election on their terms, but they had been preparing for this.

The seat count results did not much change the balance of power in the Commons. (If the Liberals did not beat the other parties, does that mean the Conservatives did not lose to the Liberals?) Still, below the surface of what seemed like stasis, the election revealed things. As Brooke Jeffrey points out in chapter 2, the total seat count of the parties may have been near identical to the composition of the previous parliament, but more than forty seats changed hands. There was a measure of political flux. The Liberals took two seats in Alberta, a significant development.

How the election turned out – that the Liberals were returned in a minority government – is plain for all to see. But why it turned out the way it did, and what that tells us about party politics, political representation, and policy priorities, is not so plain. Together, the chapters in this volume explain the election by examining what is not so plain. They are works of investigation and interpretation. The effort is to make the election reveal itself.

In addition to analyses of the parties, the media, the pollsters, and voting patterns, this volume trains attention on diversity and difference within the electorate and considers how the partisan machinery of electoral politics may court or ignore select communities that together make up the collective it exists to govern. Regionality is a longstanding marker of political difference (people who live in

Alberta, for example, look at the country and the world quite differently from people who live in Quebec; they get politically exercised about different things), and regionality is a motif that runs through the volume. Andrew Mattan and Tamara Small, in chapter 9, look specifically at how the parties used Facebook as an advertising tool, employing its microtargeting capabilities to tailor messages to voters along regional lines. The volume also features chapters on Indigenous issues and voting, the political characteristics of the millennial generation, the composition of the immigrant population and how its members may lean politically, and diversity of racial and ethnic representation in what has long been a decidedly nondiverse political theatre.

The volume does not include a chapter devoted to the People's Party of Canada (PPC), though the fact of the party and its electoral performance feature in any number of the chapters. The PPC failed to qualify for inclusion in the leaders' debates and once again failed to win a single seat, but the party will likely merit closer examination going forward, not only because it garnered more than twice the popular vote in this election than the Greens (4.94 per cent to 2.33 per cent – although as Éric Grenier points out in chapter 7, some polls toward the end of the campaign overestimated support for the PPC by as much as twice its eventual vote share), but because it gave voice to a strain of political sentiment notable for its vehemence. Understanding the wellsprings of the rancour the PPC represents is essential if one is to fully map the Canadian political topography.

A theme throughout the chapters that follow is the hostility that appeared to course through the election. Politicians and journalists alike seemed taken aback by the hair-trigger hatred directed toward them. Partisan politics has always been a perverse mixture of love and hate. On the one hand, voters have to be courted, to be won over, to be persuaded to plight their troth at the ballot box, and so the parties address the electorate in the language of seduction. At the same time, the parties address one another with white-hot uncompromising belligerence – the language of vendetta. Question Period in the House of Commons is like a permanent sitting of divorce court, where the point is not to negotiate political difference but to spit accusations and publicly despise one another, as viciously as the rules of parliamentary conduct will allow. It was rich, perhaps, to hear politicians express shock and dismay at the animosity of the public, given the example they set by making parliament into a public theatre of perpetual anger, no matter how much of this is playacting. Journalism, too, features a pundit class of combative personas whose quick-fire readings of the political scene – especially in the punchy milieu of social media, where seizing attention and provoking reaction is what matters – are often couched in mocking and derisive terms, a form of political heckling. Small wonder, then, that a vocal minority of the public take their cues from that example and respond to the media with savage contempt and worse. The shame is that it need not be so, even among committed partisan opponents. The podcast *The Curse of Politics* – featuring David Herle and Scott Reid, former Liberal Party operatives, and Jenni Byrne, former deputy chief of staff to Prime Minister Stephen Harper, along with weekly guests from the partisan arena – is particularly popular among the politically attentive and the chatterati. Much of its appeal is precisely the absence of venom and snark. The hosts and guests talk about politics in a way that is informed and informative, relaxed, wry, clever, and funny. People who truly detest one another over their political differences cannot josh with one another.

As to the specifics of the 2021 election – how and why it unfolded as it did – the chapters to follow unpack the salient issues and trace the contours of the campaign, each chapter not only standing alone but shedding light on the others. Brooke Jeffrey in chapter 2 shows why the Liberals thought a majority was within reach: they believed they were well ahead of their rivals on top priorities for voters (healthcare, climate change, and COVID economic recovery), while they were twenty points ahead in the polls on the perceived ability to manage the pandemic, surely the central governance issue of the day. In chapter 14, however, Harold Clarke, Thomas Scotto, and Marianne Stewart argue that this only concealed a vulnerability for the Liberals. Some 57 per cent of Canadians judged the country's economic performance negatively, and for those who believed that economic management and dealing with the menace of inflation were the utmost priorities, the Conservatives far outstripped the Liberals.

In the end, that was not sufficient for the Conservative Party to unseat the Liberals, but as Faron Ellis asks in chapter 3, which Conservative Party was in the running? In an effort to broaden its appeal in the hope of making gains in Ontario and Quebec, the Conservatives adopted policies – or, at least, the stance of policies – that angered some stalwart supporters, while the activism of social conservatives within the ranks allowed the Conservatives' enemies to portray the party as more strident than it was, and too strident for the new voters it was trying to reach. The result was a loss of support in British Columbia and Alberta, while the hoped-for gains in Ontario and Quebec failed to materialize. Taking into consideration how the demographics of the country are changing, the chapter suggests that "the long-term math is not in their [Conservatives'] favour."

Chapter 14 also points out the importance of leaders' images to voting decisions, and David McGrane in chapter 4 examines how the NDP campaign strategy was built around its leader, who was more popular than his party. The intent was to use the leader to try to win more seats by appealing to soft Liberals disenchanted with Justin Trudeau, while incumbent NDP MPs would be expected to hold their seats. But although the NDP gained vote share in Alberta and British Columbia, this was not enough for the party to take a single Liberal-held seat. In chapter 15, Jon Pammett and Lawrence LeDuc explain the "strategic configuration" that worked against the NDP but in favour of the Bloc Québécois. Canada's single member plurality electoral system – commonly known as first-past-the-post – disadvantages national third parties, which typically achieve a seat share far less than their share of the popular vote, but rewards regional parties such as the BQ, whose support is concentrated in a geographic pocket.

In chapter 5, Éric Montigny demonstrates how the geographic, cultural, and linguistic pocket of Quebec viewed the election through a prism all but incommensurable with how the contest was seen elsewhere in the country. At the outset of the campaign, the Bloc languished in the polls, partly because it was historically associated with the Parti Québécois, whose sovereigntist aspirations were out of favour, while the provincial government of the Coalition Avenir de Quebec (CAQ) remained highly popular after three years in office. But Liberal and NDP policies that were popular in the rest of Canada – proposals for a national childcare program, federal standards for long-term care facilities, a national approach to affordable housing – stirred support for the Bloc, because these were seen in Quebec as encroaching on the jurisdiction of the National Assembly, and therefore on the autonomy of Quebec. For a significant portion of Quebecers casting a vote in the federal election, it was the autonomy of their province that was paramount.

Even amid the pressing concerns of the pandemic and the economic damage it had wrought, Éric Grenier points out that climate change remained a forefront concern for Canadians. In another election, this might have been to the benefit of the Green Party. But as Sarah Everts and Susan Harada observe in chapter 6, "gone were the days when the Greens could claim ownership (and moral authority)" on the issue. The environment has become a matter that all the major parties prominently promised to address. (The inclusion of carbon pricing in the Conservative platform was one of the policy measures that angered many traditional Conservative supporters.) Chapter 6 provides a valuable comparison and assessment of the major parties' respective platforms on the environment. Election campaigns are also stress tests of parties' coherence; the chapter demonstrates how internal turmoil shredded the Greens.

Millennials – those born between 1980 and 2000 – are the most racially and ethnically diverse generation in Canadian history, David Coletto points out in chapter 13, and the pandemic had a greater impact on them in the form of job disruptions, lost income, and emotional stress. And yet overall they maintained a positive outlook. In June 2021, Coletto reports, 62 per cent of millennials described the state of the Canadian economy as "good." They were more inclined to support the Liberals because they saw the party as better at managing the issues that millennials prioritized: climate change, healthcare, and managing the pandemic. They even saw the Liberals as better positioned to address concerns over taxes and the cost of living, in contrast to the findings reported in chapter 14, which show that most Canadians judged the Conservatives best placed to manage the economy.

Together, chapters 10, 11, and 12 point up the gulf that remains still between the lived experience of minority communities in Canada and the political will to place their concerns and interests in the forefront of policy priorities. As the summer of 2021 began, evidence came to light of the unmarked graves of some two hundred Indigenous children on the grounds of the Kamloops Indian Residential School in BC, on the lands of the Tk'emlúps te Secwépemc First Nation – the first of other such discoveries to come. It was a searing reminder of the cruelty visited upon Indigenous peoples by institutions of the Canadian state and their proxies, and it shamed every Canadian possessed of a conscience. And yet, while the various parties all promised action on reconciliation and measures specific to Indigenous peoples in their platforms, over the course of the election Indigenous concerns and issues were hardly prominent in either party pronouncements or news coverage, with the odd consequence, as Chadwick Cowie and Liam Midzgain-Gobin point out in chapter 11, that the major media organizations eventually came to report "on the lack of major media coverage of Indigenous issues in the campaign."

New Canadians and immigration were also comparatively overlooked in the parties' electoral discourse, despite the fact that immigrants are a sizeable bloc of the electorate. The parties all court new voters to expand their bases. New voters (those who have never voted before) are mostly found in two (overlapping) pools: people who have never voted because they were too young to do so in the previous election, or because they were not yet citizens. In the decade between 2011 and 2021, 2.75 million immigrants settled in Canada.[5] And as a group, Stephen White observes in chapter 12, immigrants are more favourably disposed to the Liberals than the other parties, despite the fact that they are eleven percentage points more likely to rank the economy as one of their top three issues than native-born Canadians (a finding, again, at odds with the fact that overall people who rank the economy as a top issue are more likely to favour the Conservatives). The leaning of immigrants toward the Liberals is more pronounced among Asian, Latin American, and African arrivals, most of whom are racialized minorities, and their share of the immigrant population is growing. And yet, White points out, even though their votes are crucial to outcomes in local races and the larger election, campaigns pay little attention specifically to immigrant communities. Immigrant support for the Liberals should be good news for the party, but in an echo of Faron Ellis' suggestion that the long-term math does not favour the Conservatives, White wonders whether the support of immigrant Canadians for the Liberals might not simply mask an underlying weakness in the party's broader electoral appeal.

In chapter 10, similarly, Erin Tolley, Aneurin Bosley, and Nana aba Duncan find a gulf between the political rhetoric on diversity and representation and how the parties actually conducted themselves. Their tabulations show that in the 2021 election all the parties fielded a larger proportion of racialized candidates, a record number of Indigenous candidates, and all but the Greens fielded more women candidates. And yet, they point out, no party prioritized issues relating to equity and diversity, and the roster of candidates who won election means that the 44th Canadian Parliament remains predominantly male and white: the nation's political representatives do not themselves represent the range of identities and difference that comprise the Canada of 2021. It is not that the parties ignore issues of race and diversity, but that most parties "have mastered diversity rhetoric."

All elections are punishing to the parties that contest them, win or lose. They exhaust party coffers and party workers alike. They tax the attention and the patience of the electorate. Once they are over, there is little appetite or energy to repeat the experience anytime soon. In the short run, none of the parties will want to trigger a return to the campaign trail. But because they failed to win a majority, once again the Liberals will be obliged to secure the support of other parties to maintain the confidence of the House, and historically the capacity of political opponents to effect workable compromises in the Westminster system only lasts so long. The brute fact is that any minority government is just another election waiting to happen.

NOTES

1 "COVID-19 vaccination in Canada," Government of Canada, last updated 16 July 2021, https://health-infobase.canada.ca/COVID-19/vaccination-coverage/archive/2021-07-16/.

2 Arvin Joaquin, "Liberals Accuse Tories of Stalling Progress on Key Legislation," *National Observer*, 10 July 2021, https://www.nationalobserver.com/2021/06/10/news/liberal-house-leader-conservatives-blocking-legislation.

3 Ian Austen, "Why Did Justin Trudeau Call for an Early Election?" *New York Times*, 20 September 2021, https://www.nytimes.com/2021/09/20/world/canada/justin-trudeau-why-early-election.html.

4 Stephanie Taylor, "'Toxicity' and 'Obstructionism': Trudeau Tells Canadians Parliament Is Dysfunctional," 22 June 2021, https://www.thestar.com/politics/2021/06/22/toxicity-and-obstructionism-trudeau-tells-canadians-parliament-is-dysfunctional.html.

5 "Number of Immigrants in Canada from 2000 to 2021," Statista, published 17 November 2021, https://www.statista.com/statistics/443063/number-of-immigrants-in-canada/.

2

The Out-of-Control Election and the Frustrated Liberals

Brooke Jeffrey

Although the September 2021 federal election returned another Liberal minority with a very similar seat count to the previous election of 2019, the results hardly represented a return to the status quo. Moreover, the actual thirty-six-day campaign was anything but typical. This was an election in which unexpected external events, and extraordinary circumstances such as a global pandemic, altered both the normal conduct of the campaign and its outcome. Change took place quite dramatically throughout the election period, derailing the Liberal campaign from its intended course.

The status quo label may seem reasonable at first glance. The final distribution of seats in the House of Commons did closely mirror the 2019 results and the Liberals were once again denied a majority. But trend lines are also important. The Liberals obtained an even larger minority this time, increasing their seat count from 155 at dissolution to 160. By contrast, the Conservatives under Erin O'Toole lost two seats and fared worse than under Andrew Scheer in 2019. Similarly, the NDP, who were expected to improve their performance significantly under popular leader Jagmeet Singh, added only one seat, leaving them once more in fourth place behind the Bloc, which returned with the same number of seats as before. Meanwhile the Green Party, although it managed to take two seats, saw its popular support collapse as the maverick right-wing People's Party of Canada garnered more than double the Greens' vote count.

The overall similarity in seat count masked the fact that more than forty seats changed hands. Not a record by any means, but nevertheless significant for a number of reasons, including which seats were in play and why. For the Liberals, reclaiming the riding of Vancouver Granville – won in 2019 by Jody Wilson-Raybould as an Independent – was an important symbolic victory. Similarly, the Liberals retook the riding of Fredericton that had been held since 2019 by the Greens' Jenna Atwin, who had crossed the floor to the Liberals only months before the election. Even more significant is the fact that the Liberals took two seats in the Conservative stronghold of Alberta, one in Calgary, and one in Edmonton, a feat they could not accomplish in 2019.

In the end the Liberals may not have achieved their objective of a majority, but they were the only clear winners in this election. As former Trudeau adviser Gerald Butts noted succinctly, "a win is a win." Queen's University professor, Kathy Brock concurred: "The big winner in this election is Justin Trudeau, and that's because this is an example of change that is changeless. It appears that nothing has changed, but everything has changed. The seats are the same, but the dynamics are entirely different."[1]

Nevertheless, the results of this election were hardly preordained. Once seen as a near certainty, the likelihood of a Liberal majority quickly melted away in the early weeks of the campaign as an increasingly frustrated group of Liberals saw their initial plan rent asunder by countless unexpected events beyond their control, and others to which they were slow to react. At the midpoint in the campaign, it even briefly appeared the Conservatives might have a chance to win a minority. The wildly unexpected path taken to reach their eventual victory is therefore worth examining in detail in order to understand the context of the Liberals' last-minute return to power. Indeed, the road to the 2021 pandemic election began almost immediately after the dust had settled on the previous vote barely two years earlier in 2019.

THE BRIEF RETURN OF PARLIAMENT

From the beginning little if anything in the 43rd Parliament unfolded the way either the Liberals or Canadians expected. The Trudeau government was constantly caught off guard, fighting to manage a series of unanticipated developments that had played no part in their election platform. Certainly, it would be difficult to identify a comparable era where so many serious challenges beset any of their predecessors in their brief two-year stint as a minority. In this context, the Liberals' effort to maintain the outlines of that agenda was undoubtedly a primary reason for their eventual victory despite a series of gaffes and occasional lapses of judgment on the part of the prime minister.

The first of the unexpected challenges emerged within days of parliament's return. The new government suddenly found itself obliged to engage in renewed trade negotiations with the Trump administration, which was now threatening more disruptions to the North American Free Trade Agreement (NAFTA) agreement after initially having appeared to consider the matter settled. The mercurial US president returned to the charge on a range of issues. A full court press of Liberal cabinet ministers, senior officials, provincial premiers, and Deputy Prime Minister Chrystia Freeland were preoccupied with nailing down the deal despite a number of hardball tactics launched or threatened by the president. With the help of the Democrats, and several sympathetic state governors who had been assiduously courted by Canadian contacts, the deal was finally concluded and signed on 19 December 2019. At the time Ms Freeland referred to the agreement as a win-win deal, and polls demonstrated the vast majority of Canadians agreed. So did provincial premiers, who unanimously requested in writing that parliament pass the deal as quickly as possible.

Yet when the bill was tabled on the return of parliament on 29 January 2021, calls for speedy consideration and passage were opposed by the Conservatives, who initially attempted to forward the deal to six separate parliamentary committees for examination, a move that would have delayed ratification for months. This led to the first of many acrimonious debates and delays in the House. Noting that both the US and Mexico had ratified the agreement already, and that delays could potentially result in further change, the NDP sided with the government and an agreement was reached to complete examination of the bill by the trade committee alone.

Then in early February a dispute between the hereditary chiefs and elected band councils of the Wet'suwet'en First Nation, over the construction of the coastal Gas Link Pipeline (CGLP), once again spilled over into public protests and acts of civil disobedience by the chiefs and their supporters. In short order a number of similar protests were launched across the country by other First Nations sympathetic to the position of the Wet'suwet'en elders. Within a week both freight and passenger rail transportation, a primary target of the protesters, was largely shut down in most of the country.

Despite opposition calls for the federal government to intervene and take action, the Liberals maintained that the situation called for calm, and argued that conciliation talks were the best way to achieve a peaceful resolution. The prime minister also stressed that any police action to be taken in response to the various blockades was a municipal and provincial matter and it was not the role of politicians to tell the police how to do their job.[2] As the standoff dragged on into March, concern rose about supply chain disruptions and delays in the delivery of agricultural products to market. Ordinary Canadians and businesses began to lose patience at the lack of perceived progress.

Both of these issues were still dominating the agenda while the government was preparing to table its long-awaited budget on 30 March. However, neither the budget, nor the ongoing pipeline dispute, would be settled before a third and far more momentous unanticipated event – a global pandemic – overtook the Liberal government, the Canadian Parliament, and the nation.

THE PANDEMIC CHANGES EVERYTHING

By early January 2020 news broke of a deadly virus originating in the Wuhan area of China. However, World Health Organization (WHO) officials initially discounted concerns of a serious problem, and it was not until 30 January that it was elevated by them to the level of a "public health emergency of international concern." At this point only one case had been identified in Canada, and Chief Public Health Officer Dr Theresa Tam, a member of the WHO Committee, stated that "it's going to be rare, but we are expecting a few cases."[3] Nevertheless Global Affairs Minister Philippe Champagne arranged for Canadians in that area of China to be evacuated, and the Canadian Border Services Agency began to post signage raising awareness of the illness. By late February the government had established a special cabinet committee to monitor developments as a precautionary measure.

Then, after many weeks of cautious evaluation which was later widely criticized, on 11 March 2020 the WHO declared COVID-19 a global pandemic. The same day the prime minister announced a $1 billion response fund, including $500 million to go to provinces and territories, a $50 million contribution to WHO and an additional $275 million to fund COVID-19 research in Canada.[4]

By the next day virtually the whole of the federal government was involved in one way or another in the response to this crisis. On 14 March all Canadians outside of the country were urged to return home as quickly as possible. (In the end some 62,580 Canadian travellers were brought home from 109 countries by the federal government.) By 18 March the Canadian border was closed to all but Canadian citizens and permanent residents in an agreement jointly announced with the US. On 25 March a small group of parliamentarians met to approve Bill C-13, the *COVID-19 Emergency Response Act*, an $82 billion aid package with various programs designed to assist individual Canadians and businesses. This was followed on 11 April by another limited meeting of parliamentarians to pass Bill C-14, the *COVID-19 Emergency Response Act*, No. 2, which allocated substantially more funds to various programs including the Canada Emergency Response Benefit (CERB). In the interim, on 30 March the Canada-United States-Mexico Agreement (CUSMA) deal was finally ratified by the small parliamentary group present and would come into force on 1 July 2020.

With parliament recessed in the early days of the pandemic, while parliamentarians discussed the feasibility of establishing virtual or hybrid sessions, the prime minister featured very prominently in public information announcements and in offering reassurance. Justin Trudeau provided almost daily press briefings from outside his official residence, something Opposition Leader Andrew Scheer in particular was vocal in criticizing, arguing that it afforded Trudeau an unfair political advantage in public visibility while parliament was in recess. Scheer also demanded that the Commons resume sitting immediately (a position that was opposed by the leaders of all the other parties).

Scheer also criticized the Liberal government for failing to provide briefings to keep the opposition abreast of developments, something Green Party leader Elizabeth May scathingly contradicted in a formal statement.[5] Nevertheless, after his election as leader replacing Scheer, Erin O'Toole continued the Conservatives' opposition to a virtual or hybrid parliament, forcing special sittings of reduced numbers of MPs on several occasions to ensure passage of crucial COVID-support legislation.

The major federal role in the early days of the pandemic was to provide economic support to citizens, as Trudeau repeatedly told Canadians, "We've got your back." A panoply of programs produced in record time offered individuals and businesses a wide range of options to supplement their declining income or loss of jobs. Most of these plans were well received and opposition criticism tended to be limited to suggestions for extensions or additions to existing programs. However, one of these programs, designed to provide income support for postsecondary students over the summer, created serious problems for the Liberals and for Trudeau personally, as discussed below.

Throughout this period Trudeau was also attempting to encourage a team-Canada approach to the pandemic, but the common front he had originally managed to present with the premiers soon fell apart as jurisdictional and practical problems began to emerge in light of the fact that Canada's federal constitution assigns the vast majority of healthcare-related matters to the provincial level. Few Canadians either knew or cared who was responsible, which made matters worse for the federal government as it frequently took the blame for things that were strictly outside of its jurisdiction. Despite frequent calls for national solutions to problems, for example, the federal level could only intervene in most cases if asked by a premier. It is provinces that are responsible for hospitals, healthcare providers, and long-term care homes as well as patient records and various restrictions for public health and safety such as lockdowns or compulsory mask-wearing in public. The primary role of the federal government, by contrast, is much more limited, namely, to purchase and test items such as vaccines or personal protective equipment (PPE), and to enforce the federal *Quarantine Act*. In addition, it can provide additional funding to provinces through federal-provincial agreements, as it did on several occasions including the June 2020 announcement of a multibillion-dollar Safe Restart program providing provinces with funding for testing, contact tracing, and enhanced school ventilation systems in anticipation of a second wave of infection in fall 2020. As a last resort it can also send in the military at provincial request to assist in situations such as those encountered in long-term care facilities in Quebec and Ontario during the first wave, and in Alberta and Saskatchewan during the fourth wave.

As it transpired, the positive Safe Restart announcement was overshadowed by the emergence of a self-inflicted conflict-of-interest scandal in early June over the government's awarding (and then quickly cancelling) of a contract with the nonprofit WE charity to administer a specific COVID support program for students, something officials had told cabinet could not be administered internally due to a lack of specific bureaucratic expertise. Although both the prime minister and his Finance minister had attended WE events in the past, neither felt there was a conflict of interest since they had not received any remuneration and the prime minister had in fact verified his relationship with the Office of the Conflict of Interest Commissioner. However, in a scandal reminiscent of the Wilson-Raybould affair, the matter began to spin out of control in the absence of a solid government communications strategy. The opposition seized on the issue and in the end the fallout was extended to involve members of the prime minister's family, led to a parliamentary committee examining the issue, and ultimately cost Trudeau his Finance minister, Bill Morneau, who became implicated in the scandal when it was revealed that the WE organization had paid him more than $40,000 to cover travel expenses, and that one of his daughters worked for the charity. Trudeau, for his part, was obliged to indicate that he should have recused himself from the decision-making process that awarded the WE organization the contract.

With the issue still on the opposition radar, in mid-August the government elected to prorogue parliament until 23 September 2020. Although parliament was already scheduled to break for a summer recess until 20 September, the prorogation would have the extra effect of halting the work of parliamentary committees such as the one examining the WE affair. Opposition parties protested the move was a blatant attempt to change the channel on media reporting, but the Trudeau Liberals replied with a reminder of the problematic prorogation tactics employed three times by Conservative prime minister Stephen Harper, and then argued that the pandemic had entirely changed the agenda from what they had discussed with Canadians during the 2019 election and the subsequent Throne speech. Their stock line was that a reset was clearly needed so that they could inform Canadians of the new reality of pandemic governance in Canada and outline the Liberal plan for "building back better," given the many injustices the pandemic had revealed in Canadian society.

However, the safe start the Liberals had expected after providing provinces with substantial funding in June did not materialize for a number of reasons. Their optimistic plan to focus on the future faltered with the resurgence of the virus in fall 2020 as it became clear that several provinces had been overly optimistic in their relaxation of rules and procedures. As cases once again soared, the political situation became increasingly strained, with many premiers blaming the federal government for a variety of failures and a reluctance or inability to act promptly, or both. Among the most significant of these accusations related to what they saw as the slow acquisition of vaccines which were becoming available internationally in the fall of 2020. On the one hand, the federal government had signed contracts with at least four major international vaccine production companies and was promising Canadians that vaccines would be available by the end of the year. On the other hand, many observers were criticizing the fact that all vaccine production would be abroad and questioned why the government had not been able to ensure domestic production.

In fact, the Liberals had attempted to jumpstart domestic production capacity through a joint venture of the National Research Council and a Chinese vaccine producer with longstanding ties to Canada, but this plan had fallen through as a result of the Huawei-and-two Michaels standoff which was also plaguing the government at the time. Although several noted science commentators pointed out that the root of the problem lay with the Mulroney government's privatization and foreign sale of the world-class Canadian-owned Connaught Laboratories several decades earlier, the Liberals were clearly losing the public relations war on this front.[6] Worse still for them, several unexpected delays in the delivery of the foreign vaccines in the early part of 2021 increased public anxiety and dissatisfaction, as did the uneven and confusing distribution systems established by various provinces.

By March 2021 vaccine supplies appeared to be both abundant and stable, and the federal distribution of vaccines to provinces was becoming well established. By May 2021 the prime minister was predicting a one-shot spring and two-shot summer, with all eligible Canadians vaccinated before September. By mid-June Canada had become a world leader in percentage of the population vaccinated,[7] case counts were plummeting, and Canadians generally were beginning to see light at the end of the tunnel. Moreover, polls consistently demonstrated Canadians believed the federal government had done a good job in administering both the vaccines and the various economic support programs it had provided.

THE LIBERAL PLAN ENCOUNTERS OBSTACLES

As a result, it was hardly surprising from a political point of view that the Liberals would have begun to think about calling an election in spring 2021. It appeared that a majority was a very real possibility, something that would allow the party to proceed more easily and quickly to implement their ambitious postpandemic agenda. Since the life of minority governments in Canada rarely exceeded two years, they felt this they could argue this would not be much of a deviation from the norm. And, after initial difficulties in the Newfoundland and Labrador provincial election held early in the year, the positive experience of several more recent provincial and municipal elections suggested that one could be conducted safely and efficiently despite the limitations of the lingering pandemic.

Moreover, the path to a majority was becoming increasingly clear. Already holding most of the seats in Atlantic Canada and much of Ontario, and with the Prairies still likely to prove a wasteland for them, it would be necessary for the Liberals to target seats in Quebec and BC to reach 170 seats. With several Bloc seats in Quebec appearing vulnerable, and very positive ratings for the party in BC, both of these target areas seemed to offer solid possibilities.

The pandemic was fading from public concern given the rapidly declining case count and high rates of vaccination. Not only was the public mood now highly optimistic,[8] but some party strategists felt a late spring or summer election also would offer ideal conditions for the safe conduct of the campaign in mostly outdoor settings. However, in politics timing is everything. The Liberals' original plan had to be delayed repeatedly as new issues and obstacles arose. And with each delay the window for the Liberals to act on their position of strength to cement their majority was beginning to close.

For one thing they had not been able to proceed with as much of their positive prepandemic agenda as they had hoped, due to various unexpected pandemic problems and other political crises that inevitably occupied most of the past eighteen months. From the beginning there had also been frequent delays in the passage of the government's pandemic economic support packages as the Conservatives in particular repeatedly opposed the adoption of a virtual parliament until finally agreeing to a hybrid version. It was not until September 2020 that this hybrid version was finally operational, and January 2021 before electronic voting had been adopted over the Conservatives' repeated objections. With only a few sitting days during the interim period, almost entirely devoted to this emergency legislation, it was difficult for the government to pursue any of its original agenda which included issues related to climate change, Indigenous reconciliation, and childcare, among others, or specific legislation on internet regulation and cultural policy and imposing a ban on enforced conversion therapy.[9]

An additional series of crises began to preoccupy the government. In January 2021, the sexual misconduct crisis in the Canadian Forces emerged as a major ongoing issue, with one senior officer after another forced to step aside or take leave as what appeared to be an endless stream of inquiries was launched, extending up to and including the summer recess. This crisis was particularly significant for the Liberals as it reflected negatively on their self-identification as feminists with zero tolerance for such activities, and because it increasingly cast doubt on the competence of Defence Minister Harjit Sajjan, a prominent Trudeau appointee.

With the revelation at the end of May by the Tk'emlúps te Secwépemc First Nation that more than two hundred Indigenous children were buried on the grounds of a former residential school in Kamloops BC, it was clear the Liberals would have to delay any thought of an election until late summer. By 3 June parliament had passed a government motion to establish 30 September as an annual National Day of Reconciliation, and the prime minister ordered federal flags to be flown at half-mast indefinitely. The next few weeks were dominated by this issue as various Indigenous organizations and bands demanded additional federal funding to locate other such sites, and the media devoted considerable time and effort to the background work of the National Truth and Reconciliation Committee (TRC) and its December 2015 recommendations, only some of which at this point had been implemented by the government. One of the most important of these recommendations had been for the government to adopt the United Nations Declaration on the Rights of Indigenous Peoples, and after extensive negotiations the Liberals had tabled Bill C-15 to accomplish this objective in April 2021. However, the bill had encountered considerable opposition from the Conservatives, and it was not until the publicity produced by the Kamloops discovery provided sufficient impetus that the bill was passed.

No sooner had this landmark legislation been adopted than in mid-June 2021 yet another controversy arose, this time over the firing in

2019 of two visiting Chinese scientists who had been working at the National Microbiology Laboratory in Winnipeg. By now it was clear that the tone of parliamentary debate had become extremely confrontational. Although both Health Minister Patty Hajdu and the Public Health Agency of Canada (PHAC) President Iain Stewart stated that the dismissal was unrelated to any COVID-19 issues, parliamentarians demanded a full investigation and the submission of unredacted documents to a recently-created special parliamentary committee on Canada-China relations. The government demurred, stating that there were national security considerations that prevented this, and instead submitted the unredacted material to the all-party National Security and Intelligence Committee of Parliamentarians created for this purpose, whose members must have top security clearance and are bound to secrecy. With the opposition unprepared to accept this solution or to negotiate a compromise with the government, a motion was first tabled in which Speaker Anthony Rota declared the government to be in contempt of parliament, and the House then proceeded to the highly unusual step of calling the president of PHAC before the bar of the House of Commons to explain his refusal to turn over the documents.

Despite these numerous distractions and setbacks, the government had also been attempting to ensure that four of its most important pieces of legislation were passed before the House rose for its scheduled adjournment on 23 June. Speculation increased that the Liberals still hoped to trigger a federal election before the return of parliament and did not want to lose these bills as would happen if an election were called. Needless to say, there was considerably less cooperation on the part of the opposition as the time left before the recess diminished. In addition to the essential economic support bill, House Leader Pablo Rodriguez had identified Bills C-6 (banning involuntary conversion therapy), C-10 (regulating the internet and promoting Canadian content), and C-12 (the Climate Change Net-Zero Emissions Plan) as priorities. With significant opposition from the Conservatives on the first two bills in the House and additional resistance in the Senate, only the third was able to be assigned royal assent before the House adjourned for the summer recess, while the media increasingly focused on the possibility of an imminent election.

Although there was still internal debate in Liberal circles about the decision to proceed with an election, the argument that there would not likely be a better time won the day. By waiting another year, proponents of the election argued, much of the Liberals' good pandemic management would be forgotten while the costs of the recovery and support programs would start to feature prominently in public criticism. As it stood in late July, polls continued to show that a majority was a possibility, but the worst-case scenario was still a minority, something most were prepared to live with if necessary.

In addition, Trudeau had two additional policy cards up his sleeve, and played them just before he called the election. First, he announced that his government would impose a mandatory vaccination policy for all air and rail travellers within Canada, and on federal public servants and federally-regulated businesses, a move which immediately proved extremely popular. Second, he announced that his government had completed long-promised childcare agreements with eight of ten provinces, (Ontario and Alberta being the outliers but expected to sign on shortly). This too was a popular initiative, and both would prove difficult for the Conservatives to counter during the campaign.

UNIQUE TECHNICAL CHALLENGES OF A PANDEMIC ELECTION

The technically advanced Liberal campaign machine was well aware that there would be constraints and challenges in running a campaign during a pandemic. Much effort had gone into the planning in advance of alternative methods of reaching both voters and, even more importantly, volunteers. Increased use of days of action, phone contacts over door knocking, and the need to ensure all candidates and staff were fully vaccinated were pressing issues. Even the important practice of getting out the vote had to be adapted to a situation in which free rides to the polling booth were not likely to be an attractive option.

Planning had begun well in advance, on the assumption the election might be held in the spring. On 18 January 2021, the Liberal Party held a virtual election readiness meeting (the 2021 kickoff call) with riding presidents, campaign managers, and MPs, led by party president Suzanne Cowan and National Director (later Campaign Director) Azam Ishmael. Election readiness, election planning, and training sessions were on the agenda. Among other issues discussed was the need to ramp up candidate nominations, for which party staffer Derek Lipman was in charge. At the same time the national platform co-chairs, Mona Fortier and Terry Duguid, were appointed.

Also discussed was the party's upcoming policy convention set for 9–10 April. In the end some four thousand participants approved a total of twenty-six priority policy resolutions, while team-Trudeau staffers held various workshops on aspects of election readiness. The theme of the conference was "Keeping Canada Moving Forward," presaging the Liberals' election framing. Days later, on 19 April, Finance Minister Chrystia Freeland finally released a long-awaited budget titled "Keeping Canada Moving Forward," and the national campaign co-chairs, Navdeep Bains and Melanie Joly, were announced.

As in previous campaigns, the concept of national Days of Action organized by the party to recruit volunteers and contact voters had been underway for some time, although these efforts were obliged to adapt to the need for more telephone contacts and less door-knocking due to the public health restrictions of the pandemic.

Happily for them, money once again was not an obstacle for the Liberals. As senior fundraising director Lynda Taller Wakter reported, the party raised more money in August than ever before in a single campaign month. Over the course of the campaign some 22,500 individuals made donations to the Liberal cause. However, there were also concerns related to the actual conduct of the first national pandemic election. It was expected that many more voters would select the mail-in option, but the unexpected complexity of the process established by Elections Canada meant that in the end, even more would choose to vote in the advance polls. This made the Liberals' plan to unveil their platform in early September somewhat problematic, but it was decided that the advantages of waiting for their opponents' proposals would be worth it. By contrast, the Conservatives had revealed their entire platform at the beginning of the campaign. In the end, this did prove to be something of a poisoned chalice. The Liberals also revealed costing with their platform, something the Conservatives refused to do until near the end of the campaign, a move which may well have increased the credibility of the Liberals' various platform planks.

At the same time, the Liberal organization needed to depend far more on electronic media for the distribution of its platform planks as well as its message. Deputy Director Genevieve Hinse noted in one briefing that the party spent more on social media and electronic advertising than it had spent in the past two elections.[10] Perhaps most significant was the clear contrast between the Conservative strategy of staging a majority of their events virtually, with leader Erin O'Toole in a ballroom of a hotel in Ottawa, while Liberal leader Justin Trudeau engaged in countless direct interactions with supporters and ordinary Canadians, albeit in far more limited numbers and with numerous safety precautions in place. Similar outreach was practised by the NDP and Bloc Campaigns as well, making O'Toole's Conservatives the definite outlier.

Even so, as several Liberal organizers pointed out, it was exceedingly difficult to develop a sense of momentum on the campaign trail, important for energizing the leader but also for influencing the tone and tenor of media reporting. The well-known mass rallies held by Liberals with Justin Trudeau in 2015 and 2019 simply were not possible, and no number of virtual appearances of the leader with candidates would generate the same degree of enthusiasm either. As the Liberals entered the first few weeks of the campaign the importance of this limitation would become increasingly clear.

NOW OR NEVER: THE RUNAWAY ELECTION

The thrity-six-day campaign launched on 15 August 2021 may have been among the shortest in recent memory, but it was nevertheless marked by a significant number of unusual events that hardly constituted the status quo. From the beginning, with the eruption of Afghanistan as an issue on the very day the writ was dropped – a development that appeared to blindside the Liberal government as it did most other western democracies including the United States – the number of extraordinary developments and atypical actions on the part of voters and candidates alike was something to behold. These exceptional events derailed the Liberals' initial messaging plans and caused them to lose the air war for at least the first two weeks. The Conservatives in particular pounced on the bad news of the sudden Taliban takeover to portray the Liberals as more interested in gaining seats than helping stranded Canadians or securing safe passage out of the country for Afghans who had worked for the Canadian Forces during the military's mission in the country.

On the day the writ was dropped, Liberal leader Justin Trudeau described the election as "pivotal" and one of the most important in many decades, framed as offering voters a choice between two very different visions for the country. The Liberal slogan, "Forward. For

Everyone" was deliberately designed to offer hope and optimism, and to portray the Conservative alternative as moving the country backward. Clearly, Trudeau expected a positive reaction to an election about the future of the country as it emerged from the global pandemic. After all, he had spoken for months about the opportunity now afforded to "build back better" in the aftermath of the pandemic crisis, which had exposed serious injustices and deficiencies in the nation's social safety net. He also had good reason to expect voters would be supportive of the Liberals' plan for the future, given their positive views of his handling of the pandemic. This was hardly surprising, given that polls throughout the spring and early summer had continued to suggest his party was far ahead of the opposition and on track to form a majority government. As well, on three issues identified as top priorities by Canadians (healthcare, climate change, and COVID-19 economic recovery) the Liberal positions were the clear favourite. The Liberals were also more than twenty percentage points ahead of their nearest rivals in terms of their perceived ability to competently manage the pandemic.[11]

Hard as it may be to remember after the fact, these polls also demonstrated that Canadians were beginning to focus on other issues precisely because they saw the pandemic as something that had been brought under control and would soon fade in their rear-view mirror. Equally surprising in retrospect is the fact that other polls only days before the writ was dropped indicated that the vast majority of Canadians (roughly 83 per cent) were not overly concerned about whether there was an election or not, and in any event they were categorical about the fact that their feelings on this issue would not change their voting intentions.[12] And of course provincial elections had been held in three locations over the course of the pandemic without significant problems, suggesting that both the technology required and public confidence in the system would not be a problem. Despite these findings, significant change in public opinion about the need for the election did eventually occur, but only after the writ was dropped. Once again, the Liberals were faced with a problem of timing.

The election was not launched in the middle of the fourth wave of the pandemic, as some later recalled, but it was not long before the fact of the fourth wave began to be felt, another example of unfortunate timing on the part of the Liberals, who earlier had said they would not conduct an election during a pandemic. The speed with which public opinion shifted was stunning. Within a week or two of the election call, the fourth wave of the pandemic had emerged as a serious concern for the majority of Canadians, who now saw the election as both unnecessary and unwanted. The public's growing anxiety and waning optimism was exacerbated by the opposition's ability to frame the election as not only an unnecessary vanity election with a high price tag, but one that they argued had been called despite the fact the minority parliament was functioning well. Surprisingly for many, the Liberals seemed unprepared or unwilling to respond to these accusations despite a number of legitimate arguments that could have been put forward about Conservative filibustering and obstruction.

Instead, clearly hesitant to directly address their desire for a majority to accomplish their agenda, the Liberals decided to double down on their argument that citizens deserved the opportunity to choose between two very different approaches to the pandemic recovery. The problem was that this positive agenda for "building back better" had been announced several times in the first half of 2021 and much of it did not appear either new or exciting. Nor was it immediately clear to many voters how significantly the Conservative platform differed, since leader Erin O'Toole was working hard to present himself and his party as moderate centrists. Simply put, the Liberals had failed to nail down the election question.

In the early days of the campaign, with an unexceptional advertising campaign having failed to impress, the need to pivot to another approach in midcampaign largely proved difficult, especially in such a short campaign, a point national Campaign Director Azam Ishmael highlighted in an election postmortem briefing.[13] Some observers argued the Liberal advertising campaign never really recovered from the first two weeks when they clearly lost the air war. Experts examining the early ads released by the parties were not impressed with any, but least of all with the Liberals' vague focus on "Forward. For Everyone." David Rosenberg of Bensimon Byrne, the firm that orchestrated the widely regarded 2015 Liberal election ads, described the ads as "too vague" and "not saying enough" to motivate voters. Marketing strategist Clive Veroni agreed, calling the ads "very familiar ... there doesn't seem to be anything new or motivating and is fairly forgettable."[14] However, the Liberals were able to slightly sharpen their ads in the second half by focusing on specific promises, such as housing affordability, a move which most observers agreed was a step in the right direction, but too little too late to make a big difference.

As the campaign progressed, the increasing volatility of the electorate also continued to surprise pollsters and politicians alike. One unexpected result was the sudden increase in support for the People's Party of Canada led by renegade former Conservative MP Maxime Bernier, and in hand with this sudden increase in support for far-right political views the federal campaign also saw an unprecedented increase in violence and physical confrontation. One of Justin Trudeau's early scheduled events was actually cancelled due to the RCMP's determination of a credible threat. Subsequently, and throughout the thirty-six-day period, the Liberal leader's public events were routinely disrupted by a cadre of violent protesters. At one event the leader was pelted with gravel, resulting in criminal charges being laid against a former PPC riding president. Violence on the campaign trail, along with expressions of antisemitic, racist, and anti-LGBTQ rage, reached heights not seen in living memory, with incidents reported by candidates from all parties.[15]

THE UNEXPECTED IMPACT OF THE LEADERS' DEBATES AND PREMIER LEGAULT'S FATEFUL INTERVENTION

Another series of surprising developments, this time in the province of Quebec, added to the sense of electoral volatility. The Liberals had good reason to believe at the start of the campaign that they would make significant inroads in flipping Bloc-held seats, quite possibly in sufficient number to achieve a majority. In addition to solid advance work by the party at the riding level in targeted Bloc seats, Liberal leader Justin Trudeau had assiduously courted the highly popular Quebec premier, Francois Legault, with offers of various program funds and careful avoidance of criticism on a controversial piece of provincial language legislation, Bill 96. Given the apparently good relations between the two men as a result, it was widely assumed that Legault would, at a minimum, remain neutral during the federal campaign.

Yet, in another highly surprising move, the premier promptly launched a scornful attack on both the Liberals and the NDP on the eve of the English-language leaders' debate. Denouncing them as "centralist" and "dangerous," he implicitly urged Quebecers to vote for the "decentralist" Conservatives, not the Bloc. This attack, moreover, succeeded in overshadowing media coverage of the positive performance Trudeau had delivered in the French-language debate the night before, which many observers felt he had won.[16] Certainly, many viewers caught a glimpse of Trudeau's father in a noteworthy clash with Bloc leader Yves Blanchet, who suggested the federal government had no business intervening in Quebec matters, to which Trudeau responded that Blanchet seemed to forget that he, Trudeau, was a proud Quebecer and an MP representing a Quebec riding.

Since the Conservative platform placed that party on the wrong side of public opinion in Quebec with respect to top priorities such as gun control, climate change, and childcare, the premier's unexpected move astonished many observers and infuriated the Liberals. In the end the impact of Legault's meddling was to annoy many voters in the province sufficiently to prompt a backlash against the Conservatives, and pollsters began to observe support moving instead to the previously flagging Bloc campaign.[17]

A second unanticipated and exceptional development in the Quebec campaign was the outsized influence of the English-language leaders' debate. For years pundits have downplayed the importance of these debates, which in truth rarely result in one leader scoring a knockout punch and most often produce an uninspiring draw. On this occasion, however, it was not the participating leaders but the debate moderator, Shachi Kurl, who delivered what would prove to be a serious blow, in this case to the fortunes of the Liberals in Quebec. With her unexpected question to Bloc leader Yves-Francois Blanchet about what she termed the discriminatory nature of Bills 21 and 96, (which prohibited religious apparel and symbols and further promoted the use of French respectively) Kurl managed to inject new life into the Bloc campaign as furious Quebecers of all political stripes construed her approach as an attack on their character and that of Quebec's political culture.[18] The Liberals' hopes of a pathway to a majority through Quebec – once highly realistic – were effectively dashed.

Apart from such a bizarre influence on the Quebec campaign, the English-language debate also distinguished itself as badly organized, particularly in comparison with the well-managed and productive French-language debate. The chaotic and frustrating format, which essentially prevented participants from actually debating each other at all, featured the moderator herself intervening repeatedly to interrupt their responses. Despite this, two significant points managed to emerge which negatively impacted the Conservative campaign, namely their stated positions on gun control and the funding of childcare. Both of these issues would prove crucial to the Liberal revival as voters once again were reminded of the Harper era and obliged to consider the consequences of a split progressive vote.

Although leader Erin O'Toole avoided responding to repeated questioning by Trudeau on these two issues that night, media coverage of them continued unabated for several days and he was ultimately obliged to amend the party's position on both planks in an attempt to salvage his campaign. In the case of gun control, this involved the extraordinary move of changing a printed platform plank with a hastily-drawn unconvincing amendment. In the case of childcare, it involved a vague but equally unbelievable written commitment to Premier Legault that Quebec would somehow receive at least part of the funding committed by the Liberals in the event of a Conservative victory, even if other provinces did not.

CONCLUSION

Much has been made of the fact that the Liberals won the 2021 election with only 32.6 per cent of the vote, a figure not only lower than the second-place Conservatives at 33.7 per cent, but lower even than the Liberal result of 33.1 per cent in 2019.

However, these figures do not tell the whole tale. The chances of any political party wining a majority with 50 per cent of the popular vote or more have declined precipitously over recent decades. From an essentially three-party system (Liberals, Conservatives, NDP, and occasionally Social Credit) for much of the postwar era, the political landscape in Canada has altered dramatically since the collapse of the Progressive Conservative Party under Brian Mulroney in 1993. Since then, with most of the traditional Conservative votes splintered into two fringe parties for many years – the Reform Party and the Canadian Alliance in the West and the separatist Bloc Québécois in Quebec – the party system has changed considerably, as several academics have taken great pains to point out.[19] The subsequent right-wing merger fashioned by Stephen Harper has not held, as events during this election and the previous one have demonstrated. With the addition of a functioning Green Party, able to siphon off votes from the left, and the even more recently created People's Party vying effectively for votes on the far right, it is hardly surprising that the margin of victory is continuing to decline with the popular vote split so many more ways.

In this context, it is important to note that the Liberals actually gained seats in this, one of the most unusual elections of the century. Not only is their minority larger than it was in 2019, but they came within eleven ridings (and only 16,870 votes) of achieving a majority despite all of the unexpected obstacles and self-inflicted errors. (The Conservatives, by contrast, would have needed to win another forty-two seats and almost 100,000 votes to have succeeded.) These figures alone suggest that a majority was in fact well within the Liberals' grasp. They also demonstrate the success of the Liberals' ground war, as their well-oiled machine of enthusiastic organizers and volunteers did in fact get out their vote.

Moreover, as both Azam Ishmael and Deputy Director Matt Stickney pointed out in their election postmortem briefing, the party has made strides in western Canada. In addition to the two breakthrough seats in Alberta, the Liberals took fifteen seats in British Columbia, the second-highest number it has garnered there in the last fifty years. With support for separatism continuing to decline in Quebec and the Bloc highly vulnerable in the absence of an issue like Bill 21 in 2019 to promote, it was only able to resurrect itself in this election because of the extraordinary series of events outlined above.

Justin Trudeau has now won three consecutive elections and is currently the tenth-longest serving prime minister in Canadian history. Whether or not this is indicative of another Liberal dynasty remains, after three elections, a moot point, but post-election statements by Trudeau about policy priorities suggests that he, like his father before him, intends to use what may be his final term in office to pursue his agenda aggressively while he can. Of course, his father had a majority. But with the opposition in disarray, despite his minority government, Justin Trudeau may well achieve much of that policy project in the same way that Lester Pearson once did.

NOTES

1 Jesse Snyder, "Trudeau's Liberals to Their Opponents: 'We're Stuck with Each Other for a While'," *National Post*, 22 September 2021, https://nationalpost.com/news/politics/trudeaus-liberals-to-their-opponents-were-stuck-with-each-other-for-a-while.

2 Eric Atkins, Bill Curry, Les Perreaux, and Laura Stone, "Trudeau Will Not Direct Police to Break Up Pipeline Protests, Sticks to Negotiated Strategy," *Globe and Mail*, 14 February 2020, https://www.theglobeandmail.com/

canada/article-garneau-says-he-hopes-talks-will-end-anti-pipeline-protests-affecting/.

3 Kathleen Harris, "Canada Prepares Charter Flight to Bring Home Canadians in China Affected by Coronavirus Outbreak," CBC News, 29 January 2020, https://www.cbc.ca/news/politics/coronavirus-canada-china-consular-1.5444188.

4 Amanda Connolly, "Trudeau Announces $1B Coronavirus Response Fund for Provinces, Territories," Global News, 11 March 2020, https://globalnews.ca/news/6659384/coronavirus-funding-trudeau/.

5 Althia Raj, "Elizabeth May Slams Andrew Scheer's 'Partisan' Push for In Person House Sittings in Pandemic," *HuffPost*, 15 April 2020, https://www.huffpost.com/archive/ca/entry/elizabeth-may-andrew-scheer-covid-19_ca_5e96f2b8c5b6ac7eb26336c1.

6 William Thomas, "Connaught Labs – the Greatest Mistake Ever Made by a Canadian Government," *Toronto Star,* 22 February 2021, https://www.thestar.com/local-niagara-falls/opinion/columnists/2021/02/22/connaught-labs-the-greatest-mistake-ever-made-by-a-canadian-government.html; Josh Aldrich, "Failed Vaccination Program All Trudeau's Fault: O'Toole," *Winnipeg Sun*, 29 March 2021, https://winnipegsun.com/news/local-news/failed-vaccination-program-all-trudeaus-fault-otoole.

7 Sean Boynton, "Canada Tops World in Vaccinated Population as New COVID-19 Cases Fall Below 1,000," Global News, 14 June 2021, https://globalnews.ca/news/7949797/canada-covid-cases-june-14-2021/.

8 Marieke Walsh and Kelly Grant, "A Dose of Hope: Here's Why You Might Get the COVID-19 Vaccination Sooner Than You Think, *Globe and Mail*, 30 April 2021, https://www.theglobeandmail.com/politics/article-how-canada-can-prevent-a-fourth-COVID-19-wave/; John Michael McGrath, "The Case for COVID-19 Optimism This Summer," TVO, 18 May 2021, https://www.tvo.org/article/the-case-for-COVID-19-optimism-this-summer.

9 "Moving Forward Together," Government of Canada, last updated 5 December 2019, https://www.canada.ca/en/privy-council/campaigns/speech-throne/moving-forward-together.html.

10 Genevieve Hinse's debrief at the Liberal Party of Canada's Laurier Club Virtual Townhall on 20 October 2021.

11 David Lao, "COVID-19 No Longer Top Issue Facing Canadians Ahead of Possible Election: Poll," Global News, 26 July 2021, https://globalnews.ca/news/8055986/issues-ipsos-polling-federal-election/.

12 Bruce Anderson and David Coletto, "Most Canadians Won't Be Upset if Early Election Called; Liberals Lead by 9 Over Conservatives," Abacus

Data, 12 August 2021, https://abacusdata.ca/election-2021-liberals-lead-by-9/.

13 Azam Ishmael's election postmortem briefing at the Laurier Club Virtual Townhall Policy Edition event on 14 September 2021.

14 Rachel Aiello, "What's in an Ad? Dissecting the Parties' Early Campaign Messaging," CTV News, 30 August 2021, https://www.ctvnews.ca/politics/federal-election-2021/what-s-in-an-ad-dissecting-the-parties-early-campaign-messaging-1.5567100.

15 Neil Moss, "Political Leaders Need to Address Violence, Hate Seen on Campaign Trail, Say Experts," *Hill Times*, 22 September 2021, https://www.hilltimes.com/2021/09/22/political-leaders-need-to-address-violence-hate-seen-on-campaign-trail-say-experts/318261.

16 Greg Jack, "COMMENTARY: Justin Trudeau Finds His Fire during French Language Debate, Twitter Analysis Shows," Global News, 9 September 2021, https://globalnews.ca/news/8176804/french-leaders-debate-twitter-reaction/.

17 Antoni Nerestant and Marilla Steuter-Martin, "Legault Defends Coming out in Support of Conservatives, Says Majority of Quebec Voted 'Blue'," CBC News, 21 September 2021, https://www.cbc.ca/news/canada/montreal/federal-election-trudeau-legault-1.6183682; Ashley Burke, "Liberals Bristle at Legault's Suggestion He Would Prefer a Conservative Minority Government," CBC News, 11 September 2021, https://www.cbc.ca/news/politics/liberal-candidate-melanie-joly-reacts-quebec-premier-comments-election-1.6172842.

18 Sean Boynton, "Canada Tops World in Vaccinated Population as New COVID-19 Cases Fall below 1,000," Global News, last updated 21 December 2021, https://globalnews.ca/news/7949797/canada-COVID-cases-june-14-2021/.

19 R. Kenneth Carty, William Cross, and Lisa Young, *Rebuilding Canadian Party Politics* (Vancouver: UBC Press, 2000).

3

The Conservative Campaign: Erin O'Toole and the Conservative Dilemma

Faron Ellis

From a national perspective, the 2021 Conservative Party of Canada's (CPC) election campaign appeared to produce a stasis for the party. Conservatives won 119 seats, two fewer than they won in 2019 despite changing leaders and making a deliberate attempt at restructuring their voting base. Conservatives again won more votes than any other party but lost the election and failed to reduce the Liberals' seat total. Despite doing better than had been expected at the outset of the campaign, Conservatives for the most part found the election results unsatisfactory, often for very divergent reasons, and immediately after the outcome embarked upon yet another cycle of questioning their leader and his election team's campaign strategies and debating what should be the party's core principles.[1]

Beneath the surface, however, the 2021 Conservative election campaign illuminated a number of fundamental, often conflicting, characteristics that have been thirty years in the making and highly problematic for the party's electoral fortunes over most of that period. When the Reform Party fractured Canadian federal conservative politics in 1993 it was a party united primarily by its western populist ethos. It was also fiscally and socially conservative, but primarily by circumstance rather than by design.[2] The party's desire to form a national government meant jettisoning the western focus. The brief Canadian Alliance experiment discredited much of the populist element, leaving fiscal and social conservatism as the most recognizable characteristics of the Conservative Party of Canada after its founding in 2003. Under the leadership of Stephen Harper, modest nods to the social conservative elements were tolerated, but fiscal conservatism dominated. Shifting public opinion about the need for fiscal conservatism, as witnessed by the Liberal's successful 2015 campaign, weakened its marketability. The COVID-19 pandemic all but obliterated the ability to campaign on a platform of balanced budgets, lower taxes, and restrained social program spending. Hence, despite being a minority sentiment within the party and its broader voting base, social conservatism became the most recognizable, defining characteristic of the Conservative Party for many Canadian voters, leaving the party vulnerable to credible charges of harbouring hidden social conservative agendas on important issues.

After the 2019 election loss, many Conservatives believed the party needed to broaden its appeal to attract votes from a more centrist, urban Canadian voter. Who would lead the transformation and how it would happen would be determined by the Conservatives' 2020 leadership contest. This contest would also illustrate a dilemma for the party that would be fully exposed in the 2021 campaign: the conflicts and contradictions between the policy positions and commitments required to win the Conservative leadership and those required to win a federal election. The electoral consequences of the leadership race were compounded by a campaign that brazenly embraced recanting previous commitments, thereby limiting the effectiveness of a strategy based on the authenticity of the leader and his commitment to his platform promises.

Hence, while the 2021 election results appeared to preserve the status quo for Conservatives, a battle for the future of the party and of Canadian conservatism more broadly was taking place, with the 2021 election being merely the first act of a drama that will likely play out over the next several electoral cycles.

EMBRACING THE DILEMMA: THE 2020 CONSERVATIVE LEADERSHIP CONTEST

Conservatives embarked on a leadership selection process in 2020 by establishing an organizing committee co-chaired by former cabinet minister and deputy leader Lisa Raitt and former Conservative MP Dan Nowlan, who had chaired the previous Conservative leadership contest. Membership voting eligibility is established by the party constitution and based on a modified one-member one-vote selection process with each member provided a single transferable vote ballot to rank candidates in their preferred order. Votes are tabulated for each of the country's 338 electoral districts with each contributing one hundred points to the total. Candidates are awarded a share of points based on their percentage of votes in the district. The one-member one-vote provision is a holdover from the populist Reform legacy and opens the possibility an organized swamping of the membership could highjack the process. The equal weight per riding provision is a legacy of the old Progressive Conservative Party (PC) and is designed to counterbalance populist excesses, encourage candidates to have national reach, and ensure the party does not become hostage to the interests of one region of the country. Both provisions played significant roles in the outcome of the 2020 leadership contest.

Social conservatives have an established history within the party, particularly at the constituency level.[3] By activating existing local faith group networks with support from national social conservative associations, social conservatives routinely secure CPC nominations in safe, western Canadian ridings. Social conservatives demonstrated some success at applying these techniques to influence the outcome of the 2017 CPC leadership contest and began mobilizing to have an even greater influence in the 2020 contest. Ultimately, the constituency equality provision would see both of their candidates eliminated prior to the final ballot. But their ability to mobilize supporters to the one-member one-vote provisions allowed them to extract considerable concessions and commitments from all the candidates, including the eventual winner.

Leadership candidate recruitment produced formal interest from ten potential leaders, but only four ultimately completed filing requirements to appear on the ballot. As with 2017, a significant number of high-profile potential candidates chose not to run, including former interim leader Rona Ambrose, former cabinet ministers John Baird and Pierre Poilievre, and former federal PC leader and Quebec premier Jean Charest. The most widely known candidate to enter the contest, and presumed frontrunner, was former PC leader and Harper-era cabinet minister Peter MacKay. Former CPC cabinet minister and third-place finisher in the 2017 leadership contest Erin O'Toole entered the race, as did two virtually unknown candidates. Derek Sloan, a first-term MP from eastern Ontario, launched his bid as an unabashedly social conservative candidate. So did Ontario lawyer Leslyn Lewis, who demonstrated that despite her relative anonymity she could organize a very successful campaign, quickly attracting a handful of caucus endorsements and rivaling the frontrunners in fundraising efforts. Sloan established himself as the lightning rod for social conservative controversy early in the campaign and continued that strategy throughout. Lewis, although also unapologetically socially conservative, took a more articulate and less controversial approach and quickly became a significant contender.

Frontrunners MacKay and O'Toole approached the social conservative wing of the party very differently. Although MacKay made obligatory welcoming overtures to social conservatives during a campaign that frequently appeared disjointed and off-message, he could not completely distance himself from his "stinking albatross" evaluation of the social conservative problems that plagued the party during the 2019 campaign.[4] O'Toole, a known pro-choice, social moderate, countered by openly courting social conservative second- and third-ballot support. Some national social conservative associations like Campaign Life Coalition eschewed both candidates, but others bought into O'Toole's outreach because he offered them "a seat at the table" in his platform entitled "Our Country: A Call to Take Back Canada," where he described himself as a "True Blue Conservative" and played down his reputation for social moderation.

All candidates agreed on reducing the size of government, shrinking the tax burden, and cracking down on crime. All were critical of the Liberal firearms policy and promised to introduce stricter penalties for criminals while providing greater support for victims of crime. O'Toole distinguished himself most on the issue of climate change. In the first iteration of his platform, O'Toole made it clear that he intended to ensure Conservatives would not enter the next election without a serious carbon reduction plan. Like all candidates he promised to rescind the Liberal's carbon tax but stated he would support provincial carbon pricing mechanisms and get Canada to net-zero by 2050. MacKay described the plan as not something written by someone running for the Conservative leadership and took specific exception to O'Toole's promise to end fossil fuel subsidies. Employing a technique he would later use during the general election campaign, O'Toole quickly amended his official platform to omit the offending policy. O'Toole also distinguished himself by demonstrating a particular obsession with China, frequently issuing policy statements deriding the communist regime in that country for its human rights abuses and for its unfair trade and economic policies. By race's end, O'Toole boasted having the most endorsements from federal and provincial elected officials, while MacKay received more federal CPC caucus endorsements. Lewis surprised by garnering seven caucus endorsements. Sloan received none.

When results were announced it became clear that O'Toole's strategy had prevailed. He placed a close second to MacKay on first-ballot votes and points, and ahead of MacKay on both scores on the second count. Both social conservative candidates achieved more support than expected with Sloan picking up approximately 15 per cent of first-count votes and points. Lewis won nearly one-quarter of all first-choice votes and more than one-fifth of first-count points. Combined, they accounted for more than two of every five first ballot votes, accumulating more than one-third of the total points and demonstrating that social conservatives could deliver results in a one-member one-vote system. When Sloan was dropped from the second count, Lewis picked up more than 70 per cent of his supporters. MacKay picked up only one in twenty while O'Toole captured nearly one-quarter. Lewis' second count support placed her in the lead with more than sixty thousand total votes, but her distribution of votes across the 338 electoral districts meant that she received only 30 per cent of the points, placing her third and not eligible to continue to the final count. O'Toole was the clear beneficiary of Lewis' exit, securing nearly 59 per cent of total votes, 57 per cent of the points, and victory on the third count.

MANAGING THE DILEMMA: O'TOOLE, THE PARTY, AND THE CPC CAUCUS

Immediately following his victory, O'Toole introduced himself to Canadians as a pro-choice, pro-LGBTQ2+ rights leader in an effort at countering the emerging narrative he had secured the CPC leadership primarily because of social conservative support. A number of social conservative organizations took note of the purported betrayal and began organizing an end-run around the leader by attempting to have their issues incorporated into Conservative policy at its convention to be held in the spring of 2021. Sloan openly participated in their efforts and quickly became too incendiary to further tolerate. After initially defending Sloan and providing him with the opportunity to demonstrate he was a team player, in the wake of most Canadians' discomfort with outgoing US President Donald Trump's supporters storming of the American capital, O'Toole moved to clearly distinguish his brand of Canadian conservatism from that element of American conservatism. He declared that the far right had no place in his Conservative Party, and initiated proceedings to remove Sloan from the CPC caucus. First claiming that Sloan had received a donation during the leadership contest from a known white supremacist, O'Toole later modified the rationale, claiming Sloan had demonstrated a "pattern of destructive behaviour involving multiple incidents and disrespect towards the Conservative team for over a year."[5] Social conservatives were outraged, but undaunted in their efforts to secure their policy goals at the CPC convention, particularly by advancing a resolution designed to reverse the party's opposition to regulating abortion services.

When the party revealed that none of the thirty-four policy resolutions to be debated at the convention dealt with abortion, social conservatives again claimed a betrayal and set their sights on amending the party's constitution to give constituency associations the power to overrule party decisions regarding candidates, including arming constituency associations with the ability to sanction and potentially remove MPs they believe were not representing their interests. Although these efforts were thwarted by the convention managers, O'Toole continued to mollify social conservatives by recommitting to free caucus votes on matters of conscience, a strategy his caucus repeatedly seized upon prior to the 2021 election to demonstrate social conservatives did indeed have a seat at the table and could resist O'Toole's plans to broaden the party's voting base.

Early in 2020, while still leader, Andrew Scheer allowed Conservative MP Cathay Wagantall to introduce a private member's bill that would ban sex-selective abortions. Although the bill outraged all the CPC's parliamentary opponents, they also welcomed the opportunity to help social conservatives brand the CPC as anti-choice. O'Toole and most of his senior caucus members voted against the bill, but two-thirds of the CPC caucus exercised their conscience privileges and voted in favour. When the Liberal government's bill to ban conversion therapy reached third reading, O'Toole again voted with the government, but half the CPC caucus voted against the legislation. Social conservative caucus members had clearly demonstrated that they could do from within the party what the national social conservative organizations had failed to do at the party convention, providing Conservatives' opponents with ample evidence to paint the party as homophobic, anti-abortion, and more socially conservative than either its existing voting base or the expanded voting base O'Toole was seeking to recruit.[6]

Fiscal conservatives and those opposed to carbon pricing also began to take note of how far O'Toole was shifting the party away from its traditional policy positions. Most dramatically, in defiance of a membership that had voted down a policy convention resolution that would have had the party officially recognize climate change as real,[7] O'Toole released the environment plan on which he intended to campaign in the next election. It included a broad range of carbon reducing initiatives and, most importantly, a $20-per-tonne price on carbon emissions. O'Toole claimed to be fulfilling his leadership contest commitment to end the Liberals' carbon tax by replacing it with a Low Carbon Savings Account into which Canadians would pay and could then use to purchase approved low-carbon products. Although details about how the account would work were lacking, and how effective it would be debatable, the plan accomplished its primary goal in that it committed Conservatives to pricing carbon thereby allowing low-carbon advocates to claim all parties were now onboard. Not wanting to undermine that achievement meant many environmental activists were muted in their criticisms of the details.[8] Traditional Conservative supporters were not nearly as charitable. Some described O'Toole's plan as "outrageous,"[9] others claimed it was a "massive blow to his integrity and credibility."[10] Most saw it for what it was: a tax by another name. Some, however, saw virtue in having a plan, even if not a perfect plan,[11] to avoid the pitfalls encountered by Scheer in the 2019 campaign. Despite outraging many Conservatives because of the perceived betrayal, O'Toole's strategy largely succeeded in ensuring environment policy would not be as significant a drag on Conservative support in 2021 as it was in 2019.[12]

Climate was not the only policy domain O'Toole intended to alter in his base-broadening efforts. On Labour Day immediately after being elected leader, O'Toole released a video launching his blue-collar worker and union outreach. He followed that with a speech to the Canadian Club in which he chided Bay Street financiers, admonished corporations for focusing too much on shareholder value, derided bad trade deals, and took specific aim at China for causing high unemployment in a variety of Canadian industries. The strategy was designed to replicate what some USA conservatives and UK

Conservative prime minister, Boris Johnson, had succeeded at doing; convincing blue-colour labourers who were feeling left behind by the global trade revolution to vote Conservative.[13] Not having a central galvanizing component like former USA President Donald Trump's polarizing personality or Johnson's Brexit strategy to crystalize the issue, Conservative strategists believed they could manufacture one by positioning China as being symbolic of the problems and Conservatives as the only party willing to take a firm stance against that country's transgressions. Conservatives had some minor success in framing the issue when they secured all-party support for their motion declaring the Chinese government's treatment of ethnic Muslim Uighurs a genocide. But the link between China and jobs was not clearly articulated and unions prepared to openly campaign against Conservatives.[14] The anti-China rhetoric likely contributed to them losing three seats in metro Vancouver and Toronto without any corresponding surge in union votes in other ridings.[15] The strategy also led many traditional supporters to question their leader's commitment to any conservative ideology or principles,[16] his electability, and his very leadership.[17] Concerns mounted that O'Toole was building for himself an authenticity gap that would be revealed in the 2021 campaign.

CAMPAIGN TEAM AND ORGANIZATION

The campaign would be run from Ottawa more so than in previous elections with the leader spending at least parts of twelve days of the total thirty-six-day campaign in making announcements from the downtown Westin Hotel ballroom the party had converted into a television studio. O'Toole also used the studio for video production, to hold press conferences, and conduct virtual townhalls. The virtual townhall gambit was part of the party's beefed-up, targeted, direct-to-voter messaging strategy that included obtaining much more detailed information about potential supporters. These efforts were supported by digital consulting firms Topham Guerin and Stack Data Strategy, two firms that had worked for UK Prime Minister Johnson's successful 2019 campaign.[18] Sean Joudry headed up digital operations from Ottawa[19] while Kieran Moloney, associate director of the Conservatives' caucus research bureau coordinated O'Toole's tele-townhalls. O'Toole appointed two experienced Conservative operatives to lead the campaign.

Fred DeLorey chaired, and Laura Kurkimaki served as deputy chair, both of whom worked on O'Toole's two CPC leadership bids. They were based in Ottawa for the duration of the campaign. When travelling,[20] O'Toole was joined by his Opposition Leader Office (OLO) chief of staff, Tausha Michaud, director of scripting and policy, Dan Mader, as well as long-time Conservative communications director Cory Hann, who served as campaign spokesperson.[21] Rounding out the senior ranks was national campaign chair Walied Soliman and chief strategist Dan Robertson, a long-time Conservative operative who also worked on O'Toole's 2020 leadership campaign.[22] One of O'Toole's deputy chiefs of staff, Steve Outhouse, served as director of planning after having run Lewis' 2020 CPC leadership campaign and fellow social conservative Pierre Lemieux's 2017 leadership effort. Formerly a Harper government ministerial chief of staff, after the Conservatives were removed from office in 2015 Outhouse built a consulting firm whose work included helping social conservative candidates secure CPC nominations, an activity he and his firm continued to engage in with the knowledge of the leader while he was employed by O'Toole's OLO. Although those activities were counterproductive to O'Toole's efforts to broaden the party's base, his presence on the campaign team served the short-term goal of providing evidence that social conservatives did indeed have a seat at the table.

Candidate nominations proceeded with dispatch given the uncertainty of election timing. Incumbent caucus members were guaranteed their nominations provided they met certain fundraising requirements that were not burdensome for most. A Canadian Press analysis of party constituency association financing revealed Conservatives averaged $60,000 in net assets at the end of 2020, well ahead of all the other parties.[23] By the end of May, Conservatives had nominated two hundred candidates. By the start of the campaign, it boasted three hundred and would field a full slate of 338 by the time nominations closed. The national campaign would also be well financed with the Conservatives continuing to outpace their competitors in fundraising, breaking records in the second half of 2020 after O'Toole was elected leader, and outpacing their competitors during the first half of 2021.[24]

The Conservatives began preparing for the 2021 election immediately after O'Toole won the leadership by attempting to define a positive image for their new leader before the Liberals could portray him negatively. They released a number of ad campaigns designed to distance O'Toole from the true-blue Conservative he campaigned as to win the leadership. One of the most well received was undertaken in the fall of 2020. It included a series of short, get-to-know-me videos released on Twitter and the leader's YouTube channel. O'Toole opened up about his childhood, including how his mother's death became a driving force in his life, leading to a career in public service. Another campaign in the spring of 2021 entitled "Just Erin" was designed to present him as a humble, suburban family man but lacked any definitive policy content and was less well received. Others, such as the party's attempt at cheeky humour in an ad urging Canadian voters to send Justin Trudeau to the outhouse, fell flat. So did its attempt at creating a viral-ad phenomenon in the opening days of the campaign with a copyright-violating use of Trudeau's image crudely superimposed on unlicensed images from a Willy Wonka movie. Despite these efforts, O'Toole's policy shifts left most Canadian voters with either no significant impression of the leader and what he stood for, or negative impressions.[25] And with a campaign imminent, many usually friendly media commentators moved from skepticism to outright hostility.[26]

CAMPAIGN DYNAMICS

Knowing that Conservatives were divided over vaccination requirements, the Liberals primed the 2021 election campaign with a series of announcements about mandatory requirements for federal employees, those working under the federal labour code, and travellers. Illustrating O'Toole's dilemma, outgoing Conservative MP David Yurdiga called the proposals "tyrannical" while declaring "Canadians deserve the right to liberty" whether or not they chose to be vaccinated.[27] Whether leaders would require all of their candidates to become vaccinated immediately became the focus of media questions to all of the party leaders. Understanding that a sizable number of his caucus and candidates would either not get vaccinated or at minimum would not consent to publicly releasing their vaccination status, and that several would likely revolt if a mandatory vaccination order was issued, O'Toole tried to straddle the divide by encouraging all Canadians to get vaccinated but stopped short of requiring this for his candidates, travellers, or most employees. He argued that reasonable accommodations could be made in the name of public safety and expected his unvaccinated candidates to undergo daily COVID-19 testing. It appeared O'Toole had skirted the issue when the Treasury Board Secretariat posted its recommendations online stating that the federal bureaucracy would handle vaccine dissenters in nearly the same manner as O'Toole was proposing. But the reprieve was temporary as the vaccination issue would linger and then explode later in the campaign.

On day two of the campaign O'Toole released the entire Conservative platform from his Ottawa studio. Designed to look more like a men's health magazine than a campaign platform, Canada's Recovery Plan featured Erin O'Toole in a tee-shirt on its cover and through its 160 pages provided details about every conceivable initiative a new Conservative government would implement. Centred on the theme that O'Toole had a plan for Canada's post-pandemic recovery, it featured many images of O'Toole and his family, but none of other Conservative candidates. The cover itself did not include the word Conservative, although the party's new logo did appear as part of the stylized "Secure the Future" tagline. Included within the platform were twenty-three planks, twenty-two of them described as a "detailed plan" to achieve the leader's goals. Federal government finances did not appear until the final plank and was the only plank without a detailed plan.

For those not interested in wading through all 160 pages of detailed plans, the first fifteen pages of the document summarized the platform into five themes that identified the Conservatives' campaign priorities. The summary opened with jobs as the priority, followed by securing accountability, including strengthening ethics and conflict of interest requirements and penalties. Although the prime minister was not named, Liberal Party "cover-ups" were, with Trudeau's ethical and conflict issues the clear target. The third theme was designed to present a more compassionate and caring party by committing Conservatives to securing mental health. The fourth theme focused on pandemic management issues where the party believed the Liberals were vulnerable, including the lack of domestic vaccine manufacturing capacity and PPE production. Finally, the fifth theme committed the party to balancing the budget over the next decade by winding down pandemic support programs and by growing the economy to generate the revenue necessary to bring federal finances into balance without having to make cuts to valued social programs. Importantly absent was an independent costing of the plan and details of how it would be rolled out over the course of a four-year mandate or longer given many of the commitments would take more than one term to accomplish. The platform concluded with a statement assuring voters the party had internally costed its many commitments and a promise to make public the Office of the Parliamentary Budget Officer's (PBO's) evaluation in subsequent editions. Although the prospect of future editions did not receive attention at the time, that, along with the lack of costing, indicated that despite the man with a detailed plan narrative, the Conservative team viewed the platform as still somewhat of a work in progress. How much so would be revealed as the campaign unfolded.

As a communications tool, the platform was initially received as Conservatives had planned. It provided early voters with something tangible to use in evaluating a leader with whom many had little familiarity. It reinforced the image of O'Toole having a plan and committed the party to take more seriously some issues it had not adequately addressed in previous elections, such as climate change, while distancing itself from other aspects of the Party's social conservative legacy. Fiscal conservatives were unimpressed[28] but the Conservative campaign strategy was set: present a calm, reasonable, and moderate leader and his plan as the party. Almost immediately, however, the Conservatives would encounter two important drawbacks of their strategy: with all the focus on their leader, they would have to explain contradictions between what O'Toole promised while campaigning for the party leadership and what was now in his election platform; and, having included the level of specificity they did while making the entire document public early in the campaign, they had given their opponents ample opportunity to discover and exploit errors, inconsistencies, and other weaknesses.

Examples of the first drawback occurred in the opening days of the campaign. Despite O'Toole's repeated assurances that he was pro-choice and his platform explicitly stating that a Conservative government would not support any legislation to regulate abortion, the Liberals pounced on O'Toole's commitment to protect the conscience rights of healthcare professionals as evidence he was beholden to social conservatives and would restrict access to abortion by not requiring dissenting healthcare professionals to provide effective referrals. O'Toole tried to evade persistent questions about the issue for two days before unequivocally stating that the status quo would prevail, thereby reneging on one of his leadership campaign commitments that had made it into the election platform. The incident demonstrated both how far O'Toole would go in reversing past promises, ultimately undermining the credibility of his current commitments, and how far he was willing to go in ensuring the Conservative campaign mimicked Liberal policy in attempting to defuse even the slightest amount of controversy.[29]

A second example emerged when the Liberals released an edited video of O'Toole answering questions about private healthcare services during his leadership campaign. They claimed it showed O'Toole would bring private "for-profit" healthcare to Canada. Despite Twitter slapping a "manipulated media" warning on the post and Conservatives requesting an investigation by the Elections Commissioner, the Liberals pursued their attack. O'Toole neither defended his previous position (that private services can provide efficiencies within the public system), nor did he attempt to reverse the argument by questioning which of the many existing private services the Liberals would outlaw in defence of a purely public system that currently does not exist in Canada, possibly including private abortion services. Instead, he took the cautious approach of not being drawn into any debate about the mix of private and public healthcare service provision out of fear of being even tangentially associated with negative positions on the issues. He simply repeated his talking points about his support for the Canadian universal healthcare system and how he would outspend the Liberals on healthcare, promising to inject $60 billion over the next ten years. The strategy initially succeeded but would flounder later in the campaign after the Conservative platform costing was released.

Aside from these relatively small bumps along the trail, for the first half of the campaign the Conservative strategy appeared to be paying dividends. O'Toole stuck to his schedule of spending Sundays and at least parts of the first two days of the early weeks of the campaign making daily policy announcements and conducting virtual town-halls from his Ottawa broadcast studio, then heading on the road for the remainder of the week, aggressively targeting Liberal-held ridings. Convinced that the virtual components of the campaign were reaching more voters than would a traditional tour (200,000 during the first couple of weeks, thereby providing the party with invaluable voter contact information),[30] Conservatives found evidence of success in their leader's improving personal evaluations and the party's rise in public opinion polls, first with male voters and then more broadly. The Conservatives even managed to temporarily distance themselves from the negative attributes of the growing anti-vaccine mandate backlash plaguing Liberal campaign events and other public venues. O'Toole made it clear he had no common cause with anti-vax extremists or their chief political vehicle, Maxime Bernier's People's Party.[31] By midcampaign the Conservative momentum was clear.[32] With success came compliance from increasingly disenchanted fiscal and social conservatives, many of whom were sensing a bait-and-switch by the true-blue Conservative they elected only a year earlier, but who could not deny the gains being made and for the most part stayed in line.

And then things went very wrong. During the first French-language debate hosted by Quebec's TVA, O'Toole generally handled himself well, reasonably articulating his positions on vaccine mandates, healthcare, and his intention to scrap the Liberal childcare plan. But he found himself on the defensive about his platform commitment to rescind various aspects of the Liberals' firearms policies. O'Toole's detailed plan to secure public safety makes twenty-five references to firearms, the vast majority aimed at keeping guns out of the hands of criminals, enacting stiffer penalties for gun crimes, gangs, and imported illegal weapons. But it also claimed the Liberal firearms policy unfairly targeted law-abiding gun owners and that Conservatives would therefore repeal the most recent C-71 requirements for lifetime background checks and restriction on transportation. It also explicitly stated the party would rescind the Liberal cabinet's May 2020 Order in Council banning a large number of assault rifles while a Conservative government conducted an independent review the *Firearms Act*. But when under pressure from Trudeau, who pointed to the exact page of O'Toole's much promoted detailed plan where the commitment was printed, O'Toole declared the Conservatives would maintain a ban on assault weapons, directly contradicting his own platform.

O'Toole initially attempted to obfuscate by claiming that his statement was consistent with his platform because he only meant maintaining the 1977 legislation banning fully automatic weapons and that the Liberals' most recent ban was misguided in targeting farmers, hunters, and law-abiding Canadians rather than criminals. When that defence floundered and it was revealed that O'Toole's campaign manager DeLorey was once a lobbyist for the National Firearms Association, under pressure from an increasingly skeptical media[33]

O'Toole formally rescinded the platform commitment by amending his work-in-progress plan to declare the current ban would remain until he completed an independent review. But the about-face did not serve the Conservative campaign well. Initially, it was only a partial reversal. By leaving open the possibility a review may again legalize some of the banned weapons, O'Toole would have to answer questions about which firearms he would allow. He compounded the damage when he had no definitive answers, appearing evasive or even deceitful, as the Liberals would repeatedly charge through to the end of the campaign.

While it may stretch credulity to suggest the firearms issue cost the Conservatives the election, the midcampaign policy reversal, combined with the subsequent evasiveness, brought to wider public attention a credibility problem that O'Toole was already experiencing with conservatives. Reporters and commentators increasingly asked O'Toole about the Liberal narrative rather than his own. By giving more exposure to the contradictions between his leadership commitments and those in his general election platform, and now reversals of even those commitments, the Liberals' claim that O'Toole lacked principles and would say anything to get votes became more prevalent, and more credible. Even more damaging for a party that had invested everything in the leader as a man with a plan, if the plan could be that easily altered many voters were left wondering how much of the plan they could count on being fulfilled if the party were to be rewarded with government. The Conservative "rocket ride" of momentum stalled,[34] and O'Toole's personal performance evaluations peaked.[35]

Nevertheless, the Conservative team remained confident heading into the leaders' debates during the second last week of campaigning. They released the PBO's costing of their platform only hours prior to the French debate, the first of the two to be held on successive nights. In most analysts' evaluations, O'Toole performed admirably in both encounters,[36] remaining calm and respectful as he attempted to reinforce the Conservative ad campaign's assault on Trudeau's record in government,[37] his ethics, and how the prime minister abandoned his "sunny ways" disposition, replacing it with divisive wedge-issue politics in a transparent power grab by way of an unnecessary pandemic election. O'Toole even received an endorsement of sorts from Quebec Premier Francois Legault, who declared after the French debate that all parties other than the Conservatives would be dangerous to the Quebec nation and only O'Toole demonstrated a willingness to hand over more power to the province and transfer funds without conditions.[38] None of that appeared to matter when the immediate postdebate commentary shifted to criticisms of the debate format and the allegedly discriminatory question asked of Bloc Québécois leader, Yves-François Blanchet. Ultimately, the Liberals were the only party to receive a significant postdebate bump in the polls.[39]

More problematic for Conservatives, the costing of their platform came into focus at the same time O'Toole was under increasing pressure over his refusal to require all of his candidates to be vaccinated while the fourth wave of the pandemic raged, particularly in Alberta. For many voters the vaccination issue was symbolic of pandemic management and the party's position on healthcare more generally, an issue the Liberals refused to relinquish after their early unsuccessful attempts to tar O'Toole with the familiar refrain that Conservatives would privatize healthcare by creating a "two-tier" system. O'Toole had largely insulated his campaign against those charges by touting his platform commitment to pump $60 billion in additional funding into the universal healthcare system. But when the costing revealed that only $3.6 billion would flow to the provinces in the first five years of the plan, the rest backloaded to later years, the costing further eroded the credibility of O'Toole's healthcare commitments, and that of the platform more generally.[40] Similarly, O'Toole had committed to canceling the Liberals' $29.8-billion childcare plan, replacing it with what he argued was a superior plan of parental tax credits. The costing revealed, however, that O'Toole would spend one tenth what the Liberals would (only $2.6 billion). While it could have been presented as a more fiscally prudent and therefore more responsible approach, that was not how O'Toole had been promoting his plan since the start of the campaign and his credibility took another hit.

With authenticity issues mounting, the Liberals released a trio of attack ads that compiled a substantial list of O'Toole's contradictions and policy reversals. On climate change they associated O'Toole with Harper's emission reduction targets, a legacy O'Toole admitted was wanting and upon which he needed to rebuild trust. On its own the climate issue did not appear to either help or hinder Conservative support. But establishing a link between O'Toole and Harper was something the Liberals had been attempting to do without success since the beginning of the campaign. When Trudeau argued that O'Toole was disingenuous about his abortion and LGBTQ+ commitments, he cited the Conservative caucus' voting record as evidence. On firearms, Liberals claimed recent evidence suggested he was in the pocket of the gun lobby. Once costed, they credibly claimed his healthcare and childcare commitments were not real. On the environment, he led a party that did not believe climate change was real. Most damaging, however, was the charge that O'Toole's pandemic management would be suspect, at a time when voters were becoming increasingly supportive of vaccine mandates and passports.[41] When Trudeau criticized O'Toole's inability to convince his own caucus to be fully vaccinated, O'Toole provided only stock talking points in response. When Alberta premier Jason Kenney announced that he had made errors in lifting restrictions intended to curb the spread of the virus, and was therefore reinstating many of those measures, the Liberals released a video of O'Toole speaking to delegates at the CPC policy convention in which he praised Kenney for managing the pandemic better than Trudeau. Although the association with Kenney was problematic and undercut O'Toole's pandemic management message,[42] more damaging was O'Toole's refusal to provide the media with any meaningful response about whether or not he still believed Kenney had performed better than Trudeau.[43] With O'Toole again determined to stick to his talking points, headlines for the remainder of the campaign included the phrase: "O'Toole refuses to answer questions,"[44] leaving him appearing evasive and much less sincere than he had early in the contest.

With his party stalled in the polls and his leadership under attack, the Conservative campaign decided to make one last tactical shift. Gone was the critical but respectful charm offensive O'Toole adopted for most of the campaign. Instead, he opened the final week with a blistering, personal attack on Trudeau. Declaring Trudeau not a feminist, environmentalist, or a public servant, but "a man who's focused solely and squarely on himself," O'Toole went on to articulate "the stark differences" between himself and the prime minister,[45] contrasting his own record conducting military rescue missions to Trudeau's partying youth. He reminded voters of "the pictures" in an effort at resurrecting the blackface images from the 2019 campaign. O'Toole called Trudeau privileged, entitled, and always looking out for number one. He then acknowledged the modest but nevertheless significant rise in support for Bernier's People's Party by admonishing potential supporters that a vote for any party other than the Conservatives would be a vote for Trudeau and more of the same. Throughout the campaign O'Toole had resisted the temptation to outflank Bernier on the anti-vaccine issue, correctly calculating that his more nuanced position was likely already costing him more votes than he was gaining, and any move to further accommodate antilockdown voters would bleed more support than could be recouped. Undoubtedly, the PPC cost the Conservatives some seats, but not nearly enough to alter the election outcome.[46] Indeed, the Conservative vote dilemma was more profound.

CONCLUSION

In winning more votes than any other party, 33.7 per cent of the total, and 119 seats, the Conservatives appeared to have slipped marginally, but at least maintained the status quo in an election that only a few months earlier they were expected to lose badly. They lost seven seats to the Liberals and two to the NDP but picked up seven Liberal seats for a net loss of two compared to 2019. On a regional basis they also achieved some of the shifts in support they were aiming for, but these also tended to produce net losses rather than gains. As anticipated given the base-broadening strategy, the party lost vote share in all four western provinces leading to a loss of seven seats, four in BC and three in Alberta where their vote share dropped 13 per cent. But the much sought-after trade-off gains in Ontario and Quebec did not materialize. Conservatives gained only approximately 2 per cent more votes in each of those provinces than they won in 2019, netting only one additional Ontario seat. They made only modest gains in vote share in the Maritimes but increased their seats in that region by four, with one additional win in New Brunswick, two in Nova Scotia, and one in Newfoundland and Labrador. They were again shut out of Prince Edward Island and all three territories.

Indeed, the 2021 election results appear to have furthered the Conservatives' dilemma of being an increasingly rural-based party competing for votes in an increasingly urban country.[47] Canada's three largest metropolitan areas account for 116 seats, more than one-third of all ridings. Conservatives won only eight of those contests,[48] while they won more than half of the 150 least urban ridings, 81 in total. Conservatives were shut out of metropolitan Vancouver, losing two

Richmond seats they won in 2019. They were likewise shut out of the twenty-five city of Toronto seats and the eighteen that encompass the city of Montreal. But Conservative urban struggles extend beyond the cores of Canada's three largest cities. They won no seats within the cities of Ottawa, Hamilton, and Halifax, lost all six of Winnipeg's most urban ridings, and three of Edmonton's most densely populated constituencies. Most troubling for Conservatives, the party also fared poorly in the small city and suburban areas of southern Ontario, winning only one of the twelve seats in the Peel region west of Toronto, only three of the ten York region seats north of the city, and two of the five Durham regions to the east, including leader O'Toole's Durham riding.[49] Recognizing that the Canadian electoral system and resulting seat distributions magnify both regional and urban-rural differences, and that Canadian voters have as much in common as that which divides them, Canada is becoming more urban and progressive over time.[50] Elections are won and lost based on marginal differences and the long-term demographics are not in the Conservatives favour if they continue to pursue a policy agenda that appeals primarily to a shrinking rural and social conservative base.

NOTES

1 This chapter reflects, in part, interviews conducted with several individuals associated with various aspects of the Conservative campaign. Interviews were arranged and completed based on a commitment to ensure the anonymity for all participants. The author sincerely thanks all those who consented to provide their insights for helping make this a more accurate and complete analysis and takes responsibility for any errors in interpretation.

2 Faron Ellis, *The Limits of Participation* (Calgary: University of Calgary Press, 2005).

3 Faron Ellis, "Twenty-First Century Conservatives Can Continue to Succeed," in *Crosscurrents: Editors' Choice*, eds. Mark Charlton and Paul Barker (Toronto: Nelson, 2015), 17–36.

4 Jason Markusoff, "Peter MacKay: The Tories' Avatar of Unity, Hope and Renewal – but Also of Unforced Errors," *Maclean's*, 15 July 2020, https://www.macleans.ca/politics/peter-mackay-conservative-leadership-race-2020/.

5 "Statement from Conservative Leader Erin O'Toole," Conservative Party of Canada, 20 January 2021, https://www.conservative.ca/statement-from-erin-otoole-january-20/. (Note: Sloan would be denied a Conservative

Party nomination in the 2021 election and would eventually run as an independent in the Alberta riding of Banff-Airdrie, finishing a distant fifth garnering just 2.6 per cent of the vote.)

6 John Ibbitson, "Conservative MPs Caved on Conversion Therapy Bill, but They've Likely Already Accomplished Their Mission," *Globe and Mail*, 22 June 2021, https://www.theglobeandmail.com/politics/article-conservative-mps-caved-on-conversion-therapy-bill-but-theyve-likely/.

7 Keith Beardsley, "O'Toole Convention to Lead to Trudeau Victory," *Cornwall Free News*, 21 March 2021, https://cornwallfreenews.com/2021/03/21/view-from-the-hill-by-keith-beardsley-otoole-convention-to-lead-to-trudeau-victory/.

8 Brian Platt, "Conservative Climate Plan Will Impose a $20-per-Tonne Carbon Charge on Fuel," *National Post*, 15 April 2021, https://nationalpost.com/news/politics/conservative-climate-plan-will-impose-a-20-per-tonne-carbon-charge-on-fuel.

9 Franco Terrazzano, "Taxpayers Federation Slams CPC Leader Erin O'Toole for Announcing His Own Carbon Tax," Canadian Taxpayers Federation, 15 April 2021, https://www.taxpayer.com/newsroom/taxpayers-federation-slams-cpc-leader-erin-o%E2%80%99toole-for-announcing-his-own-carbon-tax.

10 Alex Boutilier and Alex Ballingall, "A Massive Blow to His Credibility and Integrity': Conservatives Blindsided by Erin O'Toole's Carbon Pricing Plan," *Toronto Star*, 15 April 2021, https://www.thestar.com/politics/federal/2021/04/15/conservative-leader-erin-otooles-climate-plan-expected-to-include-a-price-on-carbon-also-known-as-a-carbon-tax.html.

11 Andrew Leach, "O'Toole's Climate Plan Isn't a Good One, but It May Be Good Enough for Voters," *National Post*, 22 April 2021, https://nationalpost.com/opinion/andrew-leach-otooles-climate-plan-isnt-a-good-one-but-it-may-be-good-enough-for-voters.

12 Brian Platt, "Conservative Vote Likely Not Hurt – or Particularly Helped – by Carbon Pricing Plan, New Poll Finds," *National Post*, 29 September 2021, https://nationalpost.com/news/politics/election-2021/conservative-vote-likely-not-hurt-or-particularly-helped-by-carbon-pricing-plan-new-poll-finds.

13 John Ivison, "How O'Toole Changed the Conservative Playbook to Go after the Blue-Collar Vote," *National Post*, 31 August 2021, https://nationalpost.com/news/politics/election-2021/john-ivison-how-otoole-changed-the-conservative-playbook-to-go-after-the-blue-collar-vote.

14 Peter Mazerfeeuw, "Union Launches Pre-Election Ad Campaign Attacking O'Toole," *Hill Times*, 2 August 2021, https://www.hilltimes.

com/2021/08/02/union-launches-pre-election-ad-campaign-attacking-otoole/309433.

15 Daphne Bramham, "Conservatives Face Ugly Barrage over Party's China Policy," *Vancouver Sun*, 14 September 2021, https://vancouversun.com/opinion/columnists/daphne-bramham-conservatives-face-ugly-barrage-over-partys-china-policy.

16 Matthew Lau, "Erin O'Toole Owes Us a Second Policy Disclaimer," *Financial Post*, 28 January 2021, https://financialpost.com/opinion/matthew-lau-erin-otoole-owes-us-a-second-policy-disclaimer.

17 Chris Selley, "Grumbling over O'Toole's Leadership Might Be Overblown – but Not Entirely Unjustified," *National Post*, 6 March 2021, https://nationalpost.com/opinion/chris-selley-grumbling-over-otooles-leadership-might-be-overblown-but-its-not-unjustified.

18 Alex Boutilier and Stephanie Levitz, "Conservatives Plan 'Groundbreaking' Direct-to-Voter Messaging in Next Federal Election Campaign," *Toronto Star*, 26 May 2021, https://www.thestar.com/politics/federal/2021/05/26/conservatives-plan-groundbreaking-direct-to-voter-messaging-in-next-federal-election-campaign.html.

19 The party's digital director Dan Taller supported those efforts.

20 The leader's tour was directed by Allison Lamb while Patrick Harris served as tour wagon master, supported from Ottawa by policy manager Renze Nauta.

21 Virginie Bonneau and Josie Sabatino served as French and English press secretaries. Chelsea Tucker directed media relations from Ottawa with support from manager of media relations Mathew Clancy and a host of other recent OLO press secretaries. Jake Enwright ran rapid response and issues management.

22 Former CPC national councillor, Marc-Olivier Fortin, was appointed to direct the Conservative's Quebec campaign with support from campaign secretary Martin Belanger and Quebec communications team head Axel Rioux. Tannis Drysdale served as director of field operations for the national campaign.

23 The Canadian Press, "Tory Riding Associations' Net Assets Larger Than Other Parties," *Globe and Mail*, 26 July 2021, https://www.theglobeandmail.com/politics/article-tory-riding-associations-net-assets-larger-than-other-parties/.

24 Sammy Hudes and Allison Smith, "Tories Double up Liberals in First Half Fundraising," Politics Today, 4 August 2021, https://www.politicstoday.news/parliament-today/tories-double-up-liberals-in-first-half-fundraising/.

25 Ihor Korbabicz, "Abacus Election Bulletin: A Question of Leadership(s)," Abacus Data, 21 August 2021, https://abacusdata.ca/a-question-of leadership/.
26 Lorne Gunter, "Erin O'Toole Is Not Just a Dud, He's a Dishonest Dud Who Is Driving Conservative Voters Away from the Polls," *Edmonton Sun*, 27 April 2021, https://edmontonsun.com/opinion/columnists/gunter-erin-otoole-is-not-just-a-dud-hes-a-dishonest-dud-who-is-driving-conservative-voters-away-from-the-polls.
27 John Paul Tasker, "O'Toole Says All Canadians Should Get a Shot as Conservative MP Calls Mandatory Vaccinations 'Tyrannical'," CBC News, 11 August 2021, https://www.cbc.ca/news/politics/otoole-mandatory-vaccine-1.6137392.
28 John Robson, "What's Bleak Is That No One, Including Erin O'Toole, Want to Shrink Government," *National Post*, 25 August 2021, https://nationalpost.com/opinion/john-robson-whats-truly-laughable-is-the-thought-of-erin-otoole-shrinking-government.
29 Paul Wells, "Between the Leaders Debates," *Maclean's*, 9 September 2021, https://www.macleans.ca/politics/ottawa/between-the-leaders-debates/.
30 Hanna Thibedeau, "Conservatives Say Their 'Virtual' Campaign Strategy Is Paying off Already," CBC News, 27 August 2021, https://www.cbc.ca/news/politics/otoole-conservative-election-virtual-campaign-town-hall-pandemic-1.6154822.
31 Former Harper-era cabinet minister, Maxime Bernier contested the 2017 Conservative leadership against O'Toole, placing second to winner Andrew Scheer. See Faron Ellis, "The Conservative Campaign: An Opportunity Squandered," in *The Canadian Federal Election of 2019*, eds. Jon H. Pammett and Christopher Dornan (Montreal: McGill-Queen's University Press, 2020) 43–72, for a review of the 2017 CPC leadership contest, its aftermath, and Bernier's exit from the party.
32 Stephanie Levitz, "Surging Conservatives Now Poised to Win More Seats Than Liberals, Poll Analysis Says," *Toronto Star*, 1 September 2021, https://www.thestar.com/politics/federal-election/2021/09/01/surging-conservatives-now-poised-to-win-more-seats-than-liberals-poll-analysis-says.html.
33 Rachel Gilmore, "O'Toole Pledges to Keep Assault Rifle Ban. His Platform Says It'll Be Gone. Here's What We Know," Global News, 3 September 2021, https://globalnews.ca/news/8164859/canada-election-conservative-liberal-assault-rifle-ban-platform-contradict/.
34 Cameron French, "Conservatives on 'Rocket Ride' as Seat Projection Show a Close Race: Nanos," CTV News, 30 August 2021, https://www.

ctvnews.ca/politics/federal-election-2021/conservatives-on-rocket-ride-as-seat-projection-shows-close-race-nanos-1.5566606.

35 "With Two Weeks Remaining in Campaign, CPC Holds Three-Point Advantage over Liberals," Angus Reid Institute, 7 September 2021, https://angusreid.org/federal-election-pre-leaders-debate/.

36 Stephen Maher, "Federal Leaders Debate: Could It Be Prime Minister Erin O'Toole?" *Maclean's*, 10 September 2021, https://www.macleans.ca/politics/ottawa/federal-leaders-debate-could-it-be-prime-minister-erin-otoole/?utm_medium=organic&utm_source=Twitter#Echobox=1631252246-1.

37 Conservative ads included, "What do you think?" an attack on Trudeau using clips from newscasts covering events such as the fall of Afghanistan, the BC forest fires, and a mounting fourth wave of the COVID-19 pandemic. "Justin says," featured a voiceover listing Trudeau's promises contrasted with his record. These and an untitled ad were the Conservatives' response to what they argued were cynical, American-style Liberal attack ads designed to create fear and division.

38 Christopher Nardi, "Quebec Premier Francois Legault Praises Conservative Leader Erin O'Toole after Second French Debate," *National Post*, 9 September 2021, https://nationalpost.com/news/politics/election-2021/quebec-premier-praises-tory-leader-otoole-says-npd-liberals-dangerous-for-quebec.

39 Brooke Taylor, "Liberals See Jump in Support after Back-to-Back Debates: Nanos," CTV News, 11 September 2021, https://www.ctvnews.ca/politics/federal-election-2021/liberals-see-a-jump-in-support-after-back-to-back-debates-nanos-1.5581539.

40 Editorial Board, "The Conservative Platform Sure Looks Different, Now That It Has Numbers in It," *Globe and Mail*, 10 September 2021, https://www.theglobeandmail.com/opinion/editorials/article-the-conservative-platform-sure-looks-different-now-that-it-has-numbers/.

41 "Support for Vaccine Passports Grows, Seven-in-Ten Canadians Now Support It in Public Spaces," Angus Reid Institute, 8 September 2021, https://angusreid.org/vaccine-passports-covid-19-canada/.

42 Chris Selley, "On Pandemic Management, O'Toole Is Giving Away Points to Trudeau," *National Post,* 17 September 2021, https://nationalpost.com/news/politics/election-2021/chris-selley-on-pandemic-management-otoole-is-giving-away-points-to-trudeau.

43 Campbell Clark, "Erin O'Toole Makes His Jason Kenney Problem Bigger," *Globe and Mail*, 17 September 2021, https://www.theglobeandmail.com/politics/article-erin-otoole-makes-his-jason-kenney-problem-bigger/.

44 Stephanie Taylor, "Tory Leader Erin O'Toole Evades Questions About Alberta's Response to COVID-19," CP24, 16 September 2021, https://www.cp24.com/world/tory-leader-erin-o-toole-evades-questions-about-alberta-s-response-to-covid-19-surge-1.5588209?cache=yes%3F-clipId%3D89531%3B.

45 Chris Selley, "No More Mr Nice O'Toole as Conservative Leader Abruptly Changes Approach," *National Post*, 14 September 2021, https://nationalpost.com/opinion/chris-selley-no-more-mr-nice-otoole.

46 The PPC secured a large enough share of votes in twenty-one ridings where, under the extremely unlikely conditions of pure transference, the Conservatives could have secured victory. Given that only fourteen of these were Liberal victories, the Conservatives would have still lost the election, albeit by a slimmer margin. See Amanda Conolly and David Akin, "Canada Election: Did the PPC Split the Conservative Vote? Maybe – but It's Not That Simple," Global News, 22 September 2021, https://globalnews.ca/news/8212872/canada-election-conservative-vote-splitting/.

47 David A. Armstrong II, Jack Lucas, and Zack Taylor, "The Urban-Rural Divide in Canadian Federal Elections, 1896–2019," *Canadian Journal of Political Science* (August 2021): 1–23, doi:10.1017/S0008423921000792.

48 Aaron Wherry, "Two New Solitudes – Rural and Urban – Now Define the Canadian Political Landscape," CBC News, 3 October 2021, https://www.cbc.ca/news/politics/2021-election-rural-urban-conservative-liberal-1.6197095.

49 Lucas Casaletto, "Toronto, GTA Ridings: 2021 Federal Election Results," City News, 20 September 2021, https://toronto.citynews.ca/2021/09/20/toronto-gta-election-ridings-results/.

50 Peter Loewen, Sean Speer, and Stephanie Bertolo, "Fault Lines and Common Ground: Understanding the State of Canada's Urban-Rural Divide," *Public Policy Forum*, February 2021, https://ppforum.ca/wp-content/uploads/2021/02/PPF-Fault-Lines-and-Common-Ground-Feb-2021-EN.pdf.

4

Jagmeet Versus Justin: Leadership and the NDP's Political Marketing

David McGrane

This chapter looks at how and why leadership came to be the defining characteristic of the federal NDP's political marketing in the 2021 election campaign. For the purposes of this chapter, political marketing is defined as the study of activities that parties undertake to win elections: polling, policy offerings, branding, communications strategy, volunteer management, criticism of their opponents, and get-out-the-vote tactics. A small literature has recently emerged on the federal NDP's political marketing, and this chapter adds to this literature by examining the role that the party's leader plays in the NDP's political marketing.[1]

Using interviews with party operatives[2] and analysis of the party's television commercials and news releases, I argue that the NDP ran a very leader-centric campaign in the 2021 Canadian federal election based upon Singh being preferable to Trudeau. Indeed, every element of the NDP's campaign, from policies to advertising, to local organization, was structured by an obsession with might be called the Jagmeet versus Justin contrast.

PANDEMIC POLITICS: THE NDP IN 2020–21

The federal NDP had been in considerable turmoil and upheaval in the period from the beginning of 2016 to the end of 2019.[3] The divisive leadership review at its 2016 convention that ousted Tom Mulcair as leader was followed by a drawn-out leadership race, poor fundraising numbers, and a substantial changeover in senior party officials. Despite a rocky start as leader during which he was criticized as lacking substance and being unready to lead a major national political party, Jagmeet Singh ran a spirited campaign in the 2019 election, leading to the party not losing as many seats as expected.[4]

The federal NDP had a number of challenges coming out of the 2019 federal election. With twenty fewer MPs, the NDP's staff on Parliament Hill was significantly reduced. The party's postmortem for the 2019 election concluded both that the central spending of $9.3 million was insufficient for a major political party to run a national campaign, and that the election had left the party with significant debts to pay off. The party reacted to its dire financial situation by postponing its scheduled convention, laying off staff at party headquarters, and directing Elections Canada rebates from local Electoral District Associations (EDAs) to the central party.

Nonetheless, there were three positive outcomes from the 2019 election for the party. First, questions about Singh's leadership were definitively put to rest. He became viewed by his party, and his caucus, as a considerable asset rather than a liability. Second, the senior staff around Singh was solidified, with Anne McGrath leading party headquarters and Jennifer Howard leading the party's House of Commons operations as Singh's chief of staff. The leadership of these two experienced operatives had a calming effect on the party and the changeover in staff slowed down. Third, party operatives interviewed for this chapter recalled how the internal narrative going into the 2019 election was that the NDP could become irrelevant as it might be wiped out by an overwhelming Liberal majority. However, the 2019 election outcome relegated the Liberals and Prime Minister Trudeau to a minority government with the NDP holding the balance of power. In the minority parliament, the NDP was positioned to force the Liberals to make changes to legislation and command the attention of the national media, because their decisions had impacts on the timing of the next election and the agenda of the government.

The strategic context in which the NDP found itself following the 2019 federal election – Singh in a strengthened position and Trudeau in a weakened one – led it to emphasize leadership in its political marketing. The party restructured fundraising by devoting more resources to online fundraising as opposed to direct mail and brought their telephone fundraising in-house instead of using a vendor. At the same time, Singh's leadership began to be featured heavily in the party's fundraising requests. This restructuring of the NDP's fundraising worked, as the party began to bring in more money compared the period prior to the 2019 federal election, despite the difficulties of fundraising during the initial stages of the COVID-19 pandemic when asking supporters for money was frowned upon by party members and the general public.[5] The party's communications and legislative strategy in the House of Commons was very leader centric as well. When the COVID-19 pandemic emerged in March 2020, the party's communications shifted to how Singh could negotiate with Trudeau for better pandemic-related benefits for Canadians. Singh took credit for forcing the Trudeau government to increase temporary COVID-19 wage subsidies and related benefits.[6] In interviews with operatives, they noted how the NDP began to test-drive language about Singh "fighting for things that mattered" and getting real results for Canadians in the face of inaction by Trudeau. The idea that the NDP was slowly developing traction came from the perception that Prime Minister Trudeau had failed Canadians during the pandemic and that the NDP was relevant because Singh was able to improve Canadians' lives due to his kingmaker status in the minority parliament. Public domain polling started to illustrate the advantages of this strategy as the NDP routinely polled around 20 per cent of national support and Singh was found to be the most popular federal leader.[7]

The combination of the minority parliament and the COVID-19 pandemic drew the federal NDP and Canada's labour movement closer than they had been in recent years. The labour movement viewed a minority Liberal government reliant on NDP votes to pass legislation as an opportunity to achieve long-standing goals such as an overhaul of the federal labour code, a federal minimum wage, and Pharmacare. The Canadian Labour Congress (CLC) collaborated closely with the NDP on its legislative strategy at the beginning of the minority parliament. It used what it referred to as "digital first" strategy that involved recruiting labour activists on social media and through other electronic means to send emails, sign petitions, and make phone calls to pressure the Liberals to draft legislation in accordance with Singh's demands. As the pandemic made itself felt, the CLC invested even more heavily in its digital first strategy and co-operated regularly with Singh's staff in their attempts to force the Liberal government to make pandemic-related benefits more generous. Further, the new CLC president,

Bea Bruske, wanted to align unions more with federal NDP than her predecessor, who some critics had charged was too close with the Liberal government.[8]

Overall, the NDP's fortunes looked much brighter going into the 2021 election as compared to the 2019 election. The party was more organizationally and financially sound. It had a popular leader, and it was polling around 20 per cent in most national polls – a historically high level. The NDP was relevant to Canadian politics, had the clear backing of the labour movement, and media pundits and columnists were musing about how the 2021 election could be a breakthrough election for Singh and how the NDP could gain more seats, thereby denying Trudeau the majority government that he was seeking.[9]

ELECTION PREPARATIONS

In the minority parliament, NDP operatives felt that an election could be called at any moment; almost immediately after the 2019 result they began to prepare for the next campaign. While the party's postmortem on the 2019 election was clear that the NDP had lacked financial resources, the interviewees noted that it did mention some positive elements such as: the introduction of Singh to the Canadian electorate; a platform that was unabashedly left-wing and clearly "New Democrat"; and a general sense of momentum following the election due to the NDP's importance in a minority parliament. The preparations for the 2021 election focused on building upon the foundation that was laid in 2019 as opposed to tearing everything down and starting over again.

In late 2020 and early 2021, the party began to slowly put in place its staff for an eventual campaign. It was decided that Jennifer Howard, Singh's chief of staff, would again be the campaign director, filling the same role that she played in 2019. Several other key staff positions were also to be filled by the same people who had held them in the previous election. While volunteers had played important roles in terms of strategy, organization, and policy in 2019, due to scarce financial resources, senior staff performing these tasks in 2021 were exclusively professionals. As in past campaigns, the NDP's federal executive, composed of approximately thirty volunteers from different parts of Canada, advised on election preparation by meeting to discuss the postmortem for the 2019 campaign, was consulted on the party's overall strategy for the 2021 election, and approved an ambitious $25 million budget. Consultations concerning the party's campaign strategy were also held with the NDP's caucus at their annual planning session and informal discussion took place with affiliated unions and other stakeholders such as NDP-friendly social movements and think tanks.

The party's polling and focus groups, conducted in early 2021, illuminated the segments of the electorate in which the NDP was popular: women, racialized minorities, and young people (specifically, young women and young mothers). It was also revealed that Singh was more popular than the NDP. In fact, the NDP had potential supporters (particularly, in Ontario) among soft Liberals who liked Singh but were unsure of Trudeau. Singh was seen as likable, warm, positive, and empathic while Trudeau was seen as insincere, an actor playing a role, and interested in playing political games instead of focusing on improving the lives of Canadians. Further, taxing the ultrarich to pay for better social programs was an issue that resonated with NDP's targeted voters. These voters believed that rich Canadians had benefitted by making large profits during the COVID-19 pandemic, though these potential supporters were skeptical that anything could actually be done to get the ultrarich to pay their fair share. Ultimately, this market intelligence led to a clearer picture of Singh's brand and the party's messaging. Operatives talked about developing a personal brand for Singh that emphasized that he was trustworthy and understood the problems of everyday Canadians, but also focused on how he was a strong and competent leader who could deliver improvements for Canadians' lives in the next parliament, no matter what form that it took. These branding exercises and market research led to pre-election advertising, both on television and online, that emphasized how Trudeau had protected the profits of the ultrarich during the pandemic while Singh had fought in parliament for better jobs and higher COVID benefits for workers. The ads asked, "Ready for something different?" and the tagline was "Jagmeet Singh – Fighting for you."

In interviews, NDP operatives pointed out that the party's goals into the 2021 campaign were to let their incumbent MPs take care of their own seats while the central party focused on winning new ones. In contrast to the 2019 election when the NDP ran a regionalized campaign focused on the parts of Ontario, British Columbia, and Quebec, where it thought it could keep the seats that it held and add a few new ones, the party drew up an ambitious list of approximately fifty targeted seats (mostly held by the Liberals) from coast to coast that the NDP did not hold. The tactics to win these new seats reveal a leader-centric approach in NDP's political marketing; these targeted seats were to be given extra central support from party headquarters and the leader's tour would visit them so that Singh could personally highlight the contrast between himself and Trudeau for soft Liberal supporters living there. One operative admitted that it would not be hard to guess which seats the NDP was targeting; one would just look where Singh showed up.

While candidate recruitment did begin in the year prior to the election, it went quite slowly with many candidates in targeted seats not being nominated until the Summer of 2021 and only 210 out of 338 being officially nominated on the day that the writ dropped (compared to 284 for the Liberals and 304 for the Conservatives).[10] Further, the focus on Singh in the party's political marketing appeared to preclude an emphasis on a strong team of NDP candidates as part of the NDP communications strategy. With the exception of Avi Lewis (filmmaker and son of former Ontario NDP leader, Steven Lewis) and former Quebec NDP MP Ruth Ellen Brosseau, there were very few star NDP candidates in the election.

THE ELECTION PLATFORM

The 2019 platform had been drawn up by group of MPs and NDP operatives from around the country who were volunteering their time. As opposed to relying on polling and focus groups that the NDP could not afford, this group used their own values and gut instinct to create platform promises that they believed were what potential NDP voters wanted. The process of creating the 2021 NDP platform was more professionalized, with paid staff in the Policy and Platform Department at NDP headquarters doing the work using data from polling and focus groups as well as consultations with the federal council, MPs, unions, and relevant stakeholders. Singh then was given final approval of the document. Despite differences in the processes that created the two documents, the 2021 NDP platform ended up being very similar to the 2019 version. The operatives interviewed suggested that this similarity was rooted in the short time between the 2019 and 2021 elections as well as the general feeling at party headquarters and within the party that the 2019 platform had worked well, and little change was needed.

The title of the NDP's 2021 platform, *Ready for Better*, is an obvious play on the contrast between what voters had (Trudeau) and what they could have (Singh). The importance of Singh to the NDP's political marketing is illustrated in the visuals of the 115-page platform document: forty-three pictures are of Singh either by himself or interacting with voters. No NDP candidates are mentioned in the platform and there are only two pictures in which NDP candidates appear (even in these two pictures, they are accompanying Singh who is talking with a voter in their riding).

As for the ideological tenor of the platform, it was moderately to the left of the 2019 NDP platform, a document that was already more left-wing than the party's 2011 and 2015 platforms.[11] Indeed, a brief summary of the 2021 platform would be that it contained almost all of what the NDP promised in 2019 with some additional measures related to COVID-19 added that were meant to highlight the Jagmeet versus Justin contrast. Twelve out of the fourteen additional revenue streams proposed in the 2021 platform, all relating to higher taxes on corporations and wealthy individuals, also appeared in the 2019 platform. The one notable addition was a temporary COVID-19 excess profit measure that put an additional 15 per cent tax on windfall profits of large corporations during the pandemic. This new proposal was directly related to Singh's statement in pre-election advertising that Trudeau was protecting the pandemic-related profits of the rich while Singh would fight to make the rich pay their fair share of financing Canada's post-COVID-19 recovery. Out of the sixty-three promises in the NDP's 2021 platform that had new spending attached, fully forty-eight were found in the party's 2019 platform. Thus, big spending measures in the 2019 platform like universal prescription drug insurance, building 500,000 affordable homes, universal childcare, increasing public transit funding, doubling grants for postsecondary students, and universal dental care re-appeared in the 2021 platform. Additionally, new spending related to COVID-19 was introduced, such as a vaccination passport, a hiring bonus for small businesses, the nationalization of for-profit long-term care homes, changes to sick leave for workers, and more generous unemployment benefits. These pledges were meant to reinforce the NDP's claim that Singh would help out average Canadians during the COVID-19 pandemic recovery compared to Trudeau who only implemented more generous COVID-19-related benefits when he had been forced to by Singh.

A final important difference in spending between the 2019 and 2021 platforms related to Indigenous Canadians. While the NDP committed $500 million to $700 million annually over four years for new funding for the Indigenous child welfare system in its 2019 platform, it committed a full $15 billion in the first year of a NDP government in its 2021 platform to comply with a recent Canadian Human Rights Tribunal order to improve the Indigenous child welfare system and give compensation to Indigenous families harmed by the federal government's racial discrimination against their children.[12] This very large spending increase was connected to the Jagmeet versus Justin contrast, since one of Singh's most repeated attacks on the prime minister was that he had taken Indigenous children to court instead of providing them fair compensation for their suffering.[13] When all of the new spending was added up, the NDP's proposed annual new spending had increased from $30–$34 billion in the 2019 version to $40–$44 billion in the 2021 version. Given that the generation of tax revenues between the two platforms was similar but spending went up and economic growth was down during to the COVID-19 pandemic, the NDP proposed much larger deficits and debt-to-GDP (gross domestic product) ratios in its 2021 platform compared to its 2019 platform.[14]

A cursory comparison of the NDP's 2021 platform with that of the Liberals illustrates that the two parties were interested in addressing the same issues, but that the NDP was more willing to spend more, tax more, and regulate more to bring about immediate results. The NDP's leader-centric political marketing was at work here because the NDP needed concrete examples of policy offerings to illustrate how Singh was "better" than Trudeau. For instance, the Liberals proposed a temporary tax on banks and insurance companies who profited during the pandemic that would generate $1 billion, whereas the NDP's broader excess profit tax proposed to generate $14 billion. Further, while the Liberals and the NDP both proposed new spending on affordable housing, healthcare, seniors' care, postsecondary education, and Indigenous issues, the NDP spending proposals were considerably higher than Liberals. The NDP's promised regulations to bring down greenhouse gas emissions were also stricter than the Liberals' and the NDP's greenhouse gas emissions reduction targets were higher than the Liberals'.[15]

Overall, the 2021 NDP platform was a throwback to the social democracy of the 1970s, exemplified by the 1972 campaign slogan of "corporate welfare bums."[16] In many ways, the NDP's move back to postwar social democracy was driven by the emphasis on the Jagmeet versus Justin contrast in its political marketing. Trudeau had moved the Liberal Party to the left since becoming its leader and Singh needed a platform based on taxing the rich and spending big to place the NDP clearly to the left of the governing Liberals and to be able to credibly argue that he was "better" than Trudeau. The Liberals moving to the left naturally forced the NDP to move to the left further. At the same time, operatives noted that the platform was in line with the sentiment of the Canadian electorate during the fourth wave of COVID-19 and there was little pushback from the media or voters about the cost of the NDP's new spending promises and the proposal to run larger deficits. Indeed, even though the NDP proposed much higher spending than the Liberals and Conservatives, its platform forecast lower annual deficits than their two main competitors due to the NDP's more aggressive revenue-generating proposals focused on taxing the rich.[17]

THE CAMPAIGN PERIOD

Given the focus on Singh in its political marketing, the key element in the NDP's 2021 campaign was the leader's tour and daily news conference when Singh attacked Trudeau and presented himself as a "better" alternative. Operatives noted that the NDP tried to spread out its launch for two days in a row by having media availability for Singh in Montreal before the city's Pride Parade on 15 August and then a more formal launch in Toronto the next morning. In Montreal, Singh clearly laid out the Jagmeet versus Justin contrast that he would hammer on relentlessly throughout the campaign: "After six years, we know a lot about Mr Trudeau. He wants to look like he cares. He says the right thing but has no intention of doing it … I'm ready to fight for working people, to make the ultrarich and big corporations pay their fair share, and to build a recovery that works for everyone."[18] Unlike 2019, when the NDP reduced its costs by chartering a plane to fly Singh between cities and then using a bus to tour a particular region over several days, the party chartered a plane (branded with their leader's name) for Singh and his entourage for the entire campaign, allowing the leader's tour to stop in multiple provinces in a single day and to quickly move between regions that were far apart.

Singh mostly spent the first part of the campaign in Ontario, Quebec, and British Columbia with stops in three Prairie cities (Edmonton, Regina, and Winnipeg) and St John's. The focus on Quebec was due to operatives wanting Singh to bring attention to the high-profile candidacy of Ruth Ellen Brosseau,[19] Singh needing to be in Montreal for the TVA debate, and internal polling showing that the NDP was trending upwards in the province. After Labour Day, operatives saw the NDP's polling numbers in Quebec go down following Shachi Kurl's question in the English-language debate[20] and the party focused the rest of Singh's tour on Ontario and British Columbia with stops in Sackville, Edmonton, Sherbrooke, and Saskatoon. In its communications on election day, the party highlighted that Singh had visited fifty-one ridings during the campaign, almost all of which were not held by the NDP.[21]

My analysis of the itinerary of Singh's tour finds that the NDP divided his time as follows: 46 per cent in Ontario, 20 per cent in British Columbia, 17 per cent in Quebec, 5 per cent in Alberta, 5 per cent in Saskatchewan, and 2 per cent each in Manitoba, Newfoundland and Labrador, and Nova Scotia.[22] To be more precise, even though the NDP-targeted seats were spread all over Canada, the party ended up focusing most of Singh's time on Liberal-held seats in the city of Toronto, the cities immediately outside of Toronto, northern Ontario, the lower mainland of British Columbia, and the island of Montreal. Reflective of the leader-centric campaign that the NDP was running, operatives hoped that sending Singh into these Liberal seats to draw contrasts between himself and Trudeau would convince enough soft Liberal supporters to vote NDP and flip these seats from red to orange. As such, operatives noted that the NDP's media strategy remained constant throughout the entire campaign: to criticize Trudeau on his record and show that Singh was a "better" alternative.

The NDP's organizational structure during the 2021 campaign was similar to past elections. One wrinkle in the organization, compared to the 2015 and 2019 elections, was that the Quebec team operated relatively independently from the rest of the campaign, with different vendors, their own ad agency, and a separate communications strategy. The NDP's Quebec message centred around the verb "Oser [to dare]." Operatives explained that the NDP was asking Quebecers to dare to be different, dare to do the unexpected, and dare to do better. The party's Quebec message was intimately tied to Singh's leadership and personal story – instead of voting for Trudeau who represented the status quo, voters should dare to vote for a leader from a racialized minority community who wanted to tax the rich to pay for better social programs and ensure aggressive action to combat climate change.

Similar to the rest of the NDP's political marketing, its voter contact and get-out-the-vote efforts were leader centric. The pamphlets provided to local campaigns focused on Singh and the contrast between Singh and Trudeau (though criticisms of O'Toole were added in the regions like the Prairies where the NDP's main opponent was the Conservatives). In addition to local efforts, there was a phone bank in party headquarters in Ottawa calling into targeted seats with a script that emphasized Singh's leadership. Moreover, the NDP's digital outreach efforts were very much centred on Singh. The party's online advertising, social media posts, and Singh's Tik Tok feed all featured a call to action for voters to "text Jagmeet" with ideas about what music he should listen on the tour bus and recommendations for restaurants in the cities that he visited, or thoughts about the NDP's policies. Voters who texted the number supplied by the party then got what appeared to be personal texts directly from Singh on their cell phones throughout the campaign. This texting program, run out of party headquarters in Ottawa, used these pseudopersonal texts from Singh to push voters to the polls and to recruit volunteers. Volunteers recruited in this method became part of "Team Jagmeet" and they were asked to attend virtual meetings of small "Team Jagmeet" groups to learn about how they could get involved in the NDP's campaign. Singh himself would frequently pop into these virtual meetings to encourage volunteers to keep working hard and express his gratitude for their efforts.

The CLC's goals were to elect as many NDP MPs, and defeat as many Conservative MPs, as possible to ensure that workers' concerns were well-represented in deliberations over the post-COVID-19 recovery in the next parliament (particularly if there continued to be a Liberal minority government). The CLC, and its unions who were affiliated with the NDP, focused on contacting union members and contacting voters in ridings held by the Conservatives that could be flipped, with ridings held by the Conservatives with a strong NDP challenger being heavily targeted. Door-to-door canvasses for NDP candidates in these ridings were organized (twenty-seven of which were led by the new CLC president) and there were also activities that allowed activists to contact voters and fellow union members from their homes like phone banking through Call Hub and text banking. Similar to the 2019 federal election, the CLC did not run any television, radio, and print ads, preferring to focus its financial resources on online advertising. While unions and the NDP were closely collaborating prior to the campaign, rules introduced in 2018, prohibiting collusion between political parties and third parties, limited the formal involvement of union leaders and staff in strategizing with the NDP campaign during the writ period and in the three months ahead of the writ period.

The operatives interviewed had troubling recalling events that changed the dynamics of the campaign in a dramatic fashion. They mentioned that Singh's two visits to Indigenous reservations (Cowessess and Neskantaga) were powerful moments illustrating his empathy and desire to improve Indigenous Canadians' lives, compared to Trudeau who the operatives claimed talked a lot about reconciliation but accomplished very little. They also brought up how the large amount of media attention accorded to Singh's prowess with social media and his ability to connect with young Canadians gave the NDP campaign a sense of momentum. The NDP's strategy in the two French debates was to illustrate the relevance of the NDP to Quebec politics by highlighting Singh's critique of Trudeau for not delivering on his promises to improve Quebecers' lives and showcasing that Singh shared Quebecers' values. The NDP's strategy in the sole English-language debate was to hammer home the "better is possible" theme of their campaign by attempting to make the debate exclusively focus on Trudeau's record and his failures as a prime minister. While operatives were pleased with Singh's debate performances and the resulting media coverage for their party, they did not see any bump for their party in their internal polling numbers or public domain polling.

Given the relative stability of the party's polling numbers and the lack of negative reaction in the media to what the party's campaign was doing, NDP strategists decided to maintain their initial strategy throughout the campaign. As one operative put it, "we had a clearly delineated strategy that we executed from the first day to the last day of the campaign and we did not deviate from it." The main message associated with that strategy could be summed up in the ballot box question that the interviewees identified that was explicitly a comparison of Singh's and Trudeau's leadership: "Do you want someone who will fight for you in Ottawa or someone who says the right things but does not deliver?"

ADVERTISING AND NEWS RELEASES

Looking closely at the NDP's commercials and news releases allows for a deeper examination of the Jagmeet versus Justin contrast in the NDP's political marketing. All of the federal NDP's commercials and all of Singh's Tik Tok posts during the campaign were coded using the Qualitative Data Analysis Software (CAQDAS) program N-vivo 12, which calculates "percentage coverage" based on the number of characters coded into a particular theme.[23]

The most striking characteristic of figure 4.1 is how vividly it displays the NDP's campaign's emphasis on the Jagmeet versus Justin contrast. According to my analysis, NDP's English television commercials spent roughly half their time attacking Trudeau's leadership while spending the other half touting Singh's leadership. The overarching message was that Singh is a "better" alternative to what voters had in the sitting prime minister. The commercials stressed that Trudeau is "all talk, no action" because he says all the right things on important issues like COVID-19 benefits, Pharmacare, reconciliation with Indigenous peoples, and climate change, but all he is really interested in is protecting the profits of his rich friends. On the other hand, Singh is better than Trudeau – he has already delivered better COVID-19 benefits for Canadians in the recent minority parliament and, in the next parliament, he will make sure the rich pay their fair share to fund important social programs that will be needed during the post-COVID-19 recovery. Indeed, many of the commercials ended with Singh stating: "Ready for better? We're ready too."

Just as in the 2019 election, the NDP produced signficantly fewer French commercials than English commercials. However, in 2021, the NDP's French commercials did receive more air time in Quebec compared to the previous election. The party's series of three French commercials (one on taxing the ultrarich, one on the environment, and one on affordable housing) featured a casually dressed Singh standing against a brightly coloured background and talking straight into the camera. The text of each commercial had a similar pattern: a brief critique of Trudeau's inaction, lack of courage or duplicity,

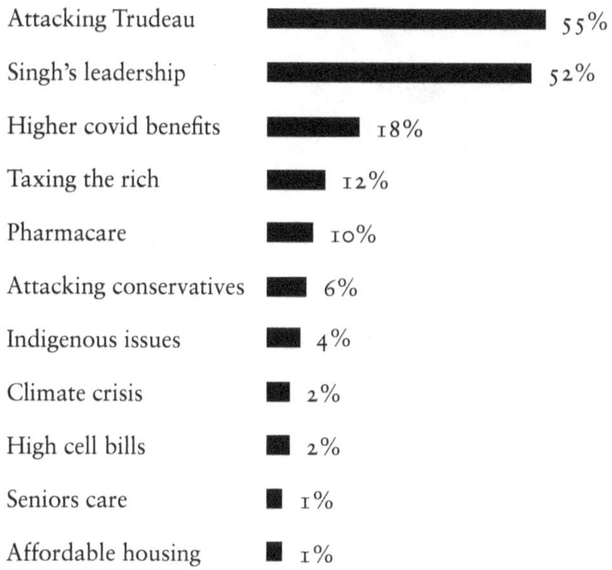

Note: percentages may total more than 100 per cent because some passages were coded twice if they implied two different themes.

Figure 4.1 | Percentage coverage of themes in NDP English TV ads (2021 election)

followed by Singh outlining his plan for the specific policy that the commercial was addressing. Since every second of every commercial had Singh talking directly to voters about his plan to improve their lives, I coded all of their text as emphasizing Singh's leadership. Trudeau was not going to act on important issues facing Quebec, the commercials argued, while Jagmeet is better – he will accelerate action to fight the climate crisis, build 500,000 affordable houses, and make the ultrarich pay their fair share. So, if Quebec voters want action on the issues that matter to them, Singh advised them at the end of the commercials that "il faut juste oser [all you have to do is dare]" to vote NDP.

Tik Tok emerged in the late 2010s as an alternative social media platform to Facebook, Twitter, and Snapchat that often involves

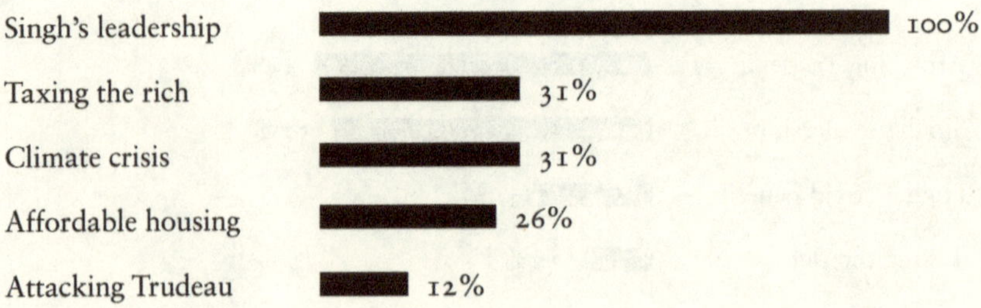

Note: percentages may total more than 100 per cent because some passages were coded twice if they implied two different themes.

Figure 4.2 | Percentage coverage of themes in NDP French TV ads (2021 election)

videos of users lip-synching and dancing, or both, to short excerpts of popular songs. While Singh continued to use Twitter to respond to his opponents' criticisms and Facebook for pushing out the party's advertising during the 2021 campaign, he used Tik Tok as a fun and less serious way to connect with voters. Singh's Tik Tok feed was often commented on by media because he was the only major party leader with a Tik Tok account and it illustrated how he was popular among young voters.[24] Indeed, by the end of the campaign, Singh had almost 850,000 Tik Tok followers and some of his posts were getting over two million views. Operatives explained how Tik Tok was essentially free for the party because it does not allow political advertising and production costs were negligible since Singh took charge of conceiving and filming his own posts on his smartphone. An operative on the NDP's leader's tour described how Singh, an avid Tik Tok user, would continually be looking for popular Tik Tok trends and when he found one that he thought he could be used to deliver his party's message, he would quickly shoot a video with minimal editing to make sure that it felt authentic and not contrived.

My analysis in figure 4.3 illustrates that the main purposes of Singh's Tik Tok feed were to encourage young people to vote and to give them a glimpse into Singh's personal life, as opposed to discussing the NDP's policy offerings. Specifically, his Tik Tok posts directed

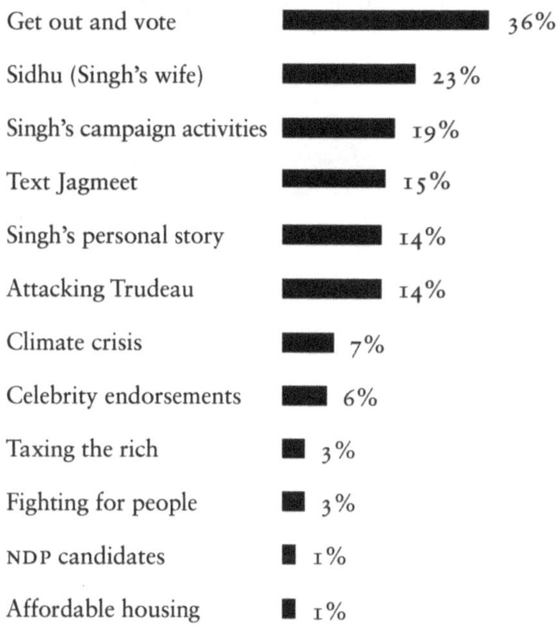

Note: percentages may total more than 100 per cent because some passages were coded twice if they implied two different themes.

Figure 4.3 | Percentage coverage of themes in Singh's TikTok (2021 election)

viewers to the NDP's website, www.howyouvote.ca, that walked them through the process of voting and asked them to text Singh a personal message that was used to contact them later to invite them to volunteer on the NDP's campaign and remind them to vote. While Singh's Tik Tok posts did directly attack Trudeau, more time was spent on Singh's background, his daily campaign routines, and humorous banter with his wife.

Table 4.1 uses the same inductive coding technique as figures 4.1 to 4.3 to analyze the news releases of the NDP during the campaign. In three important ways, it reinforces my overall analysis and confirms the information that I was given by NDP operatives. First, the Jagmeet versus Justin contrast was the overwhelmingly dominant

Table 4.1 | Percentage coverage of themes in federal NDP press releases by week

Week 1 (15 August–22 August)	Week 2 (23 August–29 August)	Week 3 (30 August–5 September)
Attacking Trudeau: 70%	Attacking Trudeau: 57%	Attacking Trudeau: 61%
Singh's leadership: 42%	Singh's leadership: 24%	Singh's leadership: 35%
Affordable housing: 21%	Taxing the rich: 16%	Affordable housing: 23%
Taxing the rich: 17%	Climate crisis: 11%	Taxing the rich: 22%
Mandatory vaccination: 17%	Student debt: 11%	Healthcare funding: 8%
Attacking Conservatives: 11%	Affordable housing: 10%	Indigenous issues: 8%
Indigenous issues: 8%	Seniors' care: 10%	Increasing Covid vaccination rates: 8%
Higher Covid-19 benefits: 7%	NDP candidates: 9%	Climate crisis: 6%
Healthcare: 7%	Lower cell bills: 8%	Quebec and federalism: 6%
Industrial strategy: 6%	Pharmacare: 8%	Dental care: 5%
Anniversary of Layton's death: 6%	Attacking Conservatives: 7%	Pharmacare: 3%
Nova Scotia election results: 4%	Afghanistan: 6%	NDP candidates: 3%
Seniors care: 4%	Privatization of healthcare: 5%	Attacking Conservatives: 3%
Drug overdose Crisis: 4%	Healthcare funding: 3%	Higher Covid benefits: 2%
Childcare: 2%	Encouragement to get out and vote: 3%	Attacking BQ: 1%
NDP candidates: 1%	Labour issues: 3%	
	Pensions: 3%	

Table 4.1 | (*continued*)

Week 4 (6 September–12 September)	Week 5 (13 September–20 September)
Attacking Trudeau: 62%	Attacking Trudeau: 84%
Singh's leadership: 38%	Singh's leadership: 33%
Taxing the rich: 24%	Taxing the rich: 21%
Climate crisis: 18%	Affordable housing: 16%
Affordable housing: 11%	Lower cell bills: 13%
Northern Ontario: 12%	Seniors care: 12%
NDP candidates: 10%	Climate crisis: 11%
Labour issues: 6%	Tougher restrictions to prevent spread of Covid-19: 5%
Indigenous issues: 4%	Indigenous issues: 4%
Guaranteed liveable income: 4%	Make protesting at hospitals illegal: 4%
NDP candidates: 3%	Attacking Conservatives: 1%
Attacking Conservatives: 5%	Pharmacare: 1%
Encouragement to get out and vote: 3%	
Lower cell bills: 2%	
Healthcare funding: 1%	
Pharmacare: 1%	
Trade issues: 1%	
LGBTQ+ rights: 0.25%	

theme in the NDP's releases in each week of the campaign. Simply put, the texts of the news releases from each day of the campaign followed the exact same pattern: critique Trudeau's failings on a particular issue and tout how Singh's plan was a better alternative. Second, NDP candidates were barely mentioned in the news releases to keep the focus firmly on Singh's leadership. Third, the theme of taxing the rich was consistently used throughout the campaign as a point of difference between Trudeau and Singh: Trudeau wanted to protect the wealth of the rich whereas Singh wanted to make them pay their fair share. Indeed, near the end of the campaign, Singh seized on Trudeau's critique of the NDP for going after the rich with "unlimited zeal" as unequivocal evidence that the Liberal leader was "on the side of billionaires."[25]

ANALYSIS OF RESULTS

When compared to their 2019 results, the NDP had a net gain of one seat in 2021, even though it centrally spent $25 million – $15 million more than the previous election. The NDP won all of the seats in 2021 that it had won in 2019, with two exceptions – it lost one seat to the Liberals (St John's East) and another seat to the Conservatives (Essex). It picked up two seats from Conservatives (Edmonton Griesbach and Port Moody-Coquitlam), and one seat from the Greens (Nanaimo-Ladysmith). The party won none of the Liberal-held seats that it targeted in Toronto and its environs, Northern Ontario, Montreal, or the BC lower mainland. The party could take some solace in that its national vote improved from 15.9 to 17.8 per cent, a gain that was driven by large increases in its vote in Alberta and British Columbia and a slight increase in Ontario.

The party's results were quite close to its historical average from 1962 to 2008 in both seats and popular vote, while the party's 2011 and 2015 results now appear to be clearly outliers. The NDP's 2021 national popular vote was only 2 per cent higher than its average national popular vote from 1962 to 2008, and the party's 2021 seat count only one higher than its average seat count from 1962 to 2008. Its seat count and popular vote in Alberta and British Columbia were higher than the 1962–2008 average, but the party reverted to a share of popular vote and share of seats similar to what it usually won from its inception in 1962 to the orange wave election of 2011in other provinces.

Table 4.2 | NDP electoral results in 1962–2008, 2011, 2015, 2019, and 2021

Province	Average Vote (1962–2008)	2011 Vote	2015 Vote	2019 Vote	2021 Vote	Average Seat Total (1962–2008)	2011 Seat Total	2015 Seat Total	2019 Seat Total	2021 Seat Total
NL	12.3%	32.6%	21.0%	23.9%	17.4%	0.1	2	0	1	0
PEI	7.0%	15.4%	16.0%	7.6%	9.2%	0.0	0	0	0	0
NS	16.9%	30.3%	16.4%	18.9%	22.1%	1.1	3	0	0	0
NB	12.0%	29.8%	18.3%	9.4%	11.9%	0.4	1	0	0	0
QC	6.9%	42.9%	25.4%	10.7%	9.8%	0.1	59	16	1	1
ON	17.5%	25.6%	16.6%	16.8%	17.8%	7.3	22	8	6	5
MB	24.0%	25.8%	13.8%	20.7%	21.4%	3.3	2	2	3	3
SK	30.0%	32.3%	25.1%	19.5%	21.1%	3.2	0	3	0	0
AB	9.7%	16.8%	11.6%	11.5%	19.1%	0.1	1	1	1	2
BC	28.1%	32.5%	25.9%	24.4%	31.0%	7.9	12	14	11	13
Territories	25.2%	27.8%	25.3%	25.6%	30.3%	0.6	1	0	1	1
National	15.9%	30.6%	19.7%	15.9%	17.8%	24.1	103	44	24	25

CONCLUSION

The NDP operatives interviewed for this chapter were very dissatisfied with their party's inability to win more seats than it had won in 2019. They described how the NDP's local ground game and its training of grassroots activists needed to be better to translate the party's increased popular vote into more seats. One mentioned that the party might have targeted too many seats, thereby spreading its central support too wide and too thin. They were also disappointed in what appeared to be a low voter turnout in the socio-demographic groups that lean towards the NDP (youth, racialized minorities, Indigenous communities, and others) and were angry about Elections Canada's decisions that increased barriers to voting for these groups, such as the decision to not have polling stations on university campuses. Nonetheless, the operatives interviewed did not question the leader-centric nature of the party's political marketing and expressed an optimism for the future. They pointed out how Singh has been established as a well-known and popular political figure in Canada and how he can use his kingmaker status in the next minority parliament to push the Liberals to deliver better social programs and to ensure that the NDP stays relevant in Canadian politics. They feel the party has a strong foundation to build upon and a clear path towards winning more seats in the future.

Still, the whole point of the Jagmeet versus Justin contrast was to convince soft Liberal voters, particularly in Liberal-held seats in certain parts of Ontario, Quebec, and British Columbia, to come over to the NDP to give the party more seats than it won in 2019. This simply did not happen. Instead of flipping seats from red to orange in 2021, the NDP actually lost a seat to the Liberals and did not succeed in winning even one Liberal-held seat. As a political strategy, the Jagmeet versus Justin contrast did not meet its intended goal. Despite all of the money and time that the NDP spent on critiquing Trudeau and building up Singh as "better," Liberal voters were generally not persuaded to switch to the NDP in this election.

This raises interesting questions for the study of the NDP. Certainly, the idea of using a popular NDP leader to entice Liberal voters (particularly in Ontario) to vote NDP is not new. A similar strategy was used during the Layton years and also under Broadbent in the 1980s.[26] Does the federal NDP keep on repeating a leader-centric strategy aimed at peeling away soft Liberal voters because it feels that there is no other option given the dominance of the Liberal Party at the federal level? Is a leader-centric strategy the only way for the federal NDP to appear relevant in the minds of voters and overcome the weaknesses associated with the party's brand? Or, have the tactics and organizations of all political parties in western democracies became increasingly leader centric[27] and the federal NDP is just following this trend? Examining the reasons why the federal NDP keeps repeating a similar strategy and why it seems to be perennially unable to persuade soft Liberal voters to migrate to the NDP would be an endeavour that would interest academics and NDP activists alike.

At a broader level, the case of the 2021 federal NDP campaign raises questions for political marketing scholars about the value of pursuing such leader-centric political marketing during elections. Is there no longer any aspect of election campaigns that remains free from the presence and influence of the party leader? For instance, technology used by the NDP in 2021 allowed its leader to be heavily involved in volunteer recruitment by sending out seemingly personalized texts directly to the phones of potential volunteers. This method of volunteer recruitment is a long way from local party activists recruiting campaign workers after church services, on university campuses, or in union halls. Finally, how effective is an overwhelming emphasis on leadership in a party's political marketing? The federal NDP in 2021 might have overspent on its advertising featuring Singh and his leader's tour while underinvesting in the recruitment and training of high-quality candidates and the building up of strong local campaigns. Studies on the effectiveness of spending on a party's air game that is usually leader focused versus the effectiveness of spending on local campaigns that are more candidate focused could be revealing.

NOTES

1 David McGrane, *The New NDP: Moderation, Modernization, and Political Marketing* (Vancouver: University of British Columbia Press, 2019); Alex Marland, "Amateurs Versus Professionals: The 1993 and 2006 Canadian Federal Elections," in *Political Marketing in Canada*, eds. Alex Marland, Thierry Giasson, and Jennifer Lees-Marshment (Vancouver: University of British Columbia Press, 2012); Jared Wesley and Mike Moyes, "Selling Social Democracy: Branding and the Political Left in Canada," in *Political Communication in Canada: Meet the Press and Tweet the Rest*, eds. Alex Marland, Thierry Giasson, and Tamara Small (Vancouver: University of British Columbia Press, 2014).

2 I conducted semi-structured interviews with NDP operatives working in the party's central campaign from 5 October 2021 to 15 October 2021. To ensure that the interviewees remained candid, I took handwritten notes, as opposed to recordings. An agreement was made with informants to publish their names but not to attribute any exact quotations or information to a particular person. The following NDP party officials graciously agreed to be interviewed: Anne McGrath (national director), George Soule (director of communications), Marie Della Mattia (political

adviser on leader's tour), and Brent Farrington (director of political action for the Canadian Labour Congress).

3 David McGrane, "Making the Best of It: Political Marketing the NDP's Fight for Relevance" in *The Canadian Federal Election of 2019*, eds. Jon Pammett and Christopher Doran (Montreal: McGill-Queen's University Press, 2020), 74–7.

4 McGrane, "Making the Best of It: Political Marketing the NDP's Fight for Relevance," 83–95.

5 In the six financial quarters from March 2018 to June 2019, the NDP brought in $7.6 million. In comparison, in the six financial quarters from March 2020 to June 2021, the NDP brought in $9.2 million.

6 Solarina Ho, "Can the NDP Take Credit for Improving Pandemic Benefits?" CBC News, 18 August 2021, https://www.ctvnews.ca/politics/can-the-ndp-take-credit-for-improving-pandemic-benefits-1.5552602.

7 "How Canadians View the Federal Party Leaders," Abacus Data, 12 July 2021, https://abacusdata.ca/party-leaders-canada-abacus-july-2021/.

8 "Canadian Labour Congress Elects New President to Lead Nation's Biggest Labour Group," CBC News, 18 June 2021, https://www.cbc.ca/news/politics/clc-new-president-1.6072291.

9 For an example, see Gary Mason, "Jagmeet Singh Is on a Roll. This Is Bad News for Justin Trudeau," *Globe and Mail*, 24 August 2021, https://www.theglobeandmail.com/opinion/article-jagmeet-singh-is-on-a-roll-this-is-bad-news-for-justin-trudeau/.

10 Sarah Turnbull, "Candidate Nominations: Where the Parties Stand on Day 1 of the Campaign," CTV News, 15 August 2021, https://www.ctvnews.ca/politics/candidate-nominations-where-the-parties-stand-on-day-1-of-the-campaign-1.5548142.

11 For a comparison of the NDP's 2019 platform with its 2011 and 2015 platforms see McGrane, "Making the Best of It: Political Marketing the NDP's Fight for Relevance," 81–3.

12 Brett Forester, "Parliamentary Budget Office Says Cost of Compensating First Nations Families Sits at $15B," APTN News, 23 February 2021, https://www.aptnnews.ca/national-news/parliamentary-budget-office-tribunal-says-cost-of-compensating-first-nations-families-sits-at-15b/.

13 Nicole Bogart and Richard Madan, "Did Trudeau's Government Take Indigenous Kids to Court?" CTV News, 10 September 2021, https://www.ctvnews.ca/politics/federal-election-2021/did-trudeau-s-government-take-Indigenous-kids-to-court-1.5581348.

14 Ryan Patrick Jones, "NDP Platform Calls for $200 billion in New Spending on Health Care, Climate Change, Indigenous Reconciliation,"

CBC News, 11 September 2021, https://www.cbc.ca/news/politics/ndp-platform-costing-1.6172629.

15 Emily Chung, "Climate Change and the Election: Compare Party Platforms," CBC News, 12 September 2021, https://www.cbc.ca/news/science/climate-platforms-1.6171619.

16 David Lewis, *Louder Voices: The Corporate Welfare Bums* (Toronto: Lorimer Publishing, 1972).

17 Jones, "NDP Platform Calls for $200 billion in New Spending."

18 "Jagmeet Singh Ready to Fight for People across Canada," New Democratic Party of Canada, 15 August 2021, https://www.ndp.ca/news/jagmeet-singh-ready-fight-people-across-canada.

19 Brosseau was a paper candidate who unexpectedly won for the NDP in 2011 in Quebec despite not living there and doing no campaigning. She went on to be a successful MP and was re-elected in 2015 only to lose a close election in 2019.

20 See chapter 5 in this book.

21 Menaka Raman-Wilms and Bill Curry, "NDP Focused on Broken Liberal Promises," *Globe and Mail*, 21 September 2021, A6.

22 Data from the CBC News website was used to make these calculations.

23 QSR International, *Nvivo 9 Basics*, (Doncaster, Australia: QSR International, 2010), 54.

24 For instance, see Raisa Patel, "Jagmeet Singh Is a TikTok Superstar. Here's What That Means for the Next Election," *Toronto Star*, 5 July 2021, https://www.thestar.com/politics/federal/2021/07/05/jagmeet-singh-is-a-tiktok-superstar-heres-what-that-means-for-the-next-election.html.

25 Jordan Press, "Leaders Argue Over How to Pay for Promises as Voters Head to Advance Polls," CTV News, 12 September 2021, https://www.ctvnews.ca/politics/federal-election-2021/leaders-argue-over-how-to-pay-for-promises-as-voters-head-to-advance-polls-1.5582262.

26 McGrane, *The New NDP*, 132–60; and Alan Whitehorn, *Canadian Socialism: Essays on the CCF-NDP* (Toronto: Oxford University Press, 1992), 211–35.

27 Thomas Poguntke and Paul Webb, *The Presidentialization of Politics in Democratic Societies: A Comparative Study of Modern Democracies* (Oxford: Oxford University Press, 2005).

5

The Bloc Québécois as a Safe Bet

Éric Montigny

At its founding convention in June 1991, the Bloc Québécois' first leader, Lucien Bouchard, asserted that the success of this nationalist party should be measured by the length of its existence.[1] In the wake of the failure of the Meech Lake Accord, it was supposed to be a temporary vehicle composed of former Conservative and Liberal MPs who joined forces to defend the unique character of Quebec until it could become sovereign.[2] In fact, to use a hockey analogy, the Bloc's existence was then part of what Quebec sovereigntists called the "three-period strategy." The 1993 federal election was the first period and was a success for the Bloc, which became the official opposition in the House of Commons. The second period was the 1994 Quebec election, which the Parti Québécois (PQ), led by Jacques Parizeau, won as it obtained a mandate to hold a referendum on sovereignty. The third period was the 1995 referendum campaign but, with a result of 49.4 per cent, the Yes option to sovereignty-partnership was defeated. There has been no rematch since, but the Bloc Québécois managed to keep a role in Ottawa. Ironically, the dean of the House of Commons is now a Bloc Québécois MP. Re-elected in 2021, Louis Plamondon has been in Ottawa since 1984. When he left the Progressive-Conservative Party, he was one of the first members of the Bloc. The founding convention of the Bloc even took place in his riding of Bécancour-Nicolet-Saurel. Like Louis Plamondon, the Bloc has crossed the ages. So how do we explain the resilience of a "temporary party" thirty years later?

It is true that the Bloc Québécois has experienced many ups and downs in its history. The orange wave of the New Democratic Party in Quebec in 2011 almost made it disappear, when Jack Layton campaigned in Quebec on the promise of asymmetrical federalism and won over many autonomists and even some sovereigntists. Consequently, only four Bloc MPs were elected and even leader Gilles Duceppe lost his seat. He returned to his role in 2015 to try to save a party that was going nowhere under Mario Beaulieu's leadership, managed to get ten MPs elected, but again failed to win his riding. A few months before the 2019 election, the Bloc once again faced an internal crisis that highlighted a clash between two visions of its role. One was resolutely pro-independence and anti-system[3] and the other was more moderate. The latter won, and Yves François Blanchet was selected as the new leader; he exceeded expectations in 2019 by winning thirty-two seats and obtained the same result in 2021, consolidating the Bloc's resurgence.

By studying the Bloc's 2021 electoral campaign, we can see its ideological evolution. We will first analyze the dynamics of its campaign. It took place in two parts, a first half where its leader sought his bearings, and a second where fortune smiled on him. We will then analyze the issue of constitutional jurisdiction as the first lifeline of his campaign. The commitments of the Liberal Party of Canada (LPC) and the NDP which intruded into the jurisdiction of the Quebec National Assembly provided an opportunity for the Bloc to take the offensive, just as it did during the leaders' debate in English. We also need to understand the importance of Premier François Legault's role in the campaign. Furthermore, in a more structural way, we will reflect on the place of the Bloc Québécois within the Quebec sovereigntist movement. For most of its existence, the BQ had been constrained by the Parti Québécois in a way that differs from other parties. It has now adapted to a new political reality in Quebec's politics in which the PQ is no longer dominant and where Quebec nationalism has evolved towards autonomy. We will conclude this analysis by explaining its role in the dual legitimacy of Quebec's elected officials.

A CAMPAIGN IN TWO PHASES

At first glance, the 2021 electoral result in Quebec was the same as that of 2019: thirty-five MPs for the Liberals, thirty-two for the Bloc Québécois, ten for the Conservatives and one for the NDP. In terms of percentage of votes, both the LPC (33 per cent) and the Bloc (32 per cent) obtained similar results. Only the Conservatives

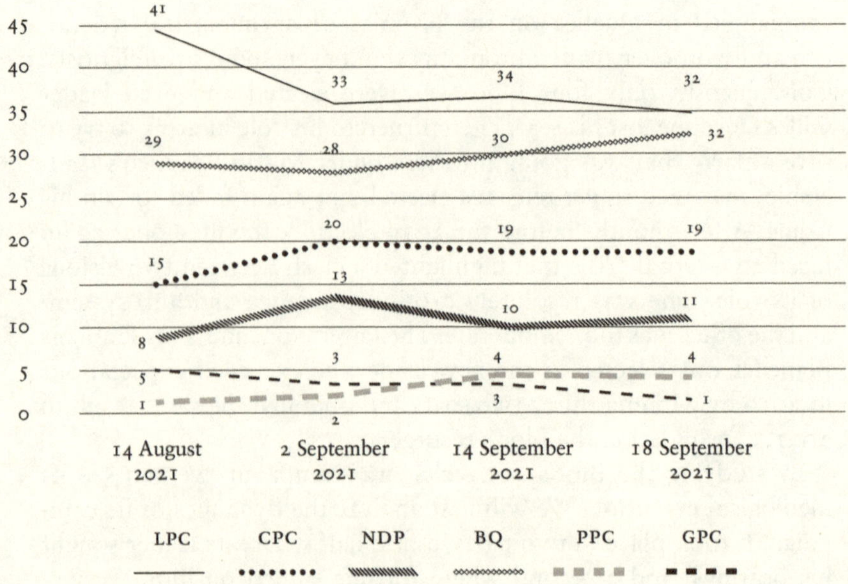

Figure 5.1 | Léger polls, Quebec only (2021 election)

made significant gains in terms of support, going from 16 to 18.5 per cent. For its part, the NDP fell below the 10 per cent mark. At 2.7 per cent Maxime Bernier's People's Party remained marginal. Strongly divided in Quebec (its Quebec wing even published a dissident program), the Green Party could only retain 1.5 per cent of popular support, 3 per cent less than 2019. However, behind these surprisingly stable numbers for the two main parties lies a much more complex reality: the poll numbers fluctuated during the campaign, and there was more electoral volatility than the results would suggest.

As the writs were dropped, observers and pollsters mostly agreed that Justin Trudeau could make substantial inroads in Quebec. That was the essence of his gamble. Winning sufficient seats to form a new majority government depended in large part on winning back seats lost to the Bloc Québécois in the 2019 election. At the beginning of the campaign, Quebec, and more precisely the territory of the 450 area code, comprising the northern and southern suburbs of Montreal, looked like fertile ground for the Grits – seven or eight highly competitive seats that could make a difference. To demonstrate that and to fully understand the evolution of the Quebec election campaign, we can analyze the evolution of the various trends observed by polling firms. Figure 5.1 shows the data published by the Léger firm for Quebec only.

The data show that the Bloc Québécois campaign had two distinct phases. When the campaign began, Blanchet and his party were in trouble. According to Léger, Justin Trudeau's Liberals had a twelve-point lead and the Bloc's support was below 30 per cent. In the early days of the campaign, the sharp drop in Liberal support that followed the election call essentially benefited the Conservatives and the NDP. Not only did the Bloc not benefit from the crumbling of Liberal support in Quebec, but it also experienced a decline in support. It was not until two weeks before the end of the campaign that the downward trend of the Bloc Québécois reversed.

A DIFFICULT START

The Bloc Québécois campaign got off to a difficult start for both circumstantial and strategic reasons. Beyond his attacks on the early start of the election, Yves François Blanchet could hardly give direction to his campaign. At its launch, he had to explain the Bloc's slogan, which was limited to one word: Québécois. Did he claim to embody the Quebec nation? He explained instead:[4] "Québécois is a model of sustainable economic development, based on Quebec's clean energy, the resources of Quebec's regions, Quebec's small and medium-sized enterprises. It is a model of development very, very Quebecois, and which is not Canadian, in that Canada remains a very oil state. Canada is almost a rogue state when it comes to the environment."[5]

He also began his campaign by making pragmatic commitments to targeted audiences without them being parts of an overarching vision. This was the case for seniors, for example, as he committed to working to increase their income. Moreover, to consolidate his support in the Quebec City area, he took a confused stance on a project initiated by the Government of Quebec for a third road link between Quebec City and Lévis. The project involved a tunnel under the St Lawrence River linking the two downtowns. This tunnel would include reserved lanes for a new public transit service integrated with a streetcar project on the north shore. This stance earned Blanchet bitter attacks from opposing groups, and even from some sovereigntists, who criticized the contradiction with his environmental position. The controversy cost him several days of campaigning as it overshadowed other policy proposals.

Moreover, Blanchet had set a very ambitious target when he declared: "I like to dream of forty [seats]."[6] Although he later downplayed his statement, a perception was created, which had the effect of raising expectations that seemed unrealistic by September. Reaching forty ridings then became a test of leadership that Blanchet could fail. It must be remembered that the Bloc Québécois began the 2019 campaign in the opposite situation. Expectations for the Bloc were low. Its campaign got off to a slow start before the issue of secularism came to the fore in the wake of the leaders' debates and the issue of abortion plagued Andrew Scheer's campaign.[7] However, the Conservatives quickly tabled a Quebec platform at the beginning of the 2021 campaign. The release of Erin O'Toole's "Covenant with Quebecers" made the Conservatives' poll numbers rise. In addition to fighting the Liberals in the Montreal area, the Bloc Québécois also had to deal with this rise of the Conservatives, mainly in the region from Trois-Rivières to Eastern Quebec.

Accordingly, the Bloc Québécois campaign was on a downward slope. Blanchet's press conferences became increasingly tense. He was even accused of arrogance by journalists and commentators[8] and his opponents also tried to define him as such. Noticing a potential flaw in the armour of her opponent, the Liberal minister Mélanie Joly was on the offensive as the second week of the campaign began: "The Bloc Québécois is currently the party of one man," she said. "A guy who is disconnected and arrogant."[9]

Nevertheless, the leader's caravan continued a day-to-day tour of Quebec, essentially on the offensive by mostly visiting winnable ridings held by opponents. The party had a very active social media strategy to get its message out directly to targeted voters. It also had enough resources to conduct a mass advertising campaign, mainly on private radio stations and on billboards with a Blanchet photo and the word "Québécois."

The first debate in French, TVA's "Face-à-Face," enabled Blanchet to reframe his message and his campaign, particularly since he found a certain balance in his tone. His campaign had been on the defensive with journalists and without a clear message. In his mother tongue, the debate allowed him to take the offensive against his opponents. As in 2019, the Bloc's leader relied on popular autonomist elements defended by François Legault to shore up support. Moreover, by wanting to make federal spending on healthcare conditional on the provinces abiding by new federal standards, Trudeau had given new ammunition to Blanchet.

AN UNEXPECTED DEBATE IN ENGLISH

Paradoxically, two elements external to its campaign strategy gave the Bloc momentum, to the point where, by the second part of the campaign, it seemed possible Blanchet might even reach his goal of forty seats. His tour then went on the offensive in several Liberal ridings, in Gaspésie and in the 450 area. He even made a detour to New Brunswick and tried to meet with the Société de l'Acadie du Nouveau-Brunswick (SANB), which ultimately cancelled the meeting at the last minute.[10]

The 9 September turned out to be a pivotal day in the campaign. Trudeau's commitments to long-term care and the hiring of family physicians, which intruded on the jurisdiction of the National Assembly, provoked Quebec Premier François Legault to publicly declare his anger at the encroachments proposed by the Liberals. "Quebecers who are nationalists," he said, "who want the Quebec nation to have more powers, must beware of three parties: the Liberal Party, the NDP, and the Green Party."[11] This statement by the Quebec premier was interpreted as indirect support for the Conservatives, though without being a disavowal of the Bloc Québécois.

That evening, another front opened unexpectedly during the leaders' debate in English, which is usually a nonevent for a Bloc Québécois leader. Chances of making gains are as small as expectations are low. But a question from moderator Shachi Kurl (the president of the Angus Reid Institute) about Quebec's *State Secularism Act* was explosive. Here is what was more of a statement than a question: "You deny that Quebec has problems with racism, but you defend laws like Bills 96 and 21, which marginalize religious minorities, anglophones, and allophones. Quebec is recognized as a distinct society, but for those outside the province, please help them understand why your party also supports these discriminatory laws."[12]

For many Quebecers, this statement was received as a serious insult and as an expression of a profound misunderstanding of Quebec. Blanchet requested apologies immediately, as Justin Trudeau and Erin O'Toole did the next day. Both the choice of the moderator and the relevance of the Leaders' Debates Commission were being questioned and both the media consortium and the Commission were put on the defensive. Less than a week before the election, on 14 September, the National Assembly unanimously adopted a motion condemning Kurl's comments and demanding an apology. A second motion, proposed by the leader of the Parti Québécois, Paul Saint-Pierre Plamondon, and by the leader of the Quebec Liberal Party, Dominique Anglade, also called for an end to this "Quebec bashing." Consequently, Blanchet was seen by many as the Quebecer whom English Canada insults and who could stand up to the intolerance of the Anglo-Canadian intelligentsia. The end of the Quebec campaign was thus characterized by a theme that the Bloc Québécois had tried unsuccessfully to put on the agenda since the beginning.

The return to issues associated with Quebec nationalism then helped the Bloc Québécois to keep the ridings it won in 2019, though not to reach the threshold of forty seats. Nevertheless, the Bloc Québécois met a crucial objective set by its leader: ensuring that the new federal government, whatever party formed it, remained a minority one.

QUEBEC AUTONOMY AND JURISDICTIONAL DISPUTES: OXYGEN FOR THE BLOC QUÉBÉCOIS

To understand the Bloc's comeback properly, we need to examine the role of the issues on constitutional jurisdiction and to contextualize the many interventions of the premier of Quebec. Tensions between Quebec and Ottawa over respecting constitutional jurisdictions were uncommon when Canada was ruled by Stephen Harper's Conservatives. The latter had adopted a more pragmatic approach to federalism. To achieve his policy and political goals, he practised a more "individualized executive federalism."[13] The lack of Quebec-Ottawa confrontation during this period had the effect of depriving the Bloc Québécois of much of its oxygen. Only two issues were thorny during this period: the federal intervention over mental health issues and the will to establish a federal securities commission.

The return of the Liberals to power in 2015 was initially characterized by a certain spirit of collaboration. The 2019 election, however, marked a shift in Trudeau's approach. He no longer hesitated to show his willingness to interfere in provincial jurisdictions and to centralize Canadian governance. An initial review showed that in the first part of the 2019 campaign, more than half of Trudeau's election commitments were directly about provincial jurisdictions.[14] In doing so, his agenda clashed with the autonomist agenda of the then-new Quebec premier elected in 2018. Legault's CAQ government has seen its role as not only defending Quebec's autonomy within Canada, but also increasing it.

These findings are even more relevant to the 2021 election. Certainly, the COVID-19 pandemic severely compromised the cooperative character of Canadian federalism, especially in its executive relations. Whether it was about jurisdictional sharing, program funding, border management, vaccine procurement, or the homologation of vaccines, stormy discussions between different levels of government shaped the daily management of the crisis. Ideally, addressing the issues at the core of the pandemic should involve not only action, but also coordination between governments that do not always see eye to eye. These various discussions and negotiations are usually conducted between the executives of the units of government within the federation and, according to the late English Canadian political scientist Ronald L. Watts, characterize executive federalism.[15] Canada's executive federalism is based on different mechanisms of communication between levels of government. The pandemic highlighted the different tools of coordination and cooperation that exist between executives, whether at the level of heads of governments, ministers, or public servants. In practice, during the pandemic direct meetings between all first ministers increased in frequency, as did meetings between ministers of Health and public health officials.

The crisis particularly shed light on certain lines of tension between Trudeau's government and Legault's. For instance, the Trudeau government was severely criticized in the early days of the pandemic for its hesitations about border management. It was not able to ensure adequate international surveillance of the evolution of the virus and the risks posed to Canada at the outbreak of the pandemic.[16] Accordingly, the Quebec government felt the need to dispatch public health services to airports to mitigate the risks related to uncontrolled international travel.

Meanwhile, Trudeau was quick to blame his provincial counterparts, and particularly Legault, for the care of seniors. With overworked staff in the long-term care centres during the first wave, Quebec and Ontario had no choice but to call on the military to lend a hand. Although only a limited number of them were deployed, the need to call in the military fed an image that provinces could not address healthcare issues alone. That reinforced Trudeau's discourse on the virtues of centralization. At the end of the mission, two Canadian military reports were made public. One noted major problems encountered in Ontario. The other, more nuanced, reported a difficult situation in Quebec.[17] Moreover, in the wake of the approval of the first two vaccines, tensions emerged between the two levels of government on the vaccination strategy and with respect to procurement. While the approval and acquisition of vaccines is a federal responsibility, their administration is done by the provinces. The first sign of tension was Trudeau's statement that too many doses were "sitting in refrigerators." Already on the defensive with the media about a shortage of vaccine supply, Trudeau opened the door to criticism from his provincial counterparts. After that, they did not hesitate to put constant pressure on Ottawa to speed up vaccine delivery. The Quebec and federal public health authorities also spoke sometimes at cross-purposes, particularly about the lapse of time required between the administration of the two doses.

Furthermore, the federal government has a significant financial capacity when compared to the provinces. It could set up several programs to provide direct support to citizens in areas of provincial jurisdiction. The collateral effects of some of these programs on the workforce were sometimes uncoordinated and were denounced by the government of Quebec and many actors of the civil society. The imbalance between federal and provincial spending powers has been particularly acute since the crisis about healthcare funding. A common front among the provinces was forged at the Council of the Federation to secure recurrent, stable, and increased funding and respect for jurisdictions. Still, Trudeau counted on signing piecemeal agreements with the provinces to break this common front so that he could impose federal standards for long-term care. That context influenced considerably the 2021 federal election in Quebec, as it affected public opinion about the Liberals and benefitted the other parties, not just the BQ.

To conduct our analysis of election commitments from a constitutional perspective, we studied all the press releases posted on the websites of the Liberal Party of Canada, the Conservative Party of Canada, and the New Democratic Party considering their respect for federal and provincial jurisdictions. More precisely, we used sections 91 of the *Constitution Act, 1867* to delineate federal jurisdiction and

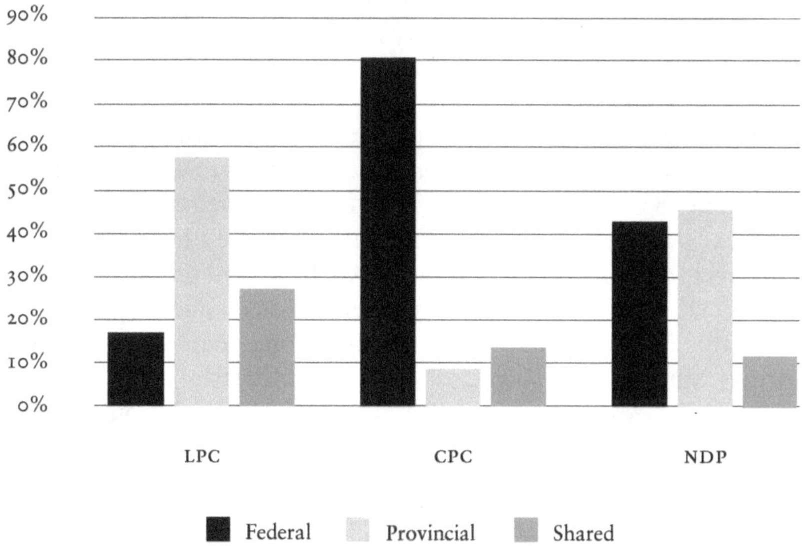

Figure 5.2 | Party election promises in areas of constitutional jurisdiction, 2021

sections 92 to 93 to delineate provincial ones. We also established a category grouping areas of shared jurisdiction. In all, we selected sixty-nine press releases for analysis. Of these, twenty-six were issued by the LPC, twenty-four by the CPC, and nineteen by the NDP.

With a ratio of fifteen to four, the Liberal Party of Canada made about four commitments on provincial matters for one on federal ones. This is followed by the nine New Democratic Party's commitments in nine areas of exclusive provincial jurisdiction compared to eight in areas of exclusive federal jurisdiction. As in the Stephen Harper era, Erin O'Toole's Conservatives remained the party with the greatest respect for constitutional jurisdictions and for provincial autonomy. Nineteen commitments were found to be within the exclusive jurisdiction of the federal government, compared to two within the exclusive jurisdiction of the provinces.

Figure 5.2 shows the percentage of commitments by jurisdiction, including those within shared jurisdictions. Of the LPC's total electoral commitments, 57 per cent were within exclusive provincial jurisdictions and only 15 per cent within exclusive federal jurisdictions. Of the commitments made by the NDP, 45 per cent were within provincial jurisdictions, while this was the case for only 8 per cent of the Conservative Party's commitments.

So, according to our data, the LPC campaign was not only differentiating itself from the CPC, but also from the NDP, which maintained a level of interference comparable to the 2019 election. The NDP reiterated commitments on dental care, long-term care centres, student scholarships, and the hiring of nurses. However, the Liberals made increased flagship commitments on provincial matters such as implementing a Canadian childcare program, enforcing federal standards in long-term care facilities, hiring family doctors, and developing initiatives on education and literacy. All three parties made commitments on housing and mental health.

Trudeau's interventionist, and somewhat confrontational, approach contrasts with Stephen Harper's, which was less interventionist and more respectful of Quebec's jurisdictions. While the Bloc Québécois could hardly push efficiently for the defence of Quebec's interests during the Harper era, the resurgence of clashes between the federal and the Quebec government has had the opposite effect. By making commitments to interfere within Quebec's jurisdictions, Trudeau helped the Bloc Québécois to put its campaign back on track. Blanchet could now go on the offensive on the axis of the centralization of the Canadian federal system and the defence of the powers of the National Assembly of Quebec. It was then easier for the BQ to justify its relevance for a large part of the Quebec electorate that is not necessarily sovereigntist.

THE BLOC QUÉBÉCOIS AND FRANÇOIS LEGAULT

The Bloc campaign cannot be analysed adequately without assessing thoroughly the Legault factor. Indeed, the Premier of Quebec's statement in which he made his demands to federal leaders was a turning point during the 2019 election. The upholding of Bill 21 on the secular nature of the Quebec state, which aims to prohibit the wearing of religious symbols by judges, police officers, and teachers, served as a spark plug for Blanchet's campaign. In contrast, Justin Trudeau refused to pledge that the federal government would not intervene in the judicial challenge process of this bill, which hurt the Grits in Quebec.

Two years later, the premier of Quebec remained extremely popular even after three years in power and the persistence of the pandemic, and could claim to be the master of the game in Quebec politics. A few days after the federal election campaign, the Léger polling firm credited the CAQ with 47 per cent support while its closest rival, the Quebec Liberal Party, had only 20 per cent.[18] The gap was even wider among francophone voters, 54 per cent of whom supported the CAQ. Noting Legault's popularity and influence, O'Toole took care to cultivate his relationship with the Quebec premier as soon as he became the Conservative leader, especially as he pledged to grant more powers to Quebec over language, taxation, and immigration matters.[19]

Still, despite tensions between them during the first waves of the pandemic, Trudeau and Legault got closer during the first months of 2021. The vaccination campaign took off. The two men made several joint economic announcements. Bill 96, which modernizes Bill 101 and ensures the constitutional recognition of the Quebec nation, was welcomed with openness by the federal government. An unconditional agreement was reached on the funding of childcare services. Trudeau even spoke of asymmetrical federalism and collaboration. Clearly, the Canadian prime minister implemented a strategy of appeasement in the months leading up to the election campaign.

On the eve of the election call, a person close to Trudeau confided to La Presse about the Liberal strategy to neutralize the Bloc Québécois: "We have demonstrated that we are capable of making deals with François Legault. All the big contentious issues have been settled ... It is certain that by making François Legault happy, we make the Bloc Québécois unhappy. It takes away a lot of ammunition! ... François Legault has no interest in helping the Bloc. Yves-François Blanchet may stick to him, but he won't give him too much credit. The link of the Bloc Québécois, it is not with the CAQ, it is with the Parti Québécois. You can see it by looking at the employees of the Parti Québécois who are running for the Bloc. In a year, the Bloc will not work to help the CAQ, it will work for the Parti Québécois."[20]

Legault had indeed chosen to be less active than in the previous election. The day before the election, the columnist Antoine Robitaille wrote that: "François Legault is likely to be more discreet in the federal election that will be called on Sunday. It will be a break with the recent past."[21]

Nonetheless, the Quebec premier was stunned to note that Trudeau's first election commitments were on new federal health-care standards. Moreover, as the campaign progressed, the Liberals contradicted the signals sent previously since its campaign, and its platform, were very interventionist and centralizing. Accordingly, Legault made four significant interventions in the campaign. The first, on 26 August, was when he made public his list of a dozen demands to the federal parties. In inviting Quebecers to read the platforms of federal parties, Legault explained that "there are two very centralizing parties,"[22] referring to the Liberals and the NDP. Furthermore, as we saw earlier, he again stepped into the campaign on 9 September. In a rare move for a premier, he urged Quebecers not to vote for the centralizing parties and highlighted that only one leader, O'Toole, could replace Trudeau. He stated that: "Justin Trudeau proposes targeted programs where he interferes in the jurisdictions of the provinces, and me, it scares me because Mr Trudeau has an approach where he wants to meddle in health, he does not want to give us power in immigration when it is important to defend our identity, our nation. He does not exclude opposing Bill 21, so this is very worrying for all Quebecers who are nationalists."[23] However, unlike René Lévesque when he took the "Beau risque," the gamble, to support Brian Mulroney's Conservatives in 1984, Legault did not put his electoral machine at the service of O'Toole's Conservatives.

Legault's third intervention took place the next day, following the English leaders' debate. He declared that Shachi Kurl's question was an attack on the Quebec nation. While welcoming Blanchet's response, Legault paraphrased Robert Bourassa's statement following the failure of the Meech Lake Accord. He then sent this message to English Canada: "No matter what is said, no matter what is done in Ottawa, Quebec is a nation free to protect its language, its values, its powers."[24] He intervened one last time two days prior to the vote, during his party's youth convention, to reassert Quebec's exclusive jurisdiction and safeguard it from federal interventionism: "Our identity as a people will always be fragile. [...] There will always be people who will lecture us and tell us that we don't have the right to impose a common language, that we don't have the right to defend Quebec values, that we don't have the right to defend our powers. [...] I will never apologize for defending our powers, defending our language, and defending our values."[25]

Therefore, Legault proved himself to be very active during the 2021 campaign as he sought to safeguard the powers of the National Assembly. Doing this, he was consistent with his autonomist vision of Quebec nationalism.

Two questions then arise. What was Legault's real influence on the Quebec vote? Moreover, and more fundamentally, how can we understand the Liberals' campaign plan and their repeated electoral commitments into provincial jurisdictions? Their strategy is hard to understand considering how careful they were to court Quebec before the writs were dropped. Still, the Liberals' hard-line on centralisation allowed the Bloc Québécois to rally, prevented the Liberals from making gains in Quebec, and likely put a majority government out of reach.

BLOC QUÉBÉCOIS: DIFFERENT PARTISAN OBJECTIVES THAN THE PARTI QUÉBÉCOIS

Despite the apparent circumstantial alliance, there are no institutional links or strategic alliances between the Bloc Québécois and the Coalition avenir Quebec. Historically, the Bloc has been closer to the PQ, since both parties theoretically support Quebec sovereignty. However, they now pursue different partisan objectives. The Bloc Québécois' 2021 campaign shed light on an important strategic gap with Paul Saint-Pierre Plamondon's Parti Québécois.

A week into the federal campaign, the Bloc Québécois unveiled its platform. Many commentators noted that it glossed over issues related to Quebec sovereignty. The word "sovereignty" appears only once, and that is in connection with Quebec's "environmental sovereignty." Although he still considers himself as a sovereigntist, Blanchet stated that he would "rather not make it a campaign theme in a context where it is not favoured by a majority of the population."[26]

Certainly, the PQ has migrated over time from a policy-seeking party to an electoral party (vote-seeking or office-seeking party).[27] From the day after the 1995 referendum until 2020, it had essentially become more concerned with adapting to its environment than with working to change it. More precisely, in the 2018 Quebec election, it sought to be more in tune with public opinion than to convince voters to become (again?) sovereigntists and to make Quebec a country. This is exactly the same strategy that the Bloc Québécois implemented in 2019 to regain its official party status in the House of Commons.[28] Instead of adopting a staunch sovereigntist agenda, when he became leader of the BQ Blanchet chose to prioritise autonomist themes such as those defended by the then-new Quebec premier François Legault.

Now embraced by the membership, this autonomist shift has characterized Blanchet's leadership. It was confirmed even more clearly in 2021. A discourse analysis highlights that, in the early days of the Bloc campaign and during the three leaders' debates, the question of Quebec sovereignty was completely absent. The Bloc Québécois instead focused on safeguarding Quebec's autonomy and its exclusive constitutional jurisdictions. For instance, to limit the federal spending power, it promised to reintroduce "a bill giving Quebec the right to automatic compensation with full indemnification when Ottawa creates federal programs in Quebec's exclusive areas of jurisdiction or seeks to attach conditions to these transfers of money."[29] So, the Bloc's platform was more about a reform of the federal framework to ensure Quebec's autonomy than about how it could be dismantled.

Paradoxically, Paul St-Pierre Plamondon was elected leader of the Parti Québécois in October 2020 with a mandate to make Quebec a sovereign state during a first electoral term. He wants the Quebec sovereigntist movement to take a different path and to uphold an assertive sovereigntist approach. After his election, Plamondon stated that: "Our independence project, we want to assume it and we want to talk about it in a proud, direct, transparent way. [This means] no more tactics, no more complicated referendum mechanics. A vote for the Parti Québécois is a vote for our country project."[30] In other words, he pledged to explain tirelessly why Quebec should become a country, even if that project was not currently in tune with Quebec public opinion.

These recent strategic choices have made the paths of the Bloc Québécois and of the Parti Québécois diverge. Although the Bloc Québécois and the Parti Québécois are distinct political and legal entities, they have a common militant base and many political staffers have worked for both parties. For instance, before leading the Bloc, Blanchet was an activist and an elected official of the Parti Québécois. Before 2019, the two political formations also boasted of making alliances during election periods. For example, Lucien Bouchard, as the Bloc's leader, campaigned for the PQ against the Action démocratique du Quebec's (ADQ) leader, Mario Dumont, in the riding of Rivière-du-Loup in 1994. However, in 2021, Plamondon did not attend the Bloc Québécois convention which launched the party's campaign. A sovereigntist activist who attended this event in Saint-Hyacinthe even deplored "the absence of a component on Quebec sovereignty" by saying: "It's all very well to have a career in Ottawa, but it's not the foundation of our party."[31]

Still, as the CAQ government and its autonomist nationalism are very popular, the Yes-No divide on sovereignty no longer structures the political debate in Quebec, which tends to marginalize overtly sovereigntist parties. To regain its prominence, the Bloc chose to adapt its approach by implementing a "vote seeking" strategy. Still, with its electoral strategy, it may be that the Bloc Québécois risks undermining the cohesion and the coherence of the sovereigntist movement's message. While the Bloc seeks to obtain more votes and seats in the short term, its strategy moves the party away from its primary objective in the longer term. For the sovereigntist movement, this is a structuring issue that goes far beyond the 2021 election. It will also be interesting to see how the Bloc Québécois will behave in the Quebec election of 2022, when the Parti Québécois campaigns for sovereignty.

CONCLUSION

Over time, for many Quebec voters, choosing the Bloc Québécois has become a safe bet. More than a sovereigntist party, it has become a genuine refuge for all those who consider that Canadian federalism, as it is, is dysfunctional and compromises the interests of Quebec. It should not be overlooked that the Bloc's origins lay in the 1982 unilateral patriation and in the failure of the Meech Lake Accord to end a persistent constitutional malaise.

The Quebec National Assembly, which represents one of Canada's founding nations and its largest minority, has had a constitution imposed on it by force and has never recognized its legitimacy. In our Quebec classrooms, we still teach our students about this constitutional power grab. The expression dedicated to this event, "The Night of the Long Knives," displays how Quebecers felt betrayed by premiers from the rest of Canada on the night of 4 November 1981. Meanwhile, as a sad example of the Canadian two solitudes, English-speaking Canadians simply remember this event as the "Kitchen Accord." Although the unilateral patriation was only made possible because of a compromise from the federal government (the integration of a notwithstanding clause to the Canadian Charter of

Rights and Freedoms – that is nowadays widely seen as discriminatory in English Canada), the inability, for forty years, to secure Quebec's place within Canada in "honor and enthusiasm" highlights why many Quebecers feel more safe to vote for the Bloc Québécois.

Initially, the Bloc Québécois was meant to be a temporary party. Then, it set out two principles to guide its action. It would defend Quebec's interests in the Canadian Parliament until it achieves its aim to see Quebec as a sovereign state. Still, nowadays, its priority is an autonomist defence of Quebec's interests. This evolution started when the anti-system vision of Martine Ouellet was rejected on the eve of the 2019 election. Then, in 2021, that change was completed when the very notion of sovereignty was evacuated from its electoral platform in favour of an autonomist nationalism akin to that fostered by the Coalition avenir Quebec.

However, in English Canada, it would be wrong to assume that the decline of the sovereigntist option ineluctably leads to that of Quebec nationalism. While the Yes-No divide on independence is no longer as decisive in structuring the political debate, a strong majority of voters remains staunchly nationalist. Nationalism has simply evolved. Its strength now relies on the popular support it generates, and which explains much of the electoral success of François Legault.

Concretely, the Quebec government's new autonomous nationalism rests on five pillars:

- Re-establishing national pride.
- Incorporating a dimension of economic success.
- Maximizing the powers of the National Assembly.
- Claiming more autonomy within the federal framework.
- Fully restoring the role of the Quebec state as promoter and protector of a common culture.[32]

To survive, the Bloc Québécois has chosen a strategy of adaptation to this new environment where the Parti Québécois is no longer the flagship of Quebec nationalism. In doing so, it has succumbed to the trap of institutionalization. That is, the Bloc is not so much trying to derail the political system as to maintain a prominent place within it.

In that vein, with the end of the Yes-No divide, Quebec voters are less loyal to federal political parties than ever before. They do some window shopping at the beginning of a federal campaign. If nothing appeals to them, it becomes tempting to fall back on a known value. For many, the Bloc Québécois is the only party that can be trusted. Furthermore, since the election of Blanchet as leader of the Bloc Québécois, the main role of the party is now linked to the principle of dual legitimacy. This is defined as follows: "Thus, when there are two levels of government, as is the case in a federal system, should we consider that the elected officials of both levels have the same legitimacy to speak and claim more powers for the same population or not? In other words, when the elected officials of two levels, from the same territory, do not share the same political vision of autonomy, are we not in the presence of a democratic impasse and a conflict of legitimacy?"[33]

In short, the existence of the Bloc Québécois boils down to the understanding that Quebec's elected representatives in the House of Commons and within the federal government could hardly claim to have the legitimacy to speak on behalf of the Quebec nation. This role is seen as reserved to members of the Quebec National Assembly and the Bloc seeks to channel their views, and not only these of the Parti Québécois' members of the Legislative Assembly.

With the end of the Yes-No divide as a structuring cleavage in Quebec' politics and independence on the back burner, what is the future role of the Bloc? Will it always be the fallback choice, as the concept of a safe bet implies, reacting to the flow of the campaign as determined by others? Or is there a more pro-active role it can play? After being almost wiped off the map in 2011 and 2015, it has since adapted by adopting an autonomist position that is much more in line with current Quebec nationalism. For now, it is Justin Trudeau's centralist approach and the NDP that gives the Bloc Québécois enough oxygen to play a dominant role in fighting centripetal forces within the federation, while the Conservatives also need to become more attractive to be more competitive in Quebec.

For now, the Bloc seems to be a safe bet for many. Beyond symbolizing the Canadian constitutional malaise, it acts as an insurance policy. It also aims to be a relay in the House of Commons of the consensus expressed in the Quebec National Assembly.

NOTES

1 Martine Tremblay, *La rébellion tranquille: Une histoire du Bloc québécois (1990–2011)* (Montreal: Quebec/Amérique, 2015).
2 Marie-France Charbonneau and Guy Lachapelle, *Le Bloc québécois: 20 ans au nom du Quebec* (Montreal: R.Vézina, 2010).
3 According to The Concise Oxford Dictionary of Politics: "A political party that wishes to change or destroy the political system in which it is operating."
4 All the sources used for this text were originally in French. For the sake of the reader's understanding, they have all been translated into English by the author.
5 Frédéric Lacroix-Couture, "Le Bloc lance sa campagne en condamnant un lancement d'"élections précipitées.'" *Le Devoir*, 15 August 2021, https://www.ledevoir.com/politique/canada/625089/le-bloc-lance-sa-campagne-en-condamnant-un-lancement-d-elections-precipitees.
6 Patrice Bergeron, "Yves-François Blanchet rêve de passer de 32 à 40 sièges," *Le Soleil*, 16 August 2021, https://www.lesoleil.com/actualite/les-elections-federales/yves-francois-blanchet-reve-de-passer-de-32-a-40-sieges-c84a5b705d1f35ef2695ac4e39de7ad3.
7 Éric Montigny, "The Battle for Quebec," in *The 2019 Canadian Federal Election*, eds. Jon H. Pammett and Christopher Dornan (Montreal: McGill-Queen's University Press, 2020), 101–27.
8 "L'attitude d'Yves-François Blanchet fait réagir," TVA Nouvelles, 1 September 2021, https://www.tvanouvelles.ca/2021/09/01/lattitude-dyves-francois-blanchet-fait-reagir.
9 Frédéric Lacroix-Couture, "Des libéraux du Quebec dénoncent 'l'arrogance' du chef du Bloc québécois," *L'Actualité*, 21 August 2021, https://lactualite.com/actualites/des-liberaux-du-quebec-denoncent-larrogance-du-chef-du-bloc-quebecois/.
10 Alix Villeneuve, "Pas besoin du Bloc québécois pour défendre les intérêts des Acadiens, dit la SANB," Radio-Canada, 15 September 2021, https://ici.radio-canada.ca/nouvelle/1824072/bloc-quebecois-acadie-societe-acadie-nouveau-brunswick-caraquet.
11 Tommy Chouinard, Fanny Lévesque, and Emlilie Bilodeau, "Legault penche pour un gouvernement conservateur minoritaire," *La Presse*, 9 September 2021, https://www.lapresse.ca/elections-federales/2021-09-09/legault-penche-pour-un-gouvernement-conservateur-minoritaire.php.
12 Raphaël Piro, "Yves-François Blanchet fustige l'animation après le débat en anglais," *Journal de Montreal*, 10 September 2021, https://www.

journaldemontreal.com/2021/09/10/yves-francois-blanchet-fustige-lanimation-apres-le-debat-en-anglais.

13 Anna Esselment, "Federal Feet and Provincial Pools: The Conservatives and Federalism in Canada," in *The Blue Print: Conservatives Parties and Their Impact on Canadian Politics*, eds. J.P. Lewis and Joanna Everitt (Toronto, Buffalo, London: University of Toronto Press, 2017).

14 Éric Montigny, "The Battle for Quebec," 101–27.

15 Ronald L. Watts, *Executive Federalism: A Comparative Analysis* (Kingston, Ontario: Institute of Intergovernmental Relations, Queen's University, 1989).

16 Alec Castonguay, *Le printemps le plus long* (Montreal: Quebec/Amérique, 2021).

17 Patrick Bellerose, "Rapport de l'armée en CSHLD: l'équipement de protection mal utilisée," *Journal de Quebec*, 27 May 2020, https://www.journaldequebec.com/2020/05/27/COVID-19-quebec-devoile-le-rapport-de-larmee-sur-la-crise-en-chsld.

18 Geneviève Lajoie, "Legault domine pas à peu près," *Le Journal de Montreal*, 2 October 2021, https://www.journaldemontreal.com/2021/10/02/sondage-leger-legault-domine-et-pas-a-peu-pres.

19 Louise Leduc, "Legault et O'Toole satisfaits de leur première rencontre," *La Presse*, 14 September 2020, https://www.lapresse.ca/actualites/politique/2020-09-14/legault-et-o-toole-satisfaits-de-leur-premiere-rencontre.php.

20 Joël-Denis Bellavance, "La belle entente avec Legault pour neutraliser le Bloc québécois," *La Presse*, 14 August 2021, https://www.lapresse.ca/actualites/analyse/2021-08-14/la-belle-entente-avec-legault-pour-neutraliser-le-bloc-quebecois.php.

21 Antoine Robitaille, "Élections fédérales: la discrétion de Legault," *Le journal de Quebec*, 14 August 2021, https://www.journaldequebec.com/2021/08/14/elections-federales-la-discretion-de-legault.

22 Mathieu Gobeil, "Plus d'argent en santé et un contrôle accru de l'immigration, demande Legault," Radio-Canada, 26 August 2021, https://ici.radio-canada.ca/nouvelle/1819501/demandes-legault-quebec-partis-federaux-election-transferts-sante-immigration.

23 Elisabeth Fleury, "Le beau risque de François Legault," *Le Soleil*, 9 September 2021, https://www.lesoleil.com/actualite/les-elections-federales/le-beau-risque-de-francois-legault-ed279479695 45e480c4e287e0f9c8079.

24 Tommy Chouinard and Mélanie Marquis, "François Legault veut des excuses pour 'l'attaque contre le Quebec'," *La Presse*, 10 September 2021, https://www.lapresse.ca/elections-federales/2021-09-10/debat-des-chefs-

en-anglais/francois-legault-veut-des-excuses-pour-l-attaque-contre-le-quebec.php.

25 Karim Ouadia, "Legault défend les champs de compétences du Quebec devant les jeunes caquistes," Radio-Canada, 19 September 2021, https://ici.radio-canada.ca/nouvelle/1825402/francois-legault-congres-releve-caq.

26 Raphaël Piro, "Le Bloc québécois mise sur l'environnement et sur l'identité," *Le Journal de Montreal*, 22 August 2021, https://www.journaldemontreal.com/2021/08/22/le-bloc-reunit-en-congres-avant-le-devoilement-de-sa-plateforme-1.

27 Éric Montigny, *Leadership et militantisme au Parti québécois: de Lévesque à Lisée* (Quebec: Presses de l'Université Laval, 2018).

28 Éric Montigny, "The Return of the Bloc Is a Mandate for Autonomy, Not Sovereignty," *Inroads*, no. 46 (2019), https://inroadsjournal.ca/the-return-of-the-bloc-is-a-mandate-for-autonomy-not-sovereignty/. And, Michel Seymour, "How Do We Explain the Return of the Bloc Québécois?," The Conversation, 28 October 2019, https://theconversation.com/how-do-we-explain-the-return-of-the-bloc-quebecois-125808.

29 "Plateforme politique Bloc 2021," Bloc Québécois, accessed 28 August 2021, https://www.blocquebecois.org/wp-content/uploads/2021/08/BQPlateforme2021webplanche.pdf.

30 Alain Gravel, "Le nouveau chef du PQ:Entrevue avec Paul St-Pierre Plamondon," Radio-Canada, 10 October 2020, https://ici.radio-canada.ca/ohdio/premiere/emissions/les-faits-dabord/segments/entrevue/204019/paul-st-pierre-plamondon-chef-parti-quebecois-pq-independance.

31 Patrice Bergeron, "Le Bloc propose un impôt spécial sur les fortunes et une péréquation verte," *Le Soleil*, 22 August 2021, https://www.lesoleil.com/actualite/les-elections-federales/le-bloc-propose-un-impot-special-sur-les-fortunes-et-une-perequation-verte-7a8a20dc5f0a85c1f34d06f-8c5827ed7.

32 Éric Montigny, "25 ans pares le referendum: le nationalisme québécois reprit par la CAQ," *Policy Options*, 30 October 2020, https://policyoptions.irpp.org/magazines/october-2020/25-ans-apres-le-referendum-le-nationalisme-quebecois-repris-par-la-caq/.

33 Éric Montigny, "Partis autonomistes et indépendantistes: paradoxes et influence institutionnelle," *Civitas Europa* 38, no. 2 (2017): 49.

6

A Climate of Chaos: How the Election Unfolded for the Environment and the Greens

Sarah Everts and Susan Harada

Just six weeks before the election, United Nations Secretary-General António Guterres called the most recent report from the Intergovernmental Panel on Climate Change (IPCC) a "Code Red for humanity." He said, "The alarm bells are deafening, and the evidence is irrefutable," he said. "Greenhouse-gas emissions from fossil-fuel burning and deforestation are choking our planet and putting billions of people at immediate risk." Not that Canadians lacked lived experience on this front: in June 2021, British Columbia reported temperatures of 49°C, the highest on record for Canada, even as nearly six hundred died from heat exposure. As the summer progressed, 1,600 forest fires burned nearly 8,700 square kilometres, pushing smoke as far as Ontario, and making the forest fire season the third worst on record, in terms of area burned. Lest voters on the east coast forget their vulnerability to extreme weather events, two weeks before the election, Hurricane Larry hit Newfoundland and Labrador overnight as a Category 1 storm.

Extreme weather events certainly contributed to the green Zeitgeist of Canadians who considered the environment a top issue, if not the top issue of the election, depending on which polling firms were reporting. In late August, when Angus Reid asked Canadians to pick the issue "most important to you personally," climate change was on top for all genders and ages, at 18 per cent.[1] Meanwhile, Nanos Research found the environment had been the top issue of concern at the beginning of 2020. But by the pandemic's March lockdown, COVID-19 angst superseded the country's still substantial eco-anxiety, a trend that their polls found would continue until the end of the 2021 election, after which the environment took precedence again.[2]

These climate concerns spoke directly to the Green Party's core mission but gone were the days when the Greens could claim ownership (and moral authority) over the environment file. Unlike 2019, when the Conservatives neglected to develop an environmental platform of any substance, the 2021 election had, for the first time, seen all the main parties[3] tabling serious environmental platforms. In fact, the two parties that could realistically form a government went further than the Greens themselves: the Liberals and Conservatives sought serious, independent scientific analysis of their environmental platforms from a respected expert.[4] As Green leader, Annamie Paul needed to be seen and heard in order to distinguish her party's platform within the climate policy fray that played out across the political spectrum. Yet instead of leading the conversation about our planet's existential crisis, Paul and her party were mired in a mutually destructive internal conflict that culminated in their grimmest federal results in twenty-one years.

LOSING THE LEADER

Running only 252 candidates out of the possible 338, Paul's Greens won less popular support than the upstart People's Party (4.9), which also fielded more candidates (312). With 2.3 per cent of the national vote, the Greens barely qualified for a partial reimbursement of election expenses. Yes, they won one new seat in Ontario – but they also lost one in BC. That they even retained their two-seat presence in parliament was something to celebrate. Not so, with respect to their leader's electoral fortunes. In spite of her near-exclusive focus on her third bid in the Liberal stronghold of Toronto Centre, Annamie Paul finished fourth, with 8.6 per cent. It was nowhere near her 2020 by-election results in that same riding, when she placed second (32.7). And while by-elections are unreliable indicators of how voter preferences will play out during a federal election, the fact that her support was slashed back to her preleadership level – when Toronto Centre voters gave her just 7.1 per cent in 2019 – was particularly crushing.

And so it was that on a sunny September day one week after she and her party were decimated at the polls, Paul – the first Black Jewish woman to lead a major national party in Canada – stepped up to a small bank of microphones to face the media in Suydam Park, a green oasis in Toronto chosen by her team for its proximity to the street.[5] It certainly made for an easier entrance and exit for the leader who had already served notice that she would take no questions after her statement. In French, she said she wanted to get in touch with the Green Party's federal council, to start the process of her resignation.[6] Shortly afterward, she tweeted in English: "I am beginning the process of stepping down as Green Party leader."[7] Short, simple statements of intent, but the resulting confusion symbolized the gap between Paul and her party. She did not explicitly say that she would retain her position until she could negotiate the terms of her departure – and senior Greens reportedly assumed, incorrectly, that she had quit on the spot.[8] She also did not say that she had already alerted the party's federal council of her intentions – yet former party leader Elizabeth May drew inaccurate conclusions in an opinion piece published days later by the *Toronto Star*: "Annamie Paul held a press conference, viewed by all national media as her resignation. She said she had notified the council. She had not."[9]

The tone of May's opinion piece – her biting assessment of Paul's leadership – laid bare the extent of the Greens' overall dysfunction: "The tragedy of Annamie Paul as leader stands out for a number of reasons. Of course, it is tragic in the Greek sense of hubris and nemesis. A brilliant woman became the first Black leader of a federal political party, finds her expectations unmet, and resigns in less than a year."[10] Paul's own summary of her treatment at the hands of the Greens – a party committed to doing politics differently – was marked by a defiant weariness as she spoke of the price she paid in becoming leader. "What people need to realise is that when I was elected and put in this role, I was breaking a glass ceiling," she said. "What I didn't realise at the time is that I was breaking a glass ceiling that was going to fall on my head and leave a lot of shards of glass that I was going to have to crawl over."[11]

Even at its best, it was never going to be easy for Paul. The political newcomer took over from May, whose outsized personality made for a difficult act to follow, particularly because she retained the role of caucus parliamentary leader. With May the longstanding go-to person for journalists seeking the party's perspective, Paul had to assert herself on the national stage. She also had to establish her leadership at a time when institutions across society, including the Greens, were grappling with systemic racism. In April 2021 some of the party's internal issues first became public in a *Toronto Star* article: "Senior

Green Officials Are Sabotaging the First Black Woman to Lead a Canadian Political Party, 'Disgusted' Insiders Say."[12] The Greens' Ombuds and Appeals Committee investigated a complaint lodged in the wake of that article and concluded that "there is systemic racism at the governance level of the Party which needs to be, but is not being, addressed."[13] Paul had earlier addressed her own experience, as leader, in being a first.

"As a new leader it is important for me to always seek to have the humility to recognize that I will make mistakes. However, often when people like me are elected or appointed to senior leadership roles, the rules of the game seem to change. Suddenly, there is a need for more oversight, heightened accountability, swifter and more severe sanctions, and a hiving off of responsibilities previously related to the role. Now, that is something that I will resist."[14]

INTO THE ELECTORAL ABYSS

A photo in Markus Harvey's social media stream, taken shortly before the 2019 election, shows the New Brunswicker on his front porch, flanked by the Greens' Fredericton candidate, Jenica Atwin, and then-leader May. Smiling broadly, the three are jammed together on a cushioned bench salvaged from a local restaurant. They were having what Harvey called "a chew" about, among other things, the increasingly flood-prone Saint John River a stone's throw from his home. May assured him, he said, that so long as Atwin stuck to the Greens' core values and platform, "she could do what was the best for the area."[15] For him that promise sealed the deal. Along with some 16,000 others, the long-time Conservative supporter voted for Atwin, whose 2019 election win as the first Green MP east of BC signalled the party's growth potential in Atlantic Canada.

But by the time election 2021 dawned, Atwin had crossed the floor to the Liberals, citing dissatisfaction with a perceived lack of support from Paul after the leader's senior adviser Noah Zatzman accused "unspecified Green MPs" of antisemitism related to the Israeli-Palestinian conflict.[16] Paul did not censure Zatzman, and Atwin's loss escalated the Greens' infighting. They plummeted to third in Fredericton, with 12.9 per cent of the vote. The locally popular Atwin retained her seat under the Liberal banner with 37 per cent. As for Harvey, he returned to the Conservatives, who finished second (35.9). Still, Fredericton was a relative success story compared to the region's other ridings. Support that had been painstakingly built nose-dived across the rest of New Brunswick (from 17.2 to 5.1 per cent of the vote), PEI (from 20.9 to 9.5) and Nova Scotia (from 11 to 1.8). The Greens could not even find candidates willing to step up in Newfoundland and Labrador. With the exception of 2019, the party had always fallen a few ridings short of a full slate of candidates under May's leadership but nowhere near the national 25 per cent shortfall of 2021.

Earlier in the year, the Greens had spelled out the need for a concerted focus on equity, diversity, and inclusion in candidate recruitment for the first time. They also made changes to the nomination approval process, giving their campaign working group the power to "approve or deny an individual's application" without a requirement to provide reasons.[17] At the same time, their operational support was weakened. According to Jo-Ann Roberts, the former interim party leader, the Greens did not hire a national campaign manager, opting instead to go with their interim executive director. "[He] had never been through an election campaign as ED," she said. "He didn't know that ... if you don't have an experienced mobilizer and you're not meeting your deadlines, you're going to end up without [because] you cannot put 100 candidates in place overnight, no matter how you look at it. And I think those are the things that got lost while the internal fighting was going on."[18]

For Darcie Lanthier, it meant an interminable delay in securing party approval to stand as a candidate. When she ran in Charlottetown back in 2019, she said she was approved and able to start campaigning a good seven months before the election call, ultimately finishing second with 23.3 per cent. Hoping to capitalize on that support and knowing a snap election could come at any time, she applied to run again as soon as the Greens opened up nominations in January 2021. But she got no response, she said. It was as if her application went into a void. Citing her health, Lanthier withdrew her application in May and tried to find another candidate. "I bought a lot of cups of coffee, and we didn't get anybody else to step up," she said. "And then they dropped the writ on August 15, and we had an emergency meeting on August 18 to come up with a candidate. And it ended up being me."[19] All things considered, she was not at her best, she said, and was relegated to fourth place (9.6 per cent). In Halifax, even Roberts' brand name recognition could not help her win more than 2.2 per cent. On the doorstep, voters made it clear they thought the party could not get its act together. "This should have been your election," she was told. "And all you've spent your time doing is fighting with yourselves."[20]

Support also collapsed on the other side of the country in BC, taking down Nanaimo-Ladysmith incumbent Paul Manly, who in a 2019 by-election became the second Green to win federal office before being re-elected months later in the federal election. It was close, but this time Manly's riding reverted to its NDP roots (28.8 per cent); the Conservatives (27.1), also with historical strength in the area, pushed Manly down to third place (25.7). Elizabeth May retained her seat in Saanich-Gulf Islands but with diminished support (from 49.1 to 37.6 per cent). In a province long receptive to electing Greens at all levels of government, the pre-election numbers were a precursor of the looming crisis. At the time of the call, the party was at approximately 7 per cent in the polls provincially,[21] down from the 12.5 per cent it won in 2019. When the votes were tallied the Greens stood at 5.4 per cent in BC. They were even lower across the Prairies, Quebec, and the Northwest Territories. There was no Green on the ballot in Nunavut.

Only in Ontario, amid an otherwise dismal popular vote of 2.2 per cent, was there a bright spot. The stars aligned in Kitchener Centre for Mike Morrice, who became the province's first Green MP. The sudden withdrawal of Liberal incumbent Raj Saini[22] – too late for the Liberals to nominate another candidate – unquestionably pushed Morrice over the top. But not to be discounted was Morrice's nonstop campaigning to build on his second-place 2019 finish, when he boosted the Greens' popular vote from 3.1 to 26 per cent. "There was already a greater sense of familiarity … a greater sense that people knew what I was about," he said.[23] He tapped into the regional well of Green support that elected long-time Ontario Green leader, Mike Schreiner as the province's first Green MPP in 2018 and snagged a public endorsement from the area's former Liberal MPP. Morrice parlayed it all into a solid win (34.9 per cent), finishing 10 per cent ahead of the second-place Conservatives.

Aside from Morrice and May, only four other Greens earned at least 10 per cent, making them eligible for a partial reimbursement of election expenses, compared to the forty-nine Green candidates in that category in 2019. In the six ridings where Greens placed second in 2019 (excluding Kitchener Centre), there seems to be no overall pattern to the way their votes scattered. In Atlantic Canada, the Liberals and Conservatives were the main beneficiaries, while in Ontario and BC the NDP picked up support. It suggests the Greens will have to formulate strategies across a gamut of fronts if they hope to rebuild. And they will have to do so while deconstructing how it came to be that they managed – in the space of two years – to largely turn back the clock on their electoral fortunes to their pre-2004 days, leaving a trail of demoralized party members, alienated voters, and ruptured political relationships in their wake.

THE ROOTS OF GREEN DISCONTENT

From the time they entered the federal political arena nearly forty years ago by running candidates in the 1984 election, the Greens have been no strangers to messy internal conflict and public controversy involving their leaders. In fact, shortly after that election, their first leader and party executive quit in frustration over the perceived inefficiency of the grassroots party's consensual decision-making process. In the years that followed, the Greens cycled through other leaders and other contentious issues, but given their status on the political margins, few Canadians were aware of such troubles. Not until 2004, when the Greens fielded a full slate of candidates and billed themselves as a national party under leader Jim Harris, did voters start taking a closer look. Dissent that used to play out behind the scenes spilled into the mainstream media. Harris had a taste of that when, after setting the party on an historic trajectory, he was publicly challenged in 2005 over what some saw as his top-down leadership tendencies.[24]

Similarly, Elizabeth May, who succeeded Harris, struggled with well-publicized missteps and conflicts. Some were not dissimilar to issues Paul faced, from how to allocate budgets (should they focus on paying down debt, or go all out to get May elected?) to how to set priorities (should May run in a riding of her choice, or in one where her chances were better?).[25] In 2018, three former staffers accused May of creating "a toxic work environment with conduct that includes yelling at employees and putting them down in front of their colleagues,"[26] although she was cleared by an independent investigator hired by the party, who found that the complaints did "not rise to the level of workplace harassment under the *Occupational Health and Safety Act*."[27]

Against this background, it was unsurprising that newly minted leader Annamie Paul would also face challenges; what was unprecedented was the scope. After an October 2020 ranked ballot vote for the leadership crown that went a whopping eight rounds, the Greens finally chose Paul – a fresh face and perceived moderate – over candidates who wanted to push the party further left.[28] Paul's uphill struggles began immediately. To begin with, she won the role during the COVID-19 pandemic, making it impossible to establish strong in-person connections with the party's federal council, its three MPs, and senior staff. She was confronted by staffing issues, with the resignation of the party's executive director (whose troubles predated her tenure),[29] followed by staff layoffs in the summer.[30] She plunged right into her Toronto Centre by-election bid, as well as the federal campaign some nine months later. And although she first ran as a Green candidate in 2019 and sat in May's shadow cabinet, Paul – a lawyer and international affairs expert with a stellar CV[31] – had little experience stickhandling internal Green politics. "I don't know if any of us really know the answer, but I think that she really had to have a greater understanding of the elements of the party that would need to be behind her," said Jo-Ann Roberts. "I think she needed to trust a few more people who wanted her to succeed and could have helped. Her team didn't have a lot of party experience. And they were up against an internal infrastructure that was fraught with internal turmoil that wasn't of her making."[32]

The extent of the challenges became evident via a series of leaks and interviews that told the tale of the growing dysfunctional relationship between Paul, federal council, and senior party executive.[33] Paul did not acquiesce to a reported "ultimatum" from federal council that she "repudiate comments from Mr Zatzman and state her support for her MPs at a news conference, or face a confidence vote on July 20."[34] Hostilities moved into the legal arena when Paul requested an arbitrator who halted the party's impending challenges to her leadership; in response, the Greens filed a notice of application for appeal in Ontario Superior Court.[35] No less potent in symbolism were the smaller scuffles: a party official reportedly had Paul's microphone muted during a federal council meeting when she tried to question the wisdom of staff cuts with a snap election looming.[36] And Paul's contract was a point of contention – not just that she asked for a salary approximately equivalent to that of an MP, but also that she wanted a more direct reporting line for the communications team. Any criticism of the latter point was a "red herring," according to Roberts, who noted that following the 2019 election, external experts recommended the party give the person in the leader's role more say over communications. "This was actually something that, in practice, both Elizabeth and I did," she said.[37] May's chief of staff, Debra Eindiguer, said that May, too, would have liked more official control over communications as leader; while she could approve fundraising letters that used her name, her formal sign-off did not extend to other material such as news releases. "She gave input ... but they had no obligation to do what Elizabeth wanted."[38]

Another flashpoint – party finances. "Green party bleeding cash amid legal battles with Annamie Paul" read the headlines, although the problem's genesis predated Paul's tenure. As reported by The Canadian Press, a senior party official noted that money issues were "due to financial decisions taken in 2019 and 2020, particularly the decision to retain staffing levels after the 2019 election."[39] Still, fundraising in the first three quarters of 2021 outpaced the same period in 2020. Elections Canada filings show the Greens raised nearly $2.7 million, approximately $1.3 million of that from 1 July to the end of September.[40] According to The Canadian Press they procured a loan of another $1.3 million for the election,[41] in line with their $1.5 million election loan in 2019. Even so, they were reportedly in a weakened financial state.[42] Paul's executive assistant, Victoria Galea, said the party held back a promised $250,000 that would have supported Paul's Toronto Centre bid in the prewrit period.[43] How much that funding would have ultimately helped is debatable: the negative narrative around Paul and the Greens was set well before the election call.

At the federal level, the campaign was almost nonexistent. Paul spent the bulk of her time in Toronto, only venturing out briefly to Kitchener Centre, PEI, and Vancouver Island, as well as the Ottawa region for the leaders' debates. Those debates, said Galea, were crucial to tipping the balance toward empathy for the embattled Paul. "Just wanting to be able to really show Canadians how talented she is was really important," Galea said. According to one poll, she "punched above her weight" and impressed across party lines.[44] One observer noted she was "the sole calm, composed, straight-shooter on the national stage."[45]

In contrast, the low-key release of the Greens' platform late in the campaign was yet another instance of timing and events working against her. Paul spent five hours almost every morning during the first two weeks of the campaign writing, editing, and adding to the party's existing document, said Galea, before seeking feedback from her shadow cabinet, whose members either wrote their own policy sections or reviewed drafts. Overall, previous housing planks were amplified with a promise to declare affordability and homelessness a national emergency. Other items included a wholesale reform of long-term care in the wake of the crisis exposed by the pandemic, and a promise to dismantle systemic racism and discrimination in areas such as the federal civil service, policing, and immigration and refugee services.

By the time it all came together it was 7 September, Rosh Hashanah, when the Jewish leader was not available to the media. Galea noted that delaying the release was not an option – Paul wanted it out before the first debate on 8 September – so she was unable to explain in a timely way why some major social policy promises, which reprised or updated existing policies such as free postsecondary education, universal pharmacare, and a guaranteed liveable income, remained uncosted by the Office of the Parliamentary Budget Officer.[46] The party finally released some, but not all, costing estimates two days before the election.[47] Even on climate policy, the Greens' raison d'être, they could not catch a break. They have always maintained that other parties joining the climate crusade was a marker of their success. Still, it was a blow when Andrew Weaver, a climate scientist and the former BC Green Party leader, singled out the Liberal climate policy as being the sole credible plan, "both bold and thoughtful."[48]

THE PRE-ELECTION CLIMATE CONTEXT

Meanwhile, Canada had not yet made much actual progress on achieving its original Paris promise of a 30 per cent reduction in greenhouse gas emissions, nor for that matter, the Liberals' newer, more ambitious 40–45 per cent commitment. The most recent data, from 2019, showed emissions down by only 1 per cent,[49] which should have been an uncomfortable elephant in the room, at least for Trudeau. Instead, he preferred to focus on a 2020 assessment by Environment and Climate Change Canada that concluded the Liberal government's proposed actions could ultimately reduce emissions "in the range of 32 per cent to 40 per cent below 2005 levels in 2030."[50] At an international summit in spring 2021, Trudeau told reporters that Canada is "now on track to blow past our old target," a cheery framing that overlooked the uncomfortable present.[51]

The planet had already warmed by an average of 1.2°C higher than pre-industrial times. Canada's warming continued, on average, at a rate twice that of the rest of the world. In fact, Canada's average land temperatures had already hit 1.7°C above those measured in 1948, when records became available, with our North already 2.3°C warmer.[52] With increasingly severe weather events becoming distressingly commonplace, public conversations about climate change sharpened in focus during the two years between federal elections. In 2019, aiming for either a 2°C or a 1.5°C limit in warming were both commonly floated by pundits and politicians alike, even as IPCC reports indicated that the more aspirational 1.5°C would still lead to alarming loss of biodiversity and harm to human life and welfare. By 2021, this catastrophic prediction had sunk into the collective consciousness, and public climate discussions increasingly focused on limiting our global warming to 1.5°C.

Just weeks before the election, to keep the 1.5°C goal within reach, an IPCC report advocated a "death knell" to coal and fossil fuels, and stat. Among the imperatives, the report noted that "[Organisation for Economic Co-operation and Development] countries ... should also end all new fossil fuel exploration and production, and shift fossil-fuel subsidies into renewable energy." With Canada's economy so deeply entwined with fossil fuels, and with some provinces so triggered by discussions of fossil fuel industry lockdowns that national unity is threatened, the Liberal government continued to subsidize the fossil fuel industry, with estimates that ranged from $1.9 billion to $18 billion in 2020, depending on whether the International Institute for Sustainable Development[53] or Environmental Defence[54] was doing the math. But while the Liberals, Bloc, NDP, and Greens all promised to end the government subsidies, the Conservatives signalled an opposite move: increased government investment in oil and gas with a proposed pipeline and a line in their platform – "the truth is that the world will still be burning oil and gas for decades to come"[55] – that suggested an alternative vision of what the future should and would hold.

THE GREENS: PUSHING THE ENVELOPE

With no chance of actually forming a government, the Greens used their platform as a place to push at the margins, to suggest policy ideas that could act as trial balloons for any party ultimately in power. On almost every environmental issue, the Greens went a step further than other parties – for example, by promising to increase the existing carbon tax to $50 per tonne and to increase it by $25 every year so as to hit $275 per tonne by 2030. Some pundits praised the platform's ambitions – both large-scale, for example to get to net-zero emissions long before the Liberal's 2050 plan, and small-scale, such as their idea to buy back internal combustion engine vehicles and promote zero-emission public transportation.

Yet valuable policy ideas notwithstanding, the Green platform was so ambitious – for example, proposing 100 per cent renewable electricity without nuclear plants by 2030, a feat that would entirely upend existing energy infrastructure in multiple provinces in only nine years – that one pundit called the Green Party agenda "Mission Improbable," noting that it would have required "a heavy-handed and top-down federal approach. It also ignores our Constitution."[56]

THE LIBERALS: A RESPECTABLE RECORD

In the run-up to the election the Liberals bolstered their climate credibility by promising an environmental platform that would go beyond the 30 per cent emission reductions that Canada had originally promised at the 2015 Paris climate summit. They upped their green ante to a 40–45 per cent reduction in emissions, and they continued to promise net-zero greenhouse gases by 2050. Ultimately climate modeller Mark Jaccard gave the Liberals the highest mark of any party for environmental platform feasibility and sincerity (eight out of ten) in the election – given that their plan was ambitious, that they seemed to have the internal willingness to put policies in place, and that those policies would not dramatically harm the economy, ultimately costing Canadians only 2 per cent growth in GDP between now and 2030. Not everyone was as positive: another economist, Jennifer Winter, at the University of Calgary's School of Public Policy, noted that despite the Liberal's "respectable record" on the environment, their 2021 platform was "unnecessarily vague."[57]

The Liberals' environmental platform did feature a dizzying array of policy promises – thirty-eight themes in total – with staccato bullet points on a wide range of topics: fighting wildfires, a zero-emission vehicle mandate, a plan for zero plastic waste by 2030, and a clean electricity standard by 2035. Buried in this platform was reference to the party's much publicized (and maligned) scheme to plant two billion trees as a way to fight climate change. Conservative pundits called it expensive greenwashing[58] because two years after the idea was first floated, there was little progress on a project that the Parliamentary Budget Office said would cost $2.78 billion more than expected.[59]

THE CONSERVATIVES: BETTER LATE THAN NEVER?

In the 2019 election, the Conservative Party entirely neglected to release a well-formulated environment platform despite the rising eco-anxiety movement led by Greta Thunberg – a faux pas that cost them credibility on the climate change front and ultimately votes. By the 2021 election, they had not only released a thorough environmental platform, they asked climate scientist Mark Jaccard to model its feasibility. He ultimately gave them high marks for achievability and low marks for ambition, in part because their goal for 2030, to reduce greenhouse gas levels by 30 per cent, would only just meet the original Paris commitment.[60] Environmental economist Jennifer Winter wryly noted that the best part of the Conservatives plan was that it existed.[61]

No longer quibbling about the need to trash a carbon tax – thanks, certainly, to a March 2021 Supreme Court ruling that found the Liberals' tax was constitutional – the federal Conservatives instead promised to reformulate and ultimately freeze it at $50 per tonne as compared to the Liberal plan to raise it to $170 by 2030. Although the platform noted – in a complete about-face from 2019 – that "the most efficient way to reduce our emissions is to use pricing mechanisms," they promised to reach Paris promises "without the government taxing working Canadians and driving jobs and investment out of the country." The idea was to recast the carbon tax as a credit scheme, wherein citizens could bank their tax payments for later purchase of low emission products. This strategy seemed rather clunky and complicated for a party supposedly committed to minimal bureaucratic red tape: the rebrand seemed like unnecessary tweaking at best and, at worst, a filibuster to delay continued implementation of the carbon tax, given that the party had rejected including in their policy documents statements to the effect that "climate change is real" and that they were "willing to act" on the issue.

THE NDP: POSTURING FOR GREEN POSTERITY?

With a target to reduce greenhouse gas emissions by 50 per cent of 2005 levels – on par with US President Joe Biden's plan[62] – the NDP's environmental platform was otherwise almost uniformly criticized as being as ambitious as it was unfeasible. Similar to 2019, readers of the 2021 platform were greeted with the same fetching photo of Jagmeet Singh in a canoe,[63] along with many of the same policy ideas. Their promises of "over a million new good jobs" and a commitment of $1 billion through to 2026 to enable the transition of oil and gas workers into greener industries were challenged on fiscal and feasibility grounds, while others faulted the platform for failing to distinguish federal and provincial jurisdictions.[64]

THE BLOC: CAUTIOUS KUDOS

Although they did not release a greenhouse gas target, previous party documents suggest the Bloc was committed, like the Green Party, to a target of 60 per cent lower than 2005 levels. Their platform was unsurprisingly Quebec-centric and progressive enough to receive cautious kudos from climate scientist Katherine Hayhoe, who noted that "the regional steps they propose – like redirecting Quebec's investments in fossil fuels into clean energy and research and replacing the national Hydrogen Strategy with Hydro-Quebec's green hydrogen program – would be plausible, assuming full collaboration with the province and the federal government."[65]

BATTLE FOR THE GLOBE, STRUGGLE FOR THE SOUL

In the weeks after the election, Nanos Research polling found that the environment, by its metrics, emerged as Canadians' topmost concern for the first time since March 2020, and that its import continued to rise. It was almost as if now that the matter of which political party would be responsible for the pandemic recovery was settled, Canadians could focus entirely on longer term concerns, all against the backdrop of global preparations for the COP26, where the world would, once again, try to find ways to curb, mitigate, and adapt to the coming climate emergency.[66]

Yet while many viewed the 2021 election as an expensive way to maintain the status quo, Trudeau's delegation of ministerial duties showed clear commitment to the climate change file, with power assigned in such a way as to "put the oil-and-gas sector on notice," as one headline put it.[67] In the role of minister of the Environment and Climate Change Canada, Trudeau put Steven Guilbeault, a former Greenpeace activist whose familiarity with the environment portfolio was certainly on point, even if the appointment poked at the existential insecurities of Canada's big oil barons. Meanwhile, the outgoing Environment minister, Jonathan Wilkinson – who by all accounts had enjoyed the portfolio and was certainly progressive on the file – was dispatched to Natural Resources, a place long criticized by environmental activists as being too friendly with the energy industry. As one columnist put it, "Justin Trudeau has fired a shot across the bow of Canada's fossil fuel industry with the appointments of a pair of climate-focused ministers in his new cabinet."[68]

Meanwhile, seven weeks after facing the media in Suydam Park, Annamie Paul terminated her party membership and officially parted ways with the Green Party.[69] If the Greens are now fortunate, they will not face another test at the polls for at least two years, giving them time to choose a new leader and begin the long road back to establishing themselves as a viable political presence. It is unclear how effectively they can accomplish the latter. The factors that previously enabled them to punch above their weight federally – the per-vote subsidy that financed their operations and gave weight to their argument that every Green vote counted, along with the enormous gaps in other parties' environmental policies – no longer apply. Short of national electoral reform that might allow them to capitalize on their traditionally diffused support, it could be that the best chance for the Greens to survive as a political entity will be at other levels of government where they have had a varying degree of electoral success and pools of regional support.

Greens are in office provincially and municipally in BC. They are the official opposition in PEI, hold three seats in New Brunswick and one in Ontario. Whether the rejection at the national level will spill over into the regions will be tested in upcoming provincial elections. Already, Ontario's Greens have distanced themselves from their federal counterparts. In a statement released soon after Paul announced her intent to resign, the party expressed its disappointment with her "painful experience": "The Ontario Green Party is determined to tear down the systemic barriers including anti-Black racism that many Ontarians and Canadians continue to face in politics. We are a wholly separate entity from the federal party with a different organizational culture and governance structure."[70]

Green activists elsewhere in the world have already started pushing for anti-racism reform within their own parties.[71] Ontario's public statement was a blunt wake-up call for Canada's national party. As its members face down their futures in the wake of the federal election, recognition that meaningful climate action demands meaningful social equity could become the ultimate tipping point in what Annamie Paul had characterized as the ongoing struggle for the party's soul.

NOTES

1 Dave Korzinski and Shachi Kurl, "Election 44: Most View This Vote as 'More Important' than 2019; Personal Stakes Involved for Three-Quarters," Angus Reid Institute, 27 August 2021, https://angusreid.org/federal-election-top-issues/.

2 Nik Nanos, "Environment Continues to Climb in Importance as Top Unprompted National Issue of Concern," Nanos Research, 12 October 2021, https://nanos.co/wp-content/uploads/2021/10/Political-Package-2021-10-08-FR-with-tabs-2817dgg122.pdf.

3 The exception being the People's Party of Canada, which we do not consider a main party. Their environmental platform consisted of primarily "long-debunked zombie myths," as one climate scientist put it. Katharine Hayhoe, "How the Federal Parties' Climate Plans Stack Up," *Chatelaine*, 14 September 2021, https://www.chatelaine.com/news/canada-election-2021-climate-plans-graded/.

4 Mark Jaccard, "Assessing Climate Sincerity in the Canadian 2021 Election," *Policy Options*, 3 September 2021, https://policyoptions.irpp.org/magazines/septembe-2021/assessing-climate-sincerity-in-the-canadian-2021-election/.

5 Susan Harada, telephone interview with Victoria Galea, then-executive assistant to Annamie Paul, 13 October 2021.

6 "Annamie Paul Announces She Is Stepping Down as Green Leader," CPAC, 27 September 2021, 01:51, https://www.cpac.ca/episode?id=22227863-67e8-4485-8e12-02e790a4ffa7.

7 Annamie Paul (@AnnamiePaul), "I am beginning the process of stepping down as Green Party Leader. When I was elected into this role, I broke a glass ceiling. I didn't realize that when I did, the shards would fall on my

head, leaving a trail of broken glass that I would have to crawl over," Twitter, 27 September 2021, https://twitter.com/AnnamiePaul/status/1442539101446623233?s=20.

8 Christopher Guly, "Where Do the Greens Go from Here?" *Tyee*, 8 October 2021, https://thetyee.ca/News/2021/10/08/Where-Greens-Go-From-Here/.

9 Elizabeth May, "Elizabeth May: Annamie Paul Told Me to Stay Silent. But Now I Must Say Something," *Toronto Star*, 3 October 2021, https://www.thestar.com/politics/political-opinion/2021/10/03/annamie-paul-told-me-to-stay-silent-but-now-i-must-say-something.html.

10 May, "Annamie Paul Told Me to Stay Silent."

11 May, "Annamie Paul Told Me to Stay Silent."

12 Alex Ballingall, "Senior Green Officials Are Sabotaging the First Black Woman to Lead a Canadian Political Party, 'Disgusted' Insiders Say," *Toronto Star*, 7 April 2021, https://www.thestar.com/politics/federal/2021/04/07/senior-green-officials-are-sabotaging-the-first-black-woman-to-lead-a-canadian-political-party-disgusted-insiders-say.html.

13 Ian Bailey, "Racism, Transphobia Big Problems in Green Party, Internal Report Says," *Globe and Mail*, 31 August 2021, https://www.theglobeandmail.com/politics/article-racism-transphobia-big-problems-in-green-party-internal-report-says/.

14 "Green Leader Annamie Paul Addresses Party Turmoil," CPAC, 16 June 2021, https://www.cpac.ca/episode?id=abada143-caa8-452c-8a3c-990900c1e0ff.

15 Susan Harada, telephone interview with Markus Harvey, 4 October 2021.

16 Janet E. Silver, "Atwin Blames Her Departure from Green Party on Leader," *iPolitics*, 11 June 2021, https://ipolitics.ca/2021/06/11/atwin-blames-her-departure-from-green-party-on-leader/. Also see, Christopher Reynolds, "Green Party Rift over Israeli-Palestinian Conflict Grows as MPs Break from Leader," *Toronto Star*, 1 June 2021, https://www.thestar.com/politics/2021/06/01/green-party-rift-over-israeli-palestinian-conflict-grows-as-mps-break-from-leader.html. And, Kevin Bissett and Christopher Reynolds, "Citing Distractions, New Brunswick Green MP Jenica Atwin Crosses Floor to Liberals," *Toronto Star*, 10 June 2021, https://www.thestar.com/politics/2021/06/10/canadian-press-news-alert-new-brunswick-mp-set-to-cross-floor-from-greens-to-liberals.html.

17 "2021 Green Party of Canada Candidate Nomination Procedures," Green Party of Canada, 19 January 2021, https://greensconnect.ca/uploads/decidim/attachment/file/58/2021_Green_Party_of_Canada_Candidate_Nomination_Procedures.pdf.

18 Susan Harada, telephone interview with Jo-Ann Roberts, former Green candidate and interim party leader, 12 October 2021.
19 Susan Harada, telephone interview with Darcie Lanthier, former Green candidate, 14 October 2021.
20 Susan Harada, telephone interview with Jo-Ann Roberts, 12 October 2021.
21 Éric Grenier, "Poll Tracker," CBC News, last modified 19 September 2021, https://newsinteractives.cbc.ca/elections/poll-tracker/canada/.
22 See, for example, Christian Paas-Lang and Ashley Burke, "Embattled Liberal Candidate Raj Saini Ends Bid for Re-Election," CBC News, 4 September 2021, https://www.cbc.ca/news/politics/raj-saini-ends-campaign-1.6165229. And, Brian Platt, "Withdrawal of Liberal MP Raj Saini Opens Door for a Green Win in Ontario Riding," *National Post*, 21 September 2021, https://nationalpost.com/news/politics/election-2021/withdrawal-of-liberal-candidate-opens-door-for-much-needed-green-win-in-ontario-riding.
23 Susan Harada, telephone interview with Mike Morrice, 11 September 2021.
24 Susan Harada, "Great Expectations: The Green Party of Canada's 2006 Campaign," in *The Canadian Federal Election of 2006*, eds. Jon H. Pammett and Christoper Dornan (Toronto: Dundurn Press, 2006), 143–70.
25 See, for example, Susan Harada, "The Promise of May: The Green Party of Canada's Campaign 2008," in *The Canadian Federal Election of 2008*, eds. Jon H. Pammett and Christopher Dornan (Toronto: Dundurn Press, 2009), 162–93.
26 Alex Ballingall, "Three Former Green Party Staffers Accuse Elizabeth May of Workplace Bullying," *Toronto Star*, 27 January 2018, https://www.thestar.com/news/canada/2018/01/27/three-former-green-party-staffers-accuse-elizabeth-may-of-workplace-bullying.html. See also, Shruti Shekar, "Green Party Launches Investigation into Elizabeth May after Hill Times, *Toronto Star* Report on Allegations of Workplace Bullying," *Hill Times*, 29 January 2018, https://www.hilltimes.com/2018/01/29/ex-green-party-canada-employee-says-investigation-leader-not-independent/132572. And, Peter Zimonjic, "Green Party Leader Elizabeth May Orders Investigation into Allegations She Bullied Staff," CBC News, 29 January 2018, https://www.cbc.ca/news/politics/elizabeth-may-allegations-investigation-1.4508997.
27 Kathleen Harris, "Harassment Claims against Elizabeth May Don't Meet Ontario's Legal Bar, Investigator Finds," CBC News, 10 May 2018, https://www.cbc.ca/news/politics/harassment-claims-green-party-may-1.4656761.

28 Alex Ballingall, "Toronto Lawyer Annamie Paul Elected Green Party of Canada Leader," *Toronto Star*, 3 October 2020, https://www.thestar.com/politics/federal/2020/10/03/toronto-lawyer-annamie-paul-elected-green-party-of-canada-leader.html. And, John Paul Tasker, "Toronto Lawyer Annamie Paul Elected Leader of the Federal Green Party," CBC News, 3 October 2020, https://www.cbc.ca/news/politics/green-party-new-leader-1.5749648.

29 Ashley Burke, "Green Party's Executive Director Resigns after Internal Probe of His Past Conduct Causes Turmoil," CBC News, 4 October 2020, https://www.cbc.ca/news/politics/green-party-executive-director-prateek-awasthi-resigns-1.5750279.

30 Allex Ballingall and Raisa Patel, "Green Party Cuts Two Staffers from Leader Annamie Paul's Office Amid Layoffs," *Toronto Star*, 7 July 2021, https://www.thestar.com/politics/federal/2021/07/07/green-party-cuts-two-staffers-from-leader-annamie-pauls-office-amid-layoffs.html.

31 "My Name Is Annamie Paul," Annamie Paul, 2020, https://www.annamiepaul.ca/about. (This website no longer exists.)

32 Susan Harada, telephone interview with Jo-Ann Roberts, 12 October 2021.

33 See, for example, Ian Bailey, "Greens President Outlines Challenges Facing Party," *Globe and Mail*, 30 June 2021, https://www.theglobeandmail.com/politics/article-greens-president-outlines-challenges-facing-party/. And, Alex Ballingall, "Is Annamie Paul Still the Green Leader? Party Members Are Left Wondering," *Toronto Star*, 15 July 2021, https://www.thestar.com/politics/federal/2021/07/15/is-annamie-paul-still-the-green-leader-party-members-are-left-wondering.html.

34 Marieke Walsh and Ian Bailey, "'It Never Felt out of Reach for Me': Annamie Paul on Her Fight to Stay as Green Party Leader," *Globe and Mail*, 19 June 2021, https://www.theglobeandmail.com/politics/article-green-leader-annamie-paul-moves-forward-amid-partys-schism/.

35 "Green Party of Canada Fund Inc. And Green Party of Canada (Applicants) and Annamie Paul (Respondent)," *Notice of Application (Pursuant to Rules 14.05 and 38 of The Rules of Civil Procedure)* (Ontario Superior Court of Justice, 2021).

36 Raisa Patel, "Green Leader Annamie Paul Muted in Virtual Meeting as She Argued against Sweeping Cuts to Party Staff," *Toronto Star*, 6 July 2021, https://www.thestar.com/politics/federal/2021/07/06/green-leader-annamie-paul-muted-in-virtual-meeting-as-she-argued-against-sweeping-cuts-to-party-staff.html.

37 Susan Harada, telephone interview with Jo-Ann Roberts, 12 October 2021.

38 Susan Harada, telephone and email interview with Debra Eindiguer, chief of staff to Elizabeth May, 25 and 26 November 2021.

39 Christopher Reynolds, "Green Party Bleeding Cash Amid Legal Battles with Annamie Paul," *Toronto Star*, 28 July 2021, https://www.thestar.com/politics/2021/07/28/green-party-bleeding-cash-amid-legal-battles-with-

40 "Registered Party Quarterly Financial Returns," Elections Canada, last modified 10 November 2021, https://www.elections.ca/WPAPPS/WPF/EN/PP/Index?act=C76&reportOption=2&selectedReportType=3&returnStatus=1&displayIntroduction=False&displayDescription=False.

41 Reynolds, "Green Party Bleeding Cash."

42 See, for example, Alex Ballingall, "Green Party near a Financial 'Tipping Point,' Council Warned in Recorded Meeting," *Toronto Star*, 28 July 2021, https://www.thestar.com/politics/federal/2021/07/28/green-party-finances-near-a-tipping-point-recording-of-meeting-reveals.html. And, Christopher Reynolds, "Green Party Lays Off Core Staff Members Amid Financial Drought, Internal Strife," *Toronto Star*, 19 October 2021, https://www.thestar.com/politics/2021/10/19/green-party-lays-off-core-staff-members-amid-financial-drought-internal-strife.html.

43 Susan Harada, telephone interview with Victoria Galea, 13 October 2021.

44 "Election 44: Two-Thirds of Debate Watchers Say Exercise Was Informative, Will Help Them Make Their Choice," Angus Reid Institute, 15 September 2021, https://angusreid.org/44th-federal-election-debate-reaction/.

45 Fatima Syed, "Annamie Paul Was the Unexpected Hero of the Leaders' Debate," *Maclean's*, 10 September 2021, https://www.macleans.ca/opinion/federal-leaders-debate-listening-to-annamie-paul/.

46 Peter Zimonjic, "Green Platform Promises Big, Largely Uncosted Social Programs, End to Fossil Fuel Industry," CBC News, 7 September 2021, https://www.cbc.ca/news/politics/annamie-paul-green-party-platform-1.6167167.

47 "44th General Election PBO Estimates," Office of the Parliamentary Budget Officer, accessed 20 October 2021, https://www.pbo-dpb.gc.ca/en/epc-estimates--estimations-cpe?epc-cmp--eid=44). And, Peter Zimonjic, "Greens Release Partial Costing of Platform Promising $210B in New Spending over Next Five Years," CBC News, 18 September 2021, https://www.cbc.ca/news/politics/green-party-platform-partial-costing-1.6181386.

48 Joan Bryden, "Former BC Green Leader Endorses Liberal Climate Plan, Slams Green Infighting," *Toronto Star*, 2 September 2021, https://www.thestar.com/politics/federal-election/2021/09/02/former-bc-green-leader-endorses-liberal-climate-plan-slams-green-infighting.html.

49 "Greenhouse Gas Emissions," Government of Canada, last modified 29 October 2021, https://www.canada.ca/en/environment-climate-change/services/environmental-indicators/greenhouse-gas-emissions.html.

50 "A Healthy Environment and a Healthy Economy," Government of Canada, last modified 8 April 2021, https://www.canada.ca/en/services/environment/weather/climatechange/climate-plan/climate-plan-overview/healthy-environment-healthy-economy.html.

51 John Paul Tasker and Aaron Wherry, "Trudeau Pledges to Slash Greenhouse Gas Emissions by at Least 40% by 2030," CBC News, 22 April 2021, https://www.cbc.ca/news/politics/trudeau-climate-emissions-40-per-cent-1.5997613.

52 E. Bush and D.S. Lemmen, eds., *Canada's Changing Climate Report* (Ottawa: Government of Canada, 2019), 444.

53 Vanessa Corkal, "Federal Fossil Fuel Subsidies in Canada: COVID-19 Edition," International Institute for Sustainable Development, 25 February 2021, https://www.iisd.org/publications/fossil-fuel-subsidies-canada-COVID-19.

54 Julia Levin, "Paying Polluters: How Much Canada Gave in Federal Financial Support for Oil and Gas in 2020," *Environmental Defence*, 15 April 2021, https://environmentaldefence.ca/2021/04/15/paying-polluters-much-canada-gave-federal-financial-support-oil-gas-2020/.

55 Sarah Cox, "Fossil Fuel Subsidies Are One of Canada's Biggest Climate Conundrums: Where Do the Parties Stand?" *Narwhal*, 16 September 2021, https://thenarwhal.ca/federal-election-2021-fossil-fuel-subsidies/.

56 Jennifer Winter, "Green Party Climate Platform Is Both Ambitious and Unrealistic," CBC News, 16 September 2021, https://www.cbc.ca/news/opinion/opinion-election-green-party-climate-platform-1.6175939.

57 Jennifer Winter, "Liberal Party Continues Balancing Act with Unnecessarily Vague Plan on Climate," CBC News, 10 September 2021, https://www.cbc.ca/news/opinion/opinion-election-liberal-party-climate-platform-1.6168763.

58 Diane Francis, "Trudeau's Promise to Plant 2 Billion Trees Nothing but Greenwashing," *Financial Post*, 31 August 2021, https://financialpost.com/diane-francis/diane-francis-trudeaus-two-billion-tree-promise-nothing-but-greenwashing.

59 Stephanie Taylor, "Liberal Tree-Planting Pledge Still Sparse on Details after Two Years, Tory Critic Says," *Globe and Mail*, 30 April 2021, https://www.theglobeandmail.com/politics/article-liberal-tree-planting-pledge-still-sparse-on-details-after-two-years/.

60 Mark Jaccard, "Assessing Climate Sincerity in the Canadian 2021 Election," *Policy Options*, 3 September 2021, https://policyoptions.irpp.org/magazines/septembe-2021/assessing-climate-sincerity-in-the-canadian-2021-election/.

61 Jennifer Winter, "Conservative Climate Plan Better Than before, but Still Full of Inconsistencies," CBC News, 30 August 2021, https://www.cbc.ca/news/opinion/opinion-election-conservative-party-climate-platform-1.6155156.

62 John Paul Tasker and Aaron Wherry, "Trudeau Pledges to Slash Greenhouse Gas Emissions by at Least 40% by 2030," CBC News, 22 April 2021, https://www.cbc.ca/news/politics/trudeau-climate-emissions-40-per-cent-1.5997613.

63 "Protecting Our Air, Land, and Water, Securing Our Future," New Democratic Party, accessed 2 November 2021, https://www.ndp.ca/climate-action.

64 Katharine Hayhoe, "How The Federal Parties' Climate Plans Stack Up," *Chatelaine*, 14 September 2021, https://www.chatelaine.com/news/canada-election-2021-climate-plans-graded/.

65 "2021 Canadian Federal Election," Federal Party Survey on Environmental Platforms, https://election2021envirosurvey.ca/responses/.

66 Nik Nanos, "Environment Continues to Climb in Importance as Top Unprompted National Issue of Concern," Nanos Research, 12 October 2021, https://nanos.co/wp-content/uploads/2021/10/Political-Package-2021-10-08-FR-with-tabs-2817dgg122.pdf

67 Adam Radwanski, "Trudeau's Cabinet Choices Put the Oil-and-Gas Sector on Notice," *Globe and Mail*, 27 October 2021, https://www.theglobeandmail.com/politics/article-trudeaus-cabinet-choices-put-the-oil-and-gas-sector-on-notice/.

68 Radwanski, "Trudeau's Cabinet Choices Put the Oil-and-Gas Sector on Notice."

69 Alex Ballingall, "Green Party Formally Accepts Annamie Paul's Resignation as Leader," *Toronto Star*, 15 November 2021, https://www.thestar.com/politics/federal/2021/11/15/green-party-formally-accepts-annamie-pauls-resignation-as-leader.html.

70 "Ontario Greens Statement on Racism, Sexism, and Antisemitism," Green Party of Ontario, 8 October 2021, https://gpo.ca/2021/10/08/ontario-greens-statement-on-racism-sexism-and-antisemitism/.

71 Samie Jeraj, "Anti-Racist Politics in Practice: Greens and Black Lives Matter," *Green European Journal*, 18 September 2020, https://www.greeneuropeanjournal.eu/anti-racist-politics-in-practice-the-greens-and-black-lives-matter/.

7

Polling in the 2021 Federal Election

Éric Grenier

If Prime Minister Justin Trudeau decided to call an early election in 2021 to secure a majority government for his party, it might have been because public opinion polls showed that such a victory was within his grasp. But even though the Liberals failed to achieve that goal, the polls nevertheless accurately gauged public opinion over the course of the five-week campaign and, by the end of it, signalled that the country was heading to another minority government.

As was the case for governments in many provinces across Canada, the federal Liberal government's handling of the COVID-19 pandemic coincided with a surge in support for both the Liberals and Trudeau – one that marked a shift from the prepandemic period. There had been no honeymoon for the Liberals after their 2019 victory, with post-election polls in the months following suggesting the Liberals and Conservatives remained neck and neck in national support. But when the pandemic shut the country down in March 2020, support for the Liberals shot up, rising to over 40 per cent in most polls between May and July 2020 and awarding the party a lead of at least 10 percentage points over the opposition Conservatives.[1] While just 32 per cent of Canadians said they held a positive impression of the prime minister in a poll conducted shortly before the country was locked down, Trudeau's positive ratings soared to 47 per cent shortly afterwards, thereby erasing the damage that had been done to his personal brand in 2019 over the SNC-Lavalin affair and the blackface scandal.[2]

These high levels of support could not be sustained indefinitely, however. The WE Charity controversy in 2020 dropped Liberal support to about 35–36 per cent, but that nevertheless gave the Liberals a lead of four to six percentage points over the Conservatives, now under the leadership of Erin O'Toole. Those numbers held relatively steady throughout the remainder of 2020 until the summer of 2021, when the Liberals' lead over the Conservatives increased to about seven points on average. Some surveys even awarded the Liberals a lead of ten points or more once again, kicking off speculation by the media that the government might consider calling an early election to take advantage of the party's strong polling numbers. At the time, Trudeau was also comparing favourably to O'Toole, with one survey showing 27 per cent of Canadians thinking Trudeau would make the best prime minister, compared to just 11 per cent for O'Toole. NDP Leader Jagmeet Singh placed second in the poll with 19 per cent, despite the New Democratic Party trailing in third place in national support.[3] Heading into a potential campaign, O'Toole's own personal brand looked to be extremely problematic for the Conservatives. According to an Abacus Data survey conducted just prior to the election call, only 22 per cent of Canadians held a positive impression of the Conservative leader, compared to 41 per cent who held a negative impression. In the same survey, 41 per cent said they held a positive impression of Trudeau with 39 per cent holding a negative impression.[4] While Trudeau's numbers were not nearly as good as they had been at the height of the pandemic (or as good as Singh's 40 per cent positive to 24 per cent negative ratings), they were still relatively strong for an incumbent prime minister after six years in office.

What the main issue of an early election would be, however, was not clear from the polling. A survey conducted by Nanos Research in the four weeks before the election was called showed 24 per cent of Canadians naming (unprompted) the coronavirus pandemic as the top issue of national concern, followed by 12 per cent who said jobs and economy, 12 per cent the environment, 9 per cent healthcare, and 6 per cent housing and cost of housing.[5] But another poll by the Angus Reid Institute showed the pandemic trailing as a top-three issue at 27 per cent behind healthcare (36 per cent), environment and climate change (36 per cent), housing affordability (27 per cent), and the economy (27 per cent).[6] The numbers suggested that while all of these issues would be important to some voters, it was unlikely that there would be a single ballot-box question upon which the 2021 election would be decided.

THE POLLING LANDSCAPE IN 2021

More polls were published during the 2021 election than any other Canadian election campaign. In all, over 150 national voting intentions surveys were published over the thirty-six-day campaign for an average of 4.3 surveys per day, not including separate poll releases focusing on various election issues or individual regions.[7] By comparison, just under 120 polls were published in 2019, similar to the number of surveys published in 2006, 2008, and 2015, and more than the eighty-one published in 2011.[8] The high volume of polls was primarily due to three polling firms (Nanos Research for *The Globe and Mail* and CTV News, Mainstreet Research for iPolitics, and EKOS Research on its website and on the *Curse of Politics* podcast) publishing daily tracking polls that featured three- or four-day roll-ups, with the oldest day of polling being dropped whenever a new day of polling was conducted. In addition to these daily poll releases, Abacus Data, the Angus Reid Institute, Ipsos (for Global News), and Léger (for The Canadian Press and Postmedia) put out new releases on at least a weekly basis. Abacus also put out a daily tracking poll for the last week of the campaign, while Campaign Research, Counsel Public Affairs, Forum Research, Innovative Research Group, Research Co., and regional polling firms Narrative Research in Atlantic Canada and Insights West in British Columbia also published multiple surveys during the campaign. Only Nanos conducted its polling over the telephone with live callers, while Forum, EKOS, and Mainstreet used the interactive voice response mode of contact. All other pollsters conducted their surveys over the internet (Ipsos also published some surveys with mixed online and telephone samples).

In recent decades, the polling industry has had to adapt to the new realities caused by dropping response rates and the move from landline telephones to mobile phones. Along with cost savings and the ability to customize surveys to a greater extent, this is one of the reasons why polling online has become more and more common. The online polling firms take great care in building and replenishing their online panels, using an array of methods – including traditional telephone recruitment – to keep their panels demographically representative, something that has been of particular concern after the difficulties faced by American pollsters in recent presidential elections. The issue of response bias, especially between Interactive

Voice Response (IVR) and online pollsters, will be explored later as it relates to support for the People's Party of Canada. Of those pollsters who did conduct their surveys over the telephone or via interactive voice response, few published response rates. But the final survey conducted by Nanos Research reported a response rate of 6 per cent. IVR response rates are often even lower. Despite the challenges faced by pollsters in assembling representative panels and combating dropping response rates, their accuracy in the 2021 campaign – as in most Canadian elections – was quite high.

As has become common in Canadian elections, several media outlets also published polling aggregates, along with seat projections, rather than entering into a relationship with individual pollsters. These aggregates were widely viewed and shared. The CBC published the Poll Tracker, featuring a poll aggregation and seat projection model maintained by the author, which received thirteen million page views during the campaign.[9] Philippe J. Fournier published the 338Canada.com website, which received over ten million page views, and collaborated with *Maclean's* and *L'actualité* magazines,[10] while the *Toronto Star* published the Signal, run by Vox Pop Labs.[11] A number of polling firms and other websites also published seat projections during the campaign.[12] By election day, despite the tight margins in national support between the Liberals and Conservatives, these models provided useful context to the horserace polls by projecting another sizeable Liberal minority, with a majority government seen as an unlikely outcome.

IMPACT OF THE ELECTION CALL

A minority outcome was not the consensus projection when the election was officially called on 15 August. The last surveys conducted by a number of polling firms before the dissolution of parliament awarded the Liberals between 35 and 40 per cent support, followed by the Conservatives at 25 to 31 per cent, and the NDP at 17 to 20 per cent. The Bloc Québécois was registering 5 to 7 per cent nationally, with the Greens at 3 to 7 per cent and the People's Party at 2 to 5 per cent. The Liberals held an average lead of six percentage points in British Columbia, eight in Quebec, nine in Ontario and twenty in Atlantic Canada. The Conservatives held leads in only Alberta, Saskatchewan, and Manitoba. These numbers put the Liberals in range of winning at least the 170 seats needed to form a majority government.

However, the Liberals lost their comfortable lead almost immediately. Coming on the same day as news broke of the fall of Kabul, the capital of Afghanistan, to the Taliban, Trudeau's visit to the governor general to call the election was generally perceived as an opportunistic political move. According to a survey by Léger, only 21 per cent of Canadians said they thought "now is a good time to have an election," while 69 per cent said "the election could have waited until next year or later." Worse for the Liberals, 34 per cent said the early call would make them less likely to vote for the party, including 13 per cent of respondents who said they were supporting the Liberals at the time. The poll suggested voters were not buying the prime minister's claim that the election was about the big choices that had to be made, as 41 per cent said the main reason for the call was because the prime minister thought "it's the Liberal Party's best chance to win a majority government." Only 19 per cent said it was because "Canadians deserve a voice and a vote on the plans for Canada's post-pandemic recovery." Even a plurality of Liberal voters believed the call was primarily motivated by a desire to win a majority government.[13]

The perceived cynicism of the election call had an immediate impact on public opinion. The share of voters saying they held a negative impression of Trudeau jumped immediately from 39 to 44 per cent[14] and one early-campaign survey showed the share of Canadians saying their views of the prime minister were worsening outpaced those who said their views were improving by a margin of more than seven-to-one. In the CBC's Poll Tracker aggregate, the margin between the Liberals and Conservatives in national support decreased by three percentage points in the first week. Compounding the bad situation for the Liberals was that O'Toole's personal ratings improved over the first few days of the campaign, with the share of those with a positive impression increasing by six points to 26 per cent after the first week and eventually increasing to 31 per cent in polling by Abacus Data, making O'Toole no longer the drag on the Conservative Party that he appeared he might be prior to the campaign's kickoff.[15]

With the Liberal leader struggling to find an answer to the question of what the election was about and both O'Toole and Singh running relatively problem-free campaigns, Trudeau and the Liberals continued to drop in public support. Within a week of the election call, the first tracking poll put the Conservatives ahead of the Liberals. By the second week of the campaign, most polls were placing the Conservatives ahead, with the party moving into first place in the Poll Tracker aggregate on 28 August. By the first week of September, the Conservatives' support would increase to 34 per cent in the aggregate, giving the party a three-point lead over the Liberals. Regionally, the Conservatives moved from third to first place in British Columbia in most polls and closed the gap on the Liberals in both Ontario and Atlantic Canada. Liberal support slid in Western Canada, allowing the NDP to move into second place throughout the region. In the Nanos three-day tracking ending on 2 September, O'Toole moved ahead of Trudeau on who Canadians preferred to be prime minister with 31 per cent to Trudeau's 27 per cent, followed by Singh at 20 per cent. Compared to Nanos' last precampaign survey, this represented a surge of 13 percentage points for O'Toole and a gain of three points for Singh, while support for Trudeau plunged eight points. This, however, would prove to be the high watermark for O'Toole.

THE TVA DEBATE AND NEW ISSUES EMERGE

A number of issues which emerged at the midpoint of the campaign coincided with a halt, and then reversal, of the Conservatives' upward trend in the polls: private healthcare, gun control, and vaccination against COVID-19. These three issues were all brought up during the first leaders' debate of the campaign, organized by Quebec's French-language network TVA on 2 September.

The debate itself appeared to have little direct impact on voting intentions. Among those who watched or heard about the debate in Quebec, Abacus Data found that all leaders left more of a positive than a negative impression. But Trudeau and Bloc Québécois Leader Yves-François Blanchet reaped the most benefits, with 48 and 49 per cent of respondents, respectively, saying the leaders made a positive impression on them, compared to 23 and 15 per cent, respectively, who said they made a negative impression. On the questions of which leader did the most to earn or lose their vote, Blanchet had the best net result at plus ten, compared to plus three for Trudeau and minus four for O'Toole. The same share of respondents said Singh did the most to earn or lose their vote.[16]

But some of the issues discussed at the debate were not particularly good ones for O'Toole. The Liberal charge that O'Toole favoured more privatization of the healthcare system was perhaps the least effective, as Léger found that 71 per cent of Canadians said they were "fine with private clinics operating in my province so long as there continues to be universal access to quality care." The Liberals were more on target when they highlighted a promise in the Conservative platform to repeal some of the Liberal government's gun control measures. Léger found that 51 per cent of Canadians supported tougher gun laws and increased regulation, compared to 9 per cent who wanted looser laws and decreased regulations. Tougher laws were particularly popular among Liberal voters (70 per cent) and NDP voters (58 per cent).[17] The Conservative opposition to mandatory vaccination for travellers and their unwillingness to require their candidates to be vaccinated was offside with an even greater share of the population. Léger found that 80 per cent of Canadians supported vaccine passports[18] while Nanos Research found 85 per cent of Canadians saying they were comfortable or somewhat comfortable with requiring proof of vaccination to travel by air and 82 per cent saying they were comfortable with requiring it for long-distance train travel.[19] Polling by Ipsos found a similar share (82 per cent) supporting proof of vaccination for travel.[20] Forcing the Conservatives on the defensive on these issues put the party onside with the minority – and in some cases a tiny minority – of public opinion. Even a majority of Conservative voters, according to Ipsos, favoured mandatory vaccination for teachers, federal public servants, and healthcare workers.[21]

The doubts the Liberals tried to instil in voters' minds about the Conservative leader appeared to have an effect. From more voters saying their views of O'Toole were improving rather than worsening over the first few weeks of the campaign, more voters were now saying their views were worsening.[22] In Abacus Data's polling, O'Toole's positive ratings hit a ceiling at 31 per cent, while his negative ratings started to increase once more. After declining from 42 to 39 per cent over the first few weeks, the share saying they held a negative impression of O'Toole would rise again to 43 per cent by the end of the campaign, which now shifted from one in which the Conservatives were rising in the polls to one where the race was tightening. By 11 September, little more than a week after the TVA debate, the Liberals and Conservatives were back in a tie in the Poll Tracker aggregate with about 31 or 32 per cent support apiece. The two parties would hold at this level of support for the rest of the campaign, as the Liberals regained a wide lead in Atlantic Canada and moved from a near-tie in Ontario to a steady four- or five-point lead. The Liberals remained stuck in their position as the third-place party in Western Canada, however.

Politicizing the debate over vaccination, as widely supported as vaccination might have been, nevertheless had some repercussions on the campaign trail. At multiple events, Trudeau was dogged by anti-vaccination, anti-mask mandate, or antilockdown protesters. At one of these events, a person in the crowd hurled gravel at the Liberal leader as he was boarding his campaign bus. These protests, along with rising COVID-19 case numbers in some parts of the country, refocused some of the campaign's attention onto the pandemic. The protests themselves appeared to have increased sympathy for the prime minister, as 50 per cent of Canadians told Léger they "felt sorry for the prime minister having his events disrupted by the protesters," including a majority of Liberal, Bloc, NDP, and Green voters. Less than a third of Conservative or PPC supporters agreed.[23]

But more and more Canadians were saying they were planning to vote for the People's Party, which had captured just 1.6 per cent of the vote in the 2019 election under Maxime Bernier's leadership. The pandemic, however, had given the PPC a raison d'être that it lacked prior to the campaign, when the party appeared stuck at around 2–3 per cent support. One survey suggested that 60 per cent of PPC voters said the pandemic was an issue that motivated their vote choice, far more than supporters of any other party.[24] Another survey conducted after the election said the main issue that drove them to the polls on election day was the party's opposition to vaccine and mask mandates.[25] From hovering around 3 per cent at the outset, the PPC cleared 4 per cent in the Poll Tracker aggregate by the beginning of September, when they had already surpassed the moribund Green Party in national support. The PPC was averaging over 5 per cent on 9 September, 6 per cent on 11 September and finished the campaign averaging around 7 per cent in the polls. There were some significant discrepancies over where the PPC's support really stood, with the IVR tracking polls putting the PPC as high as 9–12 per cent support. The online surveys, however, never put the PPC at more than 7 per cent. Regardless of where the PPC's support really stood in the final weeks of the campaign, Bernier's support was too low at the beginning of the campaign to warrant his participation in the two debates organized by the Leaders' Debates Commission on 8–9 September.

THE IMPACT OF THE FINAL DEBATES

In 2019, former governor general David Johnston, who headed-up the Leaders' Debates Commission, decided to include Bernier in the debates after commissioning polls in some targeted PPC ridings to determine whether the party had a chance of electing candidates, which was then one of the criteria for participation. In 2021, the commission rejigged the criteria. For parties without a seat in the House of Commons or that did not earn at least 4 per cent of the vote in the previous election, such as the People's Party, the commission set a threshold of 4 per cent in national polls conducted over the first week of the campaign for participation. The PPC failed to meet that bar, and so Bernier was excluded from the two debates.

Despite the crowded and cacophonous nature of the debates, particularly the one in English, the debates still had an impact on public opinion. As in 2019, the winners identified in postdebate polling were Blanchet (in French) and Singh (in English). In terms of who did the most to earn or lose their votes, Blanchet emerged as the winner among francophones with a net plus nine rating, compared to plus four for Trudeau, plus one for O'Toole, minus one for Singh, and minus six for Green Leader Annamie Paul, according to Abacus Data. Among anglophones, Singh was a plus fourteen, Trudeau was minus four and Blanchet was minus eleven. Both O'Toole and Paul had the same share saying they had done the most to earn or lose their votes in English.[26] Unlike in 2019, however, Singh's debate performance did not coincide with a spike in support for the New Democrats, who remained consistently in the 19–21 per cent range until the campaign's final days.

But the English-language debate had a significant impact on voting intentions in Quebec when Shachi Kurl, the debate moderator (and president of the Angus Reid Institute polling organization), began the debate with a question to Blanchet concerning Bills 21 and 96 in Quebec, bills which Kurl called "discriminatory." The first banned the wearing of head coverings for public servants and the second was aimed at the protection of the French language in the province. Her question exposed a difference of opinion between Quebecers and other Canadians. According to Léger, which polled on the question shortly after the debate, just 26 per cent of Quebecers (and 18 per cent of francophones) said Bills 21 and 96 were discriminatory, compared to 41 per cent of respondents in the rest of

Canada (and 42 per cent of anglophones). On the wording of the debate question itself, which Léger provided to survey-takers, 65 per cent of Quebecers said it was inappropriate, while 69 per cent of respondents in the rest of the country said it was appropriate.[27] Blanchet, who said the question painted all Quebecers as racist, suddenly had an issue that he could use to galvanize his party's support, which had slipped to around 25 per cent in Quebec on the eve of the English-language debate. In the days that followed, the Bloc's support would increase to an average of 29 per cent and inched up to 30 per cent by election day, removing one of the paths to a majority government that still remained to the Liberals. Polls suggest the debates were very important to driving Bloc voters to the ballot boxes, with 50 per cent saying they influenced their vote (more than double that of any other party's supporters),[28] 30 per cent saying they made up their minds to vote for the Bloc in the days after the debate (double the rate of NDP and Liberal voters and more than triple the rate of Conservative voters), and 12 per cent saying the debates changed their minds toward voting Bloc (double the rate of Liberal, Conservative, and NDP voters).[29] Interestingly, the English-language debate might have proven to be the most important event of the Bloc Québécois campaign.

POLLS IN THE FINAL DAYS

With the polls showing a neck-and-neck race between the Liberals and Conservatives, and the New Democrats unable to take advantage of the popularity of their leader, the decisions that would be made by uncommitted voters in the last days had the potential to make all the difference. As is often the case, the Liberals used these days to pitch to NDP and, to a lesser extent, Green voters to support Liberal candidates to block the Conservatives from government. But the Conservatives, too, had a strategic-voting card to play with the PPC. These NDP, Green, and PPC voters were up for grabs, since they were more likely than Liberal or Conservative voters to say they could change their mind before election day.[30] By wide margins, NDP supporters and those wavering between the Liberals and NDP said the possibility of a Conservative victory would make them more likely to vote Liberal than Conservative. By more than a twelve-to-one margin, PPC voters said it would make them more likely to vote Conservative.[31] As the actual results for both the NDP and PPC failed to live up to their final polls of the campaign, it is very possible that some of their supporters were peeled off to the Liberals or Conservatives because of strategic voting.

The last surveys published before voting day suggested it was going to come down to the wire, though the Liberals' distribution of support at the regional level pointed to them being more likely to win the most seats. Polls by Research Co., Nanos Research, and Abacus Data gave Trudeau (31 to 35 per cent) a lead of just three or four percentage points over O'Toole (27 to 32 per cent) on who Canadians preferred to be prime minister, with Singh in third at between 19 and 22 per cent.[32] The issue set at the beginning of the campaign was nearly identical to where it was at the end, with Abacus finding the only significant increase was a three-point jump in the number of Canadians listing "getting more people vaccinated and back to normal quicker" as a top issue. Reducing cost of living (36 per cent), improving the healthcare system (25 per cent), dealing with climate change (21 per cent), and making housing more affordable (20 per cent) ranked about as highly as they did five weeks earlier.[33] The Liberals led on healthcare and climate change by relatively small margins, but had a fifteen-point lead over the Conservatives on vaccinations, suggesting this issue was a big vote winner for them. The Conservatives were favoured on reducing the cost of living, growing the economy, and managing the federal budget deficit and debt, while the NDP led on housing affordability.

The final polls put support for the Liberals between 29 and 33 per cent and the Conservatives between 28 and 33 per cent. In the aggregate, the polls had the two parties exactly tied. The NDP trailed with between 16 and 21 per cent as some final polls showed their support sagging, while the Bloc had between 6 and 8 per cent, the PPC between 4 and 10 per cent, and the Greens between 2 and 5 per cent. With the exception of the increase in support for the PPC, the polls at the end of the campaign showed effectively identical levels of support to where Canadians had been on election night in 2019.

THE ACCURACY OF THE POLLS

On average, the final polls by the 11 polling firms that surveyed Canadians in the last week of the campaign awarded both the Liberals and the Conservatives 31.4 per cent of the vote. This represented an underestimation of 2.3 points for the Conservatives and

Table 7.1 | Final surveys of all national polling firms by total error

Polling Firm	Field Dates	Decided Sample	Mode	LPC	CON	NDP	BQ	PPC	GPC	Total Error
Léger	14–17 Sept.	1,943	Online	32	33	19	7	6	2	4.5
Research Co.	18–19 Sept.	1,650	Online	32	32	19	7	6	4	6.9
Nanos Research	19 Sept.	766	Telephone	32.4	31.2	17.5	7.5	6.6	4.5	7.0
Abacus Data	17–19 Sept.	1,894	Online	31	32	19	7	6	4	7.9
Angus Reid Institute	15–18 Sept.	2,042	Online	30	32	20	7	5	3	7.9
Ipsos	15–18 Sept.	2,009	Online & Telephone	31	32	21	7	4	3	8.7
Campaign Research	13–16 Sept.	4,727	Online	31	31	21	7	5	4	9.9
Mainstreet Research	17–19 Sept.	2,177	IVR	33.4	30.4	18.1	6	9.3	2.1	10.6
Counsel Public Affairs	16–18 Sept.	3,298	Online	31	30	19	7	7	4	10.9
YouGov	8–13 Sept.	925	Online	29	32	19	6	5	5	10.9
Forum Research	19 Sept.	1,181	IVR	29.4	33	16.2	6.9	10.3	2.9	12.2
EKOS Research	16–19 Sept.	1,492	IVR	32.5	28.4	18.2	6.9	9.5	3.6	12.4
Innovative Research Group	10–12 Sept.	2,026	Online	33	28	22	7	4	4	13.5

Table 7.2 | Average overestimation (+) and underestimation (–) of each party's support in the final polls of the campaign

Party	Canada	BC	AB	SK & MB	ON	QC	Atlantic
CPC	-2.3	-0.5	-6.2	-7.4	-3.0	-0.8	-4.0
LPC	-1.2	-2.1	+1.5	+2.5	-1.2	-1.3	-3.1
NDP	+1.1	+0.8	+0.6	-0.5	+1.3	+1.7	+3.9
BQ	-0.7					-1.9	
PPC	+1.9	+0.4	+2.6	+3.7	+1.3	+2.3	+1.9
GPC	+1.1	+1.1	+0.6	+1.4	+0.9	+1.0	+0.8

1.2 points for the Liberals, very similar to what occurred in 2019 when the Conservatives were underestimated by 2.7 points and the Liberals by 1.2 points.[34] But the error in the margin between the two parties was just 1.1 points, better than the 1.5-point error in the Conservative-Liberal margin from the 2019 federal election.[35] Some pollsters were even closer to the mark, as shown in Table 7.1, with Léger having the smallest total error and missing no party by more than a percentage point. Along with Léger, Abacus Data and Ipsos also accurately pegged the Conservative margin of victory in the national vote at one percentage point. Additionally, polling was quite accurate at the regional level, with nearly every poll awarding the Liberals the most support in Ontario, showing a close race between the Liberals and Bloc Québécois in Quebec, and placing the Conservatives, NDP, and Liberals first, second, and third, respectively, in British Columbia. Where sample sizes were smaller, such as in Alberta, the Prairies, and Atlantic Canada, the polls were less accurate but nevertheless gave the Conservatives comfortable leads

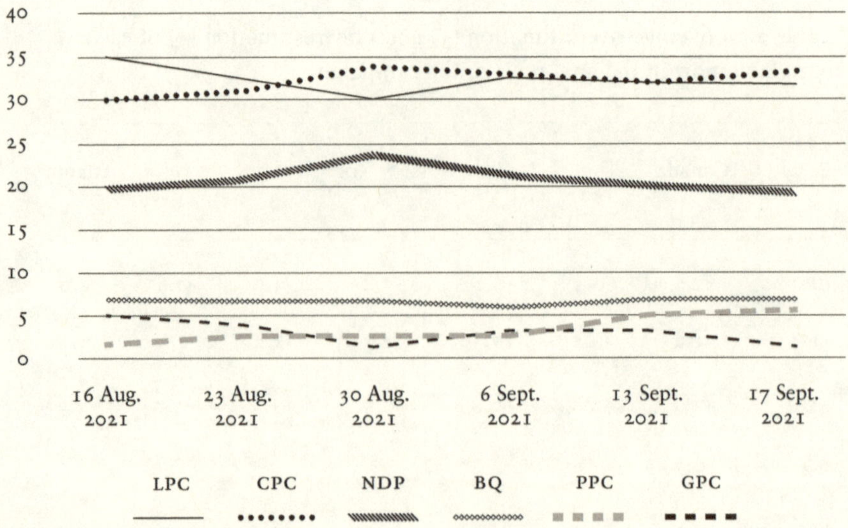

Figure 7.1 | Polling by Léger during the 2021 federal election

in their traditional strongholds in Western Canada and the Liberals a wide advantage in Atlantic Canada. On the whole, the accuracy of the polls in the 2021 federal election campaign was impressive. Increased rates of voting in advance polls and through the mail did not seem to impact pollsters' accuracy, in part because the final polls of the campaign generally asked respondents who they would or, if they had already voted, who they did support, taking these locked-in votes into account.

As in 2019, there were some common patterns in where the polls got things wrong. The Conservatives were underestimated by every polling firm and, on average, in every region of the country. Once again, the error was greatest in Alberta and the Prairies, where Conservative support was underestimated by 6.2 and 7.4 points, respectively, as shown in Table 7.2. The polls also undershot the Conservatives by three points in Ontario and four points in Atlantic Canada. This would have had a bigger impact on the projections of seat results had the polls not also underestimated the Liberals in most regions, by a little more than a point in both Ontario and Quebec, 2.1 points in BC, and 3.1 points in Atlantic Canada. Only

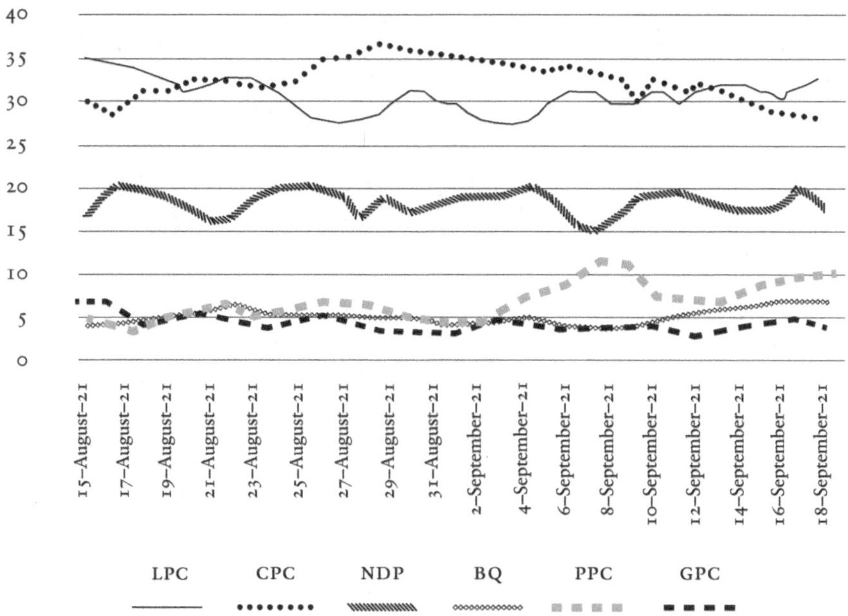

Figure 7.2 | Polling by EKOS Research during the 2021 federal election

in Alberta and the Prairies, where the Liberals were in contention for few seats, did the polls overestimate Liberal support. The New Democrats were overestimated by an average of 1.1 points, less than the 2.7-point error from 2019. The only significant errors were in Atlantic Canada (3.9 points) and Quebec (1.7 points), again in areas where the party was not in contention for more than a handful of seats. The Bloc Québécois beat its polls by just under two percentage points in Quebec, while the Greens were overestimated by about a point in every region of the country. This is most likely explained by the Greens' failure to nominate candidates in a quarter of ridings, which reduced the share of the vote the party was capable of earning. The People's Party was also overestimated, by 1.9 points nationwide and by as much as 3.7 points, on average, in the Prairies and 2.6 points in Alberta. This likely contributed to the underestimation of support for the Conservatives in these regions.

That the PPC was overestimated by as much as double its actual support raises the question of whether the more dramatic polling swings that occurred during the election were mirages. The trend line for Léger's online polling during the campaign, as shown in figure 7.1, is relatively steady. The Conservatives had a modest increase from their 30–31 per cent support in the first weeks of the campaign to the 32–34 per cent in the final weeks, while the Liberals dropped somewhat from the 35 per cent they had at the starting point. After Léger's first survey of 16 August, however, neither party experienced a variation of more than three points throughout the campaign, while the NDP registered between 19 and 21 per cent in all but one survey. The PPC's rise is an obvious trend, but it was only from 3 per cent at the midpoint of the campaign to 6 per cent at the end.

By comparison, EKOS's daily tracking poll (figure 7.2) conducted via interactive voice response shows more dramatic swings, though the trend lines are fairly similar. Support for the Conservatives dropped as low as 27 per cent in EKOS's polling and reached as high as 37 per cent, a variation of ten points over the campaign. The Liberals registered as low as 28 per cent and as high as 35 per cent, while the PPC hit as much as 12 per cent – and over 20 per cent in Alberta – at one point during the campaign.[36] Mainstreet Research, another firm using IVR, awarded the Conservatives a lead as wide as 9.5 points and showed similarly noticeable shifts in its daily tracking. As the overall trend lines were generally the same between the more stable online polls and the more variable IVR surveys, it seems plausible that both methods were gauging the general thrust of the campaign correctly. That the IVR surveys, in the field every day and subject to normal random sampling error, would show more volatility is perhaps understandable. But the daily coverage of the IVR surveys, as opposed to the weekly coverage of the online polls, might have given the impression of a more volatile campaign than was actually the case.

POST-ELECTION POLLING

With the results nearly matching those of the 2019 election, polls conducted after the votes were tallied showed mixed feelings about the outcome. According to Léger, 34 per cent of Canadians were either happy or comfortable with the outcome, with another 9 per cent saying they "prefer minority governments anyway." But 18 per cent said they were either angry or not comfortable with the outcome, with another 24 per cent saying they were "unhappy with the outcome but life goes on."[37] With the benefit of five weeks on the campaign trail, Canadians were no less unequivocal on whether the election was a good use of time as they had been at the outset, with 80 per cent of Canadians, including 60 per cent of people who voted for the Liberal Party, saying the election was "a waste of time and money, and it should not have been called." Only 20 per cent said it was a "good opportunity for Canadians to have their say."[38] Regardless of what they thought about the outcome, most Canadians had their decisions locked in well before election day. Léger found 49 per cent had made up their mind before the election was called and another 18 per cent made up their minds in the first two weeks of the campaign. Only 18 per cent made up their minds over the last weekend or on election day, with PPC supporters being the most likely to have waited until the end. At 29 and 31 per cent, respectively, Bloc and PPC voters were also the most likely to say they switched to their final choice over the course of the campaign, roughly double the number of those who voted for the Liberals, Conservatives, or NDP who said they switched to those parties.[39]

For Liberal voters, Léger found that the main motivations for supporting the party were to avoid a Conservative government (25 per cent), because Trudeau was the best political leader to lead the country (23 per cent), or because the Liberals best represented their values and beliefs (23 per cent). Only 11 per cent said it was because of how the Liberals had handled the pandemic. The main reasons for voting Conservative were to get rid of the Liberal government (39 per cent), because the Conservatives best represented their values or beliefs (21 per cent), or because O'Toole was the best leader to lead the country (14 per cent). Nearly half of NDP voters (48 per cent) were motivated to support the party because it best represented their values or beliefs, far outpacing any other reason, while 35 per cent of Bloc voters said their main reason for supporting that party was because it was "there to defend Quebec's interests." Only 10 per cent said it was because the Bloc supports Quebec's independence, which was hardly discussed on the campaign trail, while 7 per cent said it was "because of the question related to racism in the English-language debate." For People's Party voters, 32 per cent said they supported the party because it was against mask and vaccine mandates, while another 27 per cent said it was because the PPC best represented their values and beliefs. One-fifth said they voted PPC because of disappointment with the Conservative campaign or leader.[40]

THE MOST-POLLED CAMPAIGN IN CANADIAN HISTORY

With more than 150 voting intentions surveys published throughout the 2021 federal election, the campaign was the most (publicly, at least) polled election in Canadian history. It is somewhat ironic, however, that a campaign that inspired so little attention (on a scale of zero to ten, respondents rated their interest at 6.9 in an Abacus survey conducted just before the vote, lower than when the election had been called[41]) featured so few dramatic shifts in public opinion, and ended with only a few seats changing hands, would have been studied and dissected to such an extent. But the accuracy and volume of the polls, just as in 2019, meant that the dynamics of the campaign were largely well understood, and the suspense on election night was limited to a few close races – if one believed that the polls could be trusted at all. That the polls conducted before the election showed strength for the Liberals and weakness for the Conservatives and proved misleading might lead to some reticence in the future about calling an early election, but 2021 was not the first – and will almost certainly not be the last – instance of an incumbent government misjudging its chances of winning an election based on public opinion polls. It is a useful reminder of the adage that polls are just a snapshot in time and not a prediction of the future.

NOTES

1 Unless otherwise specified, polling figures for the parties are drawn from Éric Grenier, "Poll Tracker," CBC News, last modified 19 September 2021, https://newsinteractives.cbc.ca/elections/poll-tracker/canada/.

2 Bruce Anderson and David Coletto, "Months into COVID-19 Pandemic, Canadians Would Re-elect Liberal and the Prime Minister's Image Improves Markedly," Abacus Data, 21 May 2020, https://abacusdata.ca/political-update-polling-canadian-politics-may2020/.

3 Léger in collaboration with the Association for Canadian Studies (ACS), "Canadian Federal Politics – August 3, 2021," Léger, 3 August 2021, https://leger360.com/surveys/legers-north-american-tracker-august-3-2021/.

4 "Abacus Data's Final Poll: Conservatives and Liberals Are Statistically Tied on the Eve of Election Day in Canada," Abacus Data, 19 September 2021, https://abacusdata.ca/election-2021-final-poll-abacus-data/.

5 Nik Nanos, "Coronavirus Top issue Followed by Environment and Jobs – Environment Hits 17 Month High in Nanos Tracking," Nanos, 17 August 2021, https://nanos.co/wp-content/uploads/2021/08/Political-Package-2021-08-13-FR-with-tabs.pdf
6 "Politics and the Fourth Wave: As Concern over COVID Rises, Are the Liberals Poised to Benefit?" Angus Reid Institute, 12 August 2021, https://angusreid.org/federal-politics-fourth-wave/.
7 Éric Grenier, "How the Polls Did in the 2021 Election," The Writ, 29 September 2021, https://www.thewrit.ca/p/pollster-accuracy-2021-election.
8 David Coletto, "Polling and the 2015 Federal Election," in The Canadian Federal Election of 2015, eds. Jon H. Pammett and Christopher Dornan (Toronto: Dundurn, 2016), 307.
9 "CBC Is Canada's Choice for Election Coverage," CBC, 21 September 2021, https://www.cbc.ca/mediacentre/press-release/cbc-is-canadas-choice-for-election-coverage.
10 Phillipe J. Fournier, "338Canada | Poll Analysis & Electoral Projections," 338Canada, last modified 30 January 2022, https://338canada.com/.
11 "The Campaign Is Nearly Over. Here's Who Has the Momentum," Toronto Star, https://www.thestar.com/politics/federal-election/polls/2021/election-forecast.html.
12 Anthony Piscitelli, "Evaluating the 2021 Federal Election Projections," ThreeHundredThirtyEight.com, 25 September 2021, [Is this distinct from 338Canada?]https://threehundredthirtyeight.com/evaluating-the-2021-federal-election-projections.
13 "The Federal Ballot: A Postmedia-Léger Poll," Léger, 24 August 2021, https://leger360.com/surveys/the-federal-ballot-a-postmedia-leger-poll/.
14 Abacus Data, "Final Poll."
15 Abacus Data, "Final Poll."
16 Bruce Anderson and David Coletto, "Conservatives and Liberals Locked in a Tie; TVA Debate Has Limited Impact," Abacus Data, 7 September 2021, https://abacusdata.ca/election-2021-conservatives-liberals-tied/.
17 Christian Bourque, "The 2021 Federal Election: The Conservatives Are in the Lead – August 31, 2021," Léger, 31 August 2021, https://leger360.com/surveys/legers-north-american-tracker-august-31-2021/.
18 Léger in collaboration with the Association for Canadian Studies (ACS), "Vaccine Passports, Back-to-School Concerns and the Delta Variant – September 3, 2021," Léger, 3 September 2021, https://leger360.com/surveys/legers-north-american-tracker-september-3-2021/.

19 "Nanos Internal Pandemic Populated Report with Tabs," Nanos, August 2021, https://nanos.co/wp-content/uploads/2021/08/2021-1952-Nanos-Internal-Pandemic-Populated-report-with-tabs.pdf.

20 Darrell Bricker, "Strong Majority of Canadians Support Vaccination Mandates; Open to Measures Including Vaccine Passports," Ipsos, 19 August 2021, https://www.ipsos.com/en-ca/news-polls/majority-of-canadians-support-vaccination-mandates.

21 Bricker, "Strong Majority of Canadians Support Vaccination Mandates."

22 "The Federal Ballot – September 8, 2021: A Postmedia-Léger Poll," Léger, 8 September 2021, https://leger360.com/surveys/the-federal-ballot-september-8-2021-a-postmedia-leger-poll/.

23 "The 2021 Federal Election – September 18, 2021," Léger, 18 September 2021, https://leger360.com/surveys/the-2021-federal-election-september-18-2021/.

24 Léger, "The 2021 Federal Election."

25 "The 2021 Federal Election: The Aftermath," Léger, 28 September 2021, https://leger360.com/surveys/legers-north-american-tracker-september-28-2021/.

26 Bruce Anderson and David Coletto, "One Week to Go: Conservatives and Liberals Still Locked in a Tie but Liberals Open Up Clear Leads in Ontario and Quebec," Abacus Data, 13 September 2021, https://abacusdata.ca/election-2021-conservatives-liberals-tied-again/.

27 "The Federal Leaders' Debate: The French Language and Bills 21 and 96 in Quebec – September 15, 2021," Léger, 15 September 2021, https://leger360.com/surveys/federal-leaders-debate-french-language-bills-21-96-quebec/.

28 Léger, "The 2021 Federal Election – September 18, 2021."

29 Léger, "The 2021 Federal Election: The Aftermath."

30 Léger, "The 2021 Federal Election – September 18, 2021."

31 Abacus Data, "Final Poll."

32 Eliana Carrillo, "Canadians Pick Trudeau to Manage Pandemic, O'Toole for Jobs," ResearchCo, 16 September 2021, https://researchco.ca/2021/09/16/elxn44-leaders/; Nik Nanos, "#Elxn44 Nightly Ballot Tracking," Nanos, 19 September 2021, https://nanos.co/wp-content/uploads/2021/09/2021-1947-ELXN44-Nightly-Tracking-Report-Election-Call.pdf.; and Abacus Data, "Final Poll."

33 Abacus Data, "Final Poll."

34 Éric Grenier, "A Close Race from Start to Finish: Polling in the 2019 Federal Election," in The Canadian Federal Election of 2019, eds. Jon H.

Pammett and Christopher Dornan (Montreal and Kingston: McGill-Queen's University Press, 2020), 167.

35 Éric Grenier, "How the Polls Did in the 2021 Election."

36 "Liberals Headed to Form Government," EKOS Politics, 19 September 2021, https://www.ekospolitics.com/index.php/2021/09/liberals-headed-to-form-government-2/.

37 Leger, "The 2021 Federal Election: The Aftermath."

38 "Federal Politics: Three-in-Five Canadians Would Have Preferred Outcome of Election Held Using Proportional Distribution," Angus Reid Institute, 15 October 2021, https://angusreid.org/federal-politics-proportional-representation/.

39 Leger, "The 2021 Federal Election."

40 Leger, "The 2021 Federal Election."

41 Abacus Data, "Final Poll."

8

The Media: The Narratives that Defined the Mainstream Election Coverage

Brett Popplewell

The stories that defined the 2021 federal election reached the Canadian public through the usual mainstream mediums of print and broadcast news. A master narrative emerged early in the campaign and became central to the coverage. From the beginning of the campaign to the end, mainstream outlets across the media spectrum (those to the left, those to the right, and those generally considered to be in the middle) all covered the campaign with a high degree of cynicism. As a result, Canadians were told repeatedly that this election was self-serving, unnecessary, and, on several occasions, damaging to the country.

As was the case with the previous election, the 2021 contest featured an added complexity of disinformation and factual distortions which played out online. Mainstream coverage in the press and on broadcast news tended to focus on the mainstream parties while fringe media outlets operating mostly online generated increased attention for the People's Party of Canada. Though the outcome of the election proved a vindication of the mainstream polling, the campaign itself presented unprecedented challenges to several politicians and mainstream journalists who were confronted by an increasingly polarized Canadian electorate. Much of the public anger and rage expressed during the campaign was directed not only at specific candidates, but toward journalists as well. Whereas the vitriol that was seen during the previous election of 2019 was largely contained to social media, the 2021 campaign saw angry protestors disrupt campaign stop after campaign stop, berating reporters and politicians alike. The result was an election plagued by a public hostility that at times overshadowed the message from politicians and consumed the mainstream news coverage. As was the case in the lead up to the previous election, there was much speculation and fear that the mainstream national media might be overwhelmed by malicious bots and trolls.[1] But the public anger that ultimately revealed itself was unexpected and took many political journalists by surprise.

Before the campaign began, many in the media questioned what impact the ongoing COVID-19 pandemic would have on the campaign itself, while others reversed the question and asked what impact the campaign would have on the pandemic. COVID-19 infections were on the rise in the lead-up to the campaign and public health officials warned that a fourth wave was beginning to take shape. For eighteen months prior to the election, many political reporters had been working primarily from home due to pandemic regulations. Some reporters had not set foot in their newsrooms in more than a year. Those who took to the campaign trail with the leaders soon became accustomed to daily rapid COVID-19 tests, socially distant scrums, and an increased number of outdoor rallies that were often overrun by protestors. As was the case in the previous election, disinformation on social media became an increasingly disruptive force in the information flow to voters, and journalists from mainstream outlets were routinely subjected to racist and misogynist personal attacks. But unlike 2019, the attacks in 2021 seemed to be more orchestrated.

What follows is an account of the major narratives in the national English-language media coverage of the 2021 campaign. For the purpose of this chapter, the national media's coverage of the election has been analyzed chronologically. Specific attention has been paid to the coverage of the parliamentary bureaus of the country's three largest, nationally-focused newspapers (*The Globe and Mail*, *National Post*, and *Toronto Star*). Each of these news outlets views the political landscape in Canada through an ideological lens markedly different from one another, offering competing, and incompatible, readings of the election, while each claiming that their coverage is true to events. Analysing the coverage of the right leaning *National Post*, left leaning *Toronto Star* and the more centrist *The Globe and Mail* has been done in order to create a fulsome portrait of what the journalists covering the campaign themselves considered important enough to transmit to their audiences. Coverage by the country's major broadcast networks has also been incorporated as has reporting from The Canadian Press, the wire service that provides coverage to media outlets across the country.

THE MAINSTREAM NEWS AGENDA

This analysis is by no means a comprehensive study of election coverage. Reporting by local, regional, and small-market news outlets has been largely omitted. Though legacy media outlets have lost much of their impact on the daily public discourse due to diminished resources and dwindling stature, large scale general interest newspapers like the *Toronto Star*, *National Post*, and *The Globe and Mail* remain part of what scholars have called "keystone" outlets for the way they have traditionally set the agenda for web, radio, and TV. Coverage by the CBC, the most robust news organization in the country, has been analyzed across its multiple platforms; however this chapter does not represent a comprehensive account of the CBC's election coverage, for the CBC's coverage alone could take up its own chapter. Instead, this chapter pays specific attention to the commentary of print journalists who appeared on the CBC's TV, radio, and news podcasts to discuss the election. In many cases these were the same print reporters whose coverage set the agenda of concern at the country's three main national newspapers. This cross-platform punditry creates a reverberating effect that serves to amplify certain narratives in the mainstream media across all channels, creating a seemingly homogenous news agenda that can assign undue value to certain issues over others.

For the purpose of this chapter, research has been guided by two specific questions:

1. What narratives emerged in the election coverage of the national news media?
2. How did these narratives contribute to the trajectory of the election itself?

As this chapter highlights, reporters and columnists at media outlets focused their attentions on similar narratives throughout the election, creating a collective discourse that set the mainstream news agenda. The objective is not to criticize any of the journalists highlighted in this study, but rather to explore how their work simultaneously drove and responded to a collective discourse, and therefore gave form to the prevailing stories through which the public was invited to understand this election.

HOW IT STARTED

Speculation that Prime Minister Justin Trudeau would call a snap election had circulated in the media through the spring and into the summer as reporters and columnists responded to advanced polls suggesting the Liberals had received a boost in popularity as a result of their handling of the pandemic. Preliminary coverage across mainstream platforms created a narrative that Trudeau would likely trigger the election in the hope of gaining the majority that had eluded him in 2019. That narrative would remain part of the coverage throughout the entire campaign and would become the focus of several attack ads from opposition parties.

By midsummer, political journalists were beginning to talk of the election as if it were foreordained. The third wave of the COVID-19 pandemic had finally subsided. The preconditions for the Liberals to call a snap election appeared to be in place. The vaccine shortages and delays that had plagued the government in the early spring had been resolved and businesses across the country were beginning to open. Meanwhile, Conservative Party leader, Erin O'Toole was still considered to be relatively unknown by the general public. Election speculation finally turned to confirmation on 12 August as sources close to Trudeau told members of the Canadian Parliamentary Press Gallery that the prime minister was about to request that newly appointed Governor General Mary Simon dissolve parliament.

The *Toronto Star*'s Tonda MacCharles was among the reporters to get the tip. The story she wrote that day captured much of the mainstream media's preliminary discourse surrounding the election, particularly the unknown impact that the pandemic would have on the campaign.[2] MacCharles' report posed the question of whether it was even safe to hold a federal campaign and posited that this campaign, by virtue of its timing amid the ongoing pandemic, would be markedly different from 2019. "Much has been learned by Elections Canada and by the parties about holding elections in a pandemic," MacCharles wrote. "And the three main federal parties – Liberals, Conservative, and New Democrats – are pledging to do just that: respect health guidelines as they look to bring pandemic practices – including maximizing digital tools and virtual outreach – to the campaign trail. There will be leaders' tours, but don't expect to see the massive cheek-by-jowl rallies of the past even if attendees are fully vaccinated."

The *Star* paired MacCharles' story with published results of a poll which indicated that 65 per cent of respondents thought it was not a good time to have an election. The poll had been commissioned by Torstar and conducted by Mainstreet Research over two days during that same week.[3] Preliminary election coverage was much the same across the other nationally focused news outlets centring a narrative that this was an election that Canadians did not want. It was assumed by many journalists, however, that the Liberals must have had possession of their own polling data that indicated Canadians would respond favourably to their party if an election were called.

ENTER VERUCA SALT

It did not take long for the first political ads to filter out of the various party headquarters. None, however, captured more media attention in the forty-eight hours before the dissolution of parliament than a thirty-seven-second Twitter video, produced by the Conservative Party, which quickly became known as the Willy Wonka ad. In the ad, the prime minister's face is shoddily pasted over that of Veruca Salt, a spoiled child and one of the main antagonists in the 1971 film *Willy Wonka and the Chocolate Factory*. The ad, which featured the Trudeau or Veruca Salt character slipping into a tantrum song, offered a simple message: "The only reason for an election is that Trudeau wants a majority." The whole thing went over poorly, especially in the mainstream media where it was largely ridiculed. Several Conservative MPs quickly lamented the ad's existence, calling it embarrassing, tasteless, and appalling for having kicked off the election on such a negative, trolling tone.

Three days after its release, the ad remained central to the mainstream election coverage. Writing in the *National Post* on 16 August, John Ivison argued: "The Conservatives need to be sharper than they've been, and that's without commenting on the execrable Veruca Salt attack ad."[4] By 17 August, the ad had been deleted from the Conservative Party's official Twitter feed, an action which The Canadian Press's Maan Alhmidi reported was the potential result of a copyright infringement claim made against the party.[5]

THE CAMPAIGN NO ONE WANTED OR CARED ABOUT

Week One – 15 to 21 August

As Justin Trudeau made his way to Rideau Hall on 15 August to request the dissolution of parliament, Canada's national news outlets were focused on a rapidly developing story 10,000 kilometres from Ottawa in the city of Kabul, where Taliban forces were quickly taking control of the capital. It took only a day for the city to fall, igniting a humanitarian crisis, altering the international and national news agenda, and limiting the mainstream media's attention on the opening stage of the election. From the moment the writ dropped, the situation in Afghanistan was part of the election coverage as journalists and opposition leaders questioned the prime minister's logic of triggering a snap election at the exact moment that an international humanitarian crisis was spiralling out of control. While the country's three leading English-language newspapers continued to publish reports that cast the election as unnecessary and opportunistic, the prevailing narrative was not much different on the country's airwaves. On 16 August, the day after the election was called, Elamin Abdelmahmoud, guest host of CBC's *Front Burner* news podcast, centred the episode's election coverage on the question of "Why Now?"

Abdelmahmoud's guest that day was Aaron Wherry of the CBC's Parliament Hill bureau. Author of a biography of Justin Trudeau, Wherry cast the prime minister's motivations in a cynical light: "It's very fair to say that if the Liberals were not leading in the polls right now, Justin Trudeau wouldn't have gone to Rideau Hall and asked for an election," Wherry said. "Election timing is almost always political."

As Wherry later pointed out, "The opposition leaders are stuck in an almost odd position of having to complain that an election was called but to also say that now that we're having an election, now that you mention it, maybe we should vote these guys out ... For the most part, we spend the first few days or week fussing over whether there should be an election and then we all sort of come to terms with the fact that there is an election, and we get on with it."

The CBC would not devote another episode of *Front Burner* to the election for another eight days. In the meantime, the daily news agenda focused on the ongoing crisis in Kabul, an earthquake in Haiti, and climate change. All the while, other mainstream news outlets were still trying to decipher what impact the pandemic would have on the election itself. One preliminary line of thought discussed in the *Toronto Star* was whether the urban exodus of young professionals from the downtown cores of major cities like Toronto might redistribute left-leaning voters into the suburban ridings, perhaps resulting in stronger support for the Liberals and NDP in ridings that had become Conservative strongholds in previous elections.

Stephanie Levitz of the *Star*'s Ottawa Bureau wrote on 17 August: "Changing demographics offer some hope for ridings in and around Hamilton, Barrie, Niagara and others for the Liberals to wrest seats away from the Conservatives thanks to the exodus of Liberal voters from the urban core of Toronto."[6]

By the evening of 17 August, many political reporters in the country were monitoring provincial election results coming in from Nova Scotia, where the incumbent Liberals were dealt a decisive defeat that defied the polls and marked the first time in the pandemic that a provincial election did not return a governing party to power. The next day's *National Post* contained a column by Kelly McParland who was already wagering that the results in Nova Scotia should be considered an omen for the Liberals, whose polling numbers were already beginning to slip.[7] Meanwhile, *The Globe and Mail* ran a column by Lori Turnbull, director of the School of Public Administration at Dalhousie University, which attached considerably less meaning to the results.[8] Turnbull wrote: "While many have been quick to draw lessons for the federal election campaign, there are unique narratives that explain why the situation is not a victory for Erin O'Toole's Conservative Party nor a bad omen for Justin Trudeau's Liberals."

MANIPULATED MEDIA AND ANGER UNLEASHED

Week Two – 22 to 28 August

The media's coverage during week two of the campaign began with yet another Twitter distraction. This time it was the Liberal Party coming under fire for a social media misstep. On Sunday, 22 August, a video on the Twitter account of Deputy Prime Minister Chrystia Freeland was flagged by Twitter as "manipulated media." In the video in question, Conservative leader Erin O'Toole appeared to answer yes when asked if he would allow provinces to experiment with healthcare reform including private and for-profit options. In the video, O'Toole went on to discuss "public-private synergies," but the video lacked considerable context that was edited out prior to being tweeted, including remarks by O'Toole in which he said "universal access remains paramount." The Liberal Party rallied behind Freeland, while legal counsel for the Conservatives asked Elections Canada to investigate the matter. The story did not linger long in the media, though what coverage it did receive was split among those who thought it a careless act and those who thought it something deeper. The *National Post* published a particularly critical op-ed on the matter headlined "Freeland's 'manipulated' video on Twitter shows Liberals' desperation."[9] The piece, by Ben Woodfinden, a doctoral candidate and political theorist at McGill University, argued that with the Twitter distraction, "once again the Liberals have managed to step on a rake in their efforts to wedge their opponents."

As the week carried on, reporters focused their attention on what each party actually stood for in this election. Though the Liberals still had not released their platform and would not until 1 September, the NDP had released theirs three days before the writ dropped, while the Conservatives pushed theirs out on 16 August. As a result, both parties picked up early media attention while the Liberals struggled to get their election messaging out. That said, much of the initial coverage of the Conservative platform release focused on the document's cover, which featured some sort of glamour shot of Erin O'Toole in a tight-fitting T-shirt. The photo was interpreted by most in the media as an attempt to infuse the party's leader with some sex appeal.

The Globe and Mail's Lawrence Martin summarized O'Toole's strategy in a 26 August column in which he argued that he was actively borrowing from Trudeau's sunny ways image.[10] "Mr O'Toole represents a new style of leadership for the Tories, who haven't often produced leaders you'd feel comfortable having a beer with," Martin wrote. "Mr O'Toole struck a different note with the release of his platform to start the election campaign. There he was on the cover in a tight black T-shirt, beaming ear to ear, champing at the bit. With its big spending provisions, the O'Toole policy book is compassionate compared with Mr Harper's years in office, not to mention the latter's nice-guys-finish last style. With his enthusiasm, his own sunny ways, Mr O'Toole quickly put

Mr Trudeau on the defensive, turning him a bit petulant. In just a week he improved his personal standing and moved his party from well behind to neck and neck with the incumbents."

As is common in broadcast news, political journalists from the country's largest circulation newspapers served as political pundits on the nightly newscasts and on the country's most popular news podcasts. Those pundits tended to agree in their election commentary that the Conservative and NDP were tactically shrewd in getting their platforms out early. As Althia Raj of the *Toronto Star* explained in the 24 August episode of *Front Burner*, it was believed that the early release would help the parties reach out directly to those voters who would be using advanced polls as a result of the pandemic. However, the pundits were quick to follow the Liberal line of criticism, especially toward the Conservative platform, which was not properly costed out. Nevertheless, by delaying the release of their own platform and with the campaign nearly half over, the Liberals were still struggling to sell themselves to voters.

"Afghanistan has overshadowed the Liberals' ability to get their campaign message out," Raj explained. "I guess this is one of the drawbacks of being the government and having crises come at you."

The polling landscape had already shifted substantially by the time Éric Grenier, former polls analyst with the CBC's parliamentary bureau and author of the chapter on polling in this volume, told CBC listeners that: "The chances for a majority right now for the Liberals [are] not particularly good. It's still early, but certainly the trend line is not going in the right direction for them."

Grenier, who had earlier called this "The Seinfeld Election" because it was "an election about nothing," now said: "The Liberal campaign doesn't seem as sharp as the Conservative or the NDP campaign." Then Grenier offered an observation that members of the press were just beginning to note. "Support for the People's Party looks to be a bit higher than in the last campaign," he said.

As the second week of the election drew to a close, a new distraction was about to consume the campaign and those covering it. Angry protestors had been plaguing the prime minister and other senior Liberal candidates for days, drowning out the candidates at campaign stops. But on 27 August, the vitriol of protestors became the focus of the national news media when one of the prime minister's campaign rallies was cancelled due to security concerns. Susan Delacourt, national columnist for the *Toronto Star*, described how the protests had begun to threaten the campaign.[11] "It's time to talk about this rage against Justin Trudeau," she wrote. "Not just the mob spectacles on the campaign trail, but all the toxic strains of that fury simmering through Canadian politics for some time now."

Delacourt, who had travelled to the event that was ultimately cancelled, described how an "incredible scene of Trudeau haters in Bolton, Ont. their faces contorted in gleeful rage, has elevated this phenomenon from an ugly undercurrent to a force that needs to be reckoned with in the current election campaign." As Delacourt reported, Trudeau himself suggested after the incident that the growing rage was "a boiling cauldron of populist discontent, fuelled by a pandemic."

The coverage of the event and its cancellation revealed a degree of shock among the reporters who had been travelling with the prime minister and who were not accustomed to seeing such displays of public unrest on the campaign trail. "The threats are real, and they have been for as long as I've been covering federal politics," Delacourt continued. "But the poisonous rage that is directed toward Trudeau on a daily basis, churning through social media 24/7, landing as flaming parcels every day in reporters' email boxes, and now manifesting itself as a high-level security threat in small-town Ontario, is another order altogether. It is woven with threads of racism, xenophobia, sexism, conspiracy theorists and COVID/vaccine deniers. It has been emboldened by a small cottage industry of commentary that portrays a 'woke' Trudeau as the destroyer of all that holds the old Canada together."

Delacourt did not presume whether the Bolton incident would help or hurt Trudeau's electoral prospects. However, other journalists present at the Bolton event, including the *National Post*'s John Ivison, argued that the protests could ultimately help the prime minister.[12] He wrote: "The anti-vaccine protesters are a crackpot fringe. One woman in Nobleton bellowed that she had COVID. 'It's a f***ing cold,' she screamed. But they are only the most vocal representation of a significant minority of Canadians who don't want to go forward into Trudeau's brave new world; they would prefer to go backward to a world where their status and place in the world was more assured."

Ivison predicted that in the end the toxicity would backfire on the protestors and could result in increased voter support for Trudeau and the Liberal Party. "Reasonable Canadians will repudiate such tactics and look more sympathetically on Trudeau because they find the protests not only inexplicable but abhorrent," he wrote. "The agitators should reflect that all their antics are likely to achieve is the return to power of their nemesis."

Ivison's column, which appeared in the traditionally conservative *National Post*, sparked its own vitriolic response. His decision to label the protestors "a crackpot fringe" would inform and drive his subsequent reporting on the protests. As he explained in the *National Post* three days later:[13] "After a column on Friday night, I argued a 'crackpot fringe' was responsible – a descriptor that provoked a barrage of abuse directed at me and the Liberal leader," he wrote. Dan Pomerleau sent an email from Calgary: "Some of Trudeau's (semen) is sticking to your chin." Helpfully, he supplied his phone number, so I called him.

"Why would you send a complete stranger such a vile email?" I asked.

"I didn't like your pro-Trudeau position. You seem to be very anti people protesting violently against him. I think they are doing everyone a favour – he's the most divisive mother****er who laced a pair of shoes."

Pomerleau told Ivison that he was double-vaccinated but objected to vaccine mandates and did not just dislike Trudeau but also O'Toole, whom he viewed as being left of centre.

"Those were common themes in many other conversations and emails," Ivison noted. "There are echoes of Trumpism in the current protests – mainly men from the ethnic majority who feel like strangers in their own country, abandoned by progressive values they don't understand or share."

A SPOTLIGHT ON THE RAGE

Week Three – 29 August to 4 September

As the second week of the campaign closed out, Chantal Hébert, one of the country's most-read political journalists, declared in the *Toronto Star* that Justin Trudeau was in trouble. "The Liberals are losing ground to both the Conservatives and the New Democrats in Ontario," she wrote. "That trend could lead to a disaster for his party on voting day. Between now and then, the success of Trudeau's re-election bid will likely be in the hands of swing progressive voters."[14]

Hébert predicted that Trudeau would soon be hoping that "a possible Conservative government will drive at least some of those who have been looking to support the NDP and the Bloc to reconsider. Calls for progressive voters to coalesce behind the Liberals to keep the CPC at bay worked for Paul Martin in 2004 and for Trudeau in 2019. This year, both O'Toole and Singh have been trying out different strategies to counter the impact of such appeals."[15]

As the *Star*'s columnists wrote at length about the troubles befalling the Liberal Party, *The Globe and Mail*'s Kristy Kirkup was trying to analyze whether the COVID-19 protocols that were pushing politicians to hold the majority of their campaign events outdoors was itself creating a scenario that allowed the protests to spread.[16] Kirkup wrote: "Party leaders are contending with how to handle emboldened protesters on the campaign trail, where outdoor campaign events, designed to reduce the spread of COVID-19, have created security challenges. Because the events take place in public places, with few barriers to attendance, protesters have become a frequent presence."

A week after the cancellation of the Bolton event, the anger and rage spewing out of the protests continued to upstage the announcements of all parties in the mainstream coverage, especially the Liberals who finally released their platform on 1 September. Though the platform was widely parsed and reported on, the media remained focused on trying to assess and explain the discontent.

On 2 September, the CBC attempted to wrap up the week's events in an episode of the *Front Burner* podcast.[17] As the *Star*'s Althia Raj explained to host Jayme Poisson:

> It doesn't compare to past campaigns, frankly. I've never seen anything like it … It's really a level of vitriol and anger towards a politician that is unheard of and frankly makes me think of what we've seen south of the border during the Donald Trump years. […] These are far-fetched conspiracy theories. These are not people with mainstream thoughts who are consuming mainstream media that is leading them to these types of feelings, but there is a hatred of Justin Trudeau that has percolated even prior to his becoming prime minister when he was Liberal leader. I think it is also the lockdown, the anti-vaccine people. There is a sense, from just listening to them, that they need someone to blame for what has happened and they're lashing out on Justin Trudeau.

> I'm not the person to tell you why these people are there. But I think when you listen in their own words, they are there for a variety of reasons, including protesting a vaping tax. But I really think this is a very fringe part of Canadian society that is getting a megaphone during this election campaign.

A HANDFUL OF ROCKS, A QUESTION OF RACISM, AND THE PLAY FOR QUEBEC

Week Four – 5 to 11 September

As the campaign carried into its fourth week, some mainstream media outlets directed their attention toward the fundamental differences between each party's platforms – from climate change to healthcare, childcare, affordable housing, and the economy.

But the media's dissection of the platforms was quickly overshadowed by news that a People's Party of Canada supporter had thrown gravel at the prime minister during a campaign stop at a microbrewery in London, Ontario. Images quickly circulated on social media showing Trudeau getting pelted by pebbles after being escorted through an angry crowd toward his campaign bus. The chaotic scene became a lead story on the national news sites. Police would later charge a twenty-five-year-old PPC riding association president, Shane Marshall, with one count of assault with a weapon. Marshall was also expelled from his party. News stories about the incident continued to come out for days as Trudeau criticized the rhetoric of PPC leader Maxime Bernier, placing some of the blame on Bernier for the profane verbal abuse that was plaguing the campaign. The incident led to increased media attention for the fledgling PPC, which were polling at about 3 per cent support from decided voters, according to a Postmedia-Léger poll published on 8 September.[18] The same poll showed the Conservatives and Liberals tied at 33 per cent, with the NDP at 21 per cent, the Bloc Québécois at 6 per cent (27 per cent in Quebec) and the Greens at 3 per cent.

Then came the first and only English-language leaders' debate. Media analysis immediately after the debate indicated that no one seemed to have come anywhere near winning the televised contest, though the mainstream outlets all shared the view that the other leaders had spent most of their time rounding on the prime minister, who was still perceived as the candidate to beat.

Writing in the *Toronto Star*, Susan Delacourt opined: "Amid the noise and furor at the Museum of History stage though on Thursday night, it wasn't clear that any winner emerged among the four people challenging Trudeau for his job. They asked, repeatedly, why Trudeau had called the election. Standing in the centre of the group, flanked by leaders eager to remind him of all his government hadn't done in the past six years, the Liberal leader might have wondered the same."[19]

The Globe and Mail had a similar take. In a round-up piece of the night's event, Marieke Walsh, Laura Stone, and Kristy Kirkup wrote:[20] "The debate was primarily focused on Mr Trudeau, and he was put on the defensive from the start, forced to justify his decision to call an election in the middle of a pandemic and with two years left in his mandate."

The *National Post*'s Brian Platt also focused on the assault on Trudeau:[21] "Thursday night's leaders' debate had barely started when Liberal leader Justin Trudeau came under heavy fire – first from Green Party leader Annamie Paul hammering him as not a 'real feminist,' then from Conservative leader Erin O'Toole accusing him of putting his own political fortunes ahead of the well-being of Canada's Afghan allies. The heated exchanges set the tone for an English-language debate that was much feistier – and at times chaotic, with even the moderators occasionally interrupting each other – than the two French debates that preceded it."

Though there was no perceived victor from the debate, there was significant fallout from a question posed by moderator Shachi Kurl. It was a question which Kurl, a former CTV legislative reporter and current president of the Angus Reid Institute, posed to Bloc Québécois leader Yves-Francois Blanchet. "You deny that Quebec has a problem with racism," Kurl said. "Yet you defend legislation such as Bills 96 and 21, which marginalize religious minorities, anglophones, and allophones. For those outside the province, please help them understand why your party also supports these discriminatory laws." Blanchet shot back: "The question seems to imply the answer you want. Those laws are not about discrimination. They are about the values of Quebec."

Kurl would later describe in *The Globe and Mail* how in the days after the debate some party leaders tried to leverage support with blanket criticisms of the question and of her.[22] "It led the National Assembly [of Quebec] to censure me, cartoonists to ridicule me and party leaders to demand an apology," Kurl explained. "I have heard and listened to what people have said about the question, and the hurt it caused in Quebec. Could it have been phrased differently? Yes. Do I ultimately believe a change in wording would have prevented Mr Blanchet, Quebec Premier François Legault, and party leaders Justin Trudeau, Erin O'Toole and Jagmeet Singh from exploiting it all for their own purposes? No."

The release of a book by former Liberal cabinet minister Jody Wilson-Raybould (it hit bookstores five days after the debate) served as a brief distraction to the political row over Kurl's question. But even the most damning revelations from the text could not quell the columnists, pundits, journalists, and politicians alike who continued to either defend or attack Kurl, and to opine on whether Quebec has a problem with racism.

In the *Toronto Star* on 11 September, race and gender columnist Shree Paradkar wrote:[23] "It's no surprise, really, that the federal leaders failed to discuss white supremacy, systemic racism and colonialism in a serious way during the English debate on Thursday night ... Where is the focus on the people violated by laws and policies? Even a quick look at the party platforms show tackling racism is an afterthought."

Three days later in *The Globe and Mail*, Erna Paris (author of seven books on politics, history, and historical memory), called the leaders' sycophantic acceptance of Quebec's Bill 21 dangerous for all of Canada.[24] Meanwhile, Tasha Kheiriddin, a principal at Navigator, a Toronto-based public relations firm, and regular Post Media columnist, took to the pages of the *National Post* to declare the whole Kurl affair a detriment to national unity and civil discourse.[25] "Cue the outrage in Quebec," she wrote. "Where the entire political class, including the premier, lambasted Kurl for her question and English Canada, which she de facto represented, for depicting Quebecers as racist. Cue also a major voter swing to the Bloc, to the detriment of the Conservatives, and a prediction that the Bloc will now grab an additional 10 seats in Quebec."

THE INTERNATIONAL VIEW AND THE USUAL ENDORSEMENTS

Week Five – 12 to 18 September

Coverage of the last full week of the campaign began with the NDP releasing a costed-out platform just as advanced voting got under way. The following day (12 September), *The Globe and Mail*'s

Menaka Raman-Wilms, Bill Curry, and Kristy Kirkup reached out to Kevin Page, former parliamentary budget officer, to compare each of the parties' platforms (in their story Page ultimately gave the Liberal plan the highest marks for fiscal credibility).[26] As is common in the final days before a federal election, international media outlets paid increased attention to the pending outcome. Ian Austen, Ottawa-based Canada correspondent for *The New York Times*, had written about the election for his outlet throughout the campaign. Three days before the vote he remarked that Indigenous issues had been conspicuously sidelined during the debate.[27] "To a large extent, it remains an election about the need for an election," Austen wrote. "No other issues reached the point of allowing any party leaders to significantly redefine the campaign. And many important subjects were given short shrift. Exhibit A among those overlooked was Indigenous issues." Austen and *The New York Times* also profiled Conservative leader O'Toole as the candidate most likely to unseat Trudeau, with a feature that explained how O'Toole had tacked left in an effort to pull from Trudeau's base.[28] Meanwhile, in the British paper *The Observer* (the left-leaning *Guardian*'s Sunday newspaper) on 12 September, Toronto-based Leyland Cecco chose to profile Jagmeet Singh, whom *The Observer* described as an ex-lawyer and TikTok star who could topple Trudeau.[29]

By 14 September, with most in the national media predicting either a Liberal or Conservative minority, Trudeau began doing what Chantal Hébert had predicted two weeks earlier: appeal to progressive voters to come back to the Liberals.[30] Writing in the *Toronto Star* on 15 September, after the leaders had visited the newspaper's editorial board, Susan Delacourt predicted the election outcome would result in widespread disappointment among the parties and party faithful alike.[31] Delacourt described how, during those editorial board meetings, O'Toole acknowledged that some voters had been put off by the Conservatives history while Trudeau had admitted that he had "his own problems with drift and disappointment, especially among progressive voters." In her own words, Delacourt concluded: "What neither of them has confronted yet is what they will do with all this grumpiness when the election is over on Monday. Elections come and go, but bad moods like this can linger."

The editorial tone coming out of *The Globe and Mail* was not much different. In the 2019 election the newspaper had broken with tradition and not endorsed any political party; again, it withheld any editorial endorsement. On 18 September, the newspaper's editorial board remained critical of the entire contest[32]: "We have said it before, and we will say it again: This election was unnecessary. Not illegal, not illegitimate, not unconstitutional – just profoundly unnecessary. Undesired by Canadians, and undesirable for Canada."

Writing in *The Globe and Mail* on the same day, Andrew Coyne, one of the paper's most-read political columnists, wrote a 2,649-word election round-up in which he highlighted all the reasons why he believed the entire election had been ill advised.[33] "A snap election is always a risky move," he wrote. "It looks like what it most often is, a self-serving attempt to exploit a moment of advantage for the ruling party ... But to call a snap election in the middle of a pandemic looked unusually crass, not to say hazardous to public health. And to do so on the very day that Kabul fell, leaving thousands of Afghan nationals – and hundreds of Canadian citizens – to the mercies of the Taliban, looked not just opportunistic, but callous."

Not surprisingly, the *National Post* granted space in its pages to the newspaper's founder, Conrad Black, who penned a predictable endorsement of the Conservative Party.[34] "Erin O'Toole isn't exciting, but Canadian Conservative leaders rarely are. In this election, he and the Conservatives are the best we have. A vote for them won't make the heart beat faster, but it is rational." One day later, the *National Post*'s editorial board published its own lengthy endorsement of O'Toole and the Conservatives.[35] The newspaper trounced the Liberal record on the economy, national unity, climate change, and the lost war in Afghanistan, and championed the Conservatives' platform, which the editorial argued "offers a clear alternative to the Liberals, whose six years in office have yielded major scandals, empty virtue signalling, tax-and-spend irresponsibility, and failed policies." Above all, however, the *National Post*'s position was rooted in concerns about Liberal spending policies.[36] "We long ago lost faith that the Liberals put any value in the country's long-term fiscal health, after years of breaking their promises of maintaining modest deficits – and this was before the pandemic struck and times were much better. Now, based on Trudeau's track record of fuelling anger and division between regions and people, we've lost faith that he values national harmony over his own ambitions."

Finally, on the day before the election, the *Toronto Star*'s editorial board came out with their own endorsement of Trudeau and the Liberal Party. Despite the newspaper's traditional ideological support of the Liberals, the *Star* expressed its dissatisfaction at the entire process and labeled the election "unnecessary – a $610-million distraction in the middle of the worst public health crisis in a century."[37] The *Star* denounced the Liberal record on electoral reform, safe drinking water in all Indigenous communities, the government's failure to rein in the social media giants, and called for an end to the 2SLGBTQ+ blood donation ban. The editorial concluded: "We believe – albeit very reluctantly – that the Liberals are the best alternative, supported by a strong mandate for Jagmeet Singh's NDP, to address the main priority of getting Canadians through this pandemic."

POSTMORTEM COVERAGE AND THE LASTING NARRATIVE

As noted by Paul Adams, author of the chapter on the news media in *The Canadian Federal Election of 2019*, "like the contest among the parties, the story of the national media during a campaign typically confirms some expectations and confutes others."[38] While the journalistic coverage of the campaign was not the campaign itself, the coverage was itself a representation of the campaign. Collectively, the national news media highlighted certain aspects of the campaign and downplayed others.

How did the election coverage contribute to the trajectory of the election itself? Despite the media's endorsements and projections and predictions, the mainstream coverage was largely reactive to the events that played out on the campaign trail. That so many mainstream journalists were caught off guard by the public anger during the election is perhaps symbolic of a disconnect between the Parliamentary Press Gallery and the general population the gallery exists to inform. Would those assigned to cover the election have been so surprised by the vitriol if they had spent less time following the leaders and more time checking in with different sectors of the public? Perhaps. Would they have still chosen to deride those who were angry as "the crackpot fringe"? Who knows. A shift in coverage from the outset may have allowed the media to more adequately assess and explain the rising discontent that had existed before the campaign began but which did not become a central narrative of the campaign until it could no longer be ignored.

Mainstream journalists walk a delicate line in this space. Their job is not to amplify conspiracy theories and hate speech, but they cannot ignore them either. The public vitriol that emerged was directed at both the politicians and the journalists. This no doubt influenced the work of the journalists who were targeted, perhaps leading to some of the derisive language used by journalists to describe the protestors. In many cases, journalists misjudged how many Canadians shared similar sentiments to those who were protesting. Journalists also did not understand where the anger and vitriol had come from nor why it was suddenly disrupting the campaign. Those protesting the campaign and the campaign coverage were not just partisans expressing exasperation at coverage they felt was unfair to their side. Much of it was directed at journalists as a class. The resentment and anger attached to the very pretence of the journalists' work of interpreting the world to the public. This resentment and anger appear to be getting stronger while legacy media outlets continue to lose more of their impact on the daily public discourse due to diminished resources and dwindling stature.

Nevertheless, if journalism amounts to an effort to set an agenda of concern – to instruct the public on what it should consider important – this chapter charts a seismographic reading of what the journalists covering the campaign themselves considered important, what they judged merited attention and comment. What made the news media actors in the campaign was their reports and commentary, through which the majority of the public still came to apprehend the election. As demonstrated by the coverage analyzed in this chapter, different media outlets brought different analytical perspectives to bear on the campaign. The response of the media in English Canada, for example, to Kurl's debate question was markedly different from the response on the part of the media in Quebec. To some extent this may have been the result of English Canada not having been challenged by Kurl's question in the same way that French Canada appeared to be. If the media is itself a reflection of the society it covers, then the French-Canadian media may well have been challenged by the question in ways that the English-Canadian media was not.

In the end, the campaign and the coverage of the campaign remained gripped by accusations, assumptions, and conclusions that created a prevailing narrative – that the entire campaign was unnecessary. In casting the election in this way, the mainstream outlets, regardless of political leaning, ended up repeating the rhetoric of the opposition parties. How much influence this had on the final outcome is impossible to measure.

As is always the case, the election itself did not spell the end of the election coverage. For days (and at some outlets, weeks) after the outcome, columnists and reporters alike parsed the final tally, assigning or discounting meaning to all that had happened. In the end, it did not matter whether Canadians were getting their post-election news from the CBC, CTV, Global News, The Canadian Press, the *Toronto Star*, *The Globe and Mail* or the *National Post*. The narratives coming out of each mainstream media outlet were essentially the same as journalist upon journalist tried in print, on radio, podcasts, or TV to answer a simple question that had nagged at their coverage since before the writ was dropped. Was any of it worth it?

NOTES

1 Paul Adams, "The Media: Challenges of Covering the Campaign," in *The Canadian Federal Election of 2019*, eds. J.H. Pammett and Christopher Dornan (McGill-Queen's University Press, 2019), 174.

2 Tonda MacCharles, "Justin Trudeau Expected to Call a Federal Election on Sunday, as a Fourth Wave of COVID-19 Grips Canada," *Toronto Star*, 12 August 2021, https://www.thestar.com/politics/federal/2021/08/12/justin-trudeau-expected-to-call-a-federal-election-on-sunday-insiders-say.html.

3 Danica Samuel, "Nearly Two-Thirds of Canadians Don't Want a Federal Election Right Now, Mainstreet Poll Says," *Toronto Star*, 12 August 2021, https://www.thestar.com/politics/federal/2021/08/12/nearly-two-thirds-of-canadians-dont-want-a-federal-election-right-now-mainstreet-poll-says.html.

4 John Ivison, "Even Trudeau's Overblown Rhetoric Can't Justify September Election," *National* Post, 16 August 2021, https://nationalpost.com/opinion/john-ivison-even-trudeaus-overblown-rhetoric-cant-justify-election.

5 Maan Alhmidi, "Conservatives Delete 'Willy Wonka' Ad from Twitter after Copyright Complaint," CTV News, 17 August 2021, https://www.ctvnews.ca/politics/federal-election-2021/conservatives-delete-willy-wonka-ad-from-twitter-after-copyright-complaint-1.5550603.

6 Stephanie Levitz, "The Liberals Are Betting Big That They Can Win a Majority. Here's How They Plan to Do It," *Toronto Star*, 17 August 2021, https://www.thestar.com/politics/federal-election/2021/08/17/the-liberals-are-betting-big-that-they-can-win-a-majority-heres-how-they-plan-to-do-it.html.

7 Kelly McParland, "Nova Scotia Election Shows How Trudeau Could Meet

His Doom," *National Post*, 18 August 2021, https://nationalpost.com/opinion/kelly-mcparland-nova-scotia-election-shows-how-trudeau-could-meet-his-doom.

8 Lori Turnbull, "What the Nova Scotia Election Means for the Federal Campaign – and What It Doesn't," *Globe and Mail*, 19 August 2021, https://www.theglobeandmail.com/opinion/article-what-the-nova-scotia-election-means-for-the-federal-campaign-and-what/.

9 Ben Woodfinden, "Freeland's 'Manipulated' Video on Twitter Shows Liberals Desperation," *National Post*, 23 August 2021, https://nationalpost.com/opinion/ben-woodfinden-freelands-manipulated-video-on-twitter-shows-liberals-desperation.

10 Lawrence Martin, "Erin O'Toole's Sunny Ways Have Caught Justin Trudeau off Guard," *Globe and Mail*, 26 August 2021, https://www.theglobeandmail.com/opinion/article-erin-otooles-sunny-ways-have-caught-justin-trudeau-off-guard/.

11 Susan Delacourt, "It's Time to Talk about This Rage against Justin Trudeau," *Toronto Star*, 28 August 2021, https://www.thestar.com/politics/federal/2021/08/28/its-time-to-talk-about-this-rage-against-justin-trudeau.html.

12 John Ivison, "At Cancelled Trudeau Rally, a Level of Anger Not Seen Before," *National Post*, 27 August 2021, https://nationalpost.com/news/politics/election-2021/john-ivison-at-cancelled-trudeau-rally-a-level-of-anger-not-seen-before.

13 John Ivison, "These Are the People That Are so Angry at Justin Trudeau," *National Post*, 30 August 2021, https://nationalpost.com/news/john-ivison-these-are-the-people-so-angry-at-justin-trudeau.

14 Chantal Hébert, "Justin Trudeau Is in Trouble. What Are Progressive Voters to Do?," *Toronto Star*, 27 August 2021, https://www.thestar.com/politics/political-opinion/2021/08/27/justin-trudeau-is-in-trouble-what-are-progressive-voters-to-do.html.

15 Hébert, "Justin Trudeau Is in Trouble."

16 Kristy Kirkup, "Election Campaigns Facing Evolving Security Challenges in Era of Social Media and COVID-19," *Globe and Mail*, 1 September 2021,https://www.theglobeandmail.com/politics/article-election-campaigns-facing-evolving-security-challenges-in-era-of/.

17 Front Burner, "Election Watch: Anger on the Campaign Trail," CBC News, 1 September 2021, https://www.cbc.ca/radio/Front Burner/election-watch-anger-on-the-campaign-trail-1.6161986.

18 Brian Platt, "'The Worst Track Record in All the G7': Trudeau under

Heavy Fire at Final Debate before Election," *National Post*, 9 September 2021,https://nationalpost.com/news/politics/election-2021/english-language-federal-leaders-debate.

19 Susan Delacourt, "Why Did Justin Trudeau Call This Election? There's a Question He Must Be Asking Himself after That Debate," *Toronto Star*, 9 September 2021, https://www.thestar.com/politics/political-opinion/2021/09/09/why-did-justin-trudeau-call-this-election-theres-a-question-he-must-be-asking-himself.html.

20 Kristy Kirkup, Laura Stone, and Marieke Walsh, "English-Language Debate: Justin Trudeau Put on Defensive over Early Election Call, Foreign Policy," *Globe and Mail*, 9 September 2021, https://www.theglobeandmail.com/politicsarticle-english-language-debate-justin-trudeau-put-on-defensive-over-early/.

21 Platt, "The Worst Track Record."

22 Shachi Kurl, "I Was Asked to Apologize for My Question in the Leaders' Debate. I Stand by It Unequivocally," *Globe and Mail*, 25 September 2021, https://www.theglobeandmail.com/opinion/article-i-was-asked-to-apologize-for-my-question-in-the-leaders-debate-i-stand/.

23 Shree Paradkar, "Racist? Moi? Federal Leaders Miss Mark with Superficial Approach to Systemic Racism in English Debate," *Toronto Star*, 10 September 2021, https://www.thestar.com/opinion/star-columnists/2021/09/10/racist-moi-federal-leaders-miss-mark-with-superficial-approach-to-systemic-racism-in-english-debate.html.

24 Erna Paris, "The Leaders' Sycophantic Acceptance of Quebec's Bill 21 Is Dangerous for All of Canada," *Globe and Mail*, 14 September 2021, https://www.theglobeandmail.com/opinion/article-the-leaders-sycophantic-acceptance-of-quebecs-bill-21-is-dangerous-for/.

25 Tasha Kheiriddin, "Why Maxime Bernier's Rise Could Secure Trudeau's Re-Election," *National Post*, 15 September 2021, https://nationalpost.com/opinion/tasha-kheiriddin-why-maxime-berniers-rise-could-secure-trudeaus-re-election.

26 Bill Curry, Kristy Kirkup, and Menaka Raman-Wilms, "NDP Last of Three Main Parties to Release Platform Costing as Campaign Enters Final Week," *Globe and Mail*, 12 September 2021, https://www.theglobeandmail.com/politics/article-ndp-is-the-last-of-three-main-parties-to-release-platform-costing-as/.

27 Ian Austen, "Indigenous Issues Are Sidelined in Canada's Election," *New York Times*, 17 September 2021, https://www.nytimes.com/2021/09/17/world/canada/canada-election-indigenous-issues.html.

28 Ian Austen, "To Unseat Trudeau, Canada's Top Conservative Leans Left," *New York Times*, 15 September 2021, https://www.nytimes.com/2021/09/15/world/canada/trudeau-election-erin-otoole.html.

29 Leyland Cecco, "Jagmeet Singh: the Ex-Lawyer and TikTok Star Who Could Topple Trudeau," *Guardian*, 12 September 2021, https://www.theguardian.com/world/2021/sep/12/jagmeet-singh-the-ex-lawyer-and-tiktok-star-who-could-topple-trudeau.

30 Ian Bailey, Kristy Kirkup, and Laura Stone, "Trudeau Warns Progressives to Vote Liberal to Ward off Conservatives, as O'Toole Courts Quebec," *Globe and Mail*, 14 September 2021, https://www.theglobeandmail.com/politics/article-trudeau-warns-progressives-to-vote-liberal-to-ward-off-conservatives/.

31 Susan Delacourt, "Angry with Erin O'Toole? Disappointed in Justin Trudeau? Hard Feelings Will Shape Next Week's Election Result," *Toronto Star*, 15 September 2021, https://www.thestar.com/politics/political-opinion/2021/09/15/angry-with-erin-otoole-disappointed-in-justin-trudeau-hard-feelings-will-shape-next-weeks-election-result.html.

32 The Editorial Board, "Counting the Cost of an Unnecessary Election," *Globe and Mail*, 18 September 2021, https://www.theglobeandmail.com/opinion/editorials/article-counting-the-cost-of-an-unnecessary-election/.

33 Andrew Coyne, "Vote of Confidence," *Globe and Mail*, 18 September 2021.

34 Conrad Black, "There is Only One Rational Choice in This Election," *National Post*, 17 September 2021, https://nationalpost.com/opinion/conrad-black-there-is-only-one-rational-choice-in-this-election.

35 *National Post* View, "Erin O'Toole and the Conservatives Are Right for Canada," *National Post*, 18 September 2021, https://nationalpost.com/opinion/np-view-erin-otoole-and-the-conservatives-are-right-for-canada.

36 *National Post*, "Erin O'Toole and the Conservatives."

37 *Star* Editorial Board, "The *Star*'s Editorial Board Endorses Liberals for 2021 Federal Election," *Toronto Star*, 19 September 2021, https://www.thestar.com/opinion/editorials/2021/09/19/the-stars-editorial-board-endorses-liberals-for-2021-federal-election.html.

38 Paul Adams, "The Media: Challenges of Covering the Campaign," in *The Canadian Federal Election of 2019*, eds. J.H. Pammett and Christopher Dornan (McGill-Queens University Press, 2019), 174.

9

Regionalized Campaign Communication: Facebook Advertising in the 2021 Federal Election

Andrew J.A. Mattan and Tamara A. Small

In this chapter, we explore Facebook advertising by Canada's political parties in the 2021 federal election. One of the main appeals of Facebook for advertisers (political or otherwise) is the ability to target ads. Targeting, sometimes called narrowcasting or micro-targeting, is "the practice of sending particular political messages to particular people."[1] Facebook collects a multitude of data from its users including demographics, location, and other online behaviours, which allow advertisers to target ads to very specific users.[2] Facebook targeting "is driven not by a goal of making all users available to advertisers, but of making the 'right' individuals available."[3] More specifically, we consider where Canadian political parties targeted their Facebook ads. Central to our discussion is Carty, Cross, and Young's concept of regionalized campaign communication as outlined in their very important book *Rebuilding Canadian Party Politics*.[4] Published in 2001, the purpose of *Rebuilding Canadian Party Politics* was to argue that the 1993 election had created a new, fourth party system, which was defined by regionalization. With regards to campaign communication, they argued it was also regionalized. The internet, they argued, permitted political messages that differ from traditional means in their ability to facilitate the delivery of targeted messages with electronic speed to individual voters. Similar to television advertisements, these messages may be tailored to both region and a nearly endless number of sociodemographic characteristics. Unlike television advertisements, these so-called private messages to voters are not readily available to other parties, the media, or potential voters.

Through these messages the parties can send messages that may well remain below the radar screen of the national media and the opposing political parties.[5]

It is not our purpose to wade too deeply into debates about which party system is currently in place or what features define any such party system, or both. However, in looking at the election results in 2021, there is some evidence of regional bases of support for many parties (see chapter 15). The Liberals were particularly successful in Ontario and Quebec. The Conservatives continued their dominance in the Prairies. The NDP won a significant number of seats in British Columbia.

At the time Carty, Cross, and Young were making these arguments about regionalized campaign communication, fewer than 50 per cent of Canadians had regular access to the internet. Some scholars have suggested that online campaign communication in the early 2000s was quite centralized rather than regionalized.[6] This was because the main digital technology being used at that time was websites, which do not allow for widespread targeting. However, much has changed in the digital politics landscape. Statistics Canada reports that 92 per cent of Canadians regularly used the internet in the year before the election.[7] Moreover, while party websites remain important informational hubs, parties now use a variety of social media including Twitter, Facebook, and Instagram. In 2021, the NDP's Jagmeet Singh received a lot of press coverage for his use of the video-sharing social network TikTok, while the Conservatives hosted virtual town hall meetings with Erin O'Toole from a studio specially constructed for the purpose by the party.[8] We focus on Facebook ads by the main political parties during the 2021 campaign because it is one of the only applications that make location-based data available. As such, we are now able to assess the extent to which Canadian political parties engage in regionalized (or nationalized) political communication in a systematic matter. We find that Canadian parties did engage in regionalized campaign communication. Facebook ads, while viewed across the country, were developed, and purchased mainly to target users in Ontario, Quebec, and to a lesser extent British Columbia. This is likely due to the large number of seats and the level of competitiveness in these three provinces.

WHAT IS DIGITAL ADVERTISING?

During an election campaign, political parties make use of a variety of modalities to inform, mobilize and, ultimately, persuade voters. Some of these have been around a very long time and are not technological, such as lawn signs, brochures, and newspaper advertisements. More technological forms such as radio and television commercials exist alongside newer digital technologies. To be sure, some of these, such as websites and email, are no longer new. Indeed, Canadian political parties were early adopters of the internet; it is reported that one political party had a website in the 1993 federal election.[9] The internet of the 1990s was vastly different from the internet of today. In the 2021 campaign, there are far more ways that political actors can use digital technologies to communicate with voters, from social media to mobile phones to digital advertising.

Facebook campaign ads are a type of digital political advertising, which should be considered distinct from other aspects of digital campaigning, such as websites or social media feeds. Digital political advertising is defined as interactive content, placed online for a fee.[10] According to Canadian electoral law, election advertising is defined as the "transmission to the public by any means during an election period of an advertising message that promotes or opposes a registered party or the election of a candidate, including by taking a position on an issue with which a registered party or candidate is associated."[11] However, messages or communication sent for free on the internet (e.g., text messages, email, social media), online videos posted for free on a personal website or online video sites (e.g., YouTube), and content posted on a party website are not considered advertising and are, therefore, not regulated. Digital messages are only considered advertising if there is a placement cost. That is, a political actor (e.g., party, candidate, or third party) pays to place the ad or to boost content that was originally posted for free. There are many types of digital ads: content appearing in one's social media feed, a preroll before online video, a banner or page takeover on more traditional websites, or search advertising. As a form of election advertising, digital political ads are subject to the spending limit of each party in terms of the production and the transmission of message to the public. In this way, digital political advertising is more akin to television commercials than a party's Twitter feed or Facebook page.

Compared to other types of digital applications (e.g., websites, blogs, or Twitter), it is much harder to discern when political actors began using digital ads in election campaigns. This is because the former are more public or forward-facing whereas digital ads are hidden from those to whom they are not directed. Through spending data analysis, there is evidence to suggest that the 2008 presidential election in the United States was probably the first with extensive use of digital ads.[12] Since then, digital political advertising has become increasingly prevalent among campaigns worldwide. For instance, it has been reported that between the 2014 and 2018 US midterm elections, spending on digital advertising rose by 2,400 per cent.[13]

DIGITAL ADVERTISING ON FACEBOOK

As discussed in *The Canadian Federal Election of 2019*, Facebook is a particularly important application for exploring digital political advertising.[14] This is because of the Facebook Ad Library. Facebook first created the Ad Archive in 2018 as a response to several high-profile scandals, including widespread online misinformation in the 2016 United States presidential election and the Cambridge Analytica revelations in 2018. The Ad Archive, later renamed the Ad Library, is a searchable digital depository of all advertising, political or otherwise, that is purchased on any of Facebook's properties including Instagram.[15] Following these scandals, several countries, including France, Germany, the United Kingdom, and the Netherlands, either passed legislation or have submitted recommendations or proposals to their legislative bodies to eliminate or curb the practice of digital political advertising.[16] In 2019, as part of the *Electoral Modernization Act*, the Canadian government made its own effort to regulate digital platforms and bring transparency to who is purchasing online advertising. More specifically, the act required online platforms to establish an advertising registry, which must include both an electronic copy of every political advertisement posted to the platform and the name of whoever authorized its publication – whether an individual, a political party, registered association, nomination contestant, candidate, or potential candidate, or registered third party. Following the election, the registry is required to remain on the platform for two years and the information on the registry must be kept for five additional years. The failure of online platforms to publish or maintain a registry is considered an offence. The

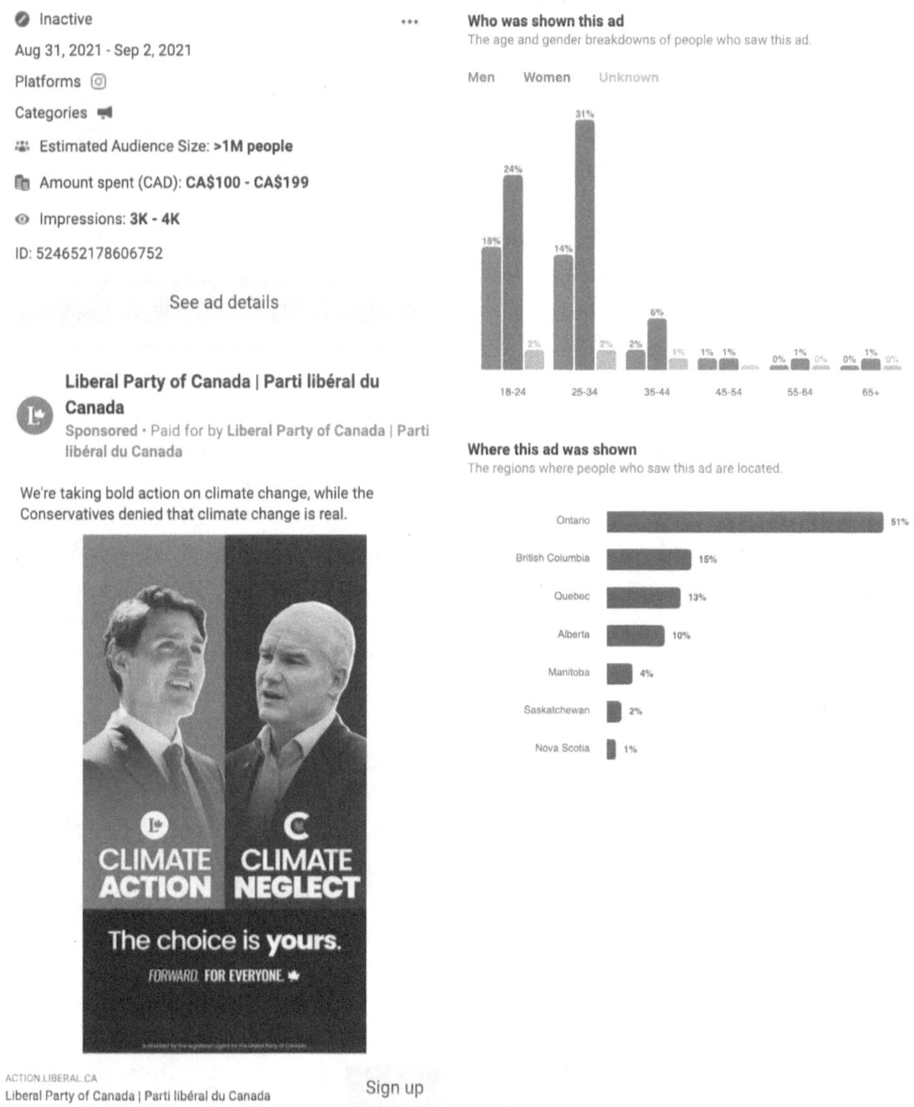

Figure 9.1 | Example of 2021 Facebook ad and summary data

Canadian version of the Ad Library allows Facebook to meet its regulatory obligations. The Ad Library exists for different countries. The other major platforms, Google and Twitter, chose not to sell digital political advertising in 2019 and 2021 in Canada, and therefore do not maintain a registry. Google Canada cited an inability to meet regulatory requirements, though Google does allow political advertising in other countries. Twitter has entirely opted out of political advertising worldwide.[17]

Facebook is extremely important to understanding digital political advertising in Canada. In addition to the ability to target, Facebook provides other benefits for political actors. First, Facebook is inexpensive compared to other more traditional forms of advertising, such as radio, television, or newspapers.[18] Second, Facebook provides access to billions of users worldwide. Facebook is the most popular social media platform in Canada. There were 27.6 million Canadian Facebook users in 2021, or around 72 per cent of the population, with twenty-five- to thirty-four-year-olds constituting the biggest group of users.[19] Finally, the Ad Library provides opportunities for researchers that were previously unavailable.[20] Now we are able to see all of the ads created by all parties, candidates and third parties in the campaign, even those that were not targeted directly to us. Additionally, as figure 9.1 shows, the Ad Library includes transparency and summary data about each ad and the sponsor including the number of ads using the same image or video and text, an estimated total money spent, impressions or the number of times the ad was seen on screen, the age and gender breakdowns of people who saw the ad and, particularly relevant to this paper, the region where people who saw the ad are located.[21] It should be noted, these data are not granular but still provide a glimpse into an advertiser's intention.[22] For instance, in figure 9.1, we see the range of dollars spent on the ad (between $100–$199 CAD) and that it reached an estimated audience of over one million views.

Accordingly, this study seeks to fill a gap by examining how political parties utilize Facebook to target specific segments of the population during the 2021 federal election. We are not the first to do so; there are Canadian studies which have utilized the Ad Library to analyze how political actors used digital advertising during the 2019 federal election. Budd and Small examined how one third party, Canada Proud, used digital political advertising to engage in populist rhetoric, discovering that they primarily directed their "attack elite" ads at older men.[23] With regards to political parties, the Digital Democracy Project provided a broad overview examining how much each of the major political parties and third parties spent on Facebook ads, whether the ads focused on the party or individual candidates, to which province the ads were directed, and to which age and sex were they were directed.[24] While taking a more focused approach, Bennett and Gordon collected party ads during two prominent days of the 2019 campaign and created a typology to capture whether the policy message, location, or demographic was being microtargeted.[25] They found that it was rare for any political ad to fulfill all three criteria. This analysis differs in its focus on one type of summary data: region. These data allow us to fully explore the relationship between digital political advertising and regionalized campaign communication.

All advertisements on Facebook properties can be manually searched using the Facebook Ad Library interface.[26] One can filter by location, ad category, and key word or advertiser in order to access grid-like lists of all advertisements (active or inactive). Additionally, these lists can be filtered by region, language, platform, media type, active status, impression, disclaimer, and potential reach. For this analysis, we searched for all advertisements related to "Issues, Elections, or Politics," created by the six major federal political parties during the 2021 writ period (15 August to 20 September 2021). In total, there were 1,150 digital ads.[27] It is worth pointing out that this is only a portion of the Facebook ads in this campaign. The party leaders have Facebook pages (separate from the Facebook pages of the main political parties) which ran ads, as did the thousands of party candidates across the country. Figure 9.1 is an example of a Facebook ad created by the Liberal Party during the election. All ads feature a text-based message at the top followed by a visual, such as an image or video. Above the ad, summary details are provided which include the ads status (inactive or active), the date range in which the ad was active, and the ad ID. Figure 9.1 shows other summary data for this particular ad relating to age, gender, and region. As should be clear, the summary data lack some specificity. Capozzi and colleagues state that summary data provide an assessment of the final reach of ads.[28] This means researchers cannot fully "distinguish between explicit targeting of the authors and the platform optimization of the ad delivery to potentially interested audience. Nevertheless, this gives … a precise measure of the final reach of the ads, and as such it is still a strong clue for investigating the ads' target audience."[29] In this analysis, we manually recorded the regional data for all the digital ads produced during the writ period by the six main political parties. Overall, this chapter is what the digital political literature refers to as "supply digital research," which focuses on the outputs from political actors and institutions on digital technologies.[30] The study does not focus on uses of those outputs by audiences (demand research) nor does it include interviews with party officials, and therefore does not make statements about these issues.

REGIONAL OR NATIONAL CAMPAIGNING?

Cochrane and Perrella remind us that there is "widespread agreement among observers of politics in Canada that the country is divided in politically consequential ways along regional lines."[31] At the same time, they note that the causes of these regional divisions are up for debate. With regards to campaign communication, many, such as Cross[32] and Flanagan,[33] point to Canada's electoral system as dictating the campaign strategies of the parties. In single member plurality (SMP), one candidate is elected in each riding using a plurality formula. SMP "tends to promote a winner-take-all mentality because there is no second prize. You either win or lose; you get elected or you don't."[34] As such, each party must determine in which ridings and regions it has a chance of winning a plurality of the vote. This results in a strategy of regional targeting. This strategy is reflected not only in which parties are competitive in which regions but also in the campaign discourse.[35] Despite this campaigning rationale, we have seen evidence of more nationalized campaign communication more recently. Looking at television commercials in the 2008 campaign, Pruysers argued that, with the exception of Quebec, the main Canadian parties focused their ads nationally.[36] Using a variety of data including the party leaders' tours, press releases, and social media activity, Stephenson and colleagues found there was "far less of a regional cast" to the 2015 election.[37] However, we argue the ability to target ads on Facebook is significantly more robust than on other technologies such as television commercials, websites, or social media. Even if there is evidence of nationalized campaign communication in other venues in this campaign, we expect Facebook to be highly regionalized.

Table 9.1 | Number of Facebook ads by party

Party	Ads
BQ	48
CPC	234
GPC	6
LPC	569
NDP	269
PPC	24
Total	1,150

Before addressing the main topic of this chapter, it is worthwhile to briefly consider the use of Facebook ads by the six main parties in this campaign. Table 9.1 shows the numbers of Facebook ads created by each party during the writ period. Overall, it is evident that different parties saw differing levels of utility of Facebook. The Liberal Party of Canada made extensive use of Facebook during the 2021 election. With 569 ads, the Liberals developed and purchased almost half of the ads in this Facebook campaign. Though less than the Liberals, the Conservatives and the NDP also developed and purchased a significant number of Facebook ads. Facebook was a less relevant advertising tool for the three smaller parties: the BQ, Greens, and PPC. This is an intriguing finding as it is often suggested that digital technologies can level or equalize the playing field for smaller and minor political actors.[38] We see little evidence of equalization in these data. Though digital ads are more cost-effective than television, radio, and newspaper, they are still costly both in terms of placement and production. Parties with limited financial capabilities may shy away from purchasing Facebook ads.

Table 9.2 provides an aggregation of summary data by geographical region for all 1,150 Facebook ads by the six political parties in the 2021 campaign. That is, for each party, we tallied and averaged "Where This Ad Was Shown" data by province (see figure 9.1). Recall this summary data shows the location of people who saw an ad by province. The bottom line in Table 9.2 is the provincial

Table 9.2 | Aggregated region summary of Facebook ads by party

Party	AB	BC	MB	NB	NL	NS	ON	PEI	QC	SK	NT	NU	YT
BQ	0.1	0.2	0.0	0.1	0.0	0.0	0.4	0.0	98.9	0.0	0.0	0.0	0.0
CPC	7.9	14.7	4.7	3.1	2.0	3.6	38.0	0.6	21.5	3.2	0.0	0.0	0.2
GPC	0.0	8.8	0.0	19.7	0.0	19.7	16.2	13.8	20.0	0.0	0.0	0.0	0.0
LPC	5.3	10.1	2.2	4.3	1.9	3.5	29.6	1.1	39.5	1.8	0.1	0.1	0.1
NDP	4.0	28.3	0.8	0.5	1.5	3.2	24.2	0.1	26.8	6.1	0.8	0.5	2.7
PPC	15.5	14.0	5.7	3.6	2.1	3.8	34.5	0.5	12.5	5.7	0.0	0.1	0.0
Average*	6.5	15.2	2.7	6.2	1.5	6.8	28.5	3.2	24.1	3.4	0.2	0.1	0.6

* Average excludes BQ
(n=1,150)

average for each party by the parties minus the Bloc Québécois. Since the BQ, unsurprisingly, only targeted its ads to people in the province of Quebec, we felt including them in the overall average skews the data.[39] We conclude that Facebook ads were regionally targeted. That is, Canadians in particular parts of the country were exposed to a lot of ads on Facebook, whereas Canadians in other parts of the country were not. The implication of this is that parties are spending money to advertise to some regions more than others. Overall, the vast majority of Facebook ads were seen by users in three provinces: Ontario, Quebec, and British Columbia (67.8 per cent of all ads). That said, as Table 9.2 shows many parties had a more distinct regional strategy, which will be discussed below. The data shows Ontarians were exposed to the most Facebook ads with 28.5 per cent of all ads being seen by people in that province. With the obvious exception of the BQ and the Greens, it was a top three target for the other four parties and the main target of the CPC and

Table 9.3 | Number of regionally dominated Facebook ads by party

Party	AB	BC	MB	NB	NL	NS	ON	PEI	QC	SK	NT	NU	YT	Total
CPC	0	0	0	0	0	0	3	0	50	0	0	0	0	53
GPC	0	0	0	0	0	0	0	0	0	0	0	0	0	0
LPC	0	16	0	6	3	5	30	0	38	0	0	0	0	98
NDP	4	58	0	0	2	6	35	0	65	9	2	1	5	187
PPC	0	0	0	0	0	0	0	0	0	0	0	0	0	0
Total	4	74	0	6	5	11	68	0	153	9	2	1	5	338

PPC. Returning to figure 9.1, this provides an example of a Liberal climate change ad that was seen across the country but mainly by those in Ontario, who accounted for 51 per cent of total impressions. In this case, the message is not targeted to Ontarians per se. However, we draw the conclusion that the Liberals believed that this negative message about Erin O'Toole's climate neglect would resonate more for some Canadians (those in Ontario and BC) compared to other parts of the country because they were willing to spend money to target them. Facebook users in Quebec saw 24.1 per cent of all party ads. It was a top three target for all six parties and the main target of the LPC and BQ (obviously). Most of these Facebook ads were in French. Éric Montigny has argued that Quebec figures prominently into the electoral strategies of most parties. This is because, with weak partisan identification, "the Quebec electorate is very volatile" and there are seventy-eight seats to be won.[40] British Columbia was also an important target for many parties at 15.2 per cent. However, much of this was driven by the NDP, which was the only party where BC was the main target (28.3 per cent). This was likely a good strategy for the party. A Léger poll found healthy support for the NDP in BC. Compared to Canadians overall, the

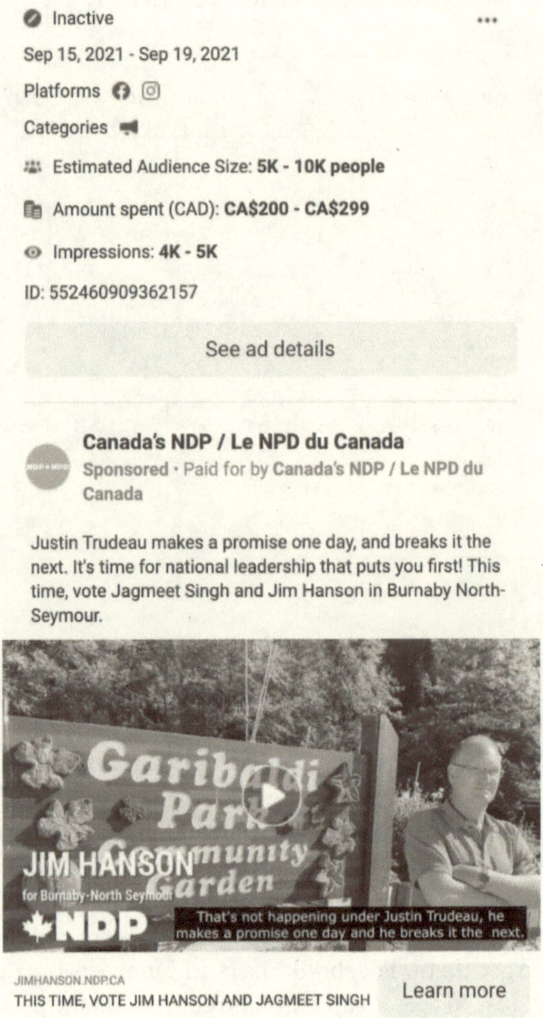

Figure 9.2 | Example of a regionally dominated Facebook ad

intention to vote for NDP was stronger in BC and the party was the preferred second choice for British Columbians.[41]

One of the stranger findings was that Facebook ads were targeted at similar rates in Nova Scotia, New Brunswick, and Alberta, at just under 8 per cent, despite Alberta having more seats than the other two provinces combined. In general, the Prairie provinces were not part of the regional targeting strategy for most parties on Facebook. The earlier discussion of the electoral system is helpful here. As mentioned, a party will focus on areas where it has a reasonable chance of finishing first. "This excludes two groups of ridings – those where the party is certain to win and those where it is certain to lose."[42] The Prairie provinces very much fit into those two categories for the main three political parties. The Prairies have long been a Conservative stronghold. In this election, the Conservatives won 83 per cent of seats in the three provinces including all the seats in Saskatchewan. Since the creation of the united Conservative Party in 2004, the NDP and the Liberals have had minimal electoral success in the Prairies. Thus, the rules of the game for campaigning under SMP provide good reasons for the lack of Facebook ads seen by voters in the Prairies despite the not unsubstantial number of seats there. That said, perhaps some extra digital attention was needed, as Conservative support fell in Alberta by nearly 14 per cent in the election compared to 2019.[43] While they failed to win any seats, smaller conservative parties such as the Maverick Party and the People's Party hurt the Conservative vote. Indeed, as Table 9.2 shows, Albertans were one of the main targets for the PPC on Facebook (15.5 per cent).

The data on New Brunswick and Nova Scotia are skewed by the Green Party's efforts. Though only purchasing six Facebook ads during the 2021 election, there is still evidence of regionalized campaign communication for the Green Party. Most people seeing these six ads were in the Maritime provinces. The Greens have had success there. In 2019, the provincial wing of the Green Party became the official opposition in Prince Edward Island. That same year, the federal Greens won a seat in New Brunswick for the first time (which they did not retain in 2021). They also won three seats in the 2020 New Brunswick election. That said, with such a small number of Facebook ads, it is difficult to provide any strong conclusion about the Greens.

Now that we have provided a broad overview of the parties' use of Facebook ads, another way to analyze the data is to consider ads that were solely targeted at individual provinces or territories and which ones were pan-national. As mentioned above, the summary data of Facebook ads cannot explicitly demonstrate intention but can provide clues about to whom the ads were directed. This is particularly the case when ads are singularly concentrated in a geographic region. Borrowing from Gitomer and colleagues, who conducted a similar study in the United States, we located the number of regionally-dominated ads – those receiving 99 per cent or more of its audience from a single region.[44] We define pan-national ads as ones where no more than 49 per cent of the audience is from one province and at least 5 per cent of the audience is found amongst three provinces.

Table 9.3 presents the number of regionally-dominated ads for five parties; the BQ is excluded as all of their ads are targeted to Quebec. It reveals that 338 (or 30.7 per cent) of the ads were regionally dominated. The use of regionally dominated ads mirrors our earlier findings that Facebook is used by political parties significantly more in some parts of the country than in others. This was particularly the case for audiences in Quebec with 115 regionally dominated ads, followed by British Columbia (seventy-four) and Ontario (sixty-five). Not all parties embraced this geographically concentrated form of advertising equally. Indeed, the Greens and PPC did not purchase a single regionally dominated ad. This seems consistent with their general reluctance to use Facebook ads altogether. Despite being the most active Facebook advertisers, the Liberals used regionally concentrated ads only 17 per cent of the time. When they did use these regionally targeted ads, they were most likely to target audiences in Quebec (thirty-eight), Ontario (thirty) or BC (sixteen). Interestingly, the CPC used regionally-dominated ads almost exclusively to advertise to audiences in Quebec (fifty of their fifty-three region-specific ads, the other three being directed to Ontario). In fact, on only six occasions did a Conservative ad find an audience in Quebec without being regionally dominated.

The NDP stood out from the other four parties, with a vast majority of their ads (69.5 per cent) being geographically concentrated. Directing regionally dominated ads to every province and territory outside of New Brunswick, Manitoba, and PEI, the NDP were also the most diverse regional advertisers. Although, like the Liberals, there was a noticeable concentration of ads in British Columbia (fifty-eight), Quebec (sixty-five) and, to a lesser extent, Ontario (thirty-five). figure 9.2 provides an example of a regionally dominated ad. In the ad, there is a region or constituency-specific text-based message encouraging voters in Burnaby North-Seymour to vote for both the NDP leader, Jagmeet Singh, and NDP candidate Jim Hanson. Included below the text is a thirty-second video of Hanson

Table 9.4 | Number and percentage of pan-national ads by party

	Number	Per cent
CPC	100	42.7
GPC	1	16.7
LPC	163	28.6
NDP	56	20.8
PPC	24	100.0
Total	344	31.2

(n=1,102)

questioning Justin Trudeau's leadership qualities and promoting region-specific issues.[45] Finally, there is a link which takes audiences to Hanson's personal NDP website. Other examples include: the Liberals' "'Sudbury Airport will receive a non-repayable contribution of $3.5 million from FedNor,' said Nickel Belt MP Marc Serré, to a round of applause inside the terminal"; and the Conservatives' "Join Erin O'Toole for his first election rally in Richmond Hill on August 17th at 6 p.m. Sign up now!" Regionally dominated ads, such as this, show the power of Facebook for political actors. These examples show that ads are not just targeted to the province but to the individual riding level. However, that is not to suggest that all or most of the regionally directed ads were tailored to local or even regional issues. In fact, many regionally directed ads had a generic message. For instance, the Conservatives produced a regionally dominated ad that attacked Justin Trudeau's economic performance using both a text-based message and image. While only shown in Ontario, there was no mention of Ontarians or locations in Ontario in the ad.[46] Another example of generic messaging was get-out-to-vote ads, like the NDP's regionally directed ad to BC which simply stated: "Early voting on Sunday, September 12 and Monday, September 13." This lack of regional or local specificity within the messaging should not take away from the fact that parties are spending more money to direct ads to certain parts of the country than others. That is, the purchasing of a generic get-out-to-vote ad solely directed at BC can speak to the parties' regional intentions as much as a regionally directed ad with messaging tailored to that province or individual riding.

Finally, we explore this data in the other direction by looking at pan-national ads (Table 9.4). Overall, we find that only around one in three Facebook ads had a broad audience, which included several provinces. It is worth noting that it was very rare that a Facebook ad was shown in every province and territory. Certainly, as Table 9.2 shows, Canadians in the territories saw very few party Facebook ads in general. The PPC had the most pan-national Facebook strategy. While most of its ads were targeted in Ontario, almost all of its twenty-four ads were seen by Canadians in every province (though not the territories). Similarly, the Conservative ads were most likely to be seen by Ontarians but around one in four was seen across the country. One example was "Four women came forward with allegations of harassment against a Liberal MP. Trudeau refuses to act," which was seen in every province except Quebec. It appears that the Conservatives hewed to a French-only advertising strategy in Quebec; only seven Conservative ads that were not in the French language were shown in Quebec. This strategy was not shared by the other parties, which purchased both English and French-language Facebook ads aimed at Quebec voters. Around one-third of Liberal Facebook ads and one-fifth of the NDP's were pan-national. Even with a very generous definition of pan-national advertising, we still find that only 31 per cent of ads had a national audience. This once more provides evidence to support our claim that in this election, the tool of paid Facebook advertising was used by the parties predominantly as a means of regional targeting.

CONCLUSIONS

In this chapter we considered one aspect of the digital campaign: Facebook ads. The Facebook Ad Library is relatively new, and therefore provided us with a unique opportunity to consider the way regionalism intersects with campaign communication. However, it is worth remembering once again the limitations of the Facebook Ad Library and that the information data remain largely the product of estimation.[47] That said, the Facebook Ad Library allows a peek behind the curtain of the targeting strategies of political actors. As such, it provides the first real ability to reflect on the claims made by Carty,

Cross, and Young more than twenty years ago. Overall, our analysis shows strong evidence of regionalized campaign communication in the use of Facebook ads by Canada's political parties in the 2021 federal election. While Facebook ads were seen by Canadians across the country, they were seen significantly more by those in particular parts of the country, namely Ontario, Quebec, and British Columbia. The implication of this is that parties are spending limited funding to ensure certain ads reach specific regions more than others. Without longitudinal data, it is difficult to know whether this regionalized approach is a feature specific to this election campaign or if parties have been using digital technologies in regionalized ways for some time. As mentioned earlier, not all digital technology (e.g., websites and Twitter feeds) has the ability to readily target geographic areas, but email, for instance, could be used to send regional messages.

In conclusion, we would like to reflect on the implications of regionalized digital ads in the Canadian campaign. First, Carty, Cross, and Young argue we should be concerned about private conversations between parties and voters: "These conversations occur beyond the radar screens of the community's national political dialogue. Parties can deliver different messages to voters in different regions or provinces and do so without the transparency and accountability inherent in the traditional media."[48] Even though the Facebook Ad Library is available to the media, researchers, and voters alike, the sheer amount of advertising produced over the thirty-six-day campaign means that it is difficult to assess the nature and content of all of it, especially in real time. This should bring to mind broader concerns in digital politics about echo chambers. An echo chamber exists when a person only encounters information or opinions that reflect and reinforce their own. In addition to purposely filtering out ideas and opinions one is uninterested in, algorithms in social media can lead to users having very different information experiences.[49] As Cass Sunstein argues, in a "well-functioning democracy, people do not live in echo chambers or information cocoons. They see or hear a wide range of topics and ideas."[50] Second, our finding about regionally-dominated ads raises concerns about campaign finance. That is, the ability to target messages to localized voters means that national parties have a means of directing advertising to particular ridings or constituencies, potentially circumventing local spending limits.[51] While regional targeting might be an effective and efficient strategy for parties, it may not be very good for Canadian democracy.

NOTES

1 Philip N. Howard, "Deep Democracy, Thin Citizenship: The Impact of Digital Media in Political Campaign Strategy," *The Annals of the American Academy of Political and Social Science* 597, no. 1 (2005): 158.

2 Amelia M. Jamison, David A. Broniatowski, Mark Dredze, Zach Wood-Doughty, DureAden Khan, and Sandra Crouse Quinn, "Vaccine-Related Advertising in the Facebook Ad Archive," *Vaccine* 38, no. 3 (16 January 2020): 512–20, https://doi.org/10.1016/j.vaccine.2019.10.066.

3 Kelley Cotter, Mel Medeiros, Chankyung Pak, and Kjerstin Thorson, "'Reach the Right People': The Politics of 'Interests' in Facebook's Classification System for Ad Targeting," *Big Data & Society* 8, no. 1 (2021): 1.

4 R. Kenneth Carty, William Cross, and Lisa Young, *Rebuilding Canadian Party Politics* (Vancouver: UBC Press, 2001).

5 Carty, Cross, and Young, *Rebuilding Canadian Party Politics*, 200–1.

6 Tamara A. Small, "Canadian Cyberparties: Reflections on Internet-Based Campaigning and Party Systems," *Canadian Journal of Political Science* 40, no. 3 (2007): 639–57.

7 "Canadian Internet Use Survey, 2020," Statistics Canada, last modified 22 June 2021, https://www150.statcan.gc.ca/n1/daily-quotidien/210622/dq210622b-eng.htm.

8 Leyland Cecco, "Jagmeet Singh: The Ex-Lawyer and TikTok Star Who Could Topple Trudeau," *Guardian*, 12 September 2021, https://www.theguardian.com/world/2021/sep/12/jagmeet-singh-the-ex-lawyer-and-tik-tok-star-who-could-topple-trudeau; and, Hannah Thibedeau, "Conservatives Say Their 'Virtual' Campaign Strategy Is Paying off Already," CBC News, 27 August 2021, https://www.cbc.ca/news/politics/otoole-conservative-election-virtual-campaign-town-hall-pandemic-1.6154822.

9 Grant Kippen, *The Use of Information Technologies by a Political Party* (British Columbia: SFU-UBC Centre for the Study of Government Business, 2000).

10 Michael M. Franz, Erika Franklin Fowler, Travis Ridout, and Meredith Yiran Wang, "The Issue Focus of Online and Television Advertising in the 2016 Presidential Campaign," *American Politics Research* 48, no. 1 (2020): 111.

11 *Canada Elections Act, Statutes of Canada* 2000, c.9.

12 Christine B. Williams and Girish J. "Jeff" Gulati, "Digital Media Expenditures in Presidential Campaigns, 2008–20," in *The Internet and*

the 2020 Campaign, ed. Jody C. Baumgartner and Terri L Towner (Lanham, MD: Lexington Books, 2021), 25–48.

13 Adina Gitomer, Pavel V. Oleinikov, Laura M. Baum, Erika Franklin Fowler, and Saray Shai, "Geographic Impressions in Facebook Political Ads," *Applied Network Science* 6, no. 1 (February 2021): 18, https://doi.org/10.1007/s41109-020-00350-7.

14 Tamara A. Small, "Digital Campaigning the Era of Misinformation," in *The Canadian Federal Election of 2019*, eds. Jon H. Pammett and Christopher Dornan (Montreal: McGill-Queen's University Press, 2020), 198–220.

15 "Registry Requirements for Political Ads on Online Platforms," Elections Canada, last modified 28 January 2022, https://www.elections.ca/content.aspx?section=pol&dir=regifaq&document=index&lang=e#q3.

16 Tom Dobber, Ronan Ó Fathaigh, and Frederik Zuiderveen Borgesius, "The Regulation of Online Political Micro-Targeting in Europe," *Internet Policy Review* 8, no. 4 (2019).

17 Small, "Digital Campaigning the Era of Misinformation."

18 Brian Budd and Tamara A. Small, "Say It Loud and Say It Proud: Populist Digital Advertising by Canada Proud in the 2019 Federal Election," (2021 CPSA Annual Conference, Virtual, 7 June 2021).

19 "Number of Facebook Users in Canada from 2017 to 2026," Statista, 25 August 2021, https://www.statista.com/statistics/282364/number-of-facebook-users-in-canada/.

20 Small, "Digital Campaigning the Era of Misinformation."

21 Liberal Party of Canada, "Liberal Party of Canada | Parti libéral du Canada," Facebook Ad Library.

22 Small, "Digital Campaigning the Era of Misinformation."

23 Budd and Small, "Say It Loud and Say It Proud: Populist Digital Advertising by Canada Proud in the 2019 Federal Election."

24 The DDP with the Online Political Transparency Project, "DDP Research Memo #6: Political Advertising on Facebook," Public Policy Forum, 10 October 2019, https://ppforum.ca/articles/ddp-research-memo-6/.

25 Colin Bennett and Jesse Gordon, "Understanding the 'Micro' in Political Micro-Targeting: An Analysis of Facebook Digital Advertising in the 2019 Federal Canadian Election," *Canadian Journal of Communication* 46, no. 3 (2021).

26 Data can also be attained by using the Ad Library API with Facebook's Github repo.

27 In total, there were 1,150 digital ads (not including duplicate ads, which were combined by the Ad Library, given their similar creative and text style).

28 Arthur Capozzi, Gianmarco De Francisci Morales, Yelena Mejova, Corrado Monti, André Panisson, and Daniela Paolotti, "Facebook Ads: Politics of Migration in Italy," in *Social Informatics*, eds. Samin Aref, Kalina Bontcheva, Marco Braghieri, Frank Dignum Fosca Giannotti, Francesco Grisolia, and Dino Pedreschi (Cham: Springer International Publishing, 2020), 43–57, https://doi.org/10.1007/978-3-030-60975-7_4.

29 Capozzi, Morales, Mejova, Monti, Panisson, and Paolotti, "Facebook Ads," 50–51.

30 Tamara A. Small and Harold J. Jansen, "Introduction: Twenty Years of Digital Politics in Canada," in *Digital Politics in Canada: Promises and Realities*, eds. Tamara A. Small and Harold J. Jansen (Toronto: University of Toronto Press, 2020).

31 Christopher Cochrane and Andrea Perrella, "Regions, Regionalism, and Regional Differences in Canada," *Canadian Journal of Political Science* 45, no. 4 (2012): 829–53.

32 William Cross, *Political Parties* (Vancouver: UBC Press, 2004).

33 Thomas Flanagan, *Winning Power: Canadian Campaigning in the 21st Century* (Montreal: McGill-Queen's University Press, 2014).

34 Flanagan, *Winning Power*, 32.

35 Cross, *Political Parties*, 129.

36 Scott Pruysers, "Canadian Party Politics in the 2000s: A Re-Examination of the Regionalization Thesis," *Canadian Political Science Review* 8, no. 1 (2014): 27–42.

37 Laura B. Stephenson, Andrea Lawlor, William P. Cross, André Blais, and Elisabeth Gidengil, *Provincial Battles, National Prize?* (Montreal: McGill-Queen's Press, 2019).

38 Rachel K. Gibson, Michael Margolis, David Resnick, and Stephen J. Ward, "Election Campaigning on the WWW in the USA and UK: A Comparative Analysis," *Party Politics* 9, no. 1 (2003): 47–75.

39 It is worth noting that 88 per cent of BQ ads were directed to Quebec. Indeed, small percentages of several ads were viewed in other provinces and even the northeastern United States. This speaks to the difference between intended and actual audiences.

40 Éric Montigny, "The Battle for Quebec," in *The Canadian Federal Election of 2019*, eds. Jon H. Pammett and Christopher Dornan (Montreal: McGill-Queen's University Press, 2020), 5.

41 "Opinions on the Upcoming Federal Election: A Postmedia-Léger Poll," Léger, 17 September 2021, https://leger360.com/surveys/opinions-on-the-upcoming-federal-election-a-postmedia-leger-poll/.

42 William Cross, Jonathan Malloy, Tamara A. Small, and Laura B. Stephenson, *Fighting for Votes* (Vancouver: UBC Press, 2015).

43 Elise von Scheel, "The Conservative Vote in Alberta Shrank. Here's Why," CBC News, 30 September 2021, https://www.cbc.ca/news/canada/calgary/conservative-vote-alberta-election-1.6194190.

44 Adina Gitomer, Pavel V. Oleinikov, Laura M. Baum, Erika Franklin Fowler, and Saray Shai, "Geographic Impressions in Facebook Political Ads," *Applied Network Science* 6, no. 1 (February 2021): 18, https://doi.org/10.1007/s41109-020-00350-7.

45 Canada's NDP, "Canada's NDP / Le NPD du Canada," Facebook Ad Library, https://www.facebook.com/ads/library/?id=552460909362157.

46 Conservative Party of Canada, "Conservative Party of Canada-Parti conservateur du Canada," Facebook Ad Library.

47 Sam Power and Ben Mason, "Mobilizing or Chasing Voters on Facebook? Analysing Echo-Chamber Effects at the UK Parliamentary General Election 2019," *Parliamentary Affairs*, no. gsab043 (July 2021), https://doi.org/10.1093/pa/gsab043.

48 Carty, Cross, and Young, *Rebuilding Canadian Party Politics*, 210.

49 Small and Jansen, "Introduction: Twenty Years of Digital Politics in Canada." While some have argued that the consequences of self-selected echo chambers have been overstated, we are here referring to algorithmic echo chambers – not information sources that individuals choose themselves, but information sources that instead choose individuals.

50 Cass R Sunstein, *#Republic: Divided Democracy in the Age of Social Media* (New Jersey: Princeton University Press, 2018), ix.

51 Damian Tambini, Sharif Labo, Emma Goodman, Martin Moore, "Media Policy Brief 19: The New Political Campaigning," LSE Media Policy Project, 2017, https://eprints.lse.ac.uk/71945/7/LSE%20MPP%20Policy%20Brief%2019%20-%20The%20new%20political%20campaigning_final.pdf.

10

Still Not There: Diversity and Inclusion in the 2021 Canadian Election Campaign

Erin Tolley, Aneurin Bosley, and Nana aba Duncan

In 2015, Prime Minister Justin Trudeau stood in front of his newly selected ministers and proclaimed it a "cabinet that looks like Canada." That cabinet had an equal number of men and women, five racialized ministers (including two who wear turbans), two Indigenous ministers, one who openly identifies as LGBTQ2, and two with disabilities. Although representational issues have always been one component of cabinet-making, Trudeau's choices and the explicitness with which they were discussed signalled a new commitment to increased diversity at the highest levels of public policy-making.

This commitment responded, in part, to steadily growing public pressure for more diversity in parliament. Increasingly, parties are recognizing the necessity for, and benefits of, institutions that reflect the demographics of the populations they serve and represent. In turn, the proportion of women, racialized and Indigenous candidates and members of parliament has risen over time.[1] Nonetheless, parties and successive governments have been accused of only paying lip service to diversity, while resisting the hard work of changing the culture of parliament and addressing systemic inequality in society. Some research suggests the media are complicit, with a predominantly white parliamentary press gallery that frequently shows a limited understanding of discrimination and its intersection with key policy areas.[2]

To understand these dynamics, we examine the 2021 campaign through the lens of diversity and inclusion. Using new data on the candidates who ran in this election, we track who ran, for which parties, and under what conditions. We then look at what diversity promises were made by each party, and how the media covered these issues. We show that incremental gains were achieved, with increases in the number of women, racialized, and Indigenous candidates. There were also important increases in the number of nonbinary and LGBTQ2 candidates standing for election. Nonetheless, the complexion of the House of Commons remained relatively unchanged, in part because a number of these candidates ran in districts that were not competitive for their parties. This pattern cements the so-called "sacrificial lamb" thesis, which shows not only that parties offer up diverse candidates in losing situations, but also that they offer them fewer resources; taken together, these tendencies stymie efforts to diversify parliament.[3]

Taking this analysis further, we examine not just who carried each party's banner, but also what the parties promised to do in areas related to diversity and inclusion, and how these issues emerged on the campaign trail. We show that in the 2021 campaign, diversity was not absent, but its presence was largely symbolic. This pattern is consistent with past elections and is why progress toward inclusion has been incremental, incomplete, and often nonexistent. Because the media have been dogged by similar challenges – including accusations of sexism and racism – parties and politicians have frequently been able to sidestep uncomfortable questions about their record on inclusion. We offer some suggestions for addressing these gaps.

THE CANDIDATES

We focus our candidate analysis on the major parties: the Liberals, Conservatives, New Democrats, Bloc Québécois, and Greens.[4] There is no centralized source of information on candidate demographics in Canada, so we tracked and recorded this information using publicly available information in candidate biographies, social media, and news reports,[5] a method that has been used elsewhere to understand who runs for office in Canadian politics.[6] Even a focus on publicly available information leaves some gaps, so we also conducted a small survey, sending the questionnaire to 113 candidates for whom we were able to identify a valid email address, but unable to find much information publicly; of these, thirty-five responded, for a response rate of 28.3 per cent. We used these responses to fill in gaps in the data set.[7] We suspect that the snap election call, shortened campaign period, and ongoing pandemic contributed to more "paper or name-on-ballot" candidates; these are individuals who run so their party can have a presence in the district, but most are not expected to win and therefore do not mount serious or sustained campaigns.

We highlight candidates' gender, racial, and Indigenous background, as well as the diversity and competitiveness of the district in which they ran.[8] Although other identities – including sexual orientation, religion, and ability – are important and politically salient, these are often not publicly disclosed or are less visible, making them more difficult to gather complete information on.[9]

DIVERSITY AMONG CANDIDATES

In total, 1,343 candidates ran for the five major parties. As is shown in Tables 10.1 and 10.2, all parties fielded a larger proportion of racialized candidates than in the previous election. Most parties also fielded a larger proportion of Indigenous candidates, though for the Bloc and Conservatives the proportion was the same. All major parties but the Greens also ran a larger proportion of women. Across all five parties, the proportion of racialized candidates rose from 17.1 per cent in 2019 to 21.9 per cent in 2021, while the proportion of Indigenous candidates went from 3.9 per cent in 2019 to 5.5 per cent in 2021.[10] The proportion of women candidates across the major parties also rose slightly between 2019 and 2021, from 41.4 per cent to 43 per cent. The proportion of candidates who identify as neither men nor women (nonbinary) also rose between 2019 and 2021, going from 0.6 per cent to 0.9 per cent, although the actual numbers are small (just twelve nonbinary candidates in 2021 and nine in 2019).

Tables 10.1 and 10.2 also show candidate data going back to 2008.[11] The pattern over the last five elections is one of incremental change in candidate diversity, with some notable jumps (for example, in the proportion of women who ran between 2015 and 2019), as well as some backsliding and plateaus.

When it comes to running racialized candidates, the Bloc and the Greens appear as laggards, although the Bloc made a sizable leap in 2021, increasing the proportion of racialized candidates on its slate from 5.1 per cent in 2019 to 11.5 per cent this time around. Even so, this result is only marginally higher than the proportion of racialized candidates they ran in 2008. The Bloc has steadily increased

Table 10.1 | Candidate race and indigeneity, 2008–21

		Indigenous		Racialized		White	
		%	(n)	%	(n)	%	(n)
BQ	2021	1.3	(1)	11.5	(9)	87.2	(68)
	2019	1.3	(1)	5.1	(4)	93.6	(73)
	2015			2.6	(2)	97.4	(76)
	2011			8.0	(6)	92.0	(69)
	2008			10.8	(8)	89.2	(66)
CPC	2021	1.8	(6)	19.7	(66)	78.5	(263)
	2019	1.8	(6)	17.5	(59)	80.8	(273)
	2015	1.2	(4)	16.3	(55)	82.5	(279)
	2011	1.6	(5)	10.4	(32)	87.9	(270)
	2008	1.6	(5)	11.4	(35)	86.9	(266)
GPC	2021	6.0	(15)	13.1	(33)	80.9	(203)
	2019	3.3	(11)	11.6	(39)	85.1	(286)
LPC	2021	7.1	(24)	25.4	(86)	67.5	(228)
	2019	4.7	(16)	18.7	(63)	76.6	(258)
	2015	5.4	(18)	17.6	(59)	77.1	(259)
	2011	1.3	(4)	9.8	(30)	88.9	(273)
	2008	2.3	(7)	11.1	(34)	86.6	(265)
NDP	2021	8.1	(27)	29.3	(98)	62.6	(209)
	2019	6.5	(22)	23.4	(79)	70.0	(236)
	2015	5.9	(20)	14.2	(48)	79.8	(269)
	2011	2.3	(7)	10.4	(32)	87.3	(269)
	2008	2.3	(7)	11.4	(35)	86.3	(264)
All major parties	2021	5.5	(73)	21.9	(292)	72.7	(971)
	2019	3.9	(56)	17.1	(244)	79.0	(1126)
	2015	3.9	(42)	15.1	(164)	81.1	(883)
	2011	1.6	(16)	10.0	(100)	88.4	(881)
	2008	1.9	(19)	11.3	(112)	86.8	(861)

Note: Data on diversity among Green Party candidates was not collected prior to 2019.

Table 10.2 | Candidate gender, 2008–21

		Men		Women		Non-binary	
		%	(n)	%	(n)	%	(n)
BQ	2021	52.6	(41)	47.4	(37)		
	2019	55.1	(43)	44.9	(35)		
	2015	71.8	(56)	28.2	(22)		
	2011	68.0	(51)	32.0	(24)		
	2008	73.3	(55)	26.7	(20)		
CPC	2021	66.7	(224)	33.3	(112)		
	2019	69.2	(234)	30.8	(104)		
	2015	80.5	(272)	19.5	(66)		
	2011	78.8	(242)	21.2	(65)		
	2008	79.2	(243)	20.8	(64)		
GPC	2021	54.8	(138)	43.3	(109)	2.0	(5)
	2019	52.4	(177)	46.2	(156)	1.5	(5)
LPC	2021	56.5	(191)	43.5	(147)		
	2019	60.4	(204)	39.3	(133)	0.3	(1)
	2015	68.9	(233)	31.1	(105)		
	2011	70.8	(218)	29.2	(90)		
	2008	63.5	(195)	36.5	(112)		
NDP	2021	47.0	(159)	50.9	(172)	2.1	(7)
	2019	50.6	(171)	48.5	(164)	0.9	(3)
	2015	57.3	(193)	42.7	(144)		
	2011	60.1	(185)	39.9	(123)		
	2008	66.6	(205)	33.4	(103)		
All major parties	2021	56.1	(753)	43.0	(577)	0.9	(12)
	2019	58.0	(829)	41.4	(592)	0.6	(9)
	2015	69.1	(754)	30.9	(337)		
	2011	69.7	(696)	30.3	(302)		
	2008	70.0	(698)	30.0	(299)		

Note: Data on diversity among Green Party candidates was not collected prior to 2019.

the number of women on their slate, second now only to the NDP. By contrast, they have historically struggled to nominate Indigenous candidates, a pattern that continued in 2021.

Despite having a Black woman leader, a factor that could encourage more candidate diversity, just 13.1 per cent of the Green Party's slate was racialized, an increase from the prior election, but still the second smallest proportion among the parties. The Greens were also the only party for whom the proportion of women candidates fell, going from 46.2 per cent in 2019 to 43.4 per cent in 2021. One factor in this shortfall could be the organizational problems the Greens encountered during the period for registering candidates (see chapter 6). Despite identifying candidates to run in every electoral district, the party struggled to collect the local nomination signatures that are required to register a candidate and ultimately fielded just 252 candidates out of a possible 338.[12] Even so, the Greens increased the number of Indigenous candidates from 3.3 per cent in 2019 to 6 per cent in 2021.

The Liberals had a large increase in the proportion of racialized candidates, going from 18.6 per cent in 2019 to 25.4 per cent in 2021, continuing the party's steady growth on this front since 2011. The number of racialized candidates running for the Liberals has steadily increased since 2011. The proportion of Indigenous candidates for the Liberals has been more variable, but in 2021 they came in second among the parties. One explanation for these trends could be that in 2016, the Liberal Party changed its nomination rules to require local associations to demonstrate they had conducted a thorough search for equity-seeking candidates before they could hold their nomination meetings. The Liberals also have made an explicit appeal to prospective women candidates through their "Ask Her" initiative. Although the direct effect of this campaign is unclear, in 2021, 43.5 per cent of the Liberal slate identified as women.

Overall, the NDP had the most diverse candidate slate, with the largest proportion of racialized candidates (29 per cent), Indigenous candidates (8 per cent), and nonbinary candidates (2.1 per cent). The NDP was also the only party to put forward a gender-equal candidate slate, with 50.9 per cent of their candidates identifying as women. The NDP is the only federal party with an explicit affirmative action policy for equity-seeking candidates, and, in this election, they were also the only party to set an explicit target, committing to a candidate slate that was at least 50 per cent women. They also

Table 10.3 | Candidate gender, race, and indigeneity, 2021

		Men		Women		Non-binary	
		%	(n)	%	(n)	%	(n)
BQ	Indigenous	100.0	(1)				
	Racialized	22.2	(2)	77.8	(7)		
	White	55.9	(38)	44.1	(30)		
CPC	Indigenous	33.3	(2)	66.7	(4)		
	Racialized	60.6	(40)	39.4	(26)		
	White	69.2	(182)	30.8	(81)		
GPC	Indigenous	33.3	(5)	66.7	(10)		
	Racialized	60.6	(20)	39.4	(13)		
	White	55.2	(112)	42.4	(86)	2.5	(5)
LPC	Indigenous	58.3	(14)	41.7	(10)		
	Racialized	58.1	(50)	41.9	(36)		
	White	55.7	(127)	44.3	(101)		
NDP	Indigenous	37.0	(10)	59.3	(16)	3.7	(1)
	Racialized	48.0	(47)	51.0	(50)	1.0	(1)
	White	47.8	(100)	49.8	(104)	2.4	(5)
All major parties	Indigenous	43.8	(32)	54.8	(40)	1.4	(1)
	Racialized	54.5	(159)	45.2	(132)	0.3	(1)
	White	57.6	(559)	41.4	(402)	1.0	(10)

required that districts with an outgoing incumbent replace that candidate with one from a historically under-represented group. Their results suggest these concrete measures to increase the diversity of the candidate slate can pay dividends.

Meanwhile, the Conservatives adopt more of a free-market approach with minimal intervention to increase candidate diversity. They saw no change in the proportion of Indigenous candidates in 2021, and of the five parties, fielded the smallest proportion of women candidates at 33.2 per cent, although this was up from 30.8 per cent in 2019. Nonetheless, the Conservatives increased the number of racialized candidates they ran, reaching 19.6 per cent in 2021, an increase from 17.5 per cent in 2019.

Across the major parties, Table 10.3 shows candidates who are white men outnumbered white women by a margin of 57.6 per cent to 41.4 per cent. That split was somewhat narrower for racialized candidates (where 54.5 per cent were men compared to 45.2 per cent women), but reversed for Indigenous candidates, where women outnumbered men by 54.8 per cent to 43.8 per cent. That margin was even larger for some parties. For example, Indigenous women candidates for the Conservatives outnumbered Indigenous men 66.7 per cent to 33.3 per cent, and in the NDP by 59.3 per cent to 37 per cent. For the NDP and the Bloc, racialized women candidates also outnumbered racialized men. The aggregate results suggest that Indigenous women may benefit from a "complementarity advantage," where their intersecting identities provide a boost over Indigenous men.[13] It is difficult to say why: it might be that parties seek to "check two boxes" with one candidate, or that they wish to increase diversity but preserve white male power by sidelining Indigenous men. These explanations are not completely persuasive, however, given that we see a different pattern for racialized men and women. Indigenous women's predominance may therefore reflect their long history of political organization and mobilization.[14]

CANDIDATE COMPETITIVENESS

Nominating diverse candidates is just part of the story; we also need to consider the contexts in which they are running. We therefore compare candidate diversity by district competitiveness. Competitiveness is measured using each party's margin of the vote in the past three elections (2015, 2019, 2021) when the number of electoral districts and their boundaries were the same. Using Elections Canada's official electoral returns, in each district, we took the difference between each party's percentage of the vote and that of the victor. A vote margin of zero indicates the party won the district, while a vote margin of thirty indicates their percentage of the vote in that district was thirty points behind that of the winner. We averaged each party's vote margin in each district over the past three elections and consider a party to be competitive in that district if the average is 10 per cent or less. This measure is straightforward albeit somewhat blunt.[15] In some cases, a party might have won a district in 2021, but it would still be considered uncompetitive if it was a long shot for the seat in the previous two elections. For example, the Conservatives won the Nova Scotia district of South Shore-St Margarets in 2021, with 40.9 per cent of the popular vote, but the Liberals won the elections in 2019 and 2015 by large margins; as a result, the Conservatives' average vote margin across the three election was 16 per cent, six points higher than our threshold. Based on this measure, the Liberals are competitive in 195 of the country's 338 districts, the highest number among the five parties, unsurprising given they have won the most seats during this time. The Conservatives are competitive in 151, the NDP in forty-three, the Bloc in forty-one, and the Greens in two districts.

As figure 10.1 shows, the Liberals ran the highest proportion of racialized candidates (25.6 per cent) in their competitive districts. Although the NDP had the largest proportion of racialized candidates overall, just 18.6 per cent of their competitive districts featured a racialized candidate. The Conservatives ran racialized candidates in 10.6 per cent of their competitive districts while the Bloc ran racialized candidates in 2.4 per cent (although this was just one candidate). The Greens ran racialized candidates in no competitive districts, although there were just two such districts for the party.

The NDP ran Indigenous candidates in the largest proportion of competitive districts, at 9.3 per cent. The Liberals ran Indigenous candidates in 4.6 per cent of the party's competitive districts, while the Conservatives ran Indigenous candidates in 2 per cent. That proportion was 2.4 per cent for the Bloc and zero for the Greens.

The NDP and the Greens were the only parties to run women candidates in at least half of their competitive districts. The NDP had women candidates in 53.5 per cent of competitive districts compared with 50.5 per cent in noncompetitive ones. The Greens ran women candidates in 50 per cent of competitive districts. However, since the Greens are only considered competitive in two districts, this 50 per cent represents one candidate, former party leader Elizabeth May in the BC district of Saanich-Gulf Islands. The other three parties ran a smaller percentage of women candidates in competitive districts. The Liberals and the Bloc had 39 per cent of competitive districts represented by women candidates, compared with 29.1 per cent for the Conservatives.

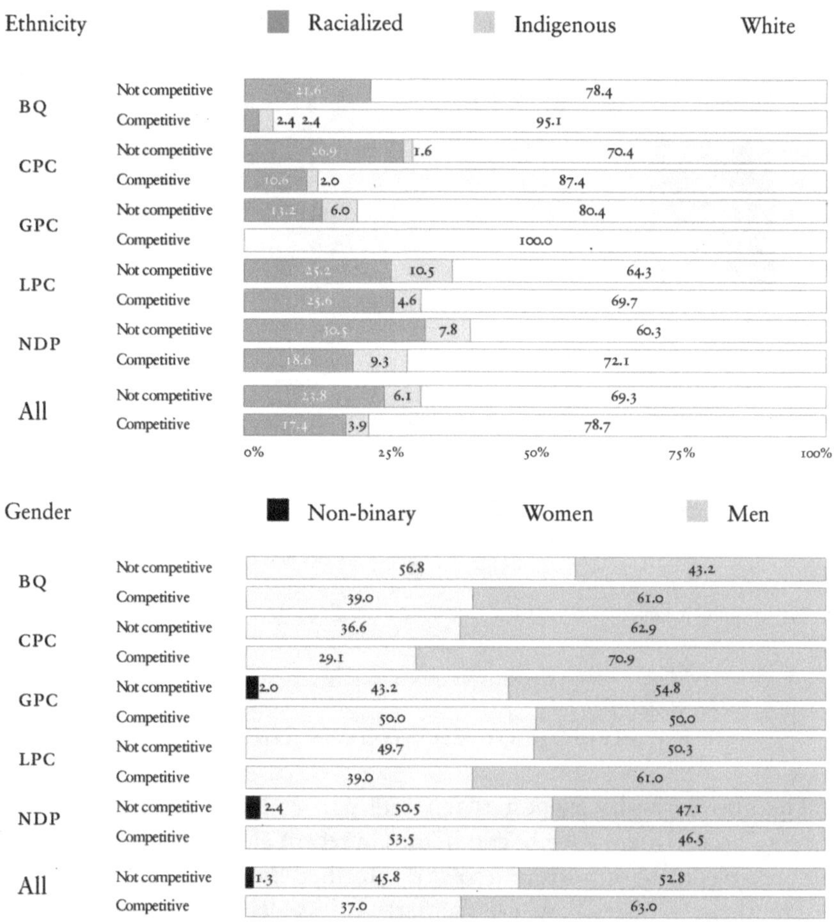

Figure 10.1 | Candidate diversity by party and district competitiveness, 2021

More men (36.1 per cent) were candidates in competitive districts than women (27.7 per cent) as were more white (35 per cent) than racialized (25.7 per cent) or Indigenous (23.3 per cent) candidates. As a result, across all districts and parties, candidates in competitive districts tend to be white and male. More specifically, in 78.7 per cent of competitive districts, candidates were white, and in 63 per cent they were men.

Figure 10.2 | Proportion of MPs by race, indigeneity, and gender, 2008–21

COMPOSITION OF THE HOUSE OF COMMONS

The above results suggest that while parties have made efforts to recruit a broader range of candidates in recent elections, those candidates' electoral opportunities are diminished by a tendency to nominate them in districts where the party is less electorally competitive. Given this, it is hardly surprising that the 2021 election resulted in a House of Commons that is represented predominantly by men and by people who are white. These are the candidates placed in districts with the best chance of winning. Although some of these privileged contenders are incumbents, and incumbents are more likely to be men and white, past research shows the effect is not simply a function of this incumbency advantage.[16]

As shown in figure 10.2, the 44th Parliament will feature a House of Commons where 15.7 per cent (n=53) of MPs are racialized, 3.8 per cent (n=13) are Indigenous and 30.5 per cent (n=103) are women. These are incremental increases in the proportion of women (28.2 per cent), racialized (15.1 per cent) and Indigenous (3 per cent) MPs who took office following the 2019 election.

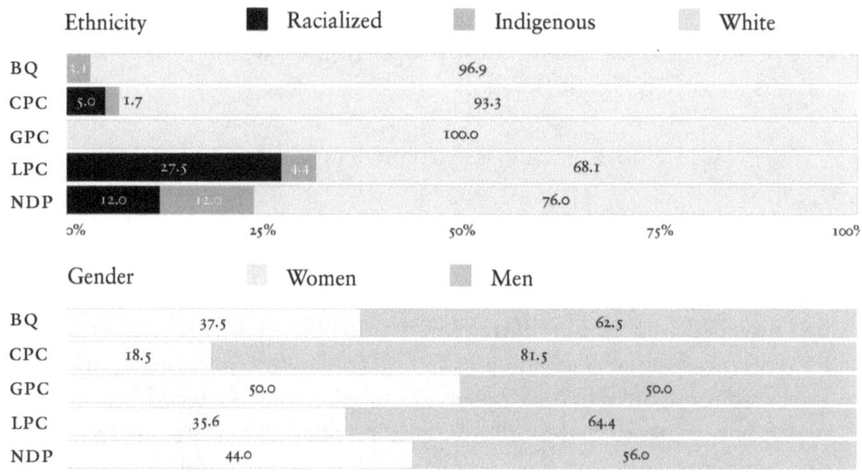

Figure 10.3 | Proportion of MPs from each party by race, indigeneity, and gender, 2021

When we tabulate gender and race together, 56.2 per cent (n=190) of MPs following the 2021 election are white men, while 24.3 per cent (n=82) are white women. Racialized women make up just 5.3 per cent (n=18) of MPs, while racialized men make up 10.4 per cent (n=35). Indigenous women make up 0.9 per cent (n=3) of MPs, while Indigenous men make up 3 per cent (n=10).

As with the overall candidate slate, some parties elected a higher proportion of women and racialized candidates to the House of Commons in 2021. figure 10.3 shows that the Liberals have the highest proportion of racialized MPs in their caucus, at 27.5 per cent (n=44), followed by the NDP at 12 per cent (n=3) and the Conservatives at 5 per cent (n=6). The Bloc and the Greens have no racialized MPs. The NDP have the largest proportion of Indigenous MPs in their caucus at 12 per cent (n=3), followed by the Liberals at 4.4 per cent (n=7), the Bloc at 3.1 per cent (n=1) and the Conservatives at 1.7 per cent (n=2). The Green caucus has the highest proportion of women MPs at 50 per cent, though this is just one member, Elizabeth May. Of the remaining parties, the NDP caucus has the highest proportion of women MPs at 44 per cent (n=11), followed by the Bloc at

37.5 per cent (n=12) and the Liberals at 35.6 per cent (n=57). The Conservatives have the smallest proportion of women MPs in their caucus at 18.5 per cent (n=22).

THE PARTIES' COMMITMENTS

The parties promoted their diverse candidate slates, but their platforms made few substantive promises on issues related to equity, discrimination, racism, or reconciliation. In late August, after the Conservatives had unveiled an animal welfare plan that proposed to ban puppy mills, CTV reporter Omar Sachedina asked O'Toole why the word "puppy" appeared more often in the Conservatives' plan than the word "racism," which is not mentioned at all. O'Toole responded that he has spoken out against racism, anti-Semitism, and Islamophobia and that he was "very proud we have the most diverse slate of candidates running for the Conservative Party."[17] The party's platform argued that "Canada's Conservatives began and led the fight for human rights in modern Canada" and includes a section on John Diefenbaker, the Tory prime minister who introduced the Canadian Bill of Rights, amendments to reduce racial discrimination in immigration laws, and the unconditional extension of the franchise to Indigenous peoples.[18]

In 2021, the Conservatives' Indigenous-focused election promises focused primarily on economic issues related to resource extraction, conservation, trade, and housing (see chapter 11). They committed funds to hire and train regional economic development officers, said they would work with Indigenous community groups to encourage Indigenous peoples to apply for positions in the public service, and promised to provide more funding to Indigenous mental health and drug treatment programs. They said they would end long-term water advisories in Indigenous communities. They also set aside money for police supports and community training programming that they propose would reduce incarceration rates among Indigenous peoples. Their immigration promises targeted reductions in administrative backlogs, the introduction of a points system into the family reunification program, and an expansion of the pathway to permanent residence for the "best and brightest" low-skilled workers. Their plan did not mention multiculturalism or anti-racism. It did commit to "enhancing the participation of women, Indigenous people, and visible minorities [in the Canadian Armed Forces] through proactive, targeted recruitment at the community level," but there were no funds for this initiative in the platform's costing.[19] The Conservatives said they would conduct an independent investigation into sexual misconduct in the military and call a public inquiry into harassment and discrimination in the armed forces. They proposed a refundable childcare tax credit for lower income families and said they would cancel existing childcare agreements between the Liberal government and some provinces; signed shortly before the election call, these agreements would increase the number of childcare space and limit fees.

The Liberals' $10-a-day childcare program was one of the party's featured campaign planks, although it simply reiterated commitments already made in the 2021 budget. Each section of the Liberals' platform included a gender and diversity impact statement, noting that many of their promises, such as the Canada Workers Benefit, would especially address challenges faced by women, racialized Canadians, Indigenous peoples, and youth. In addition, the Liberals proposed several targeted programs, including investments to address mental health and trauma among Indigenous peoples, the new Changing Narratives Fund to support Black, Indigenous, and racialized journalists and creators, and a Diversity Fellowship aimed at groups currently under-represented in hiring, appointments, and leadership positions in the federal public service. They promised new money for an anti-racism strategy, funding for Black graduate students, and a national support fund for survivors of hate-motivated crimes; they also said they would double the funding directed to women's rights organizations. The platform reiterated the party's commitment to developing a disability inclusion plan. Other commitments, such as a promise to "work to root out all sources of anti-Indigenous and anti-Black racism, LGBTQ2 prejudice, gender bias, and white supremacy in the Canadian Armed Forces" and "undertake ambitious efforts to improve the diversity of the CAF," were murkier.[20]

The NDP promised it would fully implement the UN Declaration on the Rights of Indigenous Peoples, as well as the Truth and Reconciliation Commission's ninety-four calls to action. They said they would do so by co-developing a national plan for reconciliation in collaboration with Indigenous peoples. They also promised to comply with a ruling of the Human Rights Tribunal that found Canada's child welfare system discriminates against First Nations children in care, a ruling the Liberal government had been contesting in court. The NDP said they would honour the childcare agreements already signed with the provinces. Their plan included a specific section on confronting racism, which contained promises to prioritize the collection of race-based data, a review of employment equity to help close the racialized wage gap, and a national action plan to dismantle white supremacist organizations. There was also a section on gender equity, which promised to introduce legislation to encourage political parties to nominate more women candidates; it did not mention other politically under-represented groups.[21] Their immigration plan was not a significant departure from the status quo, although it included promises to reduce administrative backlogs, as well as a commitment to eliminate the cap on applications to sponsor parents and grandparents through the family reunification program.

The Green Party did not release a fully costed platform, but they made several promises consistent with a commitment to equity and diversity and listed social justice as one of the core values in their fiscal plan. They promised to dismantle systemic discrimination in institutions, including in policing, the federal public service, and immigration and refugee services, and to address identity-based hate. The platform's section on advancing gender equality committed to pay equity legislation and an expansion of supports for low-income mothers. There was also an entire section on "decolonizing, decriminalizing, and decarcerating." A section on "diverse, truly representative democracy," that promised political parties would be required to publicly report on how they planned to recruit candidates from "under-represented groups" prior to each fixed-date election and to provide an update on their achievements.[22] The Greens said they would end water advisories and comply with the Human Rights Tribunal order on discrimination against First Nations children.

The Bloc Québécois' platform listed thirty measures to enhance Quebec's interests and identity. Most of these focused on French-language rights, culture, and increased powers for the province. However, they also committed to fully implementing the UN Declaration on the Rights of Indigenous Peoples and said they would abolish the *Indian Act*. In addition, the party's leader noted that "in the spirit of a culturally enriching coexistence, a Bloc government would give official recognition to First Nations, Inuit, and Métis languages."[23]

The parties' platforms include diversity rhetoric and advance proposals aimed at appealing to historically marginalized groups. However, many of these promises are not costed or slim on specifics, and a number are part of broader economic, environmental, or social policy goals. In this way, parties are not pursuing explicit inclusion agendas, but instead slotting diversity into issue positions or promises they would have advanced anyway. To the limited extent that diversity issues were on parties' agendas, these parts of their platforms seem to be add-ons, window-dressing, or secondary. The descriptive representation provided by an incrementally more diverse candidate slate seems not to have translated into a more robust diversity policy agenda.

THE CAMPAIGN

In many ways, the coverage of the campaign followed the parties' lead. Issues related to race, multiculturalism, and immigration have rarely figured prominently in Canadian election campaigns,[24] but they were more muted in 2021 than they had been in the previous two elections. The 2015 election was in part shaped by the Syrian refugee crisis and the Conservatives' divisive strategy to tackle so-called "barbaric cultural practices." Both were wedge issues that the parties used to distinguish themselves from one another and arguably helped shape the result.[25] In 2019, racism became part of the conversation when multiple images surfaced showing Prime Minister Trudeau in blackface. Trudeau was also dogged by allegations of "fake feminism," an accusation fuelled by two high-profile departures from his caucus: Celina Caesar-Chavannes (a Black woman and Trudeau's former parliamentary secretary) and Jody Wilson-Raybould (the country's first Indigenous minister of Justice). Although polling suggests the Liberals' electoral result was largely – and ultimately – unaffected by the revelations and allegations,[26] these nonetheless were a feature of the campaign's narrative. Issues related to race captured public attention in 2020 following the murder of George Floyd by Minneapolis police. The ensuing protests intensified demands to address systemic racism and anti-Black discrimination in the United States, Canada, and elsewhere.

Even so, race, gender equality, or diversity were scarcely seen on the electoral agenda in 2021. One news report on the first French-language debate summarized the scene succinctly, noting "Canadian Leaders Finally Talked About Racism."[27] A few days before votes were cast, Global News reporter Ahmar Khan wrote, "some voters are left wondering why the social and racial reckoning once dominating headlines has turned into a fringe issue among federal leaders."[28] There was little explicit discussion of diversity issues during the 2021 campaign, with party leaders shying away from topics that appeal to one set of so-called progressive voters, but cost them support in key battlegrounds.[29]

The most sustained reflection on race was a response to a question posed by moderator Shachi Kurl to Bloc Québécois leader Yves-François Blanchet during the English-language leaders' debate. The question read, "You deny that Quebec has problems with racism. Yet you defend legislation such as Bills 96 and 21, which marginalize religious minorities, anglophones, and allophones. For those outside the province, please help them understand why your party also supports these discriminatory laws."[30] Kurl was referring to two different pieces of provincial legislation: Bill 96 proposes updates to existing French-language rights provisions, while Bill 21 (now law) prohibits the wearing of visible religious symbols by public sector employees, including teachers, police officers, and government lawyers. Many experts say neither would survive a charter challenge, and the Quebec government seems to agree: when Bill 21 was adopted as law by the National Assembly, the notwithstanding clause was invoked, and Bill 96 includes a similar provision.[31] Even so, Blanchet has been an ardent defender of both pieces of legislation; he argues they reflect "Quebec's values" and rejects that they are an example of systemic racism (see chapter 5).

The day after the English-language debate, in a clear effort to sidestep a thorny issue that could cost them votes in Quebec, the Liberal Party leader called the question "offensive," while his Conservative counterpart characterized it as "a little unfair." Both said it was wrong to imply that Quebecers are racist.[32] Jagmeet Singh and Annamie Paul, the only racialized federal party leaders, both unequivocally characterized the legislation as discriminatory. However, Singh declared that an NDP government would not interfere in a matter of provincial jurisdiction, just as Trudeau and O'Toole both said they would respect Quebec's sovereignty on the issue. Even so, on the campaign trail, Blanchet repeatedly went after Singh, suggesting the NDP leader had not come out strongly enough against "Quebec bashing."[33] Just as the other party leaders' guarded comments were aimed at protecting their support in the province, Blanchet's strategy was undoubtedly an effort to scuttle any chance the NDP might have to repeat 2011's so-called orange wave.

Party officials suggested the campaign was the "nastiest" they had ever experienced, while the RCMP, which provides protective detail to the leaders of federal political parties, confirmed an increase in the number and intensity of security threats.[34] At a campaign stop in London, Ontario, a protester threw gravel at Trudeau; the perpetrator was a riding association president with the People's Party of Canada. He was charged, and the party's leader, Maxime Bernier, disavowed the violence. Conservative Party MP Michelle Rempel Garnier reported she had received a death threat during the campaign. In a statement, she said, "It's unfortunately an all too frequent occurrence for me and many of my colleagues, particularly women, of all political stripes."[35] Candidates reported anti-Semitic, homophobic, and racist graffiti on their signs and in communications from voters. Although election vitriol is not new, Evan Balgord, the executive director of the Canadian Anti-Hate Network, said the 2021 campaign included much more far-right activity than campaigns in recent history.[36]

Some opinion writers criticized the national debate commission's decision to exclude People's Party leader Maxime Bernier. Writing in *The Globe and Mail*, Andrew Coyne recognized the party's "toxic campaign, full of fear-mongering, inflammatory rhetoric ... and name-calling." Characterizing Bernier as a leader pandering to "crypto-racists and fringe kooks," Coyne wrote, "Those are Mr Bernier's supporters disrupting the Liberal Leader's rallies, unhinged mobs spitting venom and, increasingly, threatening violence."[37] Despite this, Coyne argued that Bernier's exclusion from the debates would only "feed his supporters' suspicions that the fix is in, not least since for once they will be right."[38] A few days later, Coyne's *Globe and Mail* colleague, John Ibbitson, said not only that the PPC's promises to decrease immigration and eliminate multiculturalism are legitimate but also that they "deserve representation." He noted, "If their voice is silenced – if PPC members fail to break through in parliament [...] – they will find another way to be heard. And you might not like their methods."[39] Observers characterized these columns as a legitimation of the party and its tactics.[40]

At the conclusion of the campaign, when journalists asked PPC officials about the party's apparent links to white nationalists and extremist agitators, Bernier doxed three reporters on social media, "calling them idiots, posting their email addresses and calling on his 160,000 followers to go after them. 'They want to play dirty, we will play dirty too,'" he wrote.[41] Several journalists – mostly racialized and women – received a torrent of racist hate mail, online harassment, and targeted threats of violence, sexual assault, harassment, and murder.[42] The disproportionate effect of such abuse on women, racialized, and Indigenous peoples, raises questions about institutional openness to diversity.

As chapter 6 details, the question of openness dogged the Green Party for most of the campaign. Annamie Paul, the first Black and Jewish woman elected to lead a federal political party,[43] faced accusations from within her own party that she led with "an autocratic attitude of hostility, superiority, and rejection," claiming Paul displayed "anger in long, repetitive, aggressive monologues."[44] These comments played on the trope of the "angry Black woman," and critics suggested the party has a "very real problem with racism."[45] Some party insiders also argued Paul's efforts to lead the party were doomed from the outset because long-time Green party members resisted her leadership style."[46] The party squabbled over Paul's request for a salary, denied her funding to support her bid to win a seat in Toronto-Centre, threatened a nonconfidence motion, and triggered a mechanism to review her membership in the party, a process that was eventually suspended. Despite performing well in the leaders' debates, Paul ultimately lost her local race. A few days later, Paul announced she would be stepping down, noting "When I was elected … I was breaking a glass ceiling. What I didn't realize at the time was that I was breaking a glass ceiling that was going to fall on my head and leave a lot of shards of glass that I was going to have to crawl over throughout my time as leader." As columnist Erica Ifill put it, "If you're being pushed off the glass cliff by your own team, you cannot really break the glass ceiling."[47]

CONCLUSION

Despite an increased number of women, racialized, and Indigenous candidates, the presence of two racialized leaders, and a context in which reconciliation, racism, and misogyny were on the public's radar, issues related to equity and diversity hardly figured in policy discussions. Certainly, no party prioritized them.[48] When pressed, leaders frequently pointed to the diversity of their candidate slates, even though their composition was not much different than in the previous election, and once the results were tallied, the House of Commons largely remained an institution of under- and un-representation. The media's coverage reflected that dynamic. As *Toronto Star* columnist Ruby Latif put it, "all we saw were performative acknowledgments by leaders and the media without substantive discussions about the systematic issues – and how we can address them."[49]

It is not as though there were not issues to talk about. The 2021 election ocurred during a pandemic that has disproportionately affected women, Indigenous peoples, and immigrants, and racialized Canadians.[50] Anti-Asian racism is on the rise.[51] In June 2021, the Afzaal family was run down by a London, Ontario driver who police later said was motivated by anti-Muslim hate; four members of the family died. Mere weeks before the start of the campaign, news coverage was dominated by images of mass graves containing the bodies of Indigenous children who had perished at residential schools. Public opinion polling suggests that one-third of Canadians say the country is "racist," and 60 per cent say that "racism is a serious issue."[52] Despite this, parties and the media have typically characterized the economy, climate change, and healthcare as issues that affect everyone, whereas "diversity" is framed as niche. Moreover, when given the opportunity to do better, parties often fall short. Prime Minister Trudeau, who while on the campaign trail boasted about his record on Indigenous issues, spent the first National Day for Truth and Reconciliation on vacation in Tofino, rather than commemorating victims and survivors of residential schools. The choice was seen by many as just more evidence that politicians prioritize symbolism over substance, performance over real policy change.[53]

This chapter suggests that the recruitment of so-called diverse candidates is just one part of the equation. Most parties have mastered diversity rhetoric, but this has not translated fully into policy action that would address systemic racism and inequality, nor has it completely altered party cultures within leaders' offices and at the district level. Parties need to rethink recruitment strategies that encourage a so-called old boys club approach by supporting and investing in candidates from historically under-represented groups. Our analysis confirms local party associations nominate diverse candidates in less electorally competitive districts; past research shows that such candidates also receive less financial support from their parties than do white men.[54] This pigeon-holing not only discourages new candidates from considering an electoral run, but also stymies their chances of victory when they do throw their hats in the ring. Parties should report data on candidate diversity at the district level, since aggregate numbers conceal the extent to which equity-deserving recruits face an uphill electoral battle in their local districts.

Parties must be receptive to different representational styles, ambitions, and visions of success. There is no point promising diverse candidates a seat at the table if their voices and policy ideas are ignored once they are there. After Treasury Board president Jane Philpott resigned from Trudeau's cabinet over his handling of the SNC-Lavalin affair, she noted, "We didn't get a seat at the table so that we would play by all the exact rules and shut up when what we had to say was not well received."[55] Policy proposals should be measured against diversity, inclusion, and equity metrics, just as environmental assessments and questions about economic impact already help to guide policy-making.

The media have a role in this: they can ask questions about these efforts, track progress, and model institutional change within their own organizations. Commentators also need to move away from old-style thinking that frames diversity as a niche or a nice-to-have add-on issue. Just as healthcare, climate change, and the economy affect all Canadians, so too are diversity, inclusion, and equity fundamental to Canada's well-being and growth. Here again, the media can be a key player because they help to shape national discourse. It was the media who led the criticism of Prime Minister Trudeau's Tofino vacation, and it was a former journalist, Shachi Kurl, who asked about race and discrimination in the English-language leaders' debate. Kurl later wrote that she had no regrets in asking the question, wondering, "What does it say about the state of our democracy that a question is deemed unaskable? … What does it say about journalism when seasoned reporters and political commentators were shocked that I dared to 'go there'?"[56] The media have also helped nudge parties toward increased diversity within their ranks by reporting on who runs and how they are treated.[57]

The media must also shift their gaze inward, given the sector's own problems with discrimination and exclusion.[58] In Canadian newsrooms, people from equity-deserving groups are often hired into positions that signal a semblance of "diversity" to employees and the public, but behind closed doors many report feeling tokenized, passed over, and unsupported. In the aftermath of George Floyd's 2020 murder and the ensuing conversation on anti-Black racism, Kathleen Newman-Bremang, a senior editor at Refinery29, wrote,

"There have been too many Black women in media (and outside of it) who have had their dreams deterred because of the bigotry of their colleagues and managers."[59]

Regardless of institution – whether it is a newsroom, a boardroom, or a parliamentary committee room – the discussion must consider questions of inclusion and equity. Unfortunately, most of the key players in politics and the media remain stuck at the diversity stage, counting who is present and considering what they look like, but not evaluating how they are treated. As Verna Myers, the vice-president of Inclusion Strategy at Netflix, puts it, "Diversity is being invited to the party. Inclusion is being asked to dance."[60] In 2015, the goal was a "cabinet that looks like Canada." Six years on, the goal needs to shift to include a parliament that looks like Canada, and one where a broad range of perspectives are included and empowered to shape a more equitable future for everyone.

NOTES

1 Anna Johnson, Erin Tolley, Melanee Thomas, and Marc-André Bodet, "A New Dataset on the Demographics of Canadian Federal Election Candidates," *Canadian Journal of Political Science* 54, no. 3 (2021): 717–25.

2 Paul Adams, "The Media: Challenges of Covering the Campaign," in *The Canadian Federal Election of 2019*, eds. Jon H. Pammett and Christopher Dornan (Montreal: McGill-Queen's University Press, 2020), 174–97; and, Erin Tolley, *Framed: Media and the Coverage of Race in Canadian Politics* (Vancouver: UBC Press, 2016).

3 Melanee Thomas and Marc André Bodet, "Sacrificial Lambs, Women Candidates, and District Competitiveness in Canada," *Electoral Studies* 32, no. 1 (2013): 153–66; Valérie Ouellet, Naël Shiab, and Sylvène Gilchrist, "White Men Make up a Third of Canada's Population but a Majority of MPs – Here's Why," CBC News, 26 August 2021, https://ici.radio-canada.ca/info/2021/elections-federales/minorites-visibles-diversite-autochtones-racises-candidats-politique/en.

4 These parties had seats in the House of Commons at the time that the election was called, and their leaders participated in the English- and French-language debates.

5 We are grateful to Nandini Gokhale, Emma Jackson, and Michelle Liang for their excellent research assistance. Funding for the data collection was provided by Carleton's School of Journalism and Communication, the

Faculty of Public Affairs, and the Canada Research Chair in Gender, Race, and Inclusive Politics. We thank Equal Voice, Philip Charbonneau, and Chadwick Cowie for their assistance in verifying parts of our coding; any errors remain our own.

6 Johnson, Tolley, Thomas, and Bodet, "A New Dataset on the Demographics of Canadian Federal Election Candidates."; Semra Sevi, "Who Runs? Canadian Federal and Ontario Provincial Candidates from 1867 to 2019," *Canadian Journal of Political Science* 54, no. 2 (2021): 471–6.

7 There is still a small percentage of candidates (0.5 per cent overall) for whom we have incomplete demographic information. This missing data is excluded from the calculations.

8 Our definition of "racialized" follows the visible minority category in the Canadian Census, which captures individuals who are not Indigenous and who are "non-Caucasian in race or non-white in colour." This includes individuals who are, for example, Black, South Asian, Chinese Canadian, or Arab. Indigenous peoples are those who identify as First Nations, Métis, or Inuit. For additional information, see Statistics Canada, *Dictionary: Census of Population* (Ottawa: Minister of Industry, 2017).

9 That said, there is some new work tracking LGBTQ2S+ candidates over the past two elections. See Mel Woods, "LGBTQ2S+ Candidates on the Issues That Matter Most This Federal Election," *Xtra*, 15 September 2021, https://xtramagazine.com/power/canada-election-lgbtq-candidates-208618.; Elizabeth Baisley and Quinn Albaugh, "District Competitiveness and the Nomination of LBGTQ Candidates," paper presented at the annual meeting of the American Political Science Association (2021); Joanna Everitt and Manon Tremblay, "Campaign Contexts and the Gendered Implications for LGBTQ Candidates," paper presented at the annual meeting of the American Political Science Association (2021).

10 Randy Boissonnault, the Liberal MP for Edmonton Centre, identifies as a "non-status adoptive Cree." See Canadian Press, "Liberal MP Randy Boissonnault: 'Amazing' How Far We Have Come on LGBTQ2 Rights'," *Saanich News*, 18 April 2017, https://www.saanichnews.com/national-news/liberal-mp-randy-boissonnault-amazing-how-far-we-have-come-on-lgbtq2-rights/. Although he is not included on PARLINFO's list of Indigenous MPs, we have coded him as Indigenous in this dataset, but recognize identification is complex and fraught, especially in cases of adoption.

11 Johnson, Tolley, Thomas, and Bodet, "A New Dataset on the Demographics of Canadian Federal Election Candidates."

12 Christopher Reynolds, "Green Party Falls Far Short of Full Slate of Election Candidates, Sources Say," CP24, 1 September 2021, https://www.cp24.com/news/green-party-falls-far-short-of-full-slate-of-election-candidates-sources-say-1.5569946.

13 Karen Celis and Silvia Erzeel, "The Complementarity Advantage: Parties, Representativeness and Newcomers' Access to Power," *Parliamentary Affairs* 70, no. 1 (2015): 43–61.

14 See, for example, Patricia E. Perkins, "Canadian Indigenous Female Leadership and Political Agency on Climate Change," in *Climate Change and Gender in Rich Countries*, ed. Marjorie Griffin Cohen (London: Routledge, 2017), 282–96.

15 For a more nuanced measure of competitiveness, see Marc André Bodet, "Strongholds and Battlegrounds: Measuring Party Support Stability," *Canadian Journal of Political Science* 46, no. 3 (2013): 575–96.

16 Melanee Thomas and Marc André Bodet, "Sacrificial Lambs, Women Candidates, and District Competitiveness in Canada."; Ouellet, Shiab, and Gilchrist, "White Men Make up a Third of Canada's Population but a Majority of MPs."; Erin Tolley, "Who You Know: Local Party Presidents and Minority Candidate Emergence," *Electoral Studies* 58 (2019): 70–9.

17 Cameron French, "O'Toole Says He's Condemned Racism in Past, When Asked Why Platform Makes No Mention of It," CTV News, 30 August 2021, https://www.ctvnews.ca/politics/federal-election-2021/o-toole-says-he-s-condemned-racism-in-past-when-asked-why-platform-makes-no-mention-of-it-1.5567086.

18 Conservative Party of Canada, *Canada's Recovery Plan* (Ottawa: Conservative Party of Canada, 2021), 106.

19 Conservative Party of Canada, *Canada's Recovery Plan*, 97.

20 Liberal Party of Canada, *Forward. For Everyone* (Ottawa: Liberal Party of Canada, 2021), 68.

21 New Democratic Party of Canada, *Ready for Better: New Democrats' Commitments to You* (Ottawa: New Democratic Party of Canada, 2021), 96.

22 Green Party of Canada, *Platform 2021: Green Future, Life with Dignity, Just Society* (Ottawa: Green Party of Canada, 2021), 79 and 88.

23 James Armstrong, "Canada Election: Complete List of Promises Made on Indigenous Reconciliation," Global News 14 September 2021, https://globalnews.ca/news/8110204/canada-election-complete-list-of-promises-made-on-Indigenous-reconciliation/#bloc-quebecois-promises.

24 Jerome H. Black and Bruce M. Hicks, "Electoral Politics and Immigration in Canada: How Does Immigration Matter?" *Journal of International Migration and Integration* 9, no. 3 (2008): 241–67.

25 Will Kymlicka, "The Precarious Resilience of Multiculturalism in Canada," *American Review of Canadian Studies* 51, no. 1 (2021): 122–42; Jon H. Pammett and Christopher Dornan, eds., *The Canadian Federal Election of 2015* (Toronto: Dundurn, 2016); Erin Tolley, "Partisan Players or Political Pawns: Immigrants, Minorities, and Conservatives in Canada," in *The Blueprint: Conservative Parties and their Impact on Canadian Politics*, eds. J.P. Lewis and Joanna Everitt (Toronto: University of Toronto Press, 2017), 101–28.

26 Éric Grenier, "A Close Race from Start to Finish: Polling in the 2019 Federal Election," in *The Canadian Federal Election of 2019*, eds. Jon H. Pammett and Christopher Dornan (Montreal: McGill-Queen's University Press, 2020), 155–73.

27 Justin Ling, "Canadian Leaders Finally Talked About Racism in Quebec and It Got Heated," *Vice*, 3 September 2021, https://www.vice.com/en/article/xgx9y4/canadian-leaders-finally-talked-about-racism-in-quebec-and-it-got-heated.

28 Ahmar Khan, "Canada Election: Black, Indigenous Voters Lament Leaders Shying Away from Race-Based Issues," Global News, 17 September 2021, https://globalnews.ca/news/8194241/black-Indigenous-voters-federal-election/.

29 Randy Besco and Erin Tolley, "Does Everyone Cheer? The Politics of Multiculturalism in Canada," in *Federalism and the Welfare State in a Multicultural World*, eds. Elizabeth Goodyear-Grant, Richard Johnston, Will Kymlicka, and John Myles (Montreal: McGill-Queen's University Press, 2018), 291–318.

30 Shachi Kurl, "I Was Asked to Apologize for My Question in the Leaders' Debate. I Stand by It Unequivocally," *Globe and Mail*, 25 September 2021, https://www.theglobeandmail.com/opinion/article-i-was-asked-to-apologize-for-my-question-in-the-leaders-debate-i-stand/.

31 Nick Wells, "Bill 96 Could Be Challenged in Court, Says Quebec Bar," CTV News, 29 September 2021, https://montreal.ctvnews.ca/bill-96-could-be-challenged-in-court-says-quebec-bar-1.5605581.

32 Catharine Tunney, "Trudeau, O'Toole Call Debate Question on Quebec's Secularism Offensive, Unfair," CBC News, 10 September 2021, https://www.cbc.ca/news/politics/trudeau-debate-blanchet-bill21-1.6171124.

33 Wells, "Bill 96."

34 Catharine Tunney, "Between Violence and Vandalism, the Parties Are Experiencing a Very Ugly Campaign," CBC News, 17 September 2021, https://www.cbc.ca/news/politics/violence-vandalism-campaign-rise-1.6177269.
35 Tunney, "Between Violence and Vandalism."
36 Tunney, "Between Violence and Vandalism."
37 Andrew Coyne, "Why Maxime Bernier and His Noxious Views Should Be at the Leaders' Debates," *Globe and Mail*, 8 September 2021, https://www.theglobeandmail.com/opinion/article-why-maxime-bernier-and-his-noxious-views-should-be-at-the-leaders/.
38 Coyne, "Maxime Bernier and His Noxious Views."
39 John Ibbitson, "The People's Party Is Far Outside the Mainstream of Canadian Politics, but It Deserves Representation," *Globe and Mail*, 14September2021,https://https://www.theglobeandmail.com/politics/article-the-peoples-party-is-far-outside-the-mainstream-of-canadian-politics/.
40 Max Fawcett, "Mainstream Media Blew Trump Coverage – and Now Risks Doing the Same with the PPC," *National Observer*, 16 September 2021, https://www.nationalobserver.com/2021/09/16/opinion/mainstream-media-trump-coverage-now-risks-same-ppc.
41 Elizabeth Renzetti, "The People's Party Showed Its True Colours with Targeting of Journalists," *Globe and Mail*, 30 September 2021, https://www.theglobeandmail.com/opinion/article-the-peoples-party-showed-its-true-colours-by-doxing-journalists-they/.
42 Canadian Association of Journalists, "CAJ Urges Government, Law Enforcement to Address Targeted Harassment of Reporters," 29 September 2021, https://caj.ca/blog/CAJ_urges_government__law_enforcement_to_address_targeted_harassment_of_reporters.
43 Vivian Barbot was appointed interim leader of the Bloc Québécois after Gilles Duceppe's resignation. She served in the role for six months until the party elected a permanent successor. Annamie Paul is the first Jewish woman to lead a federal political party.
44 Alex Ballingall, "'Will the Green Party Survive?' The Inside Story of How the Greens Toppled Annamie Paul and Tore Itself Apart in the Process," *Toronto Star*, 3 October 2021.
45 Ballingall, "The Inside Story of How the Greens Toppled Annamie Paul."
46 Ballingall, "The Inside Story of How the Greens Toppled Annamie Paul."
47 Erica Ifill, "Annamie Paul's Leadership Never Really Had a Chance," *Globe and Mail*, 1 October 2021, https://www.theglobeandmail.com opinion/article-annamie-pauls-leadership-never-really-had-a-chance/.

48 Ruby Latif, "Equity and Diversity Were Shamefully Ignored during the Election," *Toronto Star*, 3 October 2021.

49 Latif, "Equity and Diversity."

50 Statistics Canada, "Impacts on Immigrants and People Designated as Visible Minorities," *The Social and Economic Impacts of COVID-19*, 20 October 2020, https://www150.statcan.gc.ca/n1/pub/11-631-x/2020004/s6-eng.htm; Josephine Etowa and Ilene Hyman, "Unpacking the Health and Social Consequences of COVID-19 through a Race Migration and Gender Lens," *Canadian Journal of Public Health* 112, no. 1 (2021): 8–11.

51 Jon Hernandez, "More than Half of Asian Canadians Experienced Discrimination in Past Year: Survey," CBC News, 8 June 2021, https://www.cbc.ca/news/canada/british-columbia/anti-asian-discrimination-angus-reid-poll-1.6056740.

52 Reyhana Patel, "Islamophobia Must Remain Top Priority for Liberal Government," *New Canadian Media*, 4 October 2021, https://newcanadianmedia.ca/human-rights-must-remain-top-priority-for-liberal-government/.

53 *Star* Editorial Board, "C'mon Man! Trudeau's Tofino Holiday Makes a Mockery of Reconciliation Day," *Toronto Star*, 1 October 2021, https://www.thestar.com/opinion/editorials/2021/10/01/cmon-man-trudeaus-tofino-holiday-makes-a-mockery-of-reconciliation-day.html.

54 Thomas and Bodet, "Sacrificial Lambs."; Ouellet, Shiab, and Gilchrist, "White Men Make up a Third of Canada's Population but a Majority of MPs."

55 Radiyah Chowdhury, "Women of the Year 2019: Jody Wilson-Raybould, Jane Philpott, and Celina Caesar-Chavannes," *Chatelaine*, 29 November 2019, https://www.chatelaine.com/living/jody-wilson-raybould-jane-philpott-celina-caesar-chavannes-women-of-the-year-2019/.

56 Kurl, "I Stand by What I Asked in the Leaders' Debate."

57 Aedan Helmer, "'We're Not Having Our Voices Heard or Our Issues Prioritized': Researchers Say Diverse Candidates Disproportionately Underfunded," *Ottawa Citizen*, 18 September 2021.

58 Sunny Dhillon, "Journalism While Brown and When to Walk Away," *Medium*, 29 October 2018, https://level.medium.com/journalism-while-brown-and-when-to-walk-away-9333ef61de9a.

59 Kathleen Newman-Bremang, "For Black Women in Media, a 'Dream Job' Is a Myth," *Refinery* 29, 7 July 2020, https://www.refinery29.com/en-ca/2020/07/9878117/systemic-racism-canadian-media.

60 Laura Sherbin and Ripa Rashid, "Diversity Doesn't Stick Without Inclusion," *Harvard Business Review*, 1 February 2017, https://hbr.org/2017/02/diversity-doesnt-stick-without-inclusion.

11

Progress or the Status Quo? Indigenous Peoples, Participation, and Representation

Chadwick Cowie and Liam Midzain-Gobin

The Justin Trudeau Liberal government came to power in 2015 in part by promising a renewed relationship with Indigenous nations and peoples.[1] This included commitments to rebuilding a "nation-to-nation" relationship, ending long-term boil water advisories in First Nations communities, establishing a National Inquiry into the issue of Missing and Murdered Indigenous Women and Girls (MMIWG), fixing housing and other service delivery issues in First Nations and Inuit communities, as well as lifting caps on program funding for First Nations, Métis, and Inuit communities. Trudeau would go on to promise "full reconciliation" while accepting the final report of the National Truth and Reconciliation Commission as prime minister.[2]

Subsequent years have been fraught, with progress made and promises both upheld and overlooked. While still remaining hopeful and being willing participants in forums that contain the possibility of genuine change, Indigenous peoples have continued to hold the Trudeau government accountable for its promises. If anything, dissatisfaction with the federal government has continued to grow among Indigenous peoples[3] as government action on issues such as unsafe drinking water, rights to lands and resources, and funding and service delivery have not lived up to promises made.

This underlying dissatisfaction has been seen in various ways, not the least of which have been ongoing initiatives aimed at deliberately implementing Indigenous peoples' self-determination on the ground. Some examples include the Sipekne'katik First Nations' sustainable fishery, land re-occupations such as the Unist'ot'en developing a healing centre on their territory, and governance initiatives such as the Haudenosaunee Development Institute.[4] These direct-action initiatives were in the background during the lead-up to the 44th federal election, and also set the context for a summer where Indigenous issues and reconciliation took centre stage of media headlines ahead of the dissolution of parliament. Spanning the summer, Canadians, and many throughout the world (both Indigenous and not) were horrified by the confirmations of mass graves at the sites of former institutions operated through the Indian Residential School System (IRSS). Many of the graves were those of children, with the first announcement coming 28 May from the Tk'emlúps te Secwépemc nation and more announcements of findings or investigations at approximately thirty-eight sites across the country to total unmarked graves in the thousands.[5]

Many people expressed grief, shock, and horror. There were pledges from Canadian society, governments, and political parties to do more to uncover the truth of what happened in IRSS institutions, following increasing public attention to Indigenous issues and a growing public interest in seeing meaningful reconciliation.[6] Into this environment the government released its MMIWG National Action Plan on 3 June (after a year-long delay). The action plan outlines the government's plans for addressing the genocide[7] of MMIWG, and will require the long-term commitment of this government, and others, to complete. Days later the government also announced the appointment of Mary Simon as the first Inuk Governor General. An accomplished diplomat, Inuit leader, and human rights advocate, the prime minister claimed Simon's appointment represents an opportunity to "build bridges"[8] within the country and represents the highest formal office held by an Indigenous individual in Canada's history.

Leading into the federal election, then, there was a sense of both pain and possibility regarding Indigenous issues and reconciliation. The context, while sombre, also hinted at greater awareness and willingness for transformative change among Canadians. Looking back over how Indigenous peoples and policy issues were engaged in the federal election it is important to keep this in mind, as this potential was not reached. Rather, as we explore below, there was a return to longer-term trends on the part of political parties broadly supportive of the colonial status quo.

We make our argument over five parts. We open by centring Indigenous peoples, first outlining the expectations articulated by Inuit Tapirit Kanatami (ITK) and the Assembly of First Nations

(AFN), and second discussing the candidates themselves – including not only the record number who ran, but how we should understand their chances of winning individual seats. Next, we turn to the parties' policy platforms, trying to understand not only what they proposed but how they continue longer-term trends of colonial responses to Indigenous issues. We then turn our analysis to the disincentives and barriers to participation faced by Indigenous peoples, including the lack of media coverage and accessibility concerns that seem somewhat unique to this election before concluding.

INDIGENOUS PEOPLES' ENGAGEMENT

To begin, we want to outline the complicated nature of Indigenous peoples' engagement with the Canadian state and electoral system.[9] In this light, we analyze the ways that Indigenous peoples did participate in the 2021 federal election, both as organizations and individuals. On an organizational level, two National Indigenous Organizations (NIO) put out sets of priorities for what they expected the next federal government to address. Both of these flow from an understanding of Crown-Inuit and Crown-First Nation partnerships in the work ahead. Moreover, both also speak to the importance of engaging provinces and territories in this work. We first address these attempts to set the agenda before discussing the way Indigenous individuals were involved in the election as candidates.

ITK Priorities for Election 2021

On 24 August ITK released its own set of priorities for the incoming government in an attempt to set the agenda for the ongoing Inuit-Crown relationship. Like the AFN, ITK called for the priorities to be addressed in a way that both recognizes and furthers Inuit self-determination, calling for a "distinctions-based" approach to working with Inuit instead of a one-size-fits-all approach to Indigenous policymaking and program implementation.[10] Key to this is ITK's call for the finalization of the Inuit Nunangat Policy (INP) within three months of the next government taking office. Identified as the first priority, the policy has been under development with the federal government since 2015, and a central part of the Inuit-Crown Partnership Committee since its creation in 2017. Speaking to media at the end of August, ITK President Natan Obed noted the need for structural change within the federal government for further progress to be achieved.[11] It is through the finalization and implementation of this policy that ITK appears to be aiming to realize that progress.

In addition to the INP, ITK identified fourteen issue-specific priority areas, including suicide-prevention measures, food security, infrastructure and housing, health and education programming and supports, the full implementation of Inuit Land Claims Agreements, climate change, and the implementation of the United Nations Declaration on the Rights of Indigenous Peoples (UNDRIP). Many of these issues reflect longstanding areas of inaction on the part of the federal government, with issues such as infrastructure, food security, and health (among others) being those which will only continue to worsen with a changing climate. At the same time, with many of the issue areas ITK is asking the federal government to support existing ITK initiatives, or to follow through on the government's own stated priorities – highlighting that progress could be quickly achieved after the election.

Healing Path Forward: 2021 Federal Priorities for Strengthening and Rebuilding First Nations

On 31 August 2021, in keeping with previous elections, the AFN released their own set of priorities regarding the issue areas they are seeking to work with the next government on. These were:

1 Truth, reconciliation, and healing for First Nations and all Canadians.
2 Climate and conservation leadership with First Nations.
3 Economic growth, prosperity, and wealth building for First Nations.
4 Promoting peace by respecting First Nations' jurisdiction.
5 Rebuilding and strengthening First Nations.

Together, these areas touch on nearly every aspect of First Nations peoples' lives both in-community as well as outside. The underlying context of graves found at former residential institutions, and their own polling showing greater interest in reconciliation among Canadians, are used as starting points to connect many broader issues to First Nations priorities.

This is not to say that the priorities have been determined entirely by the context of 2021. Rather, as the AFN document states: "The commitments First Nations seek from the next federal government are not new. They are, at the core, about respecting First Nations' jurisdiction, Treaty rights, as well as supporting First Nations governments' fiscal capacity to exercise those rights and jurisdictions, and nation rebuilding."[12] Indeed, even in those areas that are new for 2021, such as the emphasis on recovery efforts at former residential institutions and ongoing support for intergenerational healing, the AFN is clear that success is only possible by working from an understanding of First Nations' jurisdiction.

It is in line with this approach that the document frames "reconciliation" as federal, provincial, and territorial governments coming to work alongside First Nations. That is, reconciliation cannot be achieved through truth alone, but rather through concrete, collaborative action on pressing issues such as climate change, building a sustainable economic landscape for First Nations individuals and governments, policing, health and well-being, education, infrastructure and clean drinking water, and housing, among others. Thus, it is notable that in some areas – such as priority three – there are lists of specific actions requested, while on issues of sovereignty and jurisdiction, there is only the expectation of meetings and dialogues to resolve disagreements.

Together, the priorities identified by the AFN and ITK both articulate the clear need for short-term action on specific issues, while not losing track of longer-term structural changes required to address questions of jurisdiction and funding. We caution, however, that each group's priorities reflect the specific relationships the NIOs hold with their own people and the federal government. That is, despite sharing some broad themes – including climate change, housing, education, economic well-being, healthcare, and reconciliation, among others – the emphasis and foregrounding of the themes differ across the documents. For example, ITK foregrounds the need for an INP as its first priority with climate change close to the end of the list; by contrast the AFN has foregrounded healing and reconciliation, with climate change second on its list and the sorts of policy areas covered by the INP being collected under priority five. Ultimately then, these should be seen as two articulations of how distinct Indigenous peoples envision a self-determining relationship within the Canadian state. As such they offer a clear opportunity for engagement by the next federal government.

INDIGENOUS CANDIDATES

The 2021 federal election saw a record number of Indigenous candidates (see chapter 10). Overall, at least eighty-one candidates claimed Indigenous identity.[13] Thus, 2021 marks a continued increase in the number of Indigenous candidates seeking office, with 2019 marking the second highest amount, sixty-two, and 2015 the third highest amount, fifty-four.

The New Democratic Party (NDP), as in 2019 and 2015, listed the largest number of Indigenous candidates running for office, with twenty-nine NDP candidates self-identified as Indigenous.[14] Of these, Leah Gazan, who is Lakota, was the sole incumbent, representing the riding of Winnipeg Centre; she was re-elected. The Nunavut electoral district had also been held by an Inuit NDP MP, but Mumilaaq Qaqqaq opted to end her time in federal politics, stating that the system was detrimental to her mental health and Indigenous peoples in general.[15] Although Qaqqaq opted to not seek re-election, voters opted to stick with the NDP in the 2021 federal election, electing Lori Idlout, an Inuk woman, as their MP. Joining both Gazan and Idlout on the NDP benches was a new NDP member: Blake Desjarlais, a member of the Métis nation, representing Edmonton-Griesbach. With the wins of Gazan, Idlout, and Desjarlais under the NDP banner, the election not only marked the first time three members of the NDP caucus identified as Indigenous, but also the first time the NDP caucus had representation from all three peoples: First Nations, Métis, and Inuit.

Like the NDP, the Liberal Party (LPC) also highlighted candidates who were First Nations, Métis, and Inuit. As in the 2015 and 2019 elections, the LPC registered the second largest number of Indigenous candidates for the 2021 federal election. A total of twenty-six Indigenous candidates sought a seat in the House of Commons under the LPC banner, compared to eighteen in 2019 and nineteen in 2015. Of the twenty-six Indigenous candidates running for the LPC, six were incumbents. Of the six incumbents, Yvonne Jones was first elected federally following a by-election in the electoral district of Labrador in May of 2013; Michael McLeod, Dan Vandal, Vance Badeway, and Marc Serre were each first elected in 2015 and re-elected in 2019. Jaime Battiste, the first L'nu ever elected to the House of Commons in the 2019, sought re-election in the electoral district of Sydney-Victoria.[16] Additionally, Randy Boissonnault was again looking to represent the electoral district of Edmonton-Centre, a district he had originally represented from 2015 to 2019.[17] Of the twenty-six LPC Indigenous candidates seeking seats in the 2021 federal election, the aforementioned seven were elected, leading to an increase of one Indigenous MP and thus giving the Liberals an Indigenous caucus of one L'nu, one without status but with Nehiyaw lineage, one Inuk, and four Métis MPs.

Similar to the LPC, the Conservative Party (CPC) also saw an increase in the number of Indigenous MPs elected. Prior to the 2021 federal election, the CPC had one MP who self-identified as Indigenous: Mark Dalton. Dalton, first elected in the 2019 federal election, was seeking re-election in the district of Pitt Meadows-Maple Ridge-Mission under the CPC banner and was one of eight Indigenous candidates running for the CPC, two of whom were successful in winning their seats. Alongside the successful re-election bid of Dalton was the win by Adam Chambers, a Métis candidate in the electoral district of Simcoe North. Although Chambers' win represented an increase for Indigenous representation within the CPC, the number is below the record five Indigenous MPs elected under the CPC banner in 2011.

For the Bloc Québécois, one candidate self-identified as Indigenous in the 2021 federal election. Simon-Pierre Savard-Tremblay, first elected in 2019, sought re-election in the electoral district of Saint-Hyacinthe-Bagot and easily won re-election. Unlike the BQ, CPC, LPC, and NDP, the Indigenous candidates running for the Green Party of Canada (GPC) and the People's Party failed to win in the electoral districts where they were running.[18]

Despite the lack of wins for Indigenous candidates under the Green and People's Party banners, the 2021 election did mark some political firsts for Indigenous representation. As previously highlighted, the 2021 federal election marked the first time three Indigenous MPs were elected in the same election as members of the NDP. Additionally, the 2021 election had the largest number of Indigenous candidates seeking seats. Lastly, there was an increase in Indigenous MPs elected from eleven in the 2019 and 2015 elections, to thirteen in 2021: seven Métis, four First Nations,[19] and two Inuit.

Electoral Districts and Winnability

Notwithstanding the record number of Indigenous MPs elected, of the thirteen Canadian provinces and territories, neither the Yukon nor the province of Prince Edward Island saw any Indigenous candidates. Additionally, the eighty-one candidates running for the parties were not seeking election in eighty-one of Canada's 338 federal electoral districts but rather sixty-one ridings: some electoral districts had multiple Indigenous candidates seeking to represent them.

Of the sixty-one federal electoral districts with Indigenous candidates, thirteen are located in British Columbia, eight in Alberta, seven in Saskatchewan, eight in Manitoba, twelve in Ontario, seven in Quebec, one in New Brunswick, two in Nova Scotia, and one each in Labrador, Nunavut, and the Northwest Territories. Nine of these had two Indigenous candidates running against one another, while three others saw three Indigenous candidates contesting the seat. Furthermore, in most of these sixty-one districts, the Indigenous candidate was running for a political party unlikely to win the riding.

Looking at the Indigenous NDP candidates, some were running in strong NDP ridings. For example, Gazan was seeking re-election in Winnipeg Centre. Winnipeg Centre has had a tendency to lean NDP in previous elections, though it flipped to the Liberals between 2015–19 under Robert-Falcon Ouellette – a representative with mixed Cree and Métis background. Gazan won the seat back for the NDP in 2019 and easily held it in 2021. The riding has a large urban Indigenous population.[20] The electoral district of Nunavut had also been won by the NDP in the 2019 election. Although Qaqqaq opted to not seek re-election, Idlout was able to hold the riding for the NDP by a large margin. Edmonton-Griesbach, where Desjarlais won for the NDP, was a riding the NDP was targeting, as they had placed second in both 2019 and 2015. Like Winnipeg Centre, Edmonton-Griesbach has a large Indigenous population and is also a very diverse electoral district.[21]

Therefore, in these three electoral districts Indigenous candidates had a high potential for winning. Of the other twenty-five electoral districts contested by an NDP candidate self-identified as Indigenous, twelve were electoral districts that the NDP had won in a previous election or by-election, while thirteen had never been represented by the NDP. The margins by which the other Indigenous NDP candidates lost ranged from 10 per cent to over 50 per cent. For example, in the electoral district of Edmonton-Manning there was a difference of just over 10 per cent between the CPC incumbent, who was re-elected, and the NDP's Charmaine St Germain. In the electoral district of Grande Prairie-Mackenzie, the CPC incumbent was easily re-elected by more than fifty-six percentage points over the NDP candidate. Thus, although the NDP was successful in recruiting the highest number of Indigenous candidates, the likelihood of victory was low for all but the three who actually won.

Similarly, of the twenty-six Indigenous candidates running for the Liberals, six were incumbents and easily won re-election. Of the remaining twenty, nine were running in electoral districts that the LPC had won at some point in previous elections, but all but one of these victories had been prior to 2015. For instance, Desnethe-Missinippi-Churchill River was held by Gary Maresty, a Nehiyaw individual, for the Liberals, but only from 2006 until the end of 2007. Since then, LPC candidates have finished in second or third place, with Buckley Belanger finishing third in 2021, 28 per cent behind the CPC incumbent. The only electoral district in the 2021 election in which an Indigenous candidate ran for the Liberals and that an LPC MP had held in previous periods was Edmonton Centre, where Boissonnault had previously been the incumbent from 2015 to 2019. Thus, Edmonton Centre was seen as a possible pick up for the Liberals and was a targeted electoral district by the party.

The LPC had never been victorious in any of the other eleven electoral districts in which they ran Indigenous candidates. For instance, Ron Thiering, seeking the seat of Edmonton-Wetaskiwin, finished a distant third behind the CPC incumbent with a vote share difference of 41 per cent. When assessing all nineteen electoral districts in which Indigenous LPC candidates were unsuccessful, the vote share difference ranges from 15 per cent to 62 per cent. The potential of more than seven Indigenous Liberals being elected was unlikely.

As with the LPC and NDP, many Indigenous CPC candidates also ran in electoral districts that offered them little chance of being elected. Only two ran in districts where the CPC was the incumbent party. As previously highlighted, Marc Dalton was the incumbent in Pitt Meadows-Maple Ridge-Mission, an electoral district that the CPC has traditionally won.[22] Adam Chambers, who won in Simcoe North, was a newly elected MP representing an electoral district that has favoured the CPC since the 2006 election. Four other electoral districts in which Indigenous candidates ran for the CPC, it, or its predecessors, have previously represented. That said, in 2021 the CPC placed third in three of these electoral districts and second in one. The difference in vote share in the four electoral districts between the winner and each Indigenous CPC candidate who lost ranged from 14 per cent to 31 per cent. Thus, there was limited opportunity for the CPC to see an increase in Indigenous CPC candidates winning on election night.[23]

Upon reviewing the number of Indigenous candidates seeking seats and the ridings they sought to represent, it becomes noticeable that although the 2021 election marked the largest number of Indigenous candidates, the possibility of more than thirteen being elected was minimal. In the case of the NDP, LPC, and CPC especially, a majority of their Indigenous candidates were running in so-called "unwinnable" ridings, and a total of twenty were running against one another as well. Further post-election analysis remains to be done regarding influence of Indigenous voters casting a ballot, and which ridings First Nations, Métis, and Inuit voters could potentially determine a victor,[24] analysis that might extend recent work suggesting Indigenous candidates increase turnout among Indigenous voters;[25] however, our discussion does highlight longer-term trends of parties nominating Indigenous candidates in ridings they are unlikely to win.

PARTIES AND PLATFORMS

Despite our concerns over the low numbers of Indigenous candidates running in winnable seats, the increase in candidates points to one way in which parties may be attempting to win the support of Indigenous voters. Another important aspect in any election is the proposals put forward by the political parties. Indeed, with the Trudeau government securing victory in the 2015 election in part on the strength of their ability to win the support of Indigenous voters in key regions. An important part of this is developing a platform that speaks to the priorities of Indigenous voters. However, at the same time the parties' politics on issues relevant to Indigenous peoples in Canadian elections can be seen in a different light: that parties need to be seen as serious by the electorate and national discourse increasingly attentive to questions of colonialism and inclusion in Canada. This section engages with both aspects of the national parties' policy platforms in the election, beginning with the Conservative Party of Canada before then discussing the Liberal Party of Canada, the New Democratic Party, and the Green Party of Canada[26] before closing with a collective assessment.

Conservative Party of Canada

While all parties brought forward specific policy proposals for Indigenous peoples, the CPC approach appeared to be informed by their conception of policy focused on Indigenous peoples as a "shield" issue, one that the party seeks to avoid.[27] This is also consistent with the CPC's approach to broader issues of concern for Indigenous peoples, including when related to the social safety net and climate change, resulting in a platform that is notably devoid of the type of detailed policy proposals that can be found for many other issues. The exception here is on issues of economic development, which is typically a Conservative strength. Here, the CPC's approach to policy proposals for Indigenous peoples may best be summarized as amounting to a vision of economic reconciliation.

As outlined in *Canada's Recovery Plan*,[28] the 2021 CPC policy platform, the Conservatives' vision for Indigenous policy, was largely concentrated in two sections, one focusing on Indigenous peoples specifically, the other in the section "A Detailed Plan to Secure Jobs and Economic Growth." In both, the CPC foregrounded Indigenous well-being in Canada as a function of economic prosperity and business development, especially through encouraging Indigenous organizations and governments to act as partners on resource development projects. While the platform also contained policies such as "Making Amends for Past Injustices" by implementing TRC recommendations and memorializing the victims of the IRSS, the attention continued to revert to economic issues as being at the core of ensuring reconciliation can proceed.

Liberal Party of Canada

The LPC's policy platform[29] relating to Indigenous issues, like the Conservatives', opened with the issue of reconciliation, specifically addressing the "legacy" of colonialism with a focus on residential institutions. The party's proposals also included additional support for Indigenous child and family welfare services, healthcare, clean drinking water, an Indigenous urban, rural, and northern housing strategy, and some business support, among others. Overall, while comprehensive, many of the policies proposed were articulated through the framing of continuing the work of the government as it has been in power since 2015. This is especially notable since the

LPC included in each section a list of "Key Actions" undertaken by the government, with these actions being highlighted at the front of the chapter on reconciliation and Indigenous peoples.

New Democratic Party

As many pointed out throughout the election, the NDP's platform[30] looked different than the other parties' insofar as it provided less detail in its pledges. Among concrete proposals, however, was the co-development with Indigenous peoples of an Indigenous housing strategy within the first one hundred days of their government to meet the housing needs of those in-community but also outside of communities and in more urban areas. Similarly, the NDP promised a national action plan for reconciliation, framing this as a plan focused on governance and rights and title. Other areas with explicit and concrete commitments included the implementation of initiatives proposed by First Nations leaders including Jordan's Principle[31] to equalize child and family welfare service delivery for First Nations, Shannen's Dream[32] to equalize schooling and educational spending for First Nations, and Joyce's Principle[33] to tackle systemic racism in healthcare provision, and fully funding safe drinking water infrastructure in-community. However, these commitments did not come with concrete policy measures that would have enabled their realization.

Green Party of Canada

Long criticized for a lack of substance on Indigenous policy and issues of reconciliation, in their 2021 platform[34] the Greens (GPC) showed some potential growth. The clearest engagement with Indigenous issues came in the "Reconciliation with Indigenous Peoples" section of their "Just Society" framework. In it they addressed a series of issues, including pledges to implement the recommendations of the TRC, National Inquiry into MMIWG, and even Royal Commission on Aboriginal Peoples, alongside additional promises to ameliorate healthcare services, build affordable housing and provide quality education. As with the NDP, much of the language employed by the Greens revolves around supporting Indigenous self-determination initiatives, including co-development of policy and ensuring that Indigenous peoples have decision-making power. Importantly, the GPC also envisioned a strong role for Indigenous peoples, communities, and organizations in the Greens' transition framework. Here they not only articulated the importance of incorporating Indigenous knowledge into policy to combat climate change, but noted the importance of Indigenous peoples in stopping and reversing biodiversity loss and environmental degradation.

What the Platforms Tell Us

While there is some overlap with the NIO's priorities outlined above, the parties' policy platforms offered a strong signal of where their individual focus lay. Here we examine them collectively for a more general sense of where the parties' attentions lay in 2021. As we stated at the opening of this chapter, the confirmation of mass graves at former government-sanctioned institutions was an issue that gripped Canadians leading into the election. This was reflected in the platforms insofar as each dedicated space to pledges that they would support the completion of searches of these grounds in line with the TRC's Calls to Action. However, there was much less consensus on the issue of MMIWG, where only the NDP articulated the crisis as an ongoing "genocide,"[35] and only the Liberal Party committed to implementing the Federal Pathway released in June 2021. While the NDP and GPC committed to "implement[ing] the Inquiry's Calls for Justice," the CPC only noted the existence of the National Inquiry's report, saying that it found "significant gaps in opportunity and outcome between Indigenous and non-Indigenous people"[36] while pledging to create their own national action plan.

Following this trend, the CPC was the only one of the parties analyzed here not to pledge the co-development of major policy affecting Indigenous peoples. The LPC, NDP, and GPC all pledged to co-develop major initiatives such as those on housing, climate change, and child health and well-being. While the CPC did commit to "collaborating" with Indigenous peoples and their governments, they did not go as far as either of the other parties in how they intend to develop policy.

One theme that united the parties was their pledge to implement UNDRIP, to one extent or another. The CPC was less committed as they framed it through their approach to reconciliation as an economic concern. To this end, the UNDRIP was only referred to in the section on "prosperity" with six of the seven concrete pledges relating to easing the way for further resource development.[37] This contrasts with the other parties' pledges to implement UNDRIP without this sort of minimizing framing, though the NDP then also took the additional step of invoking UNDRIP in their pledges to work with Indigenous peoples on issues such as climate change, trade, and child and family service delivery.

Related to the UNDRIP is governance capacity, an issue on which the parties were united in the need for federal support for Indigenous nations and peoples. Familiar patterns among the parties also fit here, where the CPC were most specific in applying this to the realm of economic development with corporate training, the NDP proposing its national action plan and reconciliation council, and the LPC outlining a series of commitments to continue existing work around "rebuilding," "revitalizing," and "reconstituting" nations, governance, and legal systems,[38] and the GPC promising support for self-determination and traditional governance systems though without clearly articulating a plan to do so. To some extent, both the NDP and Greens appear to go further in their stated commitments to self-determination. While we caveat that to some extent this could represent a caution on the part of the LPC and CPC, both of whom expected to form government, such ambition should not be overlooked. Indeed, the pledges can serve as useful supports for Indigenous peoples' work in shifting the perspectives and understanding of the issue. One notable distinction from this trajectory is that the LPC went furthest in outlining specific commitments to support priorities identified by First Nations, Métis, and Inuit, including on governance. While each of the parties offered some distinction between pledges specific to each group, the LPC went the furthest by including specific sections dedicated to each group, including on the INP.[39] Broadly, however, the attention by the parties to a distinctions-based approach to working with Indigenous peoples was a positive step.

Also consistent across each of the parties were pledges to end long-term drinking water advisories in First Nations communities. Unsafe water supply has been a consistent problem for Canadian federal governments, and the promises from each of the parties reflected not only the consistent attention to the issue in media, but also LPC promises from the 2015 election, which had been extended without a definite timeline by their government. Troubling, however, is the placement of these pledges in sections on reconciliation in the platforms. This reflects a tendency to group Indigenous issues together on the part of the parties, even when they would otherwise fit in a variety of other issue areas, such as, in this case, infrastructure. Moreover, referring to issues of drinking water also demonstrates an understanding of reconciliation as a project of effective service delivery, rather than the sort of political project of developing a shared future it must represent,[40] as was on display in the debates as well.

Reading the platforms both separately and together, there was a distinct sense of siloing Indigenous peoples and issues. This is especially the case with the CPC platform, where Indigenous issues were largely focused across five pages of text under the heading, "A Detailed Plan to Secure the Future of Canada's Indigenous People." The section itself touched on a variety of issues such as reconciliation, economic development, governance, clean drinking water, and other service delivery items, but what is perhaps most notable is that this was the one section of their platform where the bulk of CPC promises to Indigenous peoples were to be found. Outside of this section the platform included only references to resource development (again, in the mould of economic reconciliation outlined above), Indigenous housing needs, and fisheries policy. Other parties did slightly less of this, with the NDP and GPC especially being more attentive to the organization and placement, though all contained sections that are more specifically framed as aimed at "reconciliation," but which include a number of policy areas such as service delivery, recognition of self-governance rights, and clean drinking water. Major policy areas that were discussed elsewhere were largely confined to climate change and housing, and other areas where the federal government would be working alongside provincial governments (for example, mental health supports).

MEDIA COVERAGE

In an election that saw a record number of Indigenous candidates, and which was called on the heels of so much attention to the interlocking crises affecting those both in-community and in more urban areas, perhaps one of the strangest features was the relative neglect of Indigenous issues during the campaign itself. This was noted by many, with Indigenous leaders urging greater discussion of Indigenous priorities, and those such as AFN National Chief Roseanne

Archibald expressing disappointment and some confusion at the lack of attention to them. Speaking to CTV after the election, Archibald noted that their polling showed that "the majority of Canadians wanted to know what each of these parties was going to do to address truth and reconciliation"[41] – something confirmed by other polling. This created a somewhat strange situation, wherein media organizations were reporting on the lack of major media coverage of Indigenous issues in the campaign.[42] This is not to suggest a total lack of coverage, as individual media organizations and national outlets produced both news and opinion pieces surrounding the election. Here organizations such as Aboriginal Peoples Television News (APTN) and The Conversation especially stood out for their attention to Indigenous peoples and the issues facing them. However, as noted at the beginning, in the context of an election preceded by major media coverage of colonization and the urgent need for reconciliation, the overall silence was deafening.

One arena where coverage of Indigenous issues and reconciliation did occur was the two debates organized by the Leaders' Debates Commission. As with previous years, the debates were held on unceded Algonquin territory and incorporated questions from both journalists and the public; however, the 2021 debates saw more direct questioning of the leaders from journalists covering specific issue areas. Two questions were asked of the party leaders directly by Indigenous Canadians. First, in the French-language debate, Perry Simon asked the leaders if they would commit to making Indigenous languages official languages, with most leaders except Erin O'Toole (CPC) voicing support. Second, in the English-language debate Marek McLeod asked why any of the leaders believed they were worthy of Indigenous peoples' trust, with the leaders each largely reiterating platform promises before focusing in on Prime Minister Trudeau's (LPC) record.

There were pointed questions in the sections of the debate devoted to Indigenous issues and reconciliation. The English debate stood out, as APTN's Melissa Ridgen questioned each of the party leaders, with Trudeau especially taking exception to what he saw as Ridgen's "cynicism" while trying to defend his record. As with the questions put to them by individuals, each of the leaders sought to articulate their own platforms while criticizing the Liberals. Especially notable were Jagmeet Singh's (NDP) comments about Trudeau's lack of concrete action to address the MMIWG Inquiry's Calls to Justice, and continued inaction on the Canadian Human Rights Tribunal's orders to compensate Indigenous children and families for the systemic underfunding of child and family welfare services. Both issues had been major media problems for the government, and Trudeau's responses showed a discomfort with this, but he did not provide concrete plans for action. While the debates were generally seen to lack substance, with party leaders instead focusing on messaging, the tendency was even more pronounced in the way the leaders largely grouped all discussions relating to Indigenous peoples into the sections for reconciliation. This was mentioned above in relation to party platforms, but it was a phenomenon more pronounced in the debates themselves. Rather than speaking directly to the myriad of issue areas affecting Indigenous peoples – let alone the different issues facing different peoples – the focus on reconciliation as the most significant issue facing Indigenous peoples tends to flatten the complex and intergenerational problems. In lieu of solutions that will meaningfully engage with the interconnected issues, fixing colonialism is represented as a series of discrete policy areas to be addressed by the government without an overall vision adequate to address the need for Indigenous self-determination. Of course, this in part stems from the limits of the debates themselves – two hours for each debate with five participating leaders does not offer a great deal of time for detail. At the same time, the AFN offered to host a specific date on Indigenous issues but could not get agreement from each of the parties,[43] perhaps reflecting an unwillingness to engage more deeply from at least some.

In sum, the general lack of media coverage in 2021 was surprising given the context, and also that Indigenous peoples and issues had featured more prominently in other recent campaigns. This was especially true in 2015 when Trudeau won government in part due to grandiose promises after movements like Idle No More brought issues such as Indigenous housing, unsafe drinking water, food security, and systemic colonialism to the forefront of our national conversations. In contrast, the 2021 election saw a palpable lack of interest – to the point where this was remarked upon by many including friends, relatives, and students alongside the broader public. Given the lack of a concerted effort by national parties to articulate a message that seriously considered, and engaged with, the issues facing Indigenous peoples, perhaps we should not be surprised by this. However, considering the issues faced by those in- and out-of community, and the work of NIOs to highlight their own agendas, the muted nature of the national discussion should be understood as a disincentive to participate. When coupled with the barriers to accessibility we discuss next, this helps contextualize lower voter turnout.

VOTING AND ACCESSIBILITY

Rates of Indigenous voter participation have been a repeated topic of discussion in many of the previous elections since those recognized with status have been eligible to vote. While we do not seek to unpack this issue here, many opt not to participate in what they see as a process lending legitimacy to a colonial state, as a way to assert their national citizenship.[44] For those who do want to participate, a series of barriers have reduced the smoothness of Indigenous electors voting: fewer individuals have the required forms of identification; Indigenous individuals are less likely to be registered to vote than non-Indigenous; and Indigenous individuals reporting greater discomfort with and feeling less informed about the process.[45] The underlying context for voting accessibility for Indigenous individuals, then, reflects difficulties not typically experienced by other potential voters.

To attempt to overcome these barriers, recent elections have seen concerted efforts to build knowledge of the system and have especially focused on outreach to try to encourage participation through initiatives such as the Indigenous Rock the Vote campaign and having elected officials publicly call for their community members to vote. These efforts have been successful as Indigenous participation in a federal election jumped in 2015,[46] including 61.5 per cent of First Nations in-community voting.[47] While that dropped in 2019, momentum was still carrying forward and, in advance of the 2021 vote, the AFN identified twenty-four ridings where strong turnout from Indigenous voters could have an important impact on the results.[48]

As the 2021 election got underway, however, many people within communities began to raise concerns over decisions made by Elections Canada that lowered the accessibility of voting for many who already face barriers. The situation was particularly acute for those in more remote communities. Early concerns were raised in First Nations communities across northern Ontario, where the election day of 20 September fell during a traditional harvesting period.[49]

When accommodations were agreed to in the form of advance polls being made available, Elections Canada then cancelled the election day polling locations in at least three communities – a move leaders in those three communities claim was not communicated to them[50] – amidst other problems including polling stations opening late, or having incorrect voter lists.[51] The additional barriers and resulting confusion ultimately meant that some were not able to vote, with claims of "voter suppression" and "disenfranchisement" being raised by some of those affected in First Nations communities.[52]

Accessibility was not only a concern for First Nations, however. The accessibility of casting a ballot was also an issue across Inuit communities in Nunavut where advance polling was unavailable in at least nine communities.[53] This was further compounded by concerns over delays with mail-in ballots – concerns that were particularly acute in the more remote communities. As in First Nations, each community had some form of poll available, but during a short election the options do not appear to have been clearly articulated. As a result, opportunities to vote were fewer than they should have been, with final voter turnout numbers being substantially lower than in 2019.[54] Even when polling stations or mail-in ballots were accessible, Inuit also may have faced language barriers to participating. This was especially pronounced in Nunavut, where despite Inuktitut being an official language, and one that must be included on all signage in the Territory, only English and French were included on ballots and polling signs. With a number of Nunavummiut reporting Inuktitut as their first language, and many also reporting that they do not speak either English or French, the incongruence was noted by the senator for Nunavut, Dennis Patterson, as potentially causing some not to vote.[55]

Some of these issues, including difficulties with special mail-in ballots, can be understood in the context of a pandemic election and the ongoing difficulties that came with that. Others, such as the lack of communication regarding election-day polling stations and the lack of Inuktitut on signage, cannot. As a result of the concerns being raised, Elections Canada has formally apologized to affected First Nations, and pledged to conduct an investigation into the issues of voter accessibility.[56] Insofar as issues of accessibility relating to language, access to polling stations, election timing regarding cultural practices, and voter information and engagement remain systemic barriers to participation; removing those barriers should remain a top priority for the next federal election.

CONCLUSION

As election speculation increased throughout the summer in advance of parliament's dissolution, it would have seemed likely that First Nations, Métis, and Inuit concerns would have been top of mind for politicians and parties. Public consciousness of ongoing colonization in Canada has certainly increased over recent years, with Indigenous governance initiatives and new studies of former IRSS sites provoking increased media attention and a stated interest in transformative change among Canadians. However, as our analysis shows, the 2021 election looked even more similar to previous elections than the context might suggest. Indeed, there were few meaningful policy shifts on the part of major parties, despite the new articulation of economic reconciliation by the CPC, while the broad marginalization of Indigenous concerns to discussions of reconciliation continued.

To an extent this reflects the limits of achieving change through electoral politics. Indeed, the direct actions we opened this chapter with also point to other avenues through which First Nations, Métis, and Inuit are asserting their rights and operating through their jurisdiction. However, given the legislative barriers blocking other changes, standing for, and winning, election to the House of Commons might also offer a pathway. This is reflected in Indigenous peoples' engagement in the election. A record number of Indigenous individuals put their name forward to run as candidates, with representation from all peoples and representing each of the major parties. NIOs also worked to bring attention to their priorities, highlighting the importance of many policy areas within the federal government's power. While it is not yet possible to clearly identify to what degree the disincentives and barriers – both systemic and emergent as a result of the COVID-19 pandemic – affected turnout among Indigenous peoples, the outcry, and the subsequent investigation by Elections Canada, also point to important points of engagement and interest. This provides a good contrast with the seeming lack of interest from political parties in systemic or transformational changes in relationships with First Nations, Métis, and Inuit communities. Sustaining this interest may be crucial to Indigenous peoples playing an important role in future elections.

NOTES

1 We would like to gratefully acknowledge the work of Chelsea Gabel (McMaster University), Nicole Goodman (Brock University), and Marrissa Mathews (McMaster University), who helped organize the chapter. All errors are our own.

2 "Canada Vows 'Full Reconciliation' with Indigenous Peoples," BBC News, 15 December 2015, https://www.bbc.com/news/world-us-canada-35105339.

3 Centre of Excellence on the Canadian Federation and Environics Institute for Survey Research, "Indigenous Relations and Reconciliation – Confederation of Tomorrow 2021 Survey," Confederation of Tomorrow 2021 (Montreal: Institute for Research on Public Policy, June 2021).

4 For further background see: Haudenosaunee Confederacy, "HDI Historical Background," *Haudenosaunee Confederacy*, accessed 1 December 2021, https://www.haudenosauneeconfederacy.com/departments/haudenosaunee-development-institute/historical-background/.

5 Ka'nhehsí:io Deer, "Why It's Difficult to Put a Number on How Many Children Died at Residential Schools," CBC News, 29 September 2021, https://www.cbc.ca/news/Indigenous/residential-school-children-deaths-numbers-1.6182456.

6 Centre of Excellence on the Canadian Federation and Environics Institute for Survey Research, "Indigenous Relations and Reconciliation – Confederation of Tomorrow 2021 Survey," 9–10.

7 National Inquiry into Missing and Murdered Indigenous Women and Girls, *Reclaiming Power and Place: The Final Report of the National Inquiry into Missing and Murdered Indigenous Women and Girls* (Ottawa: National Inquiry into Missing and Murdered Indigenous Women and Girls, 2019).

8 Prime Minister of Canada Justin Trudeau, "Prime Minister's Remarks at the Installation of Her Excellency the Right Honourable Mary Simon as Canada's 30th Governor General," Government of Canada, Ottawa, Ontario, 26 July 2021, https://pm.gc.ca/en/news/speeches/2021/07/26/prime-ministers-remarks-installation-her-excellency-right-honourable-mary.

9 Chadwick Cowie, "A Vote for Canada or Indigenous Nationhood? The Complexities of First Nations, Métis, and Inuit Participation in Canadian Politics," The Conversation, 1 November 2021, https://theconversation.com/a-vote-for-canada-or-Indigenous-nationhood-the-complexities-of-first-nations-metis-and-inuit-participation-in-canadian-politics-169312.

10 Inuit Tapirit Kanatami, *ITK Priorities for Election 2021* (Inuit Tapirit Kanatami, 2021), https://www.itk.ca/itk-priorities-for-election-2021/.
11 "Inuit Tapiriit Kanatami's President Says It's 'a Transformative Time'; Here's What He Wants to Do Next," CBC News, 27 August 2021, https://www.cbc.ca/news/canada/newfoundland-labrador/q-a-with-itk-president-natan-obed-1.6152659.
12 Assembly of First Nations, *Healing Path Forward: 2021 Federal Priorities for Strengthening and Rebuilding First Nations* (Assembly of First Nations, 2021), https://www.afn.ca/the-healing-path-forward/.
13 Brittany Hobson, "Canada Election: 3 New Indigenous MPs Likely Elected for NDP, Tories," Global News, 22 September 2021, https://globalnews.ca/news/8213533/canada-election-Indigenous-mps/. Note: Although this source and others highlight seventy-eight Indigenous candidates, three additional candidates were not included in articles and research during the election (LPC candidate Randy Boissannault and two GPC candidates). Including these additional candidates brings the total to eighty-one.
14 Brittany Hobson, "Record Number of Indigenous Candidates Running in Federal Election," CTV News, 1 September 2021, https://www.ctvnews.ca/politics/federal-election-2021/record-number-of-Indigenous-candidates-running-in-federal-election-1.5570074. Note: twenty-seven Indigenous candidates ran for the NDP in 2019.
15 Shannon Proudfoot, "Mumilaaq Qaqqaq: 'It's Time to Face the Scale of Justice,'" *Maclean's*, 16 June 2021, https://www.macleans.ca/politics/ottawa/mumilaaq-qaqqaq-its-time-to-face-the-scale-of-justice/.
16 Hobson, "Canada Election."
17 Kellen Taniguchi, "Federal Election: Liberals Gain Edmonton Centre after Neck-and-Neck Race," *Edmonton Journal*, 22 September 2021, https://edmontonjournal.com/news/politics/election-2021/federal-election-edmonton-centre. Note: Randy Boissonnault is included as someone who has Nehihyaw lineage but whose lineage had been adopted out and thus Boissonnault is nonstatus, according to section 27 of the *Indian Act*.
18 For the 2021 federal election, thirteen Indigenous candidates ran for the Green Party of Canada, an increase of six from the 2019 federal election and three compared to the 2015 federal election. The People's Party of Canada had four Indigenous candidates running for them in the 2021 federal election.
19 The four First Nations MPs, when broken down by nation, include one Lakota, one L'nu, one Wendat, and one with Nehiyaw lineage but who does not have status.

20 Assembly of First Nations, *First Nations Voters Can Decide the Election Outcome in 2021* (Ottawa: Assembly of First Nations, 2021), https://www.afn.ca/wp-content/uploads/2021/08/21-08-25-First-Nations-Voters-Can-Decide-the-Election-in-2021-EN-1.pdf. See also: Loretta Smith, "Mending Fences: Increasing Aboriginal Representation in Canada," a paper presented at the 78th Annual MPSA Political Science Conference, 14–18 April 2021. Smith discusses the increase of Indigenous voter turnout when there are also Indigenous candidates seeking election. Also see Chadwick Cowie, "Validity and Potential: Dual-Citizenship and the Indigenous Vote in Canada's Federal Electoral Process," an MA thesis presented to the Political Studies Department of the University of Manitoba in August 2013.

21 Hobson, "Canada Election."

22 Between 2015–19, the electoral district was held by the LPC but had been CPC prior to that.

23 Like Chambers, the BQ incumbent for Saint-Hyacinthe-Bagot, Savard-Tremblay, was also running in a traditionally safe BQ electoral district. Thus, Savard-Tremblay's win likely had little to do with him being an Indigenous candidate as well. In relation to the thirteen Indigenous GPC candidates and two of the four PPC candidates who had information relating to their Indigenous ancestry and the electoral districts they were running in, the possibility of winning was minimal, and all placed third or lower in relation to vote share.

24 Notably, the AFN did this in their pre-election analysis; however that was specific to First Nations voters. Follow-up analysis could begin from there.

25 Simon Dabin, Jean François Daoust, and Martin Papillon, "Indigenous Peoples and Affinity Voting in Canada," *Canadian Journal of Political Science* 52, no. 1 (March 2019): 39–53. For further discussions see: Taiaiake Alfred, Brock Pitawanakwat, and Jackie Price, *The Meaning of Political Participation for Indigenous Youth. Charting the Course for Youth Civic and Political Participation* (Ottawa: Canadian Policy Research Networks, 2007); and, Kiera L Ladner, Michael McCrossan, and Elections Canada, *The Electoral Participation of Aboriginal People*, Working Paper Series on Electoral Participation and Outreach Practices (Ottawa: Elections Canada, 2007).

26 We have chosen not to include the Bloc Québécois as it only put forward candidates in Quebec, nor do we analyze the People's Party of Canada as they did not put forward a sincere engagement with Indigenous peoples, their needs, and concerns, during the election.

27 As far back as 2015, Paul Wells identified policy aimed at Indigenous peoples as a "shield" issue that the CPC preferred to avoid. See: Paul Wells, "Of Shields and Swords and Elections," *Maclean's*, 9 April 2015, https://www.macleans.ca/politics/of-shields-and-swords-and-elections/.
28 Conservative Party of Canada, *Canada's Recovery Plan* (Ottawa: Conservative Party of Canada, 2021).
29 Liberal Party of Canada, *Forward For Everyone* (Ottawa: Liberal Party of Canada, 2021).
30 New Democratic Party of Canada, *Ready for Better: New Democrat's Commitments to You* (Ottawa: New Democratic Party of Canada, 2021).
31 "Jordan's Principle," The First Nations Child & Family Caring Society, accessed 1 December 2021, https://fncaringsociety.com/jordans-principle.
32 "Shannen's Dream," The First Nations Child & Family Caring Society, accessed 1 December 2021, https://fncaringsociety.com/shannens-dream.
33 "Joyce's Princple," Principe de Joyce, accessed 1 December 2021, https://principedejoyce.com/en/index.
34 Green Party of Canada, *Green Party of Canada Platform 2021* (Ottawa: Green Party of Canada, 2021).
35 New Democratic Party of Canada, *Ready for Better*, 81.
36 Conservative Party of Canada, *Canada's Recovery Plan*, 115.
37 Conservative Party of Canada, *Canada's Recovery Plan*, 116–17.
38 Liberal Party of Canada, *Forward For Everyone*, 57.
39 Liberal Party of Canada, *Forward For Everyone*, 58–60.
40 While there are many visions of reconciliation, among the most compelling for us is that advanced by Matthew Wildcat who sees it as a process of decolonization and the creation of "new practices, structures, and attitudes where we become treaty partners." See: Team ReconciliAction YEG, "An Interview with Matthew Wildcat," *University of Alberta Law Blog*, 15 January 2018, https://ualbertalaw.typepad.com/faculty/2018/01/an-interview-with-matthew-wildcat.html.
41 Tom Yun, "Indigenous Leaders Say Issues Affecting Their Communities Largely Ignored during Election," CTV News, 21 September 2021, https://www.ctvnews.ca/politics/federal-election-2021/Indigenous-leaders-say-issues-affecting-their-communities-largely-ignored-during-election-1.5594693.
42 For example: Ian Austen, "Indigenous Issues Are Sidelined in Canada's Election," *New York Times*, 17 September 2021, https://www.nytimes.com/2021/09/17/world/canada/canada-election-Indigenous-issues.html; Amanda Coletta, "After Summer of Horrific Discoveries, Indigenous Issues Are Getting Little Attention in Canada's Election Campaign," *Washington Post*, 2 September 2021, https://www.washingtonpost.com/

world/2021/09/02/canada-election-Indigenous/.; Natalie Alcoba, "Indigenous Leaders Urge Action as Canada's Election Nears," *Aljazeera News*, 15 September 2021, https://www.aljazeera.com/news/2021/9/15/Indigenous-leaders-urge-action-as-canada-election-nears; Yun, "Indigenous Leaders Say Issues Affecting Their Communities Largely Ignored during Election."

43 Yun, "Indigenous Leaders Say Issues Affecting Their Communities Largely Ignored during Election."

44 For example, there is a complex relationship to Indigenous peoples' views on citizenship given the difficult history. See: Chadwick Cowie, "A Vote for Canada or Indigenous Nationhood? The Complexities of First Nations, Métis, and Inuit Participation in Canadian Politics," The Conversation, 1 November 2021, http://theconversation.com/a-vote-for-canada-or-Indigenous-nationhood-the-complexities-of-first-nations-metis-and-inuit-participation-in-canadian-politics-169312.

45 See: Elections Canada, "Indigenous Electors," (Ottawa: Elections Canada, 2021), https://www.elections.ca/content.aspx?section=res&dir=rec/part/abo&document=index&lang=e. It is worth noting that these issues are not necessarily a product of individuals being in-community, but reflect broader patterns of those living in urban, rural, and in-community areas.

46 Jane Gerster, "Trudeau's Liberals Benefited from Record Indigenous Voter Turnout in 2015. Can They Again?" Global News, 14 September 2019, https://globalnews.ca/news/5887701/Indigenous-voter-turnout/.

47 "On-Reserve Voter Turnout – 42nd General Election" (Ottawa: Elections Canada, 2018), https://www.elections.ca/content.aspx?section=res&dir=rec/eval/pes2015/ovt&document=index&lang=e.

48 "First Nations Voters Can Decide the Election Outcome in 2021," Assembly of First Nations, 25 August 2021, https://www.afn.ca/wp-content/uploads/2021/08/21-08-25-First-Nations-Voters-Can-Decide-the-Election-in-2021-EN-1.pdf.

49 Logan Turner, "Elections Canada Apologizes to Ontario First Nations Voters Unable to Cast Ballots Due to Issues," CBC News, 3 November 2021, https://www.cbc.ca/news/canada/thunder-bay/elections-canada-apology-kenora-1.6234598.

50 Logan Turner, "Remote First Nations See More Barriers in Voter Card Errors, Polling Station Confusion," CBC News, 21 September 2021, https://www.cbc.ca/news/canada/thunder-bay/kenora-first-nation-election-problems-1.6183246.

51 The Canadian Press, "Election Day Filled with 'Numerous and Systemic Failures' Says NDP," APTN News, 6 October 2021, https://www.aptnnews.

ca/national-news/ndp-says-errors-meant-people-including-first-nations-were-disenfranchised-on-election-day/.

52 See: The Canadian Press; Turner, "Remote First Nations See More Barriers in Voter Card Errors, Polling Station Confusion"; Turner, "Elections Canada Apologizes to Ontario First Nations Voters Unable to Cast Ballots Due to Issues." While these concerns were first, and most vociferously, raised by the NDP – and specifically in a district they had targeted as one they could potentially win – many of those who have spoken out in concern directly eschewed partisan affiliation to speak about the issue of voter accessibility as one of fairness and equity.

53 Emma Tranter, "Voting in Nunavut Challenging with Nine Communities without Advance Polls," CTV News, 18 September 2021, https://www.ctvnews.ca/politics/federal-election-2021/voting-in-nunavut-challenging-with-nine-communities-without-advance-polls-1.5590742.

54 David Lochead, "Nunavut Sees Drop in Voter Turnout during Federal Election," Nunatsiaq News, 27 September 2021, https://nunatsiaq.com/stories/article/nunavut-sees-drop-in-voter-turnout-during-federal-election/.

55 David Lochead, "Nunavut Senator Decries Lack of Inuktut Signage at Voting Stations," Nunatsiaq News, 22 September 2021, https://nunatsiaq.com/stories/article/nunavut-senator-decries-lack-of-inuktut-signage-at-voting-stations/.

56 Christopher Read, "Elections Canada Investigates First Nations 'Voter Suppression' in Ontario," APTN News, 30 October 2021, https://www.aptnnews.ca/investigates/elections-canada-investigating-voter-suppression-in-first-nation-communities-in-northern-ontario/; The Canadian Press, "Elections Canada Seeks 'Complete Picture' of Indigenous Voting Errors, Launches Probe," Global News, 4 November 2021, https://globalnews.ca/news/8350060/elections-canada-Indigenous-voting-probe/.

12

Immigrant Voting in the 2021 Canadian Federal Election

Stephen White

In the immediate aftermath of the 2021 election, there was unease within Conservative Party of Canada circles about the party's loss of support in ridings with relatively large numbers of immigrants.[1] For reasons that were not readily apparent, the Conservatives surrendered three seats to the Liberals in ridings with large concentrations of Chinese-Canadian voters. Some party members speculated leader Erin O'Toole's stance on trade and human rights issues with China hurt the party's image in the Chinese-Canadian community.[2] That a federal party would express concern about their standing within an ethnocultural minority community composed of primarily first-generation Canadians is perhaps unsurprising, as immigrants represent the largest growing segment of the voting public. The immigrant population in Canada increased 36 per cent between 1991 and 2016, from 4.3 million to 7.5 million.[3] The overwhelming majority of residents born outside of Canada are citizens eligible to vote – approximately three-quarters were Canadian citizens by naturalization in 2016,[4] and immigrant voter turnout, especially among those in Canada for more than ten years, is similar to turnout among the population born in Canada.[5]

However, the 2021 election episode regarding Conservative Party support among Chinese Canadians underscores several important currents in discourse about elections in immigrant communities. First, the concerns of immigrant-Canadian voters usually receive little attention from parties or the media during election campaigns.[6] If Chinese-Canadian voters were in fact unhappy with the Conservatives, there was little notice in the media until the votes had been counted. Perhaps privately, Conservatives expressed worries about this during or even before the campaign, but outward appearances suggest the votes of immigrant Canadians were something of an afterthought in 2021. Second, when voters born outside of Canada are discussed, there tends to be an emphasis on particular immigrant communities – namely, the largest ones – and the issues thought to be especially relevant to them. Hence, the South Asian-Canadian community or the Chinese-Canadian community often receive a good deal of attention when immigrant voters are discussed, even though they comprise only a fraction of the immigrant population. Third, the focus is typically on electoral districts, especially areas within urban centres, in which high proportions of the local population were born outside of Canada – so-called immigrant enclaves.

Although they received little attention during the election campaign, the votes of Canadians born outside of the country mattered in 2021, and not only the votes of the most populous immigrant groups, or votes in electoral districts with the highest concentrations of foreign-born voters. The immigrant-Canadian electorate is important not exclusively because of its size, but also because of its pronounced and relatively stable affinity for one federal party. The 2021 federal election echoed many earlier elections, in that predominantly racialized immigrant voters from a variety of backgrounds in Asia, Latin America, and Africa favoured the Liberal Party of Canada over other federal parties, and by a significant margin. This segment of the electorate is ever more critical to Liberal Party success, and its support is a challenge for rival parties.

This chapter explores the Canadian immigrant vote in the 44th Canadian federal election. I begin by analyzing the 2021 vote choices, issue positions, and leader evaluations of Canadians born inside and outside of the country, and then place the most recent election in broader context. Next, I estimate the impact of the Canadian immigrant vote on the 2021 election outcome. Finally, I discuss some of the implications for Canadian immigrants and the major federal parties.

IMMIGRANT VOTERS AND THE 2021 ELECTION

Immigrant Canadians were certainly not a monolithic voting bloc in 2021, but their vote choices diverged considerably from those of their Canadian-born co-citizens, as Table 12.1 shows. The broad contours of party support were comparable for immigrants and

Table 12.1 | Vote by birthplace, 2021 (%)

	Born in Canada	Born outside of Canada
Liberal Party	30	46
Conservative Party	34	36
New Democratic Party	19	14
Bloc Quebecois	10	0
Green Party	2	1
Other	5	3
Total	100	100
(n)	1453	307

Data Source: Abacus Data Post-Election Survey, 2021

non-immigrants, in that three parties – the Liberals, Conservatives, and New Democrats – received the lion's share of the votes. However, Canadians born outside of Canada were more than one and a half times likelier than Canadians born in the country to report voting for the Liberal Party (46 versus 30 per cent, respectively). Conservative Party support was similar for the two groups, with 36 per cent of voters born outside Canada backing the Conservatives compared to 34 per cent of voters born in the country. Other parties received less support from immigrant voters than those born in Canada. The gap in support for the Bloc Québécois was most striking. The party received one in ten Canadian-born votes, whereas no immigrant respondents reported voting for the Bloc. The NDP vote share was also smaller among voters born outside than in Canada (14 versus 19 per cent, respectively).

While it might be reasonable to suppose the distinctive pattern of party support among immigrants might have something to do with their opinions about political issues, or their assessments of the party leaders, there is little evidence to suggest either of those sets of considerations could explain the differences in vote choice

Table 12.2 | Most important issues by birthplace, 2021 (%)

	Born in Canada	Born outside of Canada
COVID-19 and the pandemic	49	50
Cost of living and inflation	39	42
Healthcare	38	34
The economy	29	40
The environment and climate change	29	24
Immigration	10	11
Racism and discrimination	8	8
(n)	1453	307

Data Source: Abacus Data Post-Election Survey, 2021

between those born in and outside of Canada. Immigrant Canadians were hardly different from those born in Canada with respect to the election issues they saw as most important. The Abacus post-election survey used in several chapters in this volume asked respondents to choose the three issues they believed were most important in the election.[7] Table 12.2 reports the five issues mentioned most frequently by respondents born in and outside of Canada, as well as the frequency of mentions of two other issues that seem particularly relevant: immigration, and racism and discrimination. Those born outside Canada were eleven percentage points likelier to rank the economy among their top three issues, but there were no other substantial differences between immigrants and nonimmigrants.

Nor did their positions on some of the most salient issues differ dramatically. Similar percentages of immigrants and nonimmigrants (46 and 43 per cent, respectively) rated the "current state of the economy" as "good" or "very good," and thought the Trudeau government had done a "good" or "very good" job managing the economy (50 and 45 per cent, respectively). On the issue of immigration, 19 per cent of immigrant respondents said there should be

Table 12.3 | Leader evaluations by birthplace, 2021 (%)

	Leader					
	Trudeau	O'Toole	Singh	Blanchet	Paul	Bernier
Born outside Canada (n=344)						
Very or mostly positive	45	40	44	11	17	14
Very or mostly negative	43	36	25	41	34	47
Net	2	4	18	-30	-17	-33
Born in Canada (n=1656)						
Very or mostly positive	37	33	43	20	14	13
Very or mostly negative	49	43	27	42	37	55
Net	-13	-11	16	-22	-22	-42

Data Source: Abacus Data Post-Election Survey, 2021

a lot more immigrants than there are now, compared to 15 per cent of Canadian-born respondents. The majority of those born outside Canada want about the same amount of immigration as now (and nearly as many Canadian-born respondents express the same preference).

Evaluations of the party leaders do not shed any light on differences in the vote choices of immigrant Canadians and those born in Canada either. Justin Trudeau was relatively well-liked by immigrant Canadians, as the data reported in Table 12.3 show, but so was Erin O'Toole. On balance, immigrant Canadians held more favourable views than those born in Canada about Justin Trudeau: there were 2 per cent more immigrant Canadians who had a positive impression of Trudeau than had negative impression, but 13 per cent more people born in Canada had a negative impression of the Liberal leader than had a positive impression. However, impressions of Erin O'Toole show the same dynamic: his net favourability was plus four among immigrants and minus eleven among nonimmigrants. More immigrants than nonimmigrants liked Justin Trudeau and Erin O'Toole. Moreover, both groups had a more favourable impression of NDP leader, Jagmeet Singh than Justin Trudeau or Erin O'Toole.

If issues and leader impressions seem unlikely candidates to explain the birthplace gap in party support, then why did so many more Canadians born outside of the country cast ballots for a Liberal Party candidate? Approaching an answer to that question entails looking at the 2021 election in broader context. The evidence from 2021, including the muted differences in the salience of issues and impressions of leaders, is unsurprising when viewed in historical perspective. The pattern in 2021 is a familiar one.

THE 2021 VOTE IN CONTEXT

For decades, immigrant Canadians, and especially immigrant Canadians from predominantly racialized backgrounds, have been more likely than other voters to favour Liberal candidates. Blais first called attention to the connection between racialized Canadians and the Liberal Party in 2004, and Bilodeau and Kanji subsequently documented the association between Liberal Party support and immigrants from countries outside the United States and Europe.[8] That connection has endured leadership and party system changes, as well

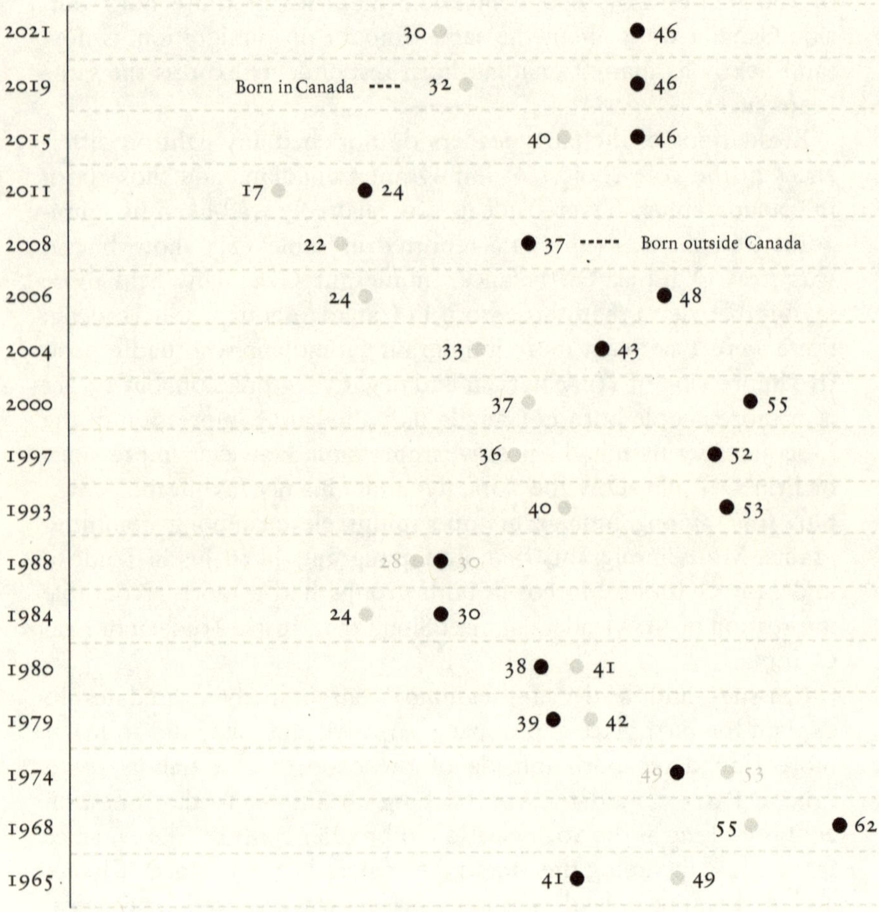

Figure 12.1 | Liberal Party vote by birthplace, 1965–2021
(Sources: Canadian Election Studies, 1965–2019; Abacus Data Post-Election Survey, 2021)

Note: Dark-shaded points represent voters born outside of Canada, light-shaded points represent voters born in Canada. Dark-shaded numbers indicate percentage differences are significant at $p < .05$.

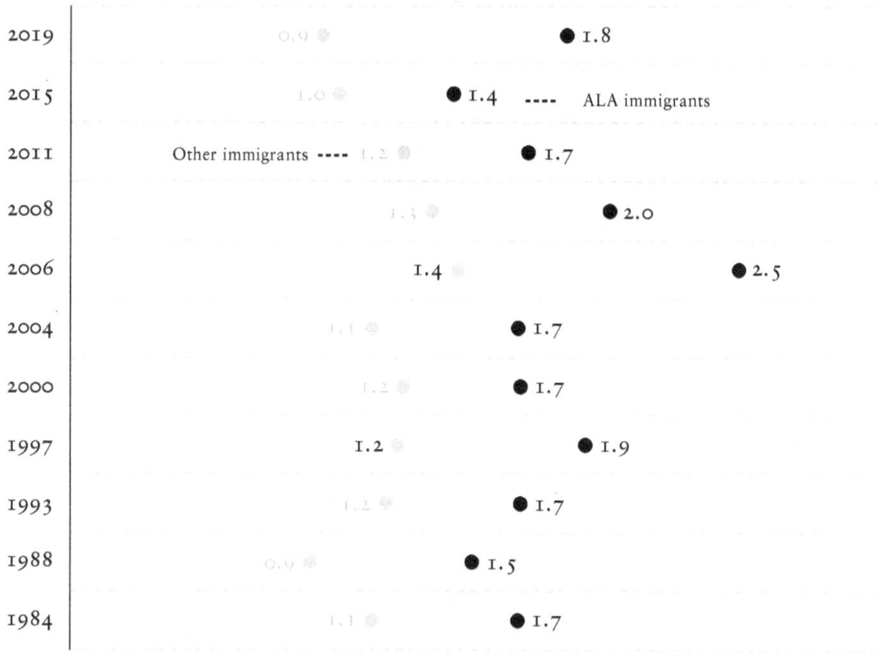

Figure 12.2 | Ratio of Liberal Party support, immigrants vs. born in Canada (Source: Canadian Election Studies, 1965–2019)

Note: Dark-shaded points represent Liberal Party support among ALA immigrants, light-shaded points represent Liberal Party support among all other immigrants. Dark-shaded numbers indicate differences significant at p < .05.

as the rise and fall of Liberal Party fortunes among the broader electorate. Figure 12.1 illustrates the robust birthplace gap in Liberal Party support in Canadian elections since 1965.[9] Until the 1990s, differences between immigrant voters and those born in Canada were modest, and, more often than not, Canadian-born voters were more likely than their immigrant Canadian counterparts to support the Liberals. That changed with the collapse of the governing Progressive Conservatives and the victory of the Liberal Party in the

1993 election, and the Liberals have enjoyed a sustained advantage in the nine elections since that time. Support for the Liberal Party among both groups has typically risen and fallen in tandem, but the long-term trend is a growing gap in Liberal Party support between immigrant Canadians and voters born in Canada: when the difference in Liberal Party support between Canadians born outside of Canada and those born in the country is regressed on election year, the estimated growth rate of the "birthplace gap" is 0.33 percentage points per year ($p < 0.001$).

The source of this growing gap is a change in composition of Canada's immigrant population. Bilodeau and Kanji, building on Blais' research demonstrating that Canadians with Asian, Latin American, and African (ALA) ethnic backgrounds are more likely than others to back the federal Liberals, showed that between the early 1980s and 2004, Liberal Party support was consistently higher among immigrants from countries outside Europe and the United States than among other voters.[10] This is illustrated in figure 12.2, which extends Bilodeau and Kanji's analysis to the 2019 federal election by showing the ratio of Liberal Party support among immigrant voters born in Asian, Latin American, and African countries to support among voters born in Canada, and the ratio of Liberal Party support among immigrant voters born in other countries to support among voters born in Canada.[11] In ten of the eleven elections between 1984 and 2019, ALA immigrants were at least one and a half times more likely than voters born in Canada to vote for the Liberal Party. Other immigrants – those born in Europe or the United States – are consistently more like voters born in Canada.

ALA immigrants, then, are more likely than other Canadian voters to support the Liberal Party, and the share of all immigrants with origins in Asian, Latin American, and African countries has grown. As of 2016, more than two-thirds of all immigrants (69 per cent) were from ALA countries.[12] Figure 12.3 shows the number of immigrants arriving from countries of origin outside Europe and the United States in each quarter, as a percentage of all immigrant admissions, between 1955 and 2013.[13] ALA immigrants were a small fraction of total admissions until the mid-1960s, after which time the proportion of immigrants arriving from these countries grew steadily and rapidly until the early 1980s. For example, ALA immigrants represented approximately 24,000 out of 147,000 admissions (16 per cent) in 1965, but approximately 66,000 out of 112,000 admissions

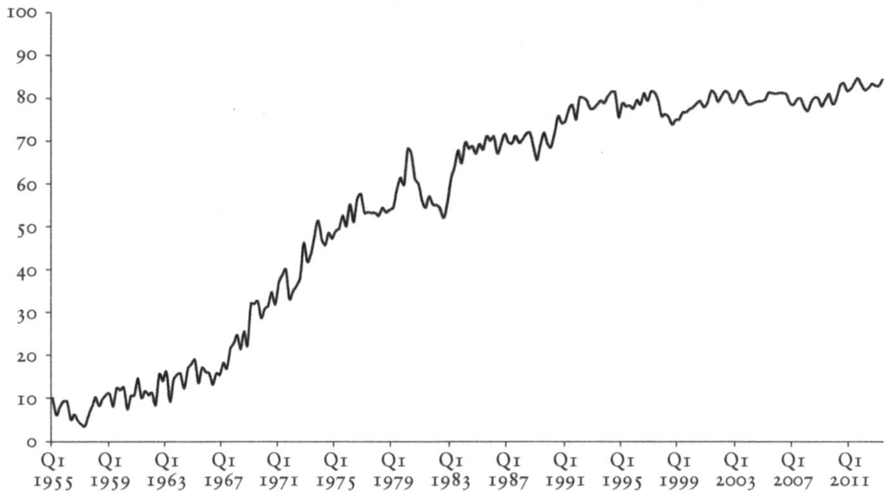

Figure 12.3 | Percentage of immigrant arrivals from ALA countries, quarterly data, 1955–2013 (Source: Statistics Canada)

(59 per cent) in 1980. By the mid-1990s, admissions had stabilized around 80 per cent, where they remained for the next two decades. In the last five years for which data are available, 1.06 of 1.3 million immigrants had ALA origins.

Why are ALA immigrants more likely than other voters to favour the Liberal Party? A definitive answer to that question remains elusive, but what is known about the nature of the relationship is nevertheless enlightening. To begin with, some potential explanations have been effectively ruled out. Neither leaders nor short-term political issues appear to be the root causes because the birthplace gap spans more than three decades. Indeed, in separate studies both Blais and Harell found that individual differences in positions on a wide range of political issues could not explain the gap in Liberal support between Canadians from ALA backgrounds and other Canadians.[14]

Perhaps outreach by the Liberal Party of Canada to different immigrant communities has been more durably successful than similar attempts by other federal parties, but it is not clear why that would be so. Liberals have long devoted considerable energy to building and strengthening ties to these communities, but so, too, have other federal parties.[15] Even as the Liberal Party was building a considerable advantage among ALA immigrants in the 1980s and 1990s, its membership was not especially diverse,[16] and in recent years other federal parties have recruited as many or more candidates from racialized backgrounds.[17]

Even so, there is evidence that party efforts to reach out to ethnocultural minority communities with large immigrant populations can mobilize votes. From 2006 to 2011, the Conservative Party made a highly visible attempt to forge links with ethnocultural minority communities, led by Minister of Citizenship and Immigration Jason Kenney.[18] Yet the Canadian Election Studies data suggest the payoffs were short-lived. From 2004 to 2006, Conservative Party support among ALA immigrants grew from 12 to 28 per cent. Then, in 2011, an estimated 39 per cent of ALA immigrants supported the Conservatives – identical to the Conservative Party share of support among voters born in Canada. In subsequent contests in 2015 and 2019, however, ALA immigrants were ten and twelve percentage points less likely than their Canadian-born counterparts to the vote for the Conservatives, as ALA immigrant voters returned to the Liberal Party.

Another possible explanation is that many perceive that the issue of multiculturalism belongs to the Liberals, which may be particularly important to ALA immigrants. That is, regardless of their specific policy positions on the issues, the Liberals have a reputation among ALA immigrants for being best able to deal with matters relating to diversity, immigration, and multiculturalism. However, there is no conclusive evidence to support that claim.[19] What we do know is that ALA immigrants are consistently more likely than other Canadians to identify with the Liberal Party.[20] On the one hand, explaining the birthplace gap in Liberal voting as a consequence of party identification is a little like kicking the can down the road, provoking the question as to why they are more likely to be Liberal partisans.[21] On the other hand, the party identification findings tell us something important about Liberal support among ALA immigrants. Party identification is generally thought to be relatively enduring at the individual level (and more stable than voter preferences), which suggests that Liberal support among this group of citizens is quite deep-seated. In fact, the evidence is that successive waves of new ALA immigrants have become progressively more Liberal in their partisan orientations.[22] The implication is that Liberal support is a standing decision for many ALA immigrants: occasionally, they might be swayed by leaders or short-term issues to vote for candidates of a different party, but most of the time the Liberal Party can count on their votes.

Most immigrants from Asian, Latin American, and African countries of origin share a common attribute already referenced, namely that they are racialized minorities. Although that finding is not an explanation per se, it is a clue that the answer to why ALA immigrants are more inclined to vote Liberal has something to do with racial background. Significantly, it also points to another important feature of ALA immigrant support for the Liberal Party: this is a wide-ranging, diverse coalition of immigrants from many different countries rather than a phenomenon spearheaded by a few large immigrant communities.

Some immigrant communities are indeed quite populous. However, one striking feature of Canadian immigration is the sheer diversity of immigrants' origins. The three most common countries of origin of immigrants from Asia, Latin America, and Africa are China, India, and the Philippines, and yet immigrants from these countries represent only 9.2, 8.9, and 7.6 per cent, respectively, of all immigrants in Canada.[23] Excluding immigrants from the United States or Europe, an additional 43 per cent of all immigrants have origins in more than 194 countries, dependencies, and territories.[24]

The empirical record shows that Liberal support among ALA immigrants is widespread, and not driven by a few large immigrant communities. Getting an accurate picture of party preferences of particular immigrant communities is a challenge because there are typically too few observations in representative samples of the Canadian population. A rare exception is the 2013 Provincial Diversity Project survey, which in addition to a nationally representative sample of Canadians included a special sample of 1,600 Canadian residents from racialized backgrounds in Quebec, Ontario, Alberta, and BC, and asked respondents "Thinking about federal politics, which party do you usually feel closest to?" Immigrant responses to that question – focusing on the three largest parties – are reported in Table 12.4, alongside responses from individuals born in Canada in the Provincial Diversity Project's nationally representative sample.[25] The immigrant sample is restricted to those from ALA countries and is divided into five groups: immigrants from the four most common countries of origin – China, Hong Kong, India, and the Philippines – and immigrants from all other ALA countries.

Table 12.4 | Party preference by country of origin, 2013 (%)

	Liberal	Conservative	NDP	(n)
Canada	32	28	25	(4120)
China	41	37	16	(76)
India	44	28	19	(73)
Hong Kong	33	49	18	(93)
Philippines	40	32	27	(46)
Other ALA	47	20	25	(394)

Data Source: Provincial Diversity Project, 2013

The survey was conducted in the winter months of 2013, when the Liberal Party of Canada appeared to be at a historical low point. The party had garnered just 19 per cent of votes and lost its role as official opposition to the NDP, in the federal election less than two years earlier. Future Prime Minister Justin Trudeau had not yet been selected as party leader (an interim leader, Bob Rae, was at the helm). Even so, there was an overwhelming preference for the Liberals among immigrants who expressed any party preference. Chinese immigrants were only slightly more likely to favour the Liberal Party over the Conservative Party (41 to 37 per cent), and Hong Kong immigrants expressed a clear preference for the Conservatives (49 per cent) over other parties. Yet these were the exceptions among immigrant groups. Immigrants originating from India and the Philippines showed a distinct preference for the Liberals, and the majority of immigrants from ALA countries – the other group – strongly favoured the Liberals (47 per cent) over the Conservatives and NDP (20 and 25 per cent, respectively). By way of comparison, just under one in three (32 per cent) of respondents born in Canada who indicated they usually felt closest to one federal party chose the Liberals – four percentage points more than the Conservatives and seven percentage points more than the New Democratic Party.

Large immigrant communities are typically the most visible, and so it is understandable if vote preferences within those groups receive the most attention from parties and political commentators. Nevertheless, putting too much emphasis on those communities risks missing the bigger picture. Immigrants from a wide range of ALA countries are much more inclined than other Canadians to support the Liberal Party, and a striking common feature of those countries is that their populations are predominantly racialized.

THE IMPACT OF IMMIGRANT VOTES IN 2021

How crucial to the Liberal Party's 2021 election performance was the support of immigrant Canadians? Put differently, how much electoral power did immigrant Canadians exercise, and to what extent do the Liberals owe their minority government to the support of citizens born outside of the country? At first blush, the answers to those questions may seem obvious: more than one in five voters are immigrants, and so their preferences must have shaped the election outcome. However, the more pertinent way of thinking about these questions is to consider what the election outcome would have looked like if immigrant voters' preferences were no different than those of the Canadian-born electorate. Given that we know immigrants make up an estimated 21.9 per cent of the population and were, according to the Abacus survey, an estimated sixteen percentage points likelier to vote Liberal (46:30), it is possible to calculate the Liberal Party share of the popular vote under a scenario in which 16 per cent fewer immigrant voters supported the Liberals. Accordingly, I estimate that the votes of immigrant Canadians translated into a Liberal advantage of about 3.5 percentage points in the popular vote (16 x 0.219). That is, the Liberals gained between three to four percentage points more of the total vote than they would have received if immigrant Canadians had been no more inclined than the rest of the electorate to vote Liberal.

Yet even that answer is insufficient. Of greater significance in Canadian elections than the popular vote is the number of seats won, given Canada's first-past-the-post electoral system. Indeed, the 2021 contest is a case in point, as the Liberals managed to claim a plurality of seats while finishing behind the Conservatives in the popular vote. The fact of the first-past-the-post electoral system therefore prompts a different set of considerations. Is the proportion of the electorate born outside of Canada sufficiently large – and sufficiently large in a sufficient number of ridings – to have delivered seats to the Liberal Party that it otherwise would not have won?

At issue is the uneven distribution of Canada's immigrant population, which is heavily concentrated in some electoral districts but sparse in many others. The great majority of immigrants settle in Greater Toronto, Vancouver, and Montreal. In 2016, the immigrant population as a proportion of the total population was more than twice the national figure of 21.9 per cent in thirty-nine electoral districts, all in the Greater Toronto (twenty-eight), Vancouver (ten), and Montreal (one) areas. Immigrants represented more than half the population in thirty-one electoral districts, with the highest foreign-born concentrations in the districts of Scarborough North (67 per cent) and Scarborough-Agincourt (66 per cent). By way of contrast, the immigrant population as a proportion of the total population was less than half the national figure in 137 electoral districts.

Whether this uneven distribution strengthens or dilutes the impact of immigrant votes is open to question. From one perspective, the geographic concentration of immigrant voters is essential to their political influence at the federal level: there are simply too many electoral districts in which immigrant voters are a sufficiently large population that the federal parties cannot ignore them and expect to win.[26] Accordingly, the Conservative Party invested considerable time and energy in appealing to immigrant communities between 2006–11.[27] However, an alternative view suggests their uneven distribution might actually weaken the influence of immigrants. It is conceivable that large numbers of immigrants in a few electoral districts gives them considerable power in those districts but diminishes their impact elsewhere. In the United States, there is ample evidence that creating majority-minority districts in which Black voters are a majority often benefits Democratic candidates within those districts, while advantaging Republicans in the more numerous surrounding districts.[28] Black voters overwhelmingly favour Democratic candidates, and altering electoral district boundaries within a state so that Black voters form a majority within some districts necessarily takes those voters out of other districts, many in which Democratic candidates would otherwise be competitive. The origins of the uneven demographic distribution are different in the American and Canadian cases: minority-majority districts are in part the conscious and often highly partisan product of redistricting in the United States; the readjustment of electoral boundaries is the responsibility of independent commissions in Canada, and instead settlement patterns are the cause of the uneven demographic distribution.[29] However, the effects might be similar. That is, because Liberal-leaning immigrant voters tend to be more heavily concentrated in a relatively small number of electoral districts in Canada, it is possible that in a small number of districts the Liberal Party gets more votes from immigrants than it needs to win – votes that could otherwise help the Liberals win in close races in many other districts. Moreover, immigrants' votes are arguably less valuable to parties because they are concentrated in dense urban ridings with large populations: in terms of its power to elect a member of Parliament, each individual vote is worth more in electoral districts with fewer voters.[30]

All of this is to say, assessing the impact of immigrant voting on the 2021 federal election requires estimating the impact of immigrant voting on electoral districts won and lost. One way to do that is to assume the national-level sixteen percentage point gap in Liberal voting between those born outside and in Canada applies across all electoral districts. Next, subtracting a fraction of those sixteen percentage points from the Liberal vote in each district equal to the proportion of the population in each district that is foreign born gives a district-level estimate of immigrant impact on the vote. That is, it tells us the percentage of the vote the Liberal candidate would have won in each district had immigrants voted in exactly the same way as the rest of the electorate. By doing the same for all other parties in each riding, it is then possible to calculate a winner in each riding if immigrant and Canadian-born voter preferences had been indistinguishable.

These estimates are reported in Table 12.5, which shows the actual election results in terms of total seats won by each party, followed by the number of seats that would have been won by each party if immigrant voters had the same preferences as all other voters. The Liberal Party would have won twenty-two fewer seats in 2021 (138 instead of 160), while the Conservative Party would have won thirteen more seats (132 instead of 119), the NDP six more seats, and the Bloc Québécois three more seats. In effect, the broad outcome of the election would have been the same, but the Liberal plurality of seats would have been considerably smaller. To put this in perspective, consider that the estimated impact of immigrant voters on the 2021 election result is almost as large as the impact of the entire province

Table 12.5 | Estimating the impact of the immigrant vote on seats won, 2021

	LPC	CPC	NDP	BQ	GPC	Total
Election 2021 result	160	119	25	32	2	338
Result if born outside of Canada vote matched born in Canada vote	138	132	31	35	2	338
Result if born outside of Canada population was distributed evenly across ridings	159	119	27	31	2	338

Data Source: Elections Canada and Statistics Canada

of Ontario: if the preferences of Ontario voters had been the same as voters in the rest of the country as a whole, the Liberal Party would have won twenty-five fewer seats, while the Conservatives and NDP would have won eighteen and eight more seats, respectively.

What about the uneven distribution of immigrants across electoral districts? To estimate its impact, I adjusted the percentage of the immigrant vote for each party in each district by a fraction of that vote equal to the difference of two proportions: the share of population in each district that is foreign born, and the share of the Canadian population that is foreign born.[31] The results, reported in the last row of Table 12.5, show that an even distribution would have made little difference to the outcome of the election: the Liberals would have lost one additional seat, the NDP would have lost two more seats, the Bloc would have gained one more seat, and the Conservatives seat total would have been unchanged. The crucial factor, then, is the sheer number of immigrant voters across Canada, rather than the way they are distributed across electoral districts.

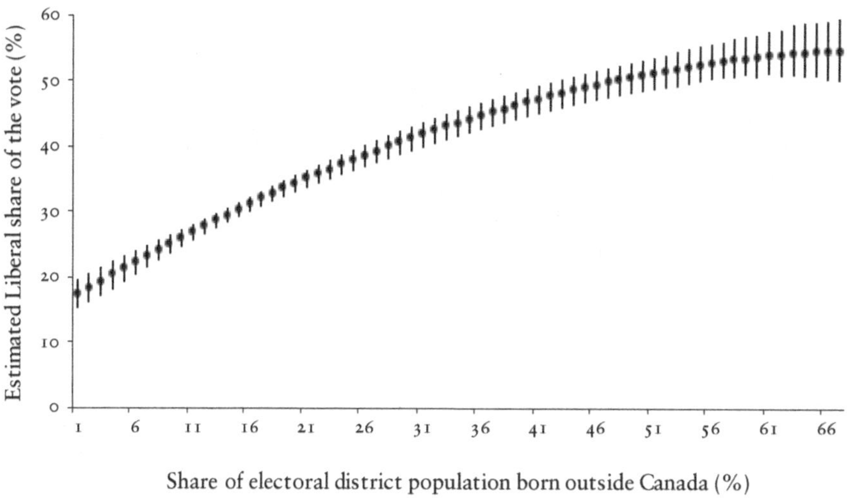

Figure 12.4 | Estimated Liberal vote share by the immigrant population in electoral districts, 2021 (Sources: Elections Canada and Statistics Canada)

Even so, this might underestimate immigrants' total impact on the vote. If the sixteen-percentage point difference in the Liberal Party vote between individual immigrants and nonimmigrants is striking, differences at the electoral district level are even more remarkable. I regressed the Liberal Party share of the 2021 vote in each riding on the proportion of the population born outside of Canada, controlling for region, population density, the proportion of the population with postsecondary education, and median income. The estimated effect of the percentage of immigrants on the Liberal share of the vote is illustrated in figure 12.4. The Liberal Party receives an estimated 17 per cent of the vote in ridings with virtually no immigrants, whereas it garners approximately 51 per cent of the vote when immigrants make up half of the riding population. There are a couple of possible reasons for this finding: to the extent the voting-age children of immigrants live in the same electoral districts, they, too, are probably more likely to support the Liberal Party; moreover, large immigrant populations likely indirectly influence the political attitudes of the rest of the population in their electoral districts.

CONCLUSION

What do the results of the 2021 election tell us about immigrant voting specifically, and the state of party competition at the federal level more generally? One vantage point for thinking about immigrant voting is through the concept of immigrant political incorporation, "the mobilization, political presence, and political influence of social groups and organizations into political institutions."[32] Are Canadian immigrants mobilized electorally? Are they salient to public officials? Are their interests considered in policymaking? Immigrants are undoubtedly mobilized, and in 2021, as in virtually every federal election for several decades, they are more inclined to support one party, the Liberals, over other parties. The question is how much political weight this electoral mobilization confers to immigrant Canadians. Election campaigns rarely seem to pay explicit attention to the large numbers of citizens born outside of the country, and yet immigrant votes are crucial to election outcomes, as the 2021 election demonstrated.

What explains that disparity? One possibility is that, because immigrant voters take into account the same voting issues and considerations as other Canadians, political parties rarely need to make tailored, explicit appeals to immigrant voters. Immigrant voters unquestionably have a significant and growing impact on elections, but from this vantage point they are not so different from the rest of the electorate and highly visible, special efforts to attract their votes are unnecessary. Another possibility is that immigrant voters do have considerable influence, but the forum of election campaigns is not where that influence is most visible. There has long been general unanimity among all of the major parties on immigration and multiculturalism issues, namely, that high immigration and Canada's official multiculturalism policy are net positives for the country. Perhaps this consensus is at least partially a consequence of immigrant voting power: it would be foolhardy for parties that wish to compete for the votes of foreign-born Canadians to break from this consensus.[33]

Finally, perhaps precisely because immigrant voters are reliably more inclined to support the Liberal Party, there is little incentive for other parties to devote special efforts to win their votes. The Conservative Party did make explicit efforts between 2006 and 2011, but their success with immigrant voters was short-lived. This seems less plausible. Regardless of how much attention the parties devote to issues related to immigrants and immigration, the continuing support of immigrant voters certainly has important implications for the Liberal Party and its competitors. If the Conservatives, NDP, or other parties want to win majority governments, it is difficult to see how that is possible without appealing more effectively to voters born outside of Canada. The challenge, however, lies in the deep-rootedness of Liberal support among this group of voters, as the Conservative Party's experience since 2006 illustrates. The party made highly visible efforts to reach out to new Canadians between 2006 and 2011, with modest success.[34] Nevertheless, for the most part any inroads the Conservatives made over that period appear to have been washed away.

At the same time, Canada's "Natural Governing Party" cannot afford to take the support of immigrant Canadians for granted. Nearly twenty years ago, Ruy Teixeira and John Judis published *The Emerging Democratic Majority*, in which they argued that along with increasing education and changing gender dynamics, the growth of Democratic Party-supporting racial minorities in the United States presented the Democratic Party with a long-term opportunity to expand its voting base.[35] In a similar fashion, the Liberal Party of Canada is increasingly reliant on the support of a growing base of immigrant Canadians. Arguably, however, the Liberal advantage among this expanding electorate has only slowed what is otherwise a significant long-term decline in party fortunes. The Liberal Party's election victories have been less and less impressive over the last fifty years, while its election losses have become more severe. The 2021 result would have been much worse for the Liberal Party of Canada without immigrant support.

NOTES

1 Brian Platt, "As Tories Review Election Loss, Weak Support in Immigrant Communities a Crucial Issue," *National Post,* 4 October 2021, https://nationalpost.com/news/politics/under-harper-the-conservatives-once-built-strong-support-in-immigrant-communities-have-they-lost-it-now.

2 Platt, "Tories Review Election Loss."

3 "Focus on Geography Series, 2016 Census," Statistics Canada, last modified 30 October 2020, https://www12.statcan.gc.ca/census-recensement/2016/as-sa/fogs-spg/desc/Facts-desc-imm-eto.cfm?LANG=Eng&GK=CAN&GC=01&TOPIC=7&.

4 Statistics Canada, *2016 Census of Population*, catalogue no. 98-400-X2016184.

5 Statistics Canada, "Reasons for Not Voting in the Federal Election, October 21, 2019," *Daily*, 26 February 2020, https://www150.statcan.gc.ca/n1/en/daily-quotidien/200226/dq200226b-eng.pdf?st=GY_foTen.

6 Jerome H. Black and Bruce M. Hicks, "Electoral Politics and Immigration in Canada: How Does Immigration Matter?" *Journal of International Migration and Integration/Revue de l'integration et de la migration internationale* 9, no. 3 (2008): 241–67.

7 Abacus Data, 2021.

8 Antoine Bilodeau and Mebs Kanji, "The New Immigrant Voter, 1965–2004: The Emergence of a New Liberal Partisan?" in *Voting Behaviour in Canada*, eds. Cameron D. Anderson and Laura Stephenson (Vancouver: University of British Columbia Press, 2011), 65–85.

9 Abacus Data, 2021; P. Converse, J. Meisel, M. Pinard, P. Regenstreif, and M. Schwartz, 1966, *The 1965 Canadian Election Survey* (microdata file), Inter-University Consortium for Political and Social Research, University of Michigan, Ann Arbor MI (producer); J. Meisel, 1968, *The 1968 Canadian Election Study* (dataset), Inter-University Consortium for Political and Social Research, University of Michigan, Ann Arbor MI (producer and distributor); H. Clarke, J. Jenson, L. LeDuc, and J. Pammett, 1980, *The 1974–80 Merged Canadian Election Study* (dataset), Toronto, Ontario, Canada: Institute for Social Research (producer and distributor); R. D. Lambert, S. D. Brown, J. E. Curtis, B. J. Kay, and J. M. Wilson, 1985, *The 1984 Canadian Election Study* (dataset), Toronto, Ontario, Canada: Institute for Social Research (producer and distributor); R. Johnston, A. Blais, H. E. Brady, and J. Crête, 1989, *The 1988 Canadian Election Study* (dataset), Toronto, Ontario, Canada: Institute for Social Research (producer and distributor); A. Blais, H. Brady, E. Gidengil, R. Johnston, and N. Nevitte, 1994, *The 1993 Canadian Election Study* (dataset), Toronto, Ontario, Canada: Institute for Social Research (producer and distributor); A. Blais, E. Gidengil, R. Nadeau, and N. Nevitte, 1998, *The 1997 Canadian Election Study* (dataset), Toronto, Ontario, Canada: Institute for Social Research (producer and distributor); A. Blais, E. Gidengil, R. Nadeau, and N. Nevitte, 2001, *The 2000 Canadian Election Study* (dataset), Toronto, Ontario, Canada: Institute for Social Research (producer and distributor); P. Fournier, D. Stolle, S. Soroka, F. Cutler, A. Blais, J. Everitt, E. Gidengil, and N. Nevitte, 2011, *The 2004–11 Merged Canadian Election Study* (dataset), Toronto, Ontario, Canada: Institute for Social Research (producer and distributor);

P. Fournier, F. Cutler, S. Soroka, and D. Stolle, 2016, *The 2015 Canadian Election Study*, (study microdata), Toronto, Ontario: Institute of Social Research (distributor); Laura B. Stephenson, Allison Harell, Daniel Rubenson, and Peter John Loewen, *The 2019 Canadian Election Study*, phone survey (dataset).

10 Bilodeau and Kanji, "The New Immigrant Voter."

11 There are too few respondents from ALA countries in Canadian Election Studies before 1984 to draw any reliable conclusions about birthplace differences in vote choice.

12 Statistics Canada, "Focus on Geography Series, 2016 Census."

13 "Immigrants to Canada, by Country of Last Permanent Residence," Statistics Canada, last modified 31 January 2022, https://www150.statcan.gc.ca/t1/tbl1/en/tv.action?pid=1710001001.

14 André Blais, "Accounting for the Electoral Success of the Liberal Party in Canada Presidential Address to the Canadian Political Science Association London, Ontario June 3, 2005," *Canadian Journal of Political Science/Revue canadienne de science politique* 38, no. 4 (2005): 821–40; and, Allison Harell, "Revisiting the 'Ethnic' Vote," in *Parties, Elections, and the Future of Canadian* Politics, eds. Royce Koop and Amanda Bittner (Vancouver: University of British Columbia Press, 2013), 140.

15 Daiva K. Stasiulis and Yasmeen Abu-Laban, "The House the Parties Built: (Re)constructing Ethnic Representation in Canadian Politics," in *Ethnocultural Groups and Visible Minorities in Canadian Politics: The Question of Access*, ed. Kathy Megyery (Toronto: Dundurn Press, 1991), 3–99; and, Inder Marwah, Triadafilos Triadafilopoulos, and Stephen White, "Immigration, Citizenship, and Canada's New Conservative Party," in *Conservatism in Canada*, eds. James H. Farney and David Rayside (Toronto: University of Toronto Press, 2018), 95–119.

16 Kenneth R. Carty, William Cross, and Lisa Young, *Rebuilding Canadian Party Politics* (Vancouver: University of British Columbia Press, 2000), 90.

17 Anna Johnson, Erin Tolley, Melanee Thomas, and Marc André Bodet, "A New Dataset on the Demographics of Canadian Federal Election Candidates," *Canadian Journal of Political Science* 54, no. 3 (2021): 722.

18 Joe Friesen and Julian Sher, "How Courting the Immigrant Vote Paid off for the Tories," *Globe and Mail*, 3 May 2011, https://www.theglobeandmail.com/news/politics/how-courting-the-immigrant-vote-paid-off-for-the-tories/article578608/.

19 Bilodeau and Kanji, "The New Immigrant Voter."

20 Stephen White and Antoine Bilodeau, "Canadian Immigrant Electoral Support in Comparative Perspective," in *Comparing Canada: Methods*

and Perspectives on Canadian Politics, eds. Luc Turgeon, Martin Papillon, Jennifer Wallner, and Stephen White (Vancouver: University of British Columbia Press, 2014), 123–46; and Harell, "Revisiting the 'Ethnic' Vote."

21 Harell, "Revisiting the 'Ethnic' Vote."

22 Stephen E. White, "Canadian Ethnocultural Diversity and Federal Party Support: The Dynamics of Liberal Partisanship in Immigrant Communities," *PS: Political Science & Politics* 50, no. 3 (2017): 708–11.

23 Statistics Canada, "Focus on Geography Series, 2016 Census."

24 Statistics Canada, "Focus on Geography Series, 2016 Census."

25 Antoine Bilodeau, L. Turgeon, S. White, and A. Henderson, 2014, *Provincial Diversity Project / Projet sur la diversité provinciale* (dataset).

26 Triadafilos Triadafilopoulos and Zack Taylor, "The Political Foundations of Canadian Exceptionalism in Immigration Policy," in *International Affairs and Canadian Migration Policy*, eds. Yiagadeesen Samy and Howard Duncan (Cham, Switzerland: Palgrave Macmillan, 2021), 13–40; and, Marwah, Triadafilopoulos, and White, "Immigration, Citizenship, and Canada's New Conservative Party."

27 Marwah, Triadafilopoulos, and White, "Immigration, Citizenship, and Canada's New Conservative Party."

28 David Lublin, "Racial Redistricting and African-American Representation: A Critique of 'Do Majority-Minority Districts Maximize Substantive Black Representation in Congress?'" *American Political Science Review* 93, no. 1 (1999): 183–6; Charles Cameron, David Epstein, and Sharyn O'Halloran, "Do Majority-Minority Districts Maximize Substantive Black Representation in Congress?" *American Political Science Review* 90, no. 4 (1996): 794–812; Kevin A. Hill, "Does the Creation of Majority Black Districts Aid Republicans? An Analysis of the 1992 Congressional Elections in Eight Southern States," *The Journal of Politics* 57, no. 2 (1995): 384–401; and, Kimball Brace, Bernard Grofman, and Lisa Handley, "Does Redistricting Aimed to Help Blacks Necessarily Help Republicans?" The *Journal of Politics* 49, no. 1 (1987): 169–85.

29 John C. Courtney, *Commissioned Ridings: Designing Canada's Electoral Districts* (Montreal: McGill-Queen's University Press, 2001).

30 Michael Pal and Sujit Choudhry, "Is Every Ballot Equal? Visible Minority Vote Dilution in Canada," *IRPP Choices* 13, no. 1 (2007): 6–7.

31 In ridings with a larger proportion of immigrants than the national proportion, that fraction of the party vote is subtracted if, according to the Abacus survey, immigrants were more likely to vote for the party, and added if immigrants were less likely to vote for the party. In ridings with a relatively smaller proportion of immigrants, that fraction of the party vote

is subtracted if immigrants were less likely to vote for the party and added if immigrants were more likely to vote for the party.

32 S. Karthick Ramakrishnan, "Incorporation Versus Assimilation," in *Outsiders No More? Models of Immigrant Political Incorporation*, eds. Jennifer Hochschild, Jacqueline Chattopadhyay, Claudine Gay, and Michael Jones-Correa (New York: Oxford University Press, 2013), 27.

33 Marwah, Triadafilopoulos, and White, "Immigration, Citizenship, and Canada's New Conservative Party."

34 John Geddes, "Harper Talks up the Conservative Grip on Immigrant Votes," *Maclean's*, 24 September 2014, https://www.macleans.ca/politics/ottawa/harper-talks-up-the-conservative-grip-on-immigrant-votes/.; Linda Diebel, "Jason Kenney: The Man Who Would Be Kingmaker," *Toronto Star*, 11 February 2011, https://www.thestar.com/news/insight/2011/02/18/jason_kenney_the_man_who_would_be_kingmaker.html.

35 John B. Judis and Ruy Teixeira, *The Emerging Democratic Majority* (New York: Simon and Schuster, 2004).

13

Not Kids Anymore: Millennials and the 2021 Election

David Coletto

In its 26 May 2011 cover story, *Time* magazine led with the headline "The Me Me Me Generation," with the subtitle "Millennials are lazy, entitled narcissists, who still live with their parents. Why they'll save us all." This idea, that an entire generation of people are all entitled, lazy, and out of touch, pervades popular culture. On YouTube, you can watch a video called "You've Gotta Love Millennials," in which musician Micah Tyler describes members of the emerging generation in a way that likely would resonate with their parents and employers. "There he sits inside your local coffee shop," the song begins. "Sporting a man bun and facial hair. Somehow, he believes although he has no job, that by his thirties he will be a millionaire." The song obviously hits a chord, playing into some common perceptions about millennials, because over the past five years, it has been watched more than seven million times.

The relentless attention millennials, the generation born between 1980 and 2000, received over the past decade is not without logic. As the largest generation in many countries, millennials are a powerful consumer group. They make up the majority of working age Canadians, and have been setting trends in technology, fashion, and other consumer product categories for years. They have even been credited or blamed for killing entire industries or product categories.[1] They have also had a major impact on politics and the outcomes of elections.

But the political impact of millennials has not occurred all at once. Because they could not all vote at the same time, their importance as a political force has gradually increased and now rivals their parents' generation – the baby boomers. More recently, they have become a kind of pot of gold at the end of the rainbow. Political parties work hard to win them over. Barack Obama was elected president of the United States because of them[2] and Hillary Clinton lost because of them[3]. In Canada, evidence suggests that Justin Trudeau and the Liberal Party would not have won a majority government in 2015 without their support[4] and might have lost government in 2019 without them.

So important was it to the political success of the incumbent Liberal government, the 2019 federal budget released by then-Finance minister Bill Morneau was termed the "millennial budget." Many of the new measures outlined in the document were meant to help millennials deal with the increasingly unaffordable housing market in Canada and appeal to them in advance of a federal election.[5]

This chapter explores the brief political history of the millennial generation in Canada with a focus on its impact on the 2021 Canadian federal election. Using survey data, it examines how Canada's largest generation was feeling heading into the 2021 campaign, how it reacted to the campaign, and how it ultimately voted. It will argue that millennials were critical to the incumbent Liberal Party's re-election, as they were in the 2019 election, and the Conservative Party's defeat in 2015. For the previous forty years, baby boomers have had a disproportionate impact on the outcome of Canadian elections. For the next forty, millennials will play the same role.

WHO ARE THE MILLENNIALS?

The word "millennial" was first used to describe the generation of Americans born in the early 1980s in historians Neil Howe and William Strauss's 1991 book *Generations*.[6] They defined millennials as those born from 1982 to 2004 and focused their attention on this cohort because "their research made it clear this generation, just eight-years old at the time, would be drastically different than the one before and therefore needed a distinct name. Plus, the oldest of them would graduate high school in 2000, a date that loomed large in the 90s."[7] Others, like *The Canadian Encyclopedia* or *Maclean's* magazine use birth years 1980 and 1996 as the limits.[8] It is not always easy or precise to establish a firm and finite demarcation point between one generation and another. For the purposes of this chapter and all the research I have conducted on generational differences, I consider millennials to be born between 1980 and 2000.

The defining characteristic of the millennial generation is the shared experience and context that comes from growing up at the same time. For millennials, who entered their adult years at the turn of the new millennium, most are the children of baby boomers, and most have experienced formative events such as the terrorist attacks on 11 September 2001, and the recession of 2008–09. These were key events which impacted everyone who lived through them but were particularly important to millennials who were forming their outlook and beginning their adult lives.

Beyond these shared experiences, as the first generation of "digital natives," millennials were also the first to integrate digital communications and technology into their lives from an early age; they were raised in less hierarchical families with lives that were more curated and programed, and received a lot of feedback at school, in extracurricular activities, and from the social media platforms they helped design and build.[9]

Millennials, also often referred to as Generation Y, are the most racially and ethnically diverse generation in Canadian history. When they entered the job market, they were also the most technologically aware and adaptive. They are also the most educated cohort in history, and the first in which more women than men are obtaining postsecondary degrees.[10] As the echo boom to the baby boomer generation, millennials also make up a disproportionately larger share of the Canadian population than the generation that preceded it – Generation X. Given the relative size of the millennial generation in the electorate and its impact on the outcome of previous elections, understanding how electors in this cohort responded to the campaign and how political actors appealed to them can add to our understanding of Canadian politics today and into the future.

A BRIEF HISTORY OF MILLENNIALS AND CANADIAN POLITICS

In the 2000 Canadian federal election, those born from 1980 to 1982 were eligible to vote for the first time. But it was not until the 2015 election that their electoral power – that is, their share of the entire eligible voting population – really began to have an impact on the outcome. From 2004 to 2015, the millennials' share of the electorate increased from 12 per cent to 29 per cent, while their share of those who voted increased from 8 per cent to 25 per cent. The 2019

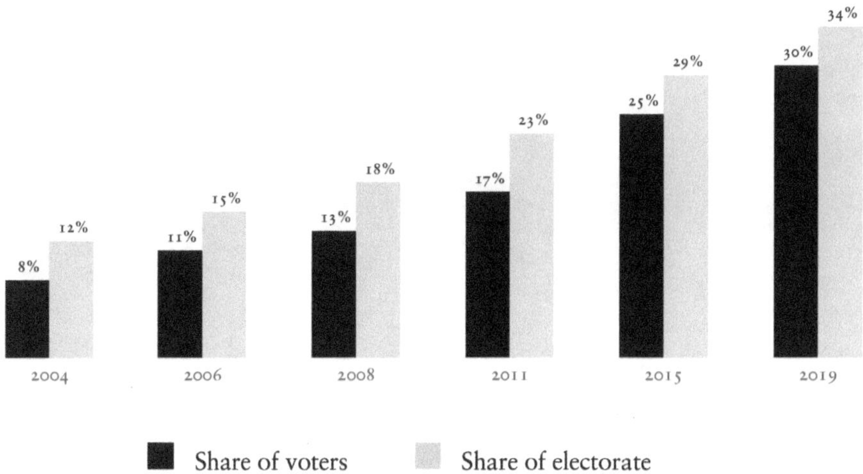

Figure 13.1 | Millennial generation share of the electorate and share of voters since 2004 (Source: Author's calculations based on data from Elections Canada)

election was the first in which every millennial Canadian was eligible to vote in a federal election. In that election, millennials represented 34 per cent of the possible electorate and 30 per cent of those who actually cast a ballot.[11]

Despite their growing generational power in the electorate, millennials have consistently voted at lower rates than older cohorts, thereby muting their potential impact as shown in figure 13.1. For example, in 2008, they made up 18 per cent of the population and yet only 13 per cent of those who cast a ballot. Even in the 2015 election, where turnout among millennials surged by sixteen percentage points over the previous election, they were still underrepresented among those who cast a ballot. The reason for this underrepresentation among the voting population is simple – voter turnout among millennials has lagged older generations throughout the time they have been eligible to vote.

This turnout gap is not new. Since the early 1980s, data suggest that the turnout differential between older and younger cohorts grew substantially. For example, self-reported turnout data from the

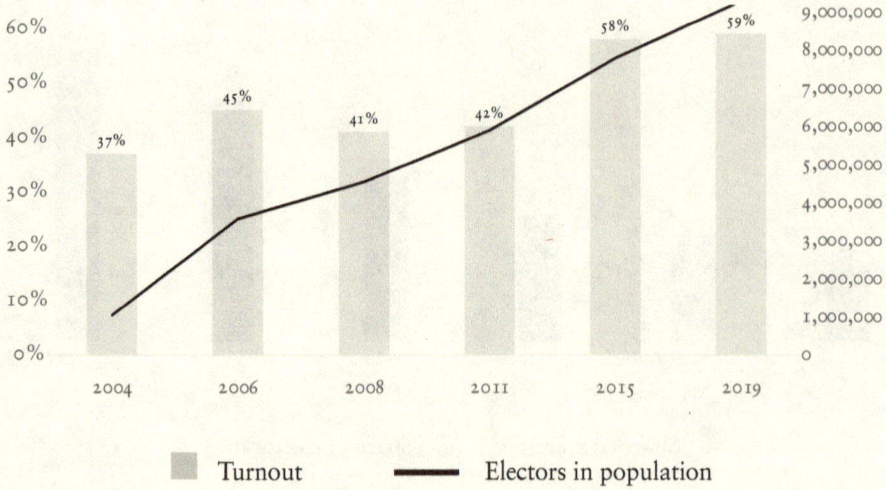

Figure 13.2 | Millennials: estimated voter turnout and number of electors since 2004 (Source: Author's calculations based on data from Elections Canada)

Canadian Election Study in 1980 found only a ten-point turnout differential between older and younger cohorts. That grew to between twenty to thirty points by 2000.[12] But as millennials entered the electorate and engaged in politics, youth voter turnout would rise.

In 2004, Elections Canada began estimating the turnout levels among different age and gender groups.[13] In 2004, 37 per cent of eligible millennial electors cast a ballot. That rose to 45 per cent in the 2006 election that saw Stephen Harper and the Conservative Party of Canada defeat the Liberals. Turnout among millennials fell again to the low forties in 2008 and 2011 but then surged by 16 percentage points in 2015 as shown in figure 13.2. In that election, Justin Trudeau and the Liberals went from third place to first, winning a majority government thanks in large part to the surge in youth voting and support for Liberal Party candidates across Canada. Higher turnout among millennials continued into the 2019 election, increasing by about a percentage point to 59 per cent. This was still, however, lower than the overall turnout rate of 66 per cent.

Table 13.1 | Millennial vote from 2011 to 2019

	2011	2015	2019
LPC	21%	45%	34%
CPC	29%	22%	28%
NDP	34%	24%	23%
BQ	6%	4%	6%
GPC	10%	4%	7%

Source: Abacus Data Post-Election Surveys, 2011, 2015, 2019

The 2015 Canadian election was a turning point for millennial participation in Canadian elections. Not only did voter turnout surge to its highest level, but a post-election survey conducted by Abacus Data found that 45 per cent of millennials voted Liberal, compared with 38 per cent of older voters. The Conservative Party came third among millennials, winning 22 per cent of the vote, compared with 36 per cent among older voters. It is likely that without such higher turnout and significant differential support from millennials versus older generations, the Liberals would not have won a majority in 2015 (Table 13.1).

During the 2015 campaign, the Liberals promised to legalize cannabis for recreational use, to reform the electoral system, and to approach governing with a more progressive agenda. Along with the appeal of leader Justin Trudeau, these ideas were quite popular among younger Canadians. As one columnist described it, Trudeau and the Liberal Party "talked about climate change, feminism, investing in infrastructure and smoking weed. He was the antithesis of everything they had known about federal politics in Canada, and he vowed to overhaul it completely – right down to the very fundamentals of how we form our governments. They trusted him, gave him their votes and arguably handed him his majority."[14] Soon after that election, recognizing the importance of youth support to his party's success, Prime Minister Justin Trudeau appointed himself the minister of Youth, the first ever federal cabinet minister to hold that title.[15]

Support for the Liberals among millennials held steady through the first two years of the Liberal mandate. In a survey published by Abacus Data in February 2017, their support for the incumbent Liberals was 42 per cent compared with 24 per cent for the Conservative Party and 19 per cent for the NDP. This was similar to the situation in the 2015 election. But the Liberals soon faced headwinds. The SNC-Lavalin controversy deeply impacted the Liberal government's approval rating[16] across all demographics. By June 2019, support for the governing Liberals had dropped to 29 per cent among millennials, only four percentage points ahead of the Conservatives. The Green Party saw a surge in support, reaching 17 per cent among millennials.

As the 2019 federal election approached, many wondered whether the Liberals could count on millennial support again or whether the disaffection created by the SNC-Lavalin controversy would suppress millennial turnout. In a regular tracking survey conducted by Abacus Data, the percentage of Canadian millennials who felt Canada was headed in the right direction dropped considerably, from 53 per cent in January 2018, to 45 per cent in January 2019, to a low of 38 per cent in June 2019.

In the end, voter turnout among millennials held, but Liberal support dropped by more than ten percentage points, with the Conservative Party making significant gains – although not enough to win more seats than the Liberals. The Liberal Party won 34 per cent of the millennial vote in 2019, five percentage points ahead of the Conservatives and eleven points ahead of the NDP. Among older generations, the Conservatives won the popular vote by four points.

One of the reasons why millennials were so important to the Liberal victory was their geographic distribution. Millennials are more likely to live in large urban centres and in communities surrounding those big cities. In the 2019 Abacus Data post-election survey, millennials were four percentage points more likely to live in an urban or suburban community and the Liberals won this group by eight points over the Conservatives. Among nonmillennials living in urban or suburban communities, the Conservatives and Liberals were essentially tied with the Conservatives at 35 per cent and the

Liberals at 34 per cent. In 2019, it appears, millennials were again critical to the Liberal victory in helping them win key districts in Canada's largest cities.

THE MILLENNIAL MINDSET IN 2021

Since January 2019, Abacus Data has conducted an annual national survey of two thousand Canadian millennials. The survey explores the attitudes and experiences of the generation through a public affairs and public policy lens. It provides insight into the mindset of the generation in the lead up to the 2021 federal election.

The election occurred while Canada and the world continued to grapple with the impacts of the global COVID-19 pandemic. As it did with every other demographic, the COVID-19 pandemic had a profound impact on the perspectives, attitudes, and behaviours of millennials. Survey data find that millennials were seventeen percentage points more likely than older generations to report having experienced economic problems because of the pandemic. Moreover, millennials were 23 per cent more likely to report having experienced emotional problems such as anxiety, depression, or suicidal thoughts than older generations.

This evidence confirms that the pandemic had a greater impact on millennials, who experienced greater job disruptions, lost income, and more severe emotional impacts. In the 2021 post-election survey conducted by Abacus Data, millennials were nine percentage points more likely to have received or live with someone in their household who received government support tied to the pandemic (31 per cent vs. 22 per cent).

But despite the impact of the pandemic, the millennial mindset remained relatively positive. Those who felt Canada was headed in the right direction consistently outnumbered those who thought it was on the wrong track. By June 2021, a slight majority were optimistic about the direction of the country. When asked to reflect on their own life, 50 per cent of millennials, in a national survey conducted in June 2021, were optimistic about their own future, substantially more than the 17 per cent who were pessimistic. This generally positive outlook was reflected in their economic outlook as well. In June 2021, 62 per cent described the current state of the Canadian economy as "good," ten percentage points higher than in February of the same year. This view was shared by millennials

Table 13.2 | Economic impact of the COVID-19 pandemic

Have you had economic problems because of the COVID-19 pandemic?

	Millennials	Other voters	Difference
Serious economic problems	21%	13%	+8
Minor economic problems	41%	32%	+9
No economic problems	38%	55%	+17

Source: Abacus Data Post-Election Survey, 22–6 September 2021 (n=709 millennials aged 21–41)

Table 13.3 | Emotional impact of the COVID-19 pandemic

Have you had emotional problems like anxiety, depression, or suicidal thoughts because of the COVID-19 pandemic?

	Millennials	Other voters	Difference
Serious emotional problems	25%	11%	+14
Minor emotional problems	41%	31%	+10
No emotional problems	34%	57%	−23

Source: Abacus Data Post-Election Survey, 22–6 September 2021 (n=709 millennials aged 21–41)

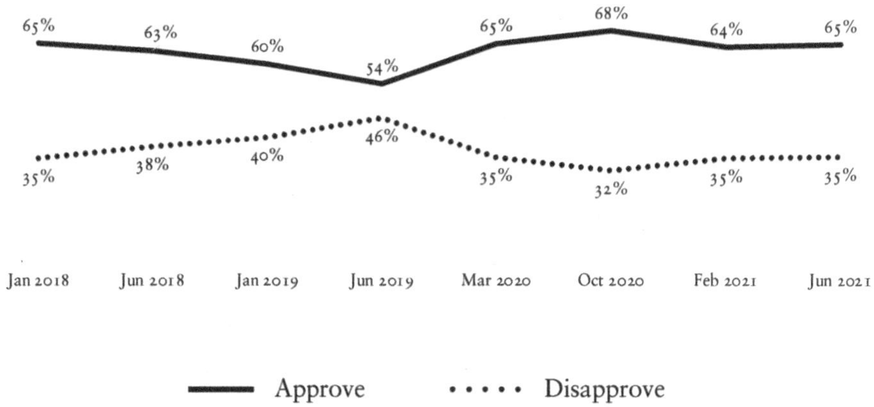

Figure 13.3 | Federal government approval rating among millennials (Source: Canadian Millennials Report, Abacus Data, National Survey of Canadians born from 1980 to 2000, n=2,000)

in all regions of the country and across older and younger cohorts. Moreover, optimism about the economy was rising. In June 2021, 52 per cent felt the Canadian economy would get better over the next six months as opposed to 15 per cent who thought it would get worse over that same period. This is in sharp contrast to the economic anxiety in the first month of the pandemic. In March 2020, 47 per cent of Canadian millennials thought the Canadian economy would get worse over the next six months, compared with 29 per cent who felt it would improve.

Beyond its immediate economic and emotional impact, the pandemic also exaggerated several existing issues for millennials. In what was already an unaffordable housing market, home prices spiked by 31 per cent in the span of twelve months from March 2020 to March 2021.[17] The cost of living increased as prices for food, fuel, and other goods climbed due to both labour shortages and disrupted supply chains. Although many relied on pandemic relief programs from the federal government and savings for some Canadians increased, the pandemic put pressures on living expenses while disrupting employment for millions of millennials.

Figure 13.4 | Top policy priorities for Canadian millennials (June 2021)
(Source: Canadian Millennials Report, Abacus Data, June 2021, n=2,000)

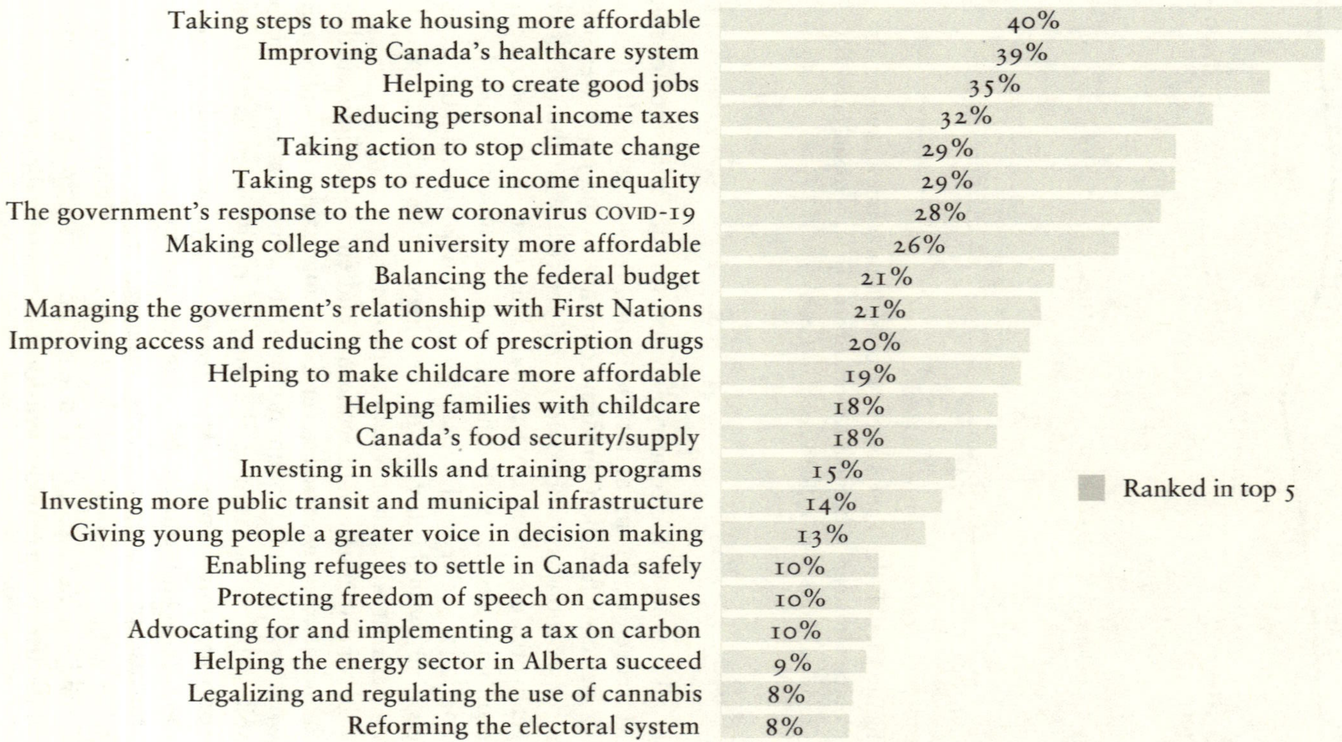

Figure 13.5 | Net federal government approval on specific policy areas (June 2021)
(Source: Canadian Millennials Report, Abacus Data, June 2021, n=2,000)

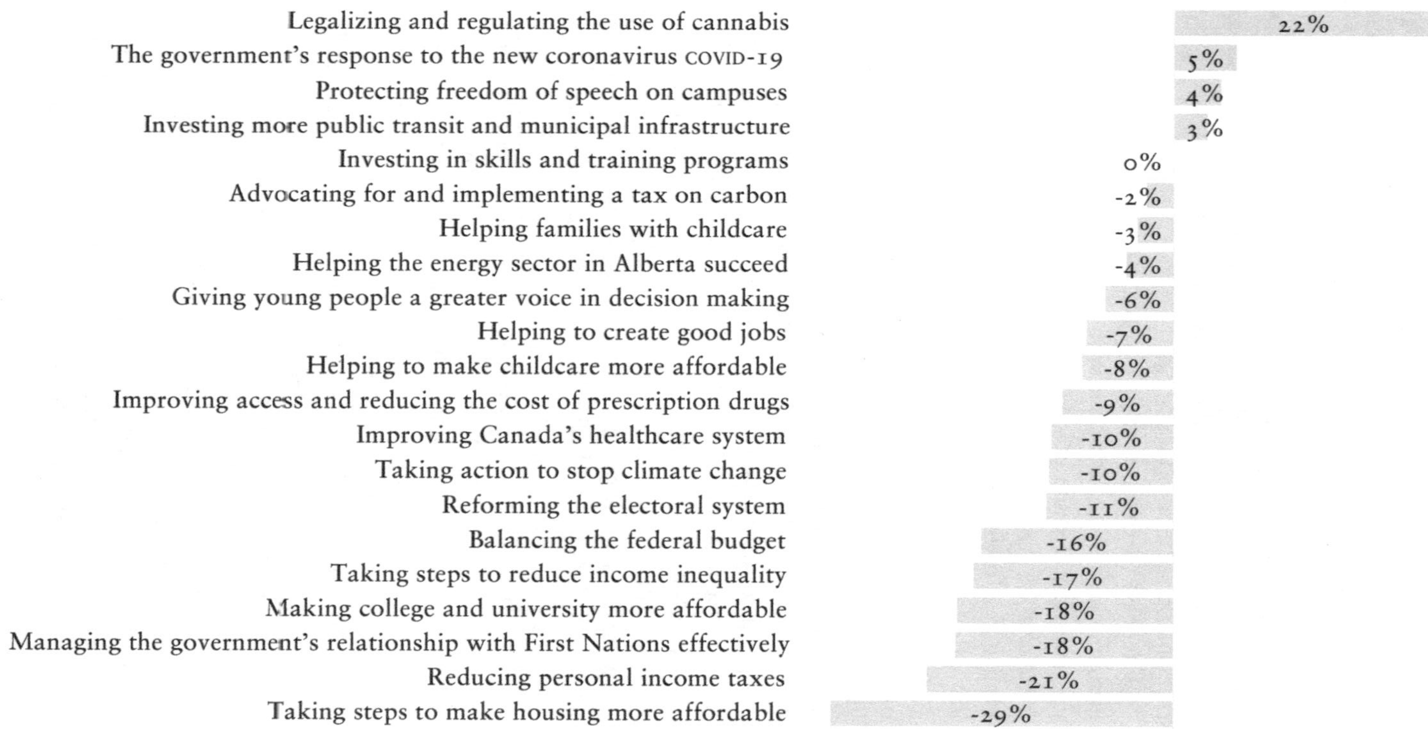

Despite the pandemic, throughout the entire pre-election and pandemic period, the federal government's approval rating among millennials was quite strong. At no point prior to March 2020 did less than 64 per cent of millennials approve of the job performance of the federal government. In June 2021, 65 per cent approved compared with 35 per cent who disapproved. But the overall goodwill millennials had towards the Liberal government masked some frustrations on specific policy areas.

When asked to rank their top five priorities for the federal government in a June 2021 survey, housing affordability, healthcare, job creation, reducing income taxes, reducing inequality, and climate change were in the top six – selected by 29 per cent or more. Housing affordability was the top issue for more millennials than any other issue.

And yet, when asked to rate the federal government's performance on the same items, the government's net approval rating was the lowest on housing affordability, reducing personal income taxes, and reducing income inequality. In fact, apart from legalizing and regulating cannabis, handling the pandemic, protecting freedom of speech on campuses, and investing in public transit and municipal infrastructure, more felt the federal government was doing a poor job than a good job on every issue or policy area tested. This suggests that while millennials generally approved of the Liberal government's performance, there was some frustration on many important issues – including housing, Indigenous reconciliation, the cost of living, and climate change.

After six years with a Liberal government and Justin Trudeau as prime minister, the promise of the 2015 election and the optimism it created among Canadian millennials was now muted. While more still had a positive impression of Prime Minister Trudeau than a negative one (38 per cent vs. 32 per cent), only 14 per cent of millennials had a very positive impression – half of what it was in the month following the 2015 Canadian election. There was far less enthusiasm for the Liberal government or the prime minister in the months leading up to the 2021 election – despite most feeling the federal government had handled the pandemic reasonably well.

One example of this comes from a survey question asked on Abacus Data's June 2021 Canadian millennial survey. It asked respondents whether they felt the policies and decisions made by the federal government benefitted older generations more than younger ones, younger generations more than older, or benefitted all generations equally. Responses were mixed. A plurality (40 per cent) felt that the policies and decisions made by the federal government benefitted older generations more than younger ones while 33 per cent felt all generations were treated equally and 27 per cent thought younger generations benefitted more than older ones. For a political party that promised to do things differently and put young Canadians at the centre of its agenda, there were many who felt reality did not match the rhetoric.

Beyond evaluations of the Liberal government's performance, millennials had mixed feelings about their alternative political options. Like other Canadians, millennials reported they did not know Conservative leader Erin O'Toole very well. Half either had a neutral view of him or did not know enough to have an opinion. The same was true for Green Party leader Annamie Paul, as 64 per cent had neither a positive nor a negative view of her. NDP leader Jagmeet Singh, on the other hand, had a generally positive image among millennials: 42 per cent had a positive impression of him compared with 16 per cent who viewed him negatively. In the months leading up to the 2021 campaign, Singh was the most popular leader among millennials.

And so, as the 2021 election approached, millennials were generally optimistic despite the economic and emotional impacts of the COVID-19 pandemic, but somewhat conflicted with their political choices. They generally approved of the performance of the federal government but were unhappy with how it had dealt with certain important issues – including climate change, housing affordability, and Indigenous reconciliation. They did not know Conservative Party Leader Erin O'Toole very well, liked but were not enthusiastic about Prime Minister Justin Trudeau, and had become quite fond of NDP Leader Jagmeet Singh.

MILLENNIALS AND THE 2021 CAMPAIGN

Given the relative size of the millennial generation in the Canadian electorate and its power to shape the outcome, it was to be expected that the political parties would position at least part of their platforms to appeal and connect with the generation. As the campaign kicked off, several issues were top of mind to millennials. In an Abacus Data survey conducted at the start of the campaign, respondents

Figure 13.6 | Top two issues impacting vote choice at the start of the 2021 election campaign

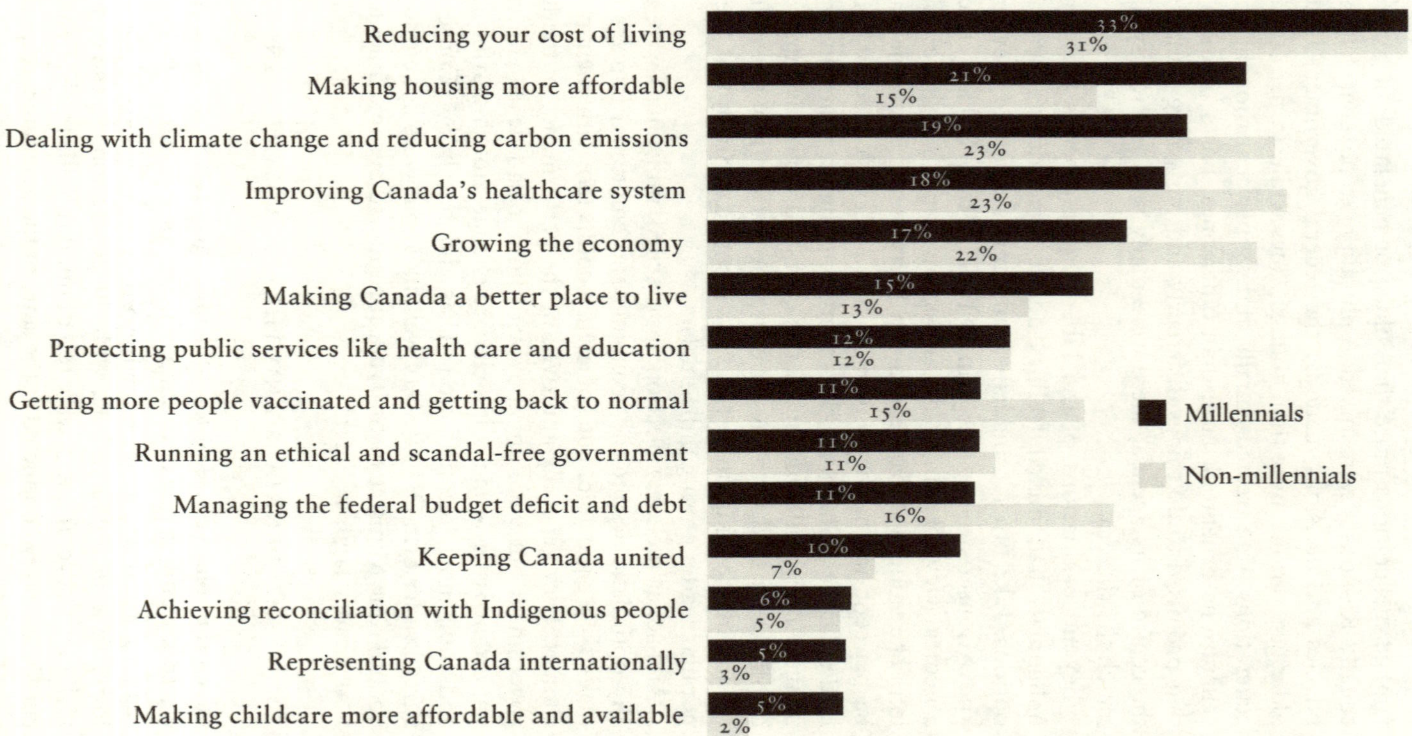

were asked to rank the top two issues that would be most important in deciding how they would vote. For all voters, reducing the cost of living, healthcare, climate change, and growing the economy were in the top five. Millennials and older generations did not fundamentally differ on their priorities. But again, as expected, millennials, given their life stage and priorities, were more likely to emphasize some issues over others. For example, housing affordability was a high priority for more millennials than those from older generations. Millennials were also more likely to rate national unity and childcare as top priorities. They were less likely to rate healthcare, growing the economy, reducing emissions, or managing the federal budget deficit as a top priority than older generations, although many did rate them as important.

These priorities were reflected in the policy proposals released by the main political parties throughout the campaign. For example, the Liberals, Conservatives, and the NDP all released comprehensive plans to address housing affordability.

The Liberal Party promised to create a "First Time Home Buyer Savings Account" that would allow Canadians under forty "to save up to $40,000 towards their first home, and to withdraw it tax-free to put towards their first home purchase with no requirement to repay it." This plan would allow people to set aside 100 per cent of funds they earn up to $40,000, deduct the savings from their income, and when the money is withdrawn, any gains in the account would be tax-free. One analyst described this policy as "candy for millennials."[18] The Liberals also promised to establish a "Home Buyers' Bill of Rights" that would criminalize blind bidding – a sales process in which prospective home buyers submit bids for homes without knowing how much others have bid on the same property – and establish the right to a home inspection as well as ban new foreign ownership for two years.

The Conservative Party platform promised to make homeownership more achievable by building a million homes in three years and by switching 15 per cent of federal real estate holdings to housing. It would also ban new foreign ownership and change mortgage rules to make it easier for homeowners to get a mortgage and reduce the costs of borrowing by encouraging a new market in seven-to-ten-year mortgages.

The NDP, which made several housing announcements throughout the campaign, promised to create half a million affordable housing units, to re-introduce a thirty-year term on insured mortgages on entry-level homes for first-time buyers while also doubling the existing Home Buyer's Tax Credit to $1,500. Their plan would have imposed a 20 per cent tax on foreign home buyers instead of banning those purchases entirely.

There were other affordability promises targeting millennials as well.

- On childcare, the Liberal Party promised to reduce childcare fees to $10 per day on average within five years and invest $30 billion over five years to create a national childcare system. The NDP also promised a $10-a-day universal childcare system. The Conservatives promised to scrap the Liberal childcare plan and implement a refundable tax credit to offset childcare costs.
- On taxes, the Conservatives promised a month-long national sales tax holiday for all purchases made at retail stores in December.
- On cellphone and internet bills, the NDP promised to impose a price cap and expand cell coverage and deliver broadband internet to every community in the country.

On climate change, all the parties proposed more ambitious plans to address the issue, but their emission targets differed. The NDP promised to reduce emissions by 50 per cent below 2005 levels by 2030, while the Liberals committed to 40 to 45 per cent reductions between 2005 levels by 2030. In contrast, the Conservatives committed to lower emissions by 30 per cent below 2005 levels by 2030. Furthermore, the Liberal Party promised to regulate oil and gas company to achieve net-zero emissions by 2050, and to protect and conserve 25 per cent of Canada's land and oceans from development by 2025 and 30 per cent by 2030. The Conservatives would scrap the federal carbon tax and replace it with an incentive program managed by the federal government that would put a levy on fossil fuels and return the funds raised to consumers to help purchase green and environmentally friendly products or home renovations.

The political parties also targeted millennials in their economic policies. The Conservative Party promised to restore one million jobs and create a new hire wage subsidy for businesses that hire new employees as part of their "Canada Job Surge Plan." It would provide a 25 per cent subsidy to all new hires for six months and top up the subsidy if an employer hires someone who has been unemployed for six months or more. It would also require gig economy companies (such as Uber) to make contributions equivalent to the national pension plan and employment insurance program. The Liberals promised to extend an existing pandemic recovery hiring program to March 2022 and provide the tourism industry with temporary wage and rent support (millennials make up a disproportionate share of the tourism and hospitality workforce). The NDP promised to raise the minimum wage to $20 per hour for federally regulated sectors, create more than one million jobs in its first mandate, and look at establishing a guaranteed livable income for all Canadians.

Finally, for those millennials who were still postsecondary students or looking to continue their education, the Liberals promised to eliminate federal interest on Canada Student Loans and Canada Apprentice Loans and invest half a billion dollars to hire up to 1,200 mental health counsellors at postsecondary institutions to address mental health issues among youth. The NDP promised to make postsecondary education more affordable by reducing tuition fees with a long-term goal of making postsecondary school completely publicly funded. It would also remove interest from federal student loans and double nonrepayable Canada Student Grants.

In short, there was a lot on offer to millennials to address their top concerns. Beyond the issues and policy promises, the political parties and leaders worked hard to connect with younger voters. Jagmeet Singh and the NDP used social media platforms TikTok and Snapchat to connect with younger voters. In June 2021, Singh had more than 690,000 followers on the platform. Throughout the campaign, Singh was viewed more positively by millennials than any of the other leaders. His net favourability score (positive impressions minus negative impressions) never fell below plus twenty-five. In contrast, Erin O'Toole was the least popular leader with net favourability scores range from a low of minus fifteen to a high of minus five throughout the campaign. Trudeau's image among millennials was more positive than O'Toole's but never approached the popularity of Singh nor his own popularity back in 2015. Throughout the campaign his net favourables were slightly positive ranging from a high of plus six to a low of plus three.

In a survey during the first week of the campaign, Abacus Data asked respondents how closely several characteristics described each of the main party leaders. Overall, Singh was viewed more

Table 13.4 | Federal party leader image: millennials vs. other Canadians

*Those who say the attributes describe the leader "completely" or "quite a bit"**

	Justin Trudeau		Erin O'Toole		Jagmeet Singh	
	Millennials	Others	Millennials	Others	Millennials	Others
Shares my values	38%	30%	36%	30%	59%	41%
Understands people like you	39%	29%	36%	30%	60%	47%
Strong leader	42%	37%	47%	37%	57%	44%
Compassionate	49%	42%	35%	32%	62%	60%
Fake	46%	45%	47%	41%	30%	23%
Untrustworthy	43%	42%	50%	40%	31%	27%

*Among those who have an opinion about the leader and attribute

Source: Abacus Data Election Survey, 17 to 22 August, n=2,000

positively by millennials and older Canadians. More than half of millennials who had an impression of Singh thought he was compassionate, empathetic, shared their values, and was a strong leader. Fewer felt he was fake or untrustworthy when compared with Trudeau or O'Toole.

In some cases, millennials were more likely to have a positive image of the Liberal leader than older respondents – for example, millennials were ten percentage points more likely to think Trudeau understands people like them and eight percentage points more likely to think he shares their values than older respondents. However, Trudeau suffered from a perception that he is fake and untrustworthy, as almost half of millennials said those characteristics described him completely or quite a bit.

Conservative leader Erin O'Toole scored about the same as Trudeau on several of the positive attributes but was seen as untrustworthy by half of millennials who had an impression of him, higher than any other leader and ten percentage points higher among millennials than older respondents.

On balance, the political parties understood the importance of the millennial cohort and offered several policies to appeal to them. Given past elections, the Liberals and the NDP needed higher turnout and high vote share from this group to help them achieve their electoral goals.

THE 2021 VOTE

In Abacus Data's weekly tracking poll during the formal campaign period, the Liberal Party was consistently ahead of the Conservatives and the NDP in vote intention among millennials. When the campaign started, the Liberals had a small four percentage point lead over the NDP (33 per cent to 29 per cent) with the Conservatives in third at 24 per cent. At no point did the Liberals lose their lead, but by the end of the campaign the NDP vote share among millennials dropped eight points lower than where it started, ending at 21 per cent. The Conservatives ended up with 29 per cent of the millennial vote, five percentage points higher than voting intentions at the start of the campaign and about what it had earned in the previous election (28 per cent). In fact, all three of the main parties earned about the same share of the millennial vote as they did in 2019, according to post-election surveys conducted by Abacus Data.

Demographically, the same poll found the Liberals winning among millennial men by twelve percentage points over the Conservatives (39 per cent to 27 per cent) and statistically tied with the Conservatives among millennial women (33 per cent to 31 per cent). There was also no statistically significant difference in how younger and older millennials voted.

For the Liberals, as with their previous two election victories, their support among millennials was likely critical to them winning the 2021 Canadian federal election. The seven-percentage point margin over the Conservatives made up for the six-percentage point lead the Conservatives had among older voters. At the time of writing this chapter, Elections Canada had not yet released voter turnout estimates by age but regardless of turnout, millennial voters were

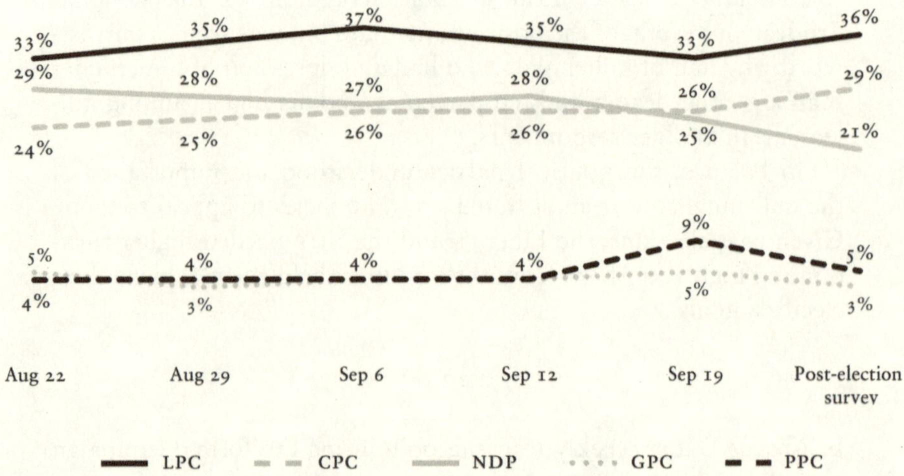

Figure 13.7 | Millennial vote intention during the 2021 Canadian federal election (Source: Abacus Data 2021 Election Surveys)

once again consequential (for some calculations from the Abacus post-election survey, see chapter 15). The Liberals likely would not have won without their support and the Conservatives did not win because they failed to grow support among this key cohort.

So why did the Liberal Party hold onto its support among millennials while the Conservative and New Democratic parties failed to make gains? The NDP had the most popular leader in Jagmeet Singh, and Conservative Leader Erin O'Toole was viewed less negatively than his predecessor Andrew Scheer.[19] Moreover, historically Trudeau's image was about the same as it was in 2019. In 2019, his net favourable was minus nine at the end of the campaign whereas it was minus ten at the end of the 2021 election. One main reason for Liberal Party success remains its advantage on issue ownership. When asked which political party is best able to manage the issue voters cared about most, the Liberals had a seven-percentage point lead over the Conservatives.

For those who said climate change and the environment was the top issue (10 per cent of millennials), the Liberals were seen as the best to manage this issue by twenty-six percentage points (42 to

Table 13.5 | Vote choice in 2021: millennials vs. other voters

	Millennials	Other voters	Difference
LPC	36%	31%	+5
CPC	29%	37%	–8
NDP	21%	16%	+5
BQ	5%	10%	–5
GPC	3%	1%	+2
PPC	5%	5%	–

Source: Abacus Data Post-Election Survey, 22 to 26 September (n=709, millennials aged 21 to 41)

16 per cent). For those who prioritized the pandemic (19 per cent of millennials), the Liberals beat the NDP by twenty-four percentage points and the Conservatives by thirty percentage points (42 per cent to 18 per cent to 12 per cent respectively). For the 9 per cent of millennials who ranked healthcare as the top issue, the Liberals beat the NDP by nineteen points and the Conservatives by twenty-two points. And finally, for those who said the cost of living and inflation was the top issue (15 per cent of millennials), the Liberals edged out the Conservatives and NDP by seven percentage points (31 per cent to 24 per cent and 24 per cent respectively). The Liberals even beat the Conservatives on taxes – an issue the Conservatives often lead on – by ten points (42 per cent to 32 per cent) among the 7 per cent of millennials who said it was their top issue. On these four key issues – the pandemic, the cost of living, climate change, and healthcare – the Liberals held a sizeable advantage.

But on one issue that was important to millennials – housing – the Liberals failed to gain an issue advantage. Among those who said housing affordability was a top issue, 31 per cent thought the NDP would do best on the issue, followed by the Conservatives at 21 per cent and the Liberals at 20 per cent. For those who said housing was a top issue and thought the NDP would do best on it, 78 per cent said they voted NDP. Had the issue become even more salient during the campaign, the NDP might have done better with millennials than it ultimately did, and the Liberals might have won enough seats to form a majority government.

The 2021 election in many ways seemed like a repeat of the 2019 election, and the role millennials played in determining the outcome was no different. The Liberals won more of the millennial vote in part because they were viewed as the best at managing issues that mattered most to millennials. Its leader was neither disliked nor loved, but seen as a better choice than Erin O'Toole, who struggled to be perceived as relevant on the critical issues of climate change, affordability, social justice, and the pandemic. NDP Leader Jagmeet Singh had by far the most positive image but that was not sufficient for the NDP to make any gains with the millennial cohort in this election. Millennials were an important part of the NDP coalition however, making up a larger share of its total vote than any other major party except for the Green Party. Based on the Abacus Data post-election survey, millennials made up 37 per cent of the voting population but made up 44 per cent of the NDP, three percentage points higher than the Liberals and twelve percentage points more than the Conservatives.

Ultimately, the 2021 Canadian election may be one of the first in which millennials transitioned from being voters attracted by a party leader's image and personality to issue voters – basing their support on the party they think will do the best job on the issues they care most about. While perceived by many to be lazy and entitled, millennials once again demonstrated that they are paying attention to important issues, more are participating in elections than in the past, and thus will continue to exert a substantial influence on Canadian election outcomes for years to come.

NOTES

1 "Fourteen Industries Experts Say Millennials Are Killing – And Why They're Wrong," CB Insights, Research Briefs, 26 February 2020, https://www.cbinsights.com/research/millennials-killing-industries/.

2 Tom Rosentiel, "Young Voters in the 2008 Election," *Pew Research Center*, 13 November 2008, https://www.pewresearch.org/2008/11/13/young-voters-in-the-2008-election/.

3 Jelani Cobb, "Hillary Clinton and the Millennial Vote," *New Yorker*, 2 October 2016, https://www.newyorker.com/magazine/2016/10/10/hillary-clinton-and-the-millennial-vote.

4 David Coletto, "The Next Canada: Politics, Political Engagement, and Priorities of Canada's Next Electoral Powerhouse: Young Canadians," Abacus Data, 19 April 2016, https://abacusdata.ca/the-next-canada-politics-political-engagement-and-priorities-of-canadas-next-electoral-powerhouse-young-canadians/.

5 Bill Curry, "Liberal Budget to Be Aimed at Younger Voters, Seniors," *Globe and Mail*, 18 March 2019, https://www.theglobeandmail.com/politics/article-liberal-budget-to-be-aimed-at-younger-voters-seniors/.

6 Neil Howe and William Strauss, *Generations: The History of America's Future, 1584 to 2069* (New York: William Morrow, 1992).

7 Samantha Sharf, "What Is a Millennial Anyway? Meet the Man Who Coined the Phrase," *Forbes*, 24 August 2015, https://www.forbes.com/sites/samanthasharf/2015/08/24/what-is-a-millennial-anyway-meet-the-man-who-coined-the-phrase/?sh=6d7501b04a05.

8 "Who Are Baby Boomers, Gen X, Millennials and Gen Z?" *Maclean's*, 8 January 2020, https://www.macleans.ca/society/who-are-baby-boomers-gen-x-millennials-and-gen-z/.

9 David Coletto, "Talking About My Generation: Why a Generational Lens Can Help Explain and Anticipate Behaviour," Abacus Data, 11 April 2018, https://abacusdata.ca/talking-about-my-generation-why-a-generational lens-can-help-explain-and-anticipate-behaviour/.

10 Richard Fry, Ruth Igielnik, and Eileen Patten. "How Millennials Today Compare with Their Grandparents 50 Years Ago," *Pew Research* Centre, 16 March 2018, https://www.pewresearch.org/fact-tank/2018/03/16/how-millennials-compare-with-their-grandparents/.

11 Author calculations based on data from Elections Canada.

12 Margaret Adsett, "Change in Political Era and Demographic Weight as Explanations of Youth 'Disenfranchisement' in Federal Elections in Canada, 1965–2000," *Journal of Youth Studies* 6, no. 3 (2003): 251.

13 "Estimation of Voter Turnout by Age Group at the 38th Federal General Election," Elections Canada, last modified 27 August 2018, https://www.elections.ca/content.aspx?section=res&dir=rec/part/estim/38ge&document=report38&lang=e.

14 Robyn Urback, "Millennials Finally Fall out of Love with Justin Trudeau after He Abandons Electoral Reform," CBC News, 9 February 2017,

https://www.cbc.ca/news/opinion/falling-out-of-love-with-trudeau-1.3972771.

15 Alex Ballingall, "Youth Minister Trudeau: Is PM Delivering on Promises?" *Toronto Star*, 7 February 2017, https://www.thestar.com/news/canada/2017/02/07/youth-minister-trudeau-is-pm-delivering-on-promises.html.

16 Brooke Jeffery, "Second Chance: The Chastened Liberals," in *The Canadian Federal Election of 2019*, eds. J.H. Pammett and Christopher Dornan (Montreal: McGill-Queen's University Press, 2020).

17 Ryan Flanagan, "Not Just the Pandemic: Why Housing Prices Are Skyrocketing, and What Could Come Next," CTV News, 10 June 2021, https://www.ctvnews.ca/canada/not-just-the-pandemic-why-housing-prices-are-skyrocketing-and-what-could-come-next-1.5464194.

18 Daniel Johnson, "First Home Savings Account Called 'Voter Candy for Millennials' by Mortgage Insider," *Financial Post*, 13 September 2021, https://financialpost.com/news/election-2021/first-home-savings-account-called-voter-candy-for-millennials-by-mortgage-insider.

19 In Abacus Data's 2019 postelection survey, Conservative Leader Andrew Scheer's net favourable rating was minus seventeen. In 2021, Erin O'Toole's was minus eight.

14

Canada Votes in a COVID Election

Harold D. Clarke, Thomas J. Scotto, and Marianne C. Stewart

When Prime Minister Justin Trudeau informed Canadians that they would be returning to the polls slightly less than two years since the last election, he justified his decision by claiming that he needed a fresh mandate to continue the country's battle against the COVID-19 pandemic: "Canadians need to choose how we finish the fight against COVID-19 and build back better, from getting the job done on vaccines to having people's back all the way to and through the end of the crisis."[1] Not everyone was convinced, and opposition parties quickly proclaimed that the new election was an unnecessary and expensive waste of time and money. The stage was set for what would prove to be a fractious, oftentimes bitter, campaign that produced an almost identical result to what had occurred in 2019.

When deciding to go to the people, Trudeau had wagered that Canadians would focus their attention on the COVID-19 crisis and reward his government for responding to it effectively. He was right to assume that voters were very concerned about the pandemic. More important from his point of view, he was also correct to conclude that most Canadians evaluated the government positively for how it was handling the situation. However, COVID-19 was not just a narrowly defined public health emergency. The pandemic had battered Canada's economy – unemployment had risen substantially, inflation had driven the cost of living sharply upwards, and the deficit had ballooned to historically high levels. As the prime minister and his party would learn, the time-tested wisdom that a healthy economy is a major prerequisite for political success still held in 2021.

Other factors were at work as well. As is typical in Canadian elections, images of the party leaders and psychological identifications with political parties joined with evaluations of party performance on important issues as the key triumvirate of forces driving the vote. To investigate the impact of these and other factors that informed electoral choice in 2021, we employ data from a national post-election survey of two thousand eligible voters conducted by Abacus Data.[2] We begin by considering how voters defined the 2021 issue agenda and how they judged party performance on the issues that mattered most to them.

ISSUES 2021: COVID VERSUS THE ECONOMY

When asked how Bill Clinton could defeat George H. W. Bush in the 1992 US presidential election, Democratic strategist James Carville famously replied, "It's the economy, stupid!"[3] Decades of research testify that Carville was correct to identify voters' reactions to economic conditions as a major factor shaping electoral decisions.[4] The economy is the canonical example of what political scientists call a valence issue.[5] Valence issues are ones where virtually everyone agrees on the goals of public policy and political debate focuses on how to achieve those goals and, more importantly, who is best able to do so. When voters assess economic conditions there is widespread agreement that an economy characterized by low rates of inflation and unemployment and vigorous, sustainable growth is the ideal.

Figure 14.1 displays Canadians' evaluations of the state of the national economy for the four federal elections held between 2011 and 2021. As shown, 72 per cent were positive about economic conditions a decade ago when the Conservatives led by Stephen Harper won a majority government. However, in 2015, shortly after the economy had tipped into recession, only 43 per cent offered positive appraisals, 57 per cent gave negative ones and Harper's Conservatives were soundly defeated by the Trudeau-led Liberals. Economic evaluations reversed again in 2019 when 57 per cent were positive about the state of the economy and 43 per cent were negative. Yet another reversal occurred in 2021 when 57 per cent reported that they judged the country's economic performance negatively and 43 per cent judged it positively. Ignoring Carville's aphorism about the importance of economic conditions as a driver of voting behaviour, Prime Minister Trudeau called the 2021 federal election in a context of substantial negativity about Canada's economy. This would prove to be risky business for the prime minister and his party.

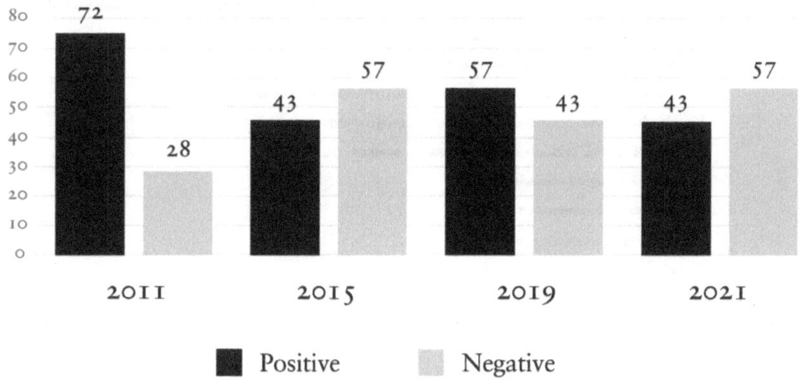

Figure 14.1 | Evaluations of the state of the Canadian economy, 2011–21 (Sources: 2011 Political Support in Canada Pre-Election Survey, 2015 Abacus Canada Pre-Election Survey, and 2019 and 2021 Abacus Data Post-Election Surveys)

Other valence issues also are frequently salient in national elections in Canada and elsewhere.[6] Healthcare is a good example, with overwhelming majorities demanding accessible and effective healthcare. Education and security are additional examples. A high quality, readily affordable education system has widespread support, as does providing security from terrorists, rogue regimes, and common criminals. Over the past decade, environmental protection has received increasing attention, and opinion polls report that sizable numbers of Canadians designate combating climate change as a high priority goal.[7]

Before the 2021 federal election was called, COVID-19 had joined this list of salient valence issues. The World Health Organization (WHO) declared a worldwide pandemic on 11 March 2020, and COVID-19 immediately became a major topic of public concern. The virus proceeded to wreak a horrific toll on public health in countries around the globe. Canada was not spared. By the time of the 2021 federal election nearly 1.6 million Canadians had contracted the disease and more than 27,000 had died from it.[8] Government efforts to reduce the pandemic's impact by encouraging "social distancing," forbidding international and, in some cases, interprovincial travel,

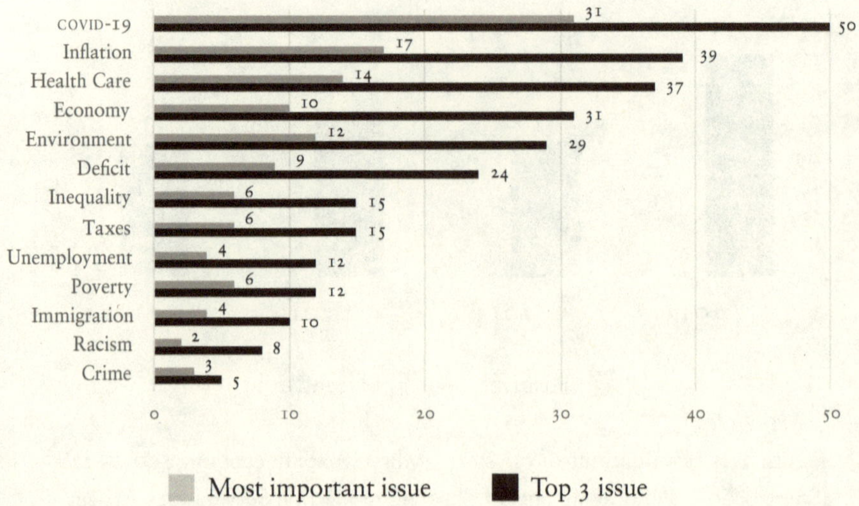

Figure 14.2 | Most important issues facing the country, 2021
(Source: 2021 Abacus Post-Election Survey)

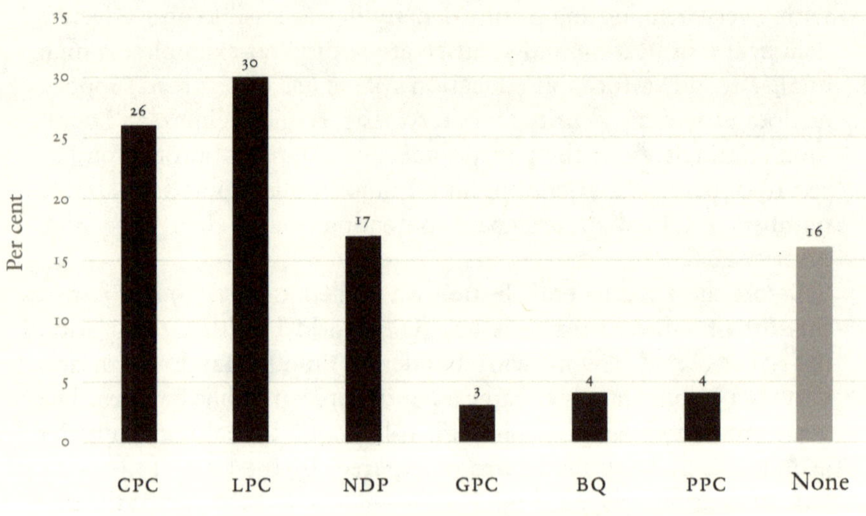

Figure 14.3 | Party best able to handle all most important issues, 2021
(Source: 2021 Abacus Post-Election Survey)

closing hospitality venues, schools, sporting events, and other public gatherings took a heavy toll on the economy. Unemployment rose from 5.6 per cent at the time of the October 2019 election to 13.7 per cent in May 2020 before retreating to a still uncomfortable 7.1 per cent when the election was called in August 2021. The cost of living was also a problem – inflation had jumped upwards from 1.9 per cent to 4.4 per cent, with housing prices in major cities escalating sharply.[9] Reacting to the mounting economic adversity, consumer confidence plummeted in the spring of 2020 and then made only a partial recovery.[10] There were adverse psychological consequences as well – 16 per cent and 35 per cent, respectively, of the respondents in Abacus' 2021 post-election survey reported that they had suffered either serious or minor psychological problems. The devastation wrought by the COVID crisis ensured the pandemic would rank high on the electoral agenda in 2021.

Figure 14.2 shows the emphasis Canadians placed on COVID-19, the economy, and several other issues at the time of the 2021 election. When presented with a list of thirteen issues and asked to designate the three most important, 50 per cent of the Abacus respondents chose COVID, 39 per cent selected inflation, and 37 per cent, 31 per cent, and 29 per cent cited healthcare, the economy generally, and the environment respectively. One-quarter picked the deficit. Other issues such as immigration, racism, and crime were cited by less than one person in twenty. When asked a follow-up question about which issue was the single most important, 31 per cent selected COVID, 17 per cent picked inflation, 14 per cent chose healthcare and 12 per cent and 10 per cent, respectively, opted for the environment or the economy generally. The salience of economic conditions is magnified if one sums the percentages mentioning inflation, the economy, or the deficit – taken together, 36 per cent cited one these issues as "most important." These data testify that COVID and economic concerns topped the 2021 issue agenda.

A plurality of the Abacus respondents thought the Liberals were best able to handle the issue respondents designated as the single most important facing the country. However, as figure 14.3 indicates, Liberal strength on these issues was not overwhelming – 30 per cent chose the Liberals, 26 per cent selected the Conservatives, and 17 per cent opted for the NDP. The BQ, the Greens, and the People's Party each were chosen by less than one person in twenty. A substantial number of the Abacus survey respondents did not designate any

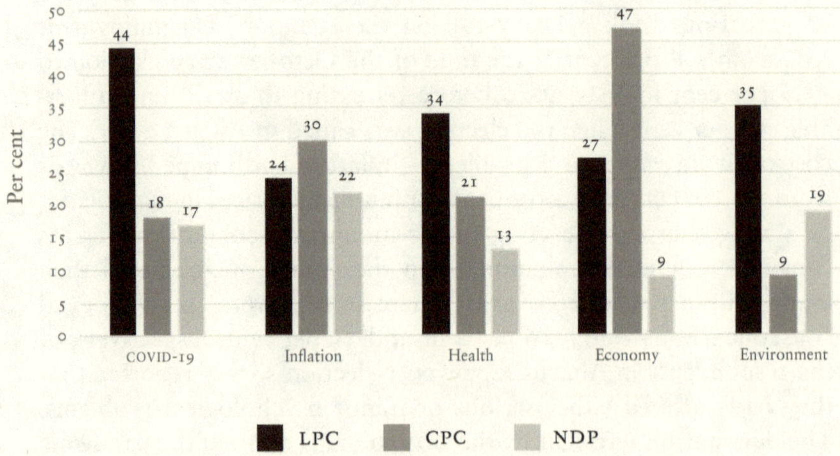

Figure 14.4 | Party best able to handle five most frequently mentioned important issues, 2021 (Source: 2021 Abacus Post-Election Survey)

"best party" – 16 per cent said none of the federal parties was able to handle important issues or that they did not know which party was best.

The data in Figure 14.3 conceal the fact that the parties selected as best able to handle important issues varied widely across issue categories. Figure 14.4 illustrates this point. If Prime Minister Trudeau based his decision to call the 2021 election on a perception that Canadians were favourably disposed towards his government's efforts to combat COVID, he was correct. When the data on party best able to handle important issues is disaggregated by specific issues, among those choosing COVID as most important, 44 per cent selected the Liberals as the most competent party, and only 18 per cent and 17 per cent, respectively, chose the Conservatives or the NDP. The Liberals also held sizable leads among people designating healthcare or the environment as their biggest concern, with the party's edge being impressive on the latter issue. Among Abacus respondents prioritizing the environment, slightly over one-third thought the Liberals were best and one in five picked the NDP. Less than one in ten of those surveyed opted for the Conservatives.

The picture is very different for economic issues. As Figure 14.4 illustrates, among respondents selecting inflation as most important, 30 per cent chose the Conservatives as best, with 24 per cent selecting the Liberals, and 22 per cent the NDP. The Conservative edge among those citing the economy generally is considerably larger. Nearly half of this group opted for the Conservatives, and just slightly over one-quarter selected the Liberals. Less than one person in ten designated the NDP.

Overall, the data in Figure 14.4 reveal that Canadians' evaluations of the competence of the federal parties varied widely on 2021's two key valence issues, COVID-19 and the economy. For COVID – the single most frequently mentioned issue – the Liberals held a big lead. However, this was offset by Conservative preferences among the large group of people emphasizing various aspects of the economy. These very different judgments about party competence on the two leading issues would make it difficult for both major parties to assemble the large electoral coalition needed to win a majority of parliamentary seats.

PARTY LEADERS

Party leader images are a key heuristic (cue) that voters use when making their electoral choices.[11] Seeking to navigate a political environment where stakes are high and uncertainty abounds, voters employ their images of the party leaders to facilitate decisions about who is best able to handle high priority issues. The importance of leader images for explaining voting behaviour was one of the important findings to emerge from the early Canadian election studies conducted in the 1960s.[12] In the half century plus since then researchers have repeatedly documented that leader images are major determinants of electoral choice.[13] And 2021 was no exception.

Summary reactions to the party leaders in the 2015, 2019, and 2021 federal elections are catalogued in Figure 14.5. A striking finding is the decline in Trudeau's ratings after 2015 when 44 per cent were favourably disposed towards him and only 30 per cent judged him negatively. In contrast, only 36 per cent in 2019 and 38 per cent in 2021, respectively, were favourable and 45 per cent and 48 per cent were unfavourable. Widespread negativity also characterized public reactions to the Conservative leaders. As Figure 14.5 shows, the balance of negative to positive feelings about them was

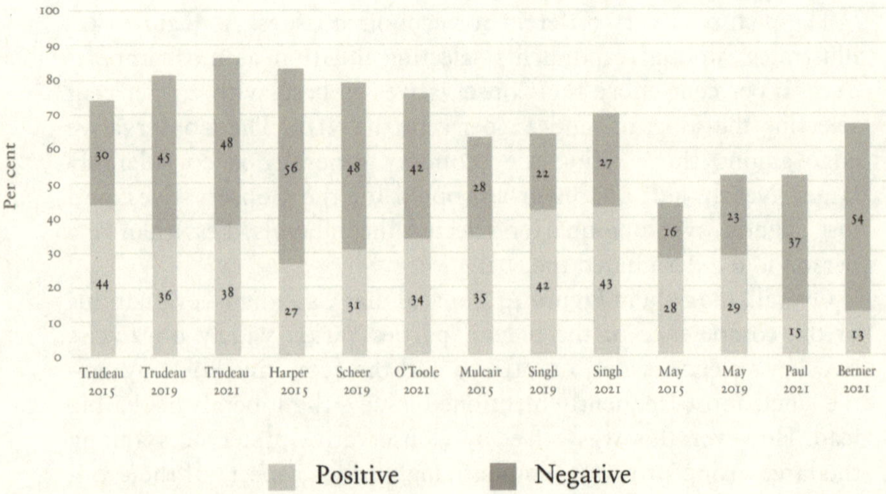

Figure 14.5 | Feelings about party leaders in 2015, 2019, and 2021 (Source: Abacus Pre- and Post-Election Surveys)

especially pronounced in 2015 when a clear majority judged Stephen Harper negatively and just over one-quarter judged him positively. The percentage of positive responses increased modestly for subsequent Conservative leaders, Andrew Scheer and Erin O'Toole. However, the latter's figure (34 per cent) meant that he had slightly fewer endorsements than Trudeau (38 per cent) when voters cast their ballots in 2021.

Public reactions to NDP Leader Jagmeet Singh were quite different. In both 2019 and then again in 2021 Singh's pluses outdistanced his minuses by wide margins. In 2019 these numbers were 42 per cent and 22 per cent respectively. His equivalent 2021 figures were 43 per cent and 27 per cent. Thus, Singh was more favourably received than the leaders of the two major parties in both of these elections. Singh's popularity also contrasts sharply with how voters reacted to leaders of the minor parties. In 2021, only 15 per cent of the electorate viewed the Green Party leader, Annamie Paul, positively and 37 per cent viewed her negatively. Reactions to People's Party leader, Maxime Bernier, were dismal – just slightly over one person in ten was positively disposed and over half judged him negatively.

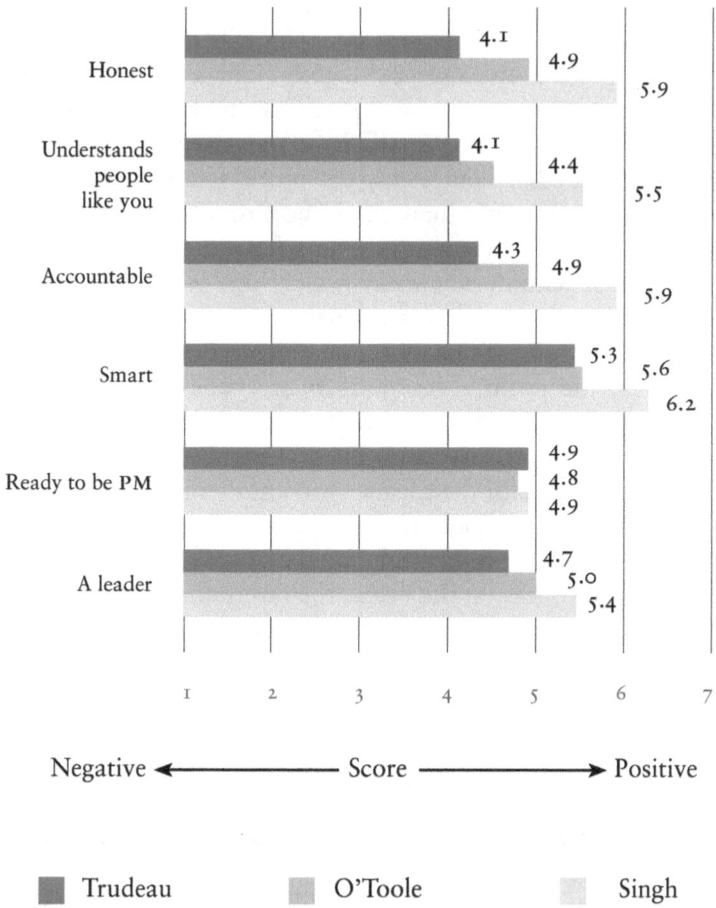

Figure 14.6 | Party leader traits: Justin Trudeau, Erin O'Toole, and Jagmeet Singh, 2021 (Source: 2021 Abacus Post-Election Survey)

Questions in the 2021 Abacus survey asking about a variety of specific traits of the party leaders provide additional insights. Figure 14.6 summarizes responses for six important traits along zero to ten scales. In terms of average ratings on these scales, Justin Trudeau fares quite badly, being outdistanced on five of six traits by O'Toole and Singh. Only on the item "ready to be prime minister" does Trudeau rank first (tied with Singh). O'Toole does somewhat better than Trudeau on the remaining five trait scales, but similar to his Liberal rival O'Toole's scores are lacklustre. In contrast, Jagmeet Singh is viewed more positively – his average trait scores place him number one in terms of leadership, intelligence, accountability, responsiveness, and honesty. Yet even in Singh's case, there is only one trait ("smart") for which he has an average score greater than six on the zero to ten scale. None of Trudeau's or O'Toole scores reach that mark.

Taken together with the summary evaluations presented in Figure 14.5, the trait ratings emphasize that many Canadians were less than enthusiastic about any the party leaders in 2021. In Trudeau's case it is clear that the positive reception many voters had given him when he first led to his party to victory in 2015 had evaporated by 2019 and did not return two years later. The widespread absence of positive endorsements for their leader was another factor that would diminish the Liberals' chances of winning a parliamentary majority in 2021, in part by not motivating voters to turn out to the polls, as chapter 15 illustrates. In the event, they were fortunate that their main rival, the Conservatives, also had a leader whose ratings were far from stellar.

PARTISANSHIP

The pioneering mid-twentieth-century election studies conducted at the University of Michigan found that most American voters had psychological attachments to political parties that strongly influenced how they viewed the political world and did much to shape the choices they made in successive elections.[14] The Michigan researchers called these attachments party identifications and contended that in the vast majority of cases they were stable long-term elements in the set of forces driving voting behaviour. Early Canadian election studies carried out in the 1960s and 1970s also found that a large majority of people identified psychologically with political parties. However, these partisan attachments frequently were "flexible." Large numbers of Canadians identified only weakly with a political party or were "inconsistent" in the sense that they identified with different parties at the federal and provincial levels of government. Also, Canadians' party identifications often were characterized by individual-level instability, with sizable minorities moving from one party to another between adjacent elections.[15]

Figure 14.7 | Federal party identification, 2011–21

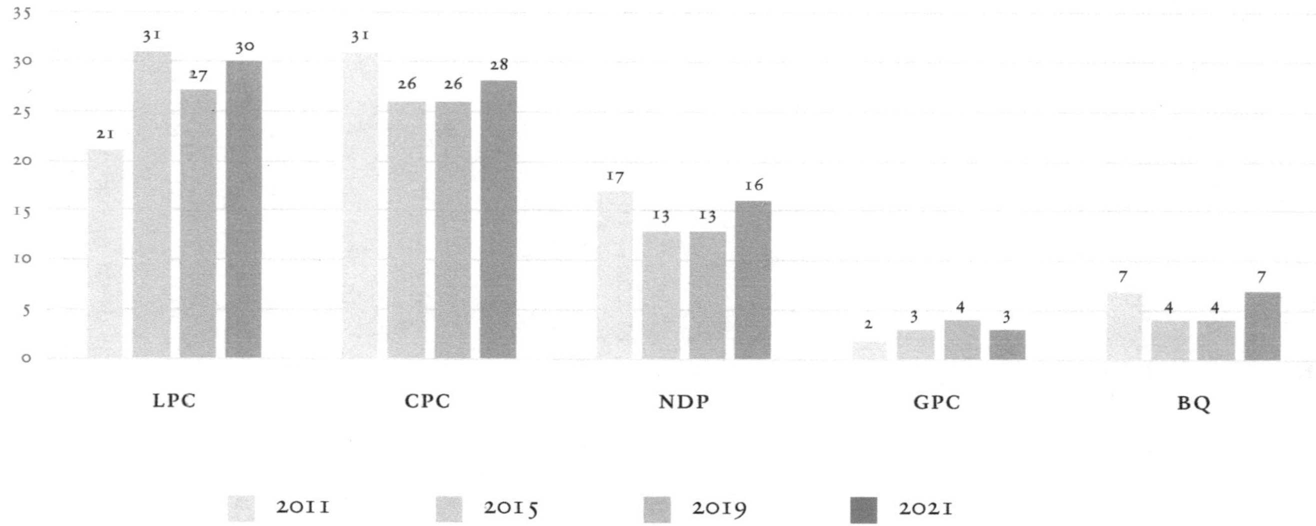

(Souce: 2011 Political Support in Canada Pre-Election, 2015 Abacus Pre-Election, 2019 & 2021 Abacus Post-Election Surveys)

Although weakness, inconsistency, and instability were features of partisanship that encouraged Canadian political scientists to reconsider the applicability of the "Michigan model" of voting behaviour, statistical analyses show that at any particular point in time, Canadian voters' psychological attachments to political parties significantly influence the choices they make.[16] Similar to citizens in other mature democracies, Canadians use their party identifications as guides for assembling and interpreting information relevant for making political decisions. Like party leader images, party identifications act as heuristics voters use when casting their ballots. Other things being equal, a party with a substantial edge in the number of party identifiers is well positioned for victory.

Figure 14.7 displays the distributions of identifications with various parties at the time of the last four federal elections. As shown, the Conservatives held a ten-point lead over the Liberals (31 to 21 per cent) in 2011, but this evaporated in 2015 and has not returned. When the 2021 election was held, 30 per cent identified with the Liberals, and slightly fewer (28 per cent) said they were Conservatives. The cohort of NDP identifiers was consistently smaller, ranging from a high of 17 per cent in 2011 to low of 13 per cent in 2015 and 2019. In 2021, 16 per cent said they were NDP partisans. Reflecting its poor performance on election day, only 3 per cent identified with the Green Party in 2021.

Viewed generally, the party identification data point up the difficulties the Liberals faced in 2021. Combined with their failure to receive widespread endorsements for handling the economy and their leader's inability to generate enthusiasm across much of the electorate, the Liberals' mediocre share of party identifiers worked to inhibit their support. With only three Canadians in ten claiming to be Liberal partisans and almost as many identifying with the Conservatives, Prime Minister Trudeau and his party faced an uphill road to secure their coveted majority government.

MAKING POLITICAL CHOICES

Multivariate statistical analyses of the Abacus survey data enable us to assess the importance of various influences on voting in 2021. Separate binomial logit models[17] of Liberal, Conservative, NDP, and People's Party voting are specified, and the effects of several predictor variables are investigated.[18] In keeping with previous research documenting the centrality of valence politics considerations as factors driving electoral choice, we include judgments about which party is best on a voter's most important issue, reactions to the party leaders, and party identifications. As discussed above, the economy and other valence issues typically dominate the issue agenda and judgments about party performance on such issues are important drivers of voting behaviour. Canadians rely heavily on their images of party leaders and their party identifications as cues regarding which party will do the best job on these issues. In addition to these valence politics variables, a measure of a voter's position on a summary left-right scale is included to determine the extent to which electoral choices are a product of general ideological orientations.

A "tactical voting" variable is included as well. This predictor assesses the possibility that some voters cast their ballots for a party that was not their first preference to keep another party from winning in their riding. An example would be a voter who prefers the NDP but judges that the New Democrats are not competitive in their riding and opts for the Liberals to help defeat the Conservatives. Another example is someone who favours the People's Party but decides to support the Conservatives to increase the likelihood that the Liberal candidate will not be successful.

Finally, several socio-demographic characteristics are included. These variables include age, education, gender, annual family income, and degree of urbanization of place of residence. Variables for region of residence are also specified.

The results of these analyses are summarized in Table 14.1. Overall, the voting models have strong explanatory power, with the percentages of voting decisions correctly classified varying from a low of 92.0 per cent for the Liberals to a high of 97.9 per cent for the People's Party. Similarly, the McKelvey R^2 goodness-of-fit statistic[19] testifies that models perform well. On a zero to one scale, the R^2's range from 0.70 for the NDP to 0.92 for the PPC. Comparable numbers for the Liberals and the Conservatives are 0.80 and 0.85, respectively.

Other entries in Table 14.1 document how the probability of voting for a party changes if a statistically significant predictor variable varies across its range while all other predictors are held constant at their average values. The results make the point that, as in other Canadian federal elections, party leader images were very important in 2021. Specifically, the probability of voting Liberal increases

Table 14.1 | Changes in probability of voting for various political parties associated with changes in statistically significant predictors

Predictor Variable	CPC	LPC	NDP	PPC
Party Leaders				
O'Toole (CPC)	.47	–.08	–.15	.11
Trudeau (LPC)	–.11	.52	–.11	–.06
Singh (NDP)			.15	
Paul (GPC)		–.05	.08	
Blanchet (BQ)	–.04	–.07		
Bernier (PPC)	–.08	.08		.28
Party best on most important issue				
CPC			–.04	–.02
LPC	–.11	.10		–.03
NDP	–.06		.13	
GPC	–.20			
BQ	–.09			
PPC	–.08	–.14	–.12	.06
Federal party identification				
CPC	.08	–.08	–.08	
LPC	–.04	.09	–.09	
NDP	–.08	–.09	.10	–.04
Other	-.06			
Left-right ideology		–.06		
Tactical voting	.08	.07	–.06	

Table 14.1 | (*continued*)

Predictor Variable	CPC	LPC	NDP	PPC
Socio-demographics				
Age				
Education				
Gender				
Income	.05		−.05	
Urban-Rural				−.03
Region of residence				
Atlantic				
Quebec	−.03	−.05	−.03	
Prairies				
British Columbia	−.06		.04	
McKelvey R^2	.85	.80	.70	.92
Per cent correctly predicted	93.2	92.0	93.3	97.9

Note: Binomial logit models; changes in probability computed by varying a statistically significant ($p < .05$) predictor across its range while holding all other predictors at their mean values.

by fully 0.52 points (on a zero to one scale) as reactions to Justin Trudeau move from very negative to very positive. The impact of views of Erin O'Toole is similarly large, with the probability of casting a Conservative ballot climbing by 0.47 points on the zero to one scale as his image becomes increasingly positive. Leader image effects on NDP and PPC voting are smaller, but still nontrivial. In the NDP case, shifts from negative to positive in Jagmeet Singh's image produce a shift of 0.15 points in the likelihood of supporting the New Democrats. The equivalent effect of changing views of Maxime Bernier on a PPC vote is 0.28 points.

There is also evidence that judgments about party performance on important issues and party identifications mattered. As expected, the probability of supporting the Conservatives decreases by 0.06 to 0.20 points if a voter thought any other party was best on the issue deemed most important. Similarly, other things being equal, the probability of voting NDP climbs by 0.17 points (0.13- minus 0.04) if the New Democrats rather the Conservatives are judged best on an important issue. As for party identification, the likelihood of supporting the Liberals increases by 0.18 points (0.09- minus 0.09) if a voter is a Liberal rather than a NDP identifier. The Conservative story is similar with the probability of voting for that party moving upwards by 0.12 points if someone identifies with the Conservatives rather than the Liberals.

Table 14.1 also documents that some of the other predictors have significant effects, but most of them are modest in magnitude. For example, there is evidence that tactical voting was at work in 2021. The probability of voting for one of the two major parties increases among voters who said they took parties' competitive positions into consideration. Thus, the probability of voting Conservative increases by 0.08 points if someone is a tactical voter, with the comparable probability of voting Liberal rising by 0.07 points. Consonant with their weaker competitive status in many ridings, the likelihood of voting NDP falls 0.07 points among tactically-minded voters. In contrast to tactical considerations, there is little evidence that left-right ideological positions directly affected voting. Left-right ideology is significant only for Liberal voting, with the probability of casting a Liberal ballot falling by 0.07 points as ideological position is shifted from left to right.

In most instances socio-demographic variables failed to exert significant effects. An exception is income – other things being equal, people with higher incomes were somewhat more likely to vote Conservative and less likely to vote NDP. People in urban areas were less likely than those in rural areas to support the PPC, but the change in probability of doing so was only 0.03 points. The impact of region of residence is also very modest, although as one might anticipate, the likelihood of supporting the Liberals, Conservatives, or NDP is smaller in Quebec where the available choices are different than elsewhere because of the presence of the Bloc Québécois.

THE TWO SIDES OF PANDEMIC POLITICS

When making his case for calling the 2021 federal election, Prime Minister Trudeau claimed that he needed a fresh mandate to complete his government's battle against COVID-19. By the time the election was held, over a million and a half Canadians had contracted the disease and thousands had died from it. Despite these grim statistics, many people judged the Trudeau government's handling of the health crisis favourably – in the Abacus survey, 42 per cent said the government had done a "good" or "very good" job, compared to 30 per cent who said it had done a "bad" or "very bad" job. These numbers suggest that Trudeau's claim that he needed to rally public support to ensure that his battle against the pandemic would be successful might resonate positively with the electorate.

However, as previously mentioned, COVID had caused major shocks to the Canadian economy. When Trudeau called the election in mid-August, unemployment remained stubbornly high, the deficit had ballooned, and inflation had made the cost of living a major concern for millions of people. As we have seen, large numbers of Canadians designated some aspect of the economy as their most important issue. Recall that evaluations of the state of the economy and the government's performance in handling it were generally unfavourable. A solid majority (57 per cent) of the Abacus survey respondents said the economy was doing poorly and almost as many (54 per cent) judged the government's economic management negatively. These numbers meant that Trudeau and his colleagues would campaign for re-election in a context where a majority of voters were unhappy with government performance on a perennially major issue. Trudeau was gambling that the electorate would attribute the country's economic difficulties to the pandemic rather than his government's policies.

To investigate the impact of voters' judgments about government efforts to curtail the pandemic and its economic management, we employ a multivariate statistical model of Liberal voting where judgments about the likelihood that COVID would be brought under control over the next year and evaluations of the state of the economy are the featured predictor variables. Other predictors include party identification, left-right ideological orientations, and the several socio-demographic characteristics in the voting models discussed above.

We investigated how the probabilities of voting Liberal change as the "COVID under control" and economic evaluation variables are varied over their ranges with other predictors held at their average values. Both of these variables have statistically significant positive effects on the likelihood of a Liberal vote but the strength of these effects differs widely. In the case of controlling COVID, the probability of voting Liberal increases by only five points (from 0.31 to 0.36 on a zero to one scale) as judgments become increasingly positive. The impact of economic evaluations is much stronger, climbing by twenty-three points (from 0.23 to 0.46) as they move from negative to positive.

Given the impressively large impact of Trudeau's image on the likelihood of Liberal voting discussed above, we replicate this analysis substituting feelings about the prime minister for Liberal voting. Judgments about bringing COVID under control and economic conditions both have positive effects, but the latter are much greater. Varying COVID judgments from negative to positive increases the probability of positive feelings about Trudeau by twelve points (0.33 to 0.45). In comparison, varying evaluations of the state of the economy from negative to positive boosts the likelihood of having positive feelings about the Liberal leader by fully 0.47 points (0.19 to 0.66).

A similar pattern emerges if we consider choice of the Liberals as best on a voter's most important issue. These results (not shown in graphic form) reveal that the COVID control variable has significant effects and varying it from negative to positive enhances the likelihood of selecting the Liberals as best on most important issue by 0.08 points (0.26 to 0.34). The impact of economic evaluations is considerably stronger – varying judgments about economic conditions from negative to positive increases the likelihood of designating the Liberals best on most important issue by 0.21 points (from 0.20 to 0.41). Once again, the problem for the party was the low number of people who gave them high marks for the economy.

Taken together, these three analyses testify that Trudeau was mistaken if he thought that appraisals of the economy would not be a major factor driving how voters reacted to him and his government in 2021. Rather than concentrating narrowly on the consequences for public health of Liberal efforts to combat the pandemic, voters also were paying attention to the battered economy. Many of them were not pleased with what they saw. Their negative economic judgments drove down the probability that they would cast a Liberal ballot.

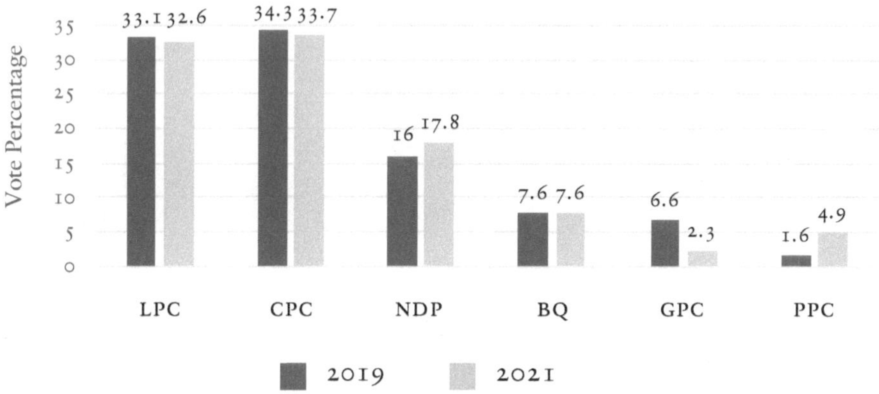

Figure 14.8 | Parties' vote shares in the 2019 and 2021 federal elections (Source: Elections Canada)

THE FLOW OF THE VOTE 2019–21

Parties' vote shares in the 2021 election were very similar to those in 2019. As Figure 14.8 illustrates, both the Liberals and the Conservatives captured slightly lower shares of the vote than they had two years earlier. The Liberal total fell from 33.1 per cent to 32.6 per cent and the Conservative total dropped from 34.3 per cent to 33.7 per cent. The Greens suffered larger losses, retreating from 6.6 per cent to only 2.3 per cent. In contrast, the NDP and the PPC saw their support climb by 1.8 per cent and 3.3 per cent respectively. The BQ stayed exactly where it had been, with 7.6 per cent of the national vote. In absolute terms, the average change for all six parties is only 1.8 per cent.

Aggregate stability in party support does not necessarily mean that the same people were voting for the same parties in the two elections. However, the Abacus survey data indicate that there was a high level of individual continuity from 2019 to 2021. Panel A of Table 14.2 indicates that fully 87.3 per cent of people voting Conservative in 2019 remained with the party two years later. Similarly, the Liberals, NDP, and BQ were supported by very large percentages of the same individuals who had voted for these parties in 2019. The Liberals' ability to retain the vote of over four-fifths of

Table 14.2 | The flow of the vote, 2019–21

A. Where the 2019 vote went in 2021 (%)

	2019 vote						
	LPC	CPC	NDP	GPC	BQ	PPC	Non-voter
2021 vote							
LPC	81.1	3.2	7.9	10.5	3.0	0.0	29.0
CPC	8.0	87.3	8.6	14.9	5.3	19.6	14.6
NDP	9.8	3.7	77.6	31.5	2.5	9,0	22.2
GPC	0.4	0.7	2.1	33.1	0.0	15.2	0.0
BQ	0.2	0.7	2.2	0.0	89.3	0.0	2.1
PPC	0.1	4.4	1.6	10.3	8.0	65.2	32.1

Note: Column percentages – number in each cell is percentage of column total

B. Combinations of voting in 2019 and 2021 as percentages of everyone voting in 2021

	2019 vote						
	LPC	CPC	NDP	GPC	BQ	PPC	Non-voter
2021 vote							
LPC	28.2	1.8	1.1	0.4	0.2	0.0	2.0
CPC	2.8	28.0	1.2	0.6	0.4	0.1	1.0
NDP	3.4	1.1	10.5	1.3	0.2	0.0	1.6
GPC	0.1	0.2	0.3	1.4	0.0	0.1	0.0
BQ	0.2	0.2	0.3	0.0	7.2	0.0	0.1
PPC	0.1	1.4	0.2	0.4	0.0	0.3	32.1

Note: cell percentages—number in each cell is percentage of everyone voting in 2021

those who had supported the party in 2019 contrasts with what had happened between 2015 and 2019. Across those two earlier elections, the Liberals held onto only slightly over three-fifths of those who had supported them four years earlier. Proportionately, the pattern for the Greens between 2019 and 2021 was even worse, with the party being abandoned by two-thirds of those who had voted for it two years earlier.

Panel A of Table 14.2 also informs us about where those abandoning their 2019 party went in 2021. The flow of the vote for the three largest parties was one of offsetting movement – 8.0 per cent of 2019 Liberals moved to the CPC and 9.8 per cent went to the NDP. Similarly, 3.2 per cent of 2019 Conservatives went to the Liberals, but 3.7 per cent opted for the NDP. Echoing these offsetting flows, 7.9 per cent of 2019 New Democrats moved to the Liberals and 8.6 per cent chose the Conservatives. In contrast, movement by erstwhile Green voters heavily favoured the NDP. As for 2019 nonvoters who chose to participate in 2021, nearly one-third opted for the PPC, nearly as many chose the Liberals, and just over one in five went NDP. Less than one in six of 2019 nonvoters supported the Conservatives in 2021.

Panel B of Table 14.2 shows the size of various groups supporting various parties in 2019 and 2021 as percentages of all those who voted in the latter election. The percentages who were stable Liberals or Conservatives are very similar, 28.2 per cent and 28.0 per cent, respectively. The cohort of stable NDP voters was much smaller at 10.5 per cent, and 7.5 per cent were stable BQ supporters. Less than one 2021 voter in fifty was either stable Green or stable PPC.

Panel B also indicates that the magnitude of most groups moving between parties was small and largely offsetting. For example, although 2.8 per cent of the active 2021 electorate were 2019 Liberals who went Conservative, 1.8 per cent were 2019 Conservatives who moved to the Liberals. Similarly, the Conservatives and the NDP exchanged just over 1 per cent of the 2021 electorate. The largest net gain occurred for moves between the Liberals and NDP, with 3.4 per cent of those voting in 2021 being 2019 Liberals who decided to go New Democrat. The percentage moving in the opposite direction was smaller, 1.1 per cent. Panel B also shows that the People's Party attracted previous nonvoters – 2.3 per cent of those who voted in 2021 did not cast a ballot in 2019 but opted for the PPC two years later.

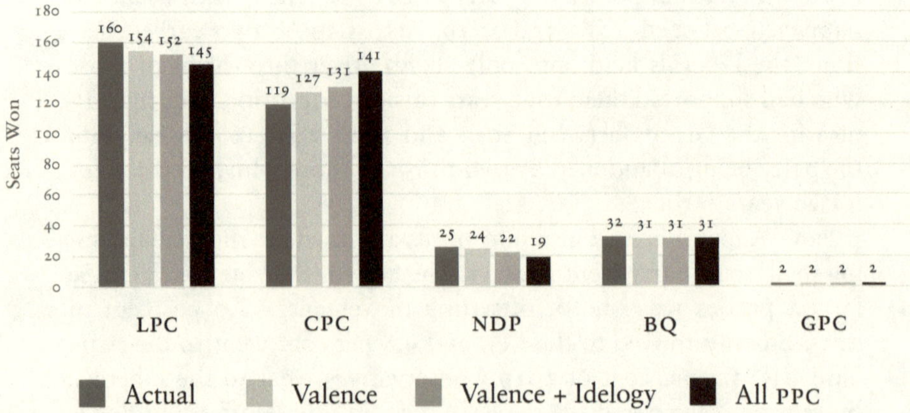

Figure 14.9 | How switching from the PPC to the CPC would have affected parties' seat shares in the 2021 federal election

Overall, the data in Table 14.2 testify to impressive levels of individual-level stability in voting choice from 2019 to 2021, indicative perhaps of the absence of significant shifts in party support between these two elections held close together. Altogether, of those participating in both elections, fully 81.3 per cent stayed with the same party. The PPC was the only party which benefitted substantially from shifts in support across the two elections. But, as we next discuss, the increase in PPC support was not sufficient to alter the 2021 election outcome.

HOW MUCH DID THE PEOPLE'S PARTY HURT THE CONSERVATIVES?

When the 2021 election outcome was announced, some observers speculated that the sizable increase in People's Party's vote – 4.9 per cent as compared to 1.6 per cent in 2019 cost the Conservatives some seats, thus raising the possibility that the PPC might even have stymied Conservative efforts to secure an election victory.[20] Is it the case that if all or even a large proportion of PPC supporters had opted for the Conservatives, they would have won more seats than the Liberals? If so, then a case can be made that the PPC played a key role in thwarting Conservative ambitions for power.

Elections Canada data on the riding-level results[21] in combination with the Abacus survey data enable us to investigate the impact of the PPC vote on the Conservatives' seat share. We consider three scenarios. In a first valence politics scenario, the Abacus data are employed to compute the percentage of PPC voters who either ranked Mr O'Toole ahead of his rival party leaders, or judged the Conservatives as best on most important issue, or identified themselves as Conservatives. This percentage of PPC voters, together with the percentage voting PPC in 2019, is reallocated to the Conservatives in each riding. As Figure 14.9 shows, the result is that the Liberal seat total falls modestly from 160 to 154 and the Conservative total climbs from 119 to 127.

The second scenario is identical to the first except that the percentage of PPC voters in the Abacus survey who place themselves on the right of the ideological spectrum is added to the valence politics percentage computed in scenario one.[22] The Liberal seat total decreases again, but only slightly to 152 with the Conservatives winning 131. In scenario three, we reallocate the entire PPC vote in each riding to the Conservative candidate. This reduces the Liberals to 145 seats, but the Conservatives still trail with 141. Thus, even if all PPC voters had redirected their support to the Conservatives, this would not have been enough to oust the Liberals from power. The conjecture that the PPC was responsible for the Conservative's 2021 defeat is not supported by the evidence.

CONCLUSION: COVID CANADA VOTES

In several respects, the 2021 federal election was an ordinary election held in extraordinary times. The COVID-19 crisis was an unprecedented intervention in the lives of Canadians. The pandemic was a grave public health emergency which had major impacts on Canada's economy and society. It had important political effects as well. Many voters judged the federal government positively for its handling of the crisis and this helped to boost support for the Liberals and Prime Minister Trudeau. However, many voters also reacted negatively to the economic dislocations caused by the pandemic. The result was that two issues with offsetting effects – COVID and the economy – dominated the political agenda in 2021. Although the presence of the COVID issue was novel, the prominence of the economy was typical of many earlier Canadian elections.

As also is typical of previous elections, the effects of voters' images of the party leaders played important roles. Much of the electorate was unenthusiastic about Prime Minster Trudeau and his principal rival, Conservative Leader Erin O'Toole. Both Trudeau and O'Toole were considerably less popular than NDP Leader Jagmeet Singh and voters rated both of them inferior to Singh on several leader image dimensions. Trudeau's unpopularity joined with negative appraisals of his government's handling of the economy as principal factors limiting Liberal support. In O'Toole's case, his unpopularity was accompanied by his party's failure to be judged positively on any major issue but the economy. And, although Singh was the most well received leader, the likelihood that voters would opt for the NDP was reduced by the party's lack of a sizable partisan base and its inability to convince voters that it could deal successfully with important issues.

The other two national parties, the Greens and the People's Party, were inhibited in multiple ways by unpopular leadership, lack of partisans, and negative appraisals of their issue competence. The Green vote, already meagre, fell sharply and only two Green MPs were elected. For its part, although the PPC managed to more than double its 2019 vote share, it again failed to elect a single MP. Also, the PPC acted as a spoiler to only a limited extent – the party's invigorated vote in 2021 was not responsible for the Conservatives' inability to win more seats than the Liberals.

In the end, the 2021 federal election produced vote and seat shares that were virtual carbon copies of those recorded two years earlier. The result was another Liberal minority government. Students of Canadian politics will recognize that this outcome is not unusual. Since the year 2000, there have been eight federal elections, and five of them have produced minority governments. Three of those five have been Liberal governments. Although the 2021 election was held in highly unusual circumstances, many of the major factors shaping the vote were familiar and worked in familiar ways. For Canadians of a certain age, the presence of a Trudeau-led government in Ottawa is eminently familiar as well.

NOTES

1 Amanda Coletta, "Canada's Trudeau Calls Snap Election in Bid to Regain Parliamentary Majority," *Washington Post*, 15 August 2021, www.washingtonpost.com/world/2021/08/15/canada-trudeau-election/.

2 We are pleased to thank David Coletto of Abacus Data for sharing this data with us. This dataset is also used in chapters 12, 13, and 15 of this book.

3 "It's the Economy, Stupid," Wikipedia, last modified 25 December 2021, en.wikipedia.org/wiki/It%s_the_economy_stupid.

4 See, for example, Michael S. Lewis-Beck, *Economics and Elections: The Major Western Democracies* (Ann Arbor, MI: University of Michigan Press, 1988). And, Raymond Duch and Randolph Stevenson, *The Economic Vote: How Political and Economic Institutions Condition Election Results* (Cambridge: Cambridge University Press, 2008).

5 Harold D. Clarke, Jane Jenson, Lawrence LeDuc, and Jon H. Pammett, *Absent Mandate: Strategies and Choices in Canadian Elections* (Toronto: University of Toronto Press, 2019); Harold D. Clarke, Allan Kornberg, and Thomas J. Scotto, *Making Political Choices: Canada and the United States* (Toronto: University of Toronto Press, 2009); and, Harold D. Clarke, David Sanders, Marianne C. Stewart, and Paul Whiteley, *Political Choice in Britain* (Oxford: Oxford University Press, 2004).

6 See, for example, Clarke, Jenson, LeDuc, and Pammett, *Absent Mandate – Strategies and Choices in Canadian Elections,* ch. 4.

7 Harold D. Clarke and Jon H. Pammett, "Environmental Issues in Recent British and Canadian Elections," *Journal of European and Russian Studies* 14 (2020): 102–8.

8 "Canada," Worldometer, last modified 31 January 2021, www.worldometers.info/coronavirus/country/Canada.

9 For time series data on the Canadian economy, see "FRED," Federal Reserve Bank of St Louis, https://fred.stlouisfed.org/.

10 "Canada – Consumer Confidence," Moody's Analytics, www.economy.com/canada/consumer-confidence. And, "Consumer Confidence Index," IBISWorld, last modified 19 January 2022, https://www.ibisworld.com/ca/bed/consumer-confidence-index/15004/.

11 On the importance of heuristics for making a wide variety of decisions, see Gerd Gigerenzer, *Rationality of Mortals: How People Cope with Uncertainty* (Oxford: Oxford University Press, 2008). On the use of party leader image and partisan heuristics inform electoral choice see Harold D. Clarke, Allan Kornberg, and Thomas J Scotto, *Making Political Choices*

(Toronto: University of Toronto Press, 2008), ch. 1; and, Harold D. Clarke, David Sanders, Marianne C. Stewart, and Paul F. Whiteley *Performance Politics and the British Voter* (Cambridge: Cambridge University Press, 2002), ch.2.

12 John Meisel, *Working Papers on Canadian Politics* (Montreal: McGill-Queen's University Press, 1973); and, Harold D. Clarke, Jane Jenson, Lawrence LeDuc, and Jon H. Pammett, *Political Choice in Canada* (Toronto: McGraw-Hill Ryerson, 1979).

13 See, for example, Clarke, Jenson, LeDuc, and Pammett, *Absent Mandate – Strategies and Choices in Canadian Elections.*

14 Angus Campbell, Warren E. Miller, Donald E. Stokes, and Phillip E. Converse, *The American Voter* (New York: John Wiley & Sons, 1960).

15 Clarke, Jenson, LeDuc, and Pammett, *Absent Mandate – Strategies and Choices in Canadian Elections,*ch. 2 – presents data on the weakness, inconsistency, and instability of partisanship. See also, Harold D. Clarke and Allan McCutcheon, "The Dynamics of Party Identification Reconsidered," *Public Opinion Quarterly* 73 (2009): 704–28.

16 See, for example, Clarke, Jenson, LeDuc, and Pammett, *Absent Mandate – Strategies and Choices in Canadian Elections,* ch. 7; and, Harold D. Clarke and Marianne C. Stewart, "From Sunny Ways to Cloudy Days: Voting in the 2019 Canadian Federal Election," in *The Canadian Federal Election of 2019*, eds., Jon H. Pammett and Christopher Dornan (Montreal: McGill-Queens' University Press, 2020).

17 J. Scott Long and Jeremy Freeze, *Regression Models for Categorical and Limited Dependent Variables* (College Station, TX: Stata Press, 2014).

18 Details concerning the measurement of various predictors are available from the authors upon request.

19 The McKelvey R^2 statistic is computed using Long and Freeze's Stata "FIT-STAT" module. The percentage of voters correctly classified is computed by cross tabulating whether a survey respondent reported voting for a party with whether they were predicted to vote for that party according to the analyses summarized in Table 14.1 Respondents with a probability of voting for a party greater than 0.5 is predicted to vote for the party in question.

20 Most analysts who expressed views on this topic judged the PPC effect on the Conservative seat share was real but limited. See, for example, Éric Grenier, "Who Is Voting for the PPC – and Will They Cost the Conservatives a Win?" The Writ, 14 September 2021, https://www.thewrit.ca/p/who-is-voting-for-the-ppc-and-will; and, John Paul Tasker, "Moving from Fringe to 4th Place, PPC Complicates the Conservatives' Path to

Power," CBC News, 14 September 2021, https://www.cbc.ca/news/politics/erin-otoole-maxime-bernier-peoples-party-1.6174014.

21 "Elections Canada," Elections Canada, last modified 22 January 2022, https://www.elections.ca/home.aspx.

22 The Abacus data shows that 55 per cent of the PPC and 51 per cent of CPC voters placed themselves on the right of the ideological spectrum. Voters for the other federal parties were far less likely to indicate that they were right of centre. The size of the right of centre groups among voters for the Liberals, NDP, Greens, and BQ are 9 per cent, 6 per cent, 22 per cent and 10 per cent, respectively. Overall, 31 per cent of the electorate placed themselves on left of centre ideologically, 44 per cent located themselves at the centre and 25 per cent said they were right of centre.

15

The Elusive Liberal Dynasty and the Continuation of Minority Government

Lawrence LeDuc and Jon H. Pammett

Coming out of the 2015 election, expectations for Justin Trudeau and the new Liberal majority government were high. Feelings toward the new prime minister were positive and slightly ahead of those toward his party. By the time of the 2019 election, those feelings had changed. Although one might have expected four years in government to have taken its toll, a number of incidents that reflected on Trudeau personally during his first term contributed to this decline. His shambles of a trip to India, the blackface scandal, and the handling of the SNC-Lavalin affair all played their part. The latter, which led to the resignation of two senior cabinet ministers, inflicted the greatest political damage, and its effects lingered on well into the 2019 election that reduced the Liberals to minority status. By the time of that election, feelings toward Justin Trudeau had turned more negative and, as measured by the thermometer scales included in the 2019 Canadian Election Study, were by then running several points behind feelings toward his party, which had also declined (Figure 15.1).

If it was primarily this decline in positive feelings toward Justin Trudeau and the Liberal Party that accounted for the loss of the Liberal majority in 2019, the period of minority government that followed provided little opportunity for recovery over the next two years. The onset of the pandemic consumed much of the government's attention and resources. But there was also further damage to Justin Trudeau's personal standing. The WE Charity scandal which involved potential family conflict of interest, like the SNC affair during the first term, lay largely at the leader's doorstep. And, like SNC, it also resulted in the resignation of a senior cabinet minister and generated effects that lingered for a considerable period of time. Concurrently, the impasse

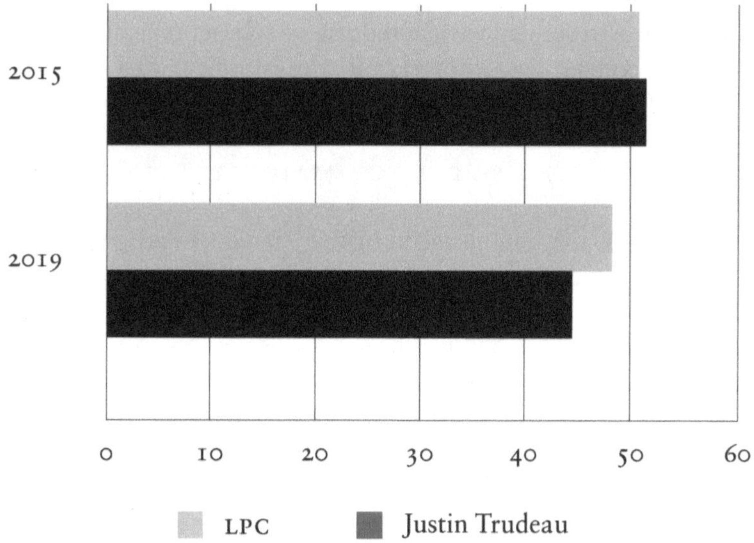

Figure 15.1 | Feelings towards Justin Trudeau and the Liberal Party (Source: CES Surveys. n [2015] = 3,892; n [2019] = 3,941)

Note: 100-point thermometer scale

brought about by the arrest of Huawei executive Meng Wanzhou on an American extradition warrant, and the subsequent lengthy retaliation initiated by the Chinese government, provided few opportunities for repair of an already tarnished image.

Given the circumstances confronting the minority Liberal government in the fall of 2021, it was a risky decision for the prime minister to call the election at that time. But, like mist from a winter breath, the clouds thrown up by minority election results can obscure the vision of Canadian government leaders. If the minority situation follows a previous change of government, the agenda is clear; some competent leadership and evidence of thwarted, popular, measures can form the basis of a new campaign to secure a majority. John Diefenbaker in 1958 famously pursued this course. However, if the minority outcome follows a previous majority, as in 2019, the path forward is much more uncertain. Is the public collectively saying that a renewed effort, correction of past mistakes, and a better governing record is needed to regain their favour? Or are the voters en route to desiring a new government altogether? But the determination of the Trudeau government to take the risk of an election call, purely in the hope of converting a stable minority government into a majority, seemed inevitable (chapter 2).

THE QUEST FOR MAJORITY

Only once in Canadian electoral history has a federal government won a majority of seats in parliament, been reduced to a minority in the following election, and come back to form another majority. That was the Liberal government led by Pierre Trudeau, who took the party to 155 of 264 seats in 1968, was reduced to a minority of 109 in the election of 1972, and came back to win 141 seats, another majority, in 1974. Justin Trudeau, born on Christmas Day in 1971, was probably too young to remember that rebound, but was not too young to remember his father's second comeback, from actual defeat in 1979, to yet another majority victory in the election of 1980. It is important to remember however, that the 1974 election came about as a result of the Trudeau government's defeat in parliament, following eighteen votes of confidence during that stormy parliamentary session.[1] Unlike 2021, the Trudeau government in 1974 could not be blamed for an ill-timed and opportunistic election call.

Pierre Trudeau was not the only prime minister to face a combined opposition majority in the House of Commons and feel the urge (and be urged by his advisers) to correct the situation. The Liberal government of Lester Pearson had come to office in 1963, defeating John Diefenbaker's Progressive Conservatives. This was a case in which the Liberals felt that they could easily gain the handful of seats necessary to turn their minority into a majority, following a two-year period of successful minority government. As it turned out, they did not, and the 1965 election produced a result almost identical with that of 1963. Elections like 1965 and 2021, in which the governing party sought a majority, and the election call was made entirely at their discretion, have historically not been successful.

The Liberals have not been the only governing party thwarted in their quest to turn a minority into a majority. In 2008, after two years as prime minister, Stephen Harper became dissatisfied with his minority situation. He felt that the opposition parties were weak, with new and untested leadership associated with unpopular policies, exemplified by Stephane Dion's proposal of a "green shift" of taxation to include carbon pricing. Harper saw his opportunity to ask for a dissolution of parliament and new elections, despite having previously passed legislation calling for fixed election dates. This search for majority status was, however, derailed by several unexpected developments, including a rapidly escalating economic crisis. Although the Harper Conservatives did improve their position in the 2008 election, the result of 143 seats fell short of a majority. And the parliamentary crisis that followed the 2008 election quickly put the second Harper minority government at risk of losing power to a coalition of opposition parties.[2]

The Conservatives were eventually able to turn their minority government into a majority in the election of 2011, as several conditions at that time were more favourable to them than had been the case in 2008. First, their administration had been defeated by the opposition in a combined vote in parliament, thus removing the stigma of opportunism from the election context. Second, the leadership of the Liberals under Michael Ignatieff was even weaker than it had been in the previous election, such that the eventual result propelled the NDP under Jack Layton past the Liberals to form the official opposition. Finally, the Harper Conservatives had eventually reacted to the economic crisis of 2008–09 with Canada's Economic Action Plan, a dramatic reversal of their previous positions regarding the need for decisive government measures to address the recession that followed.[3]

These were the precedents for Justin Trudeau as he took his minority government into the second session of the 43rd Parliament. The only instances where a sitting prime minister with a minority government had managed to turn this situation into a majority by requesting a dissolution of parliament even though the government had not been defeated in the House of Commons were those of John Diefenbaker in 1958, and Pierre Trudeau just after he took over from Lester Pearson in 1968. Both of these men were charismatic leaders with wide public popularity who had very recently come into power and could realistically reason that voters would want them to have a chance to govern for a period with a free hand. All other instances of deliberate seeking of majorities have ended in failure. For reasons which were not clear at the time, and that he was not able to adequately explain during the campaign, Justin Trudeau decided to initiate the 2021 election despite these omens from the past.

Table 15.1 | Percentages of total vote in four elections

	2021	2019	2015	1965
LPC	32.6	33.1	39.5	40.2
CPC	33.7	34.3	31.9	32.4
NDP	17.8	16.0	19.7	17.9
BQ	7.6	7.6	4.7	---
PPC	4.9	1.6	---	---
GPC	2.3	6.5	3.4	---
Social Credit*	---	---	---	8.3
All other	1.1	0.9	0.8	1.2

*Includes votes for Ralliement des Créditistes in Quebec. Data Source: Elections Canada [www.elections.ca]

STRATEGIC CONFIGURATION

The strategic configuration of Canadian electoral politics today facilitates minority government, as it has often done in the past. Five of the last seven federal elections have produced minority governments. In the last two of these (2019 and 2021) the party forming that government was not the party winning the most votes. While advocates of electoral reform have taken note of these anomalies, the prospect of electoral reform in Canada remains unlikely. The 2016 Special Committee, in its response to the Liberals 2015 electoral reform promise, made it clear in its report[4] that any acceptable reform would have to deliver at least a minimum degree of proportionality, thus ending Liberal hopes for the introduction of ranked ballots. Likewise, the current party system, while no longer the two-and-a-half party system of some years ago, nevertheless acts to make the attainment of parliamentary majorities ever more difficult. With five or more competitive parties across the country, votes, and often seats as well, are drained away from the two major competitors. With only 32.6 per cent of the total vote and 160 of the 338 House of Commons seats in 2021, the Liberals were well short of their majority objective, despite winning the election.

By strategic configuration, we mean the structure of the electoral system and party system, the interactions between them, and the strategies followed by both parties and voters as they operate within this complex institutional framework.[5] Writing in 1968, Alan Cairns took note of the effects that our single member plurality system (SMP) had in maintaining the structure of the party system, and in turn the effects of that party system on the practice of electoral politics in Canada.[6] The two larger parties, which are able to run effective national campaigns, are well served by this system, as Maurice Duverger demonstrated in developing his famous law noting the tendency of SMP electoral systems to sustain two party competition.[7] More often than not, one or both of the two major parties in Canada obtain a larger share of seats than their share of the vote would produce in more proportional systems. In the 2021 election, the Liberals obtained 47.3 per cent of the 338 seats – a share substantially larger than their 32.6 per cent share of the vote. And the Conservatives also obtained a higher proportion of seats – 35.2 per cent of the seats vs. 33.7 per cent of the vote. This pattern can be found in most federal elections. In 1965 for example, an election which bears some remarkable similarities to the most recent one (Table 15.1), the Liberals' 40.2 per cent of the vote yielded 49.4 per cent of the parliamentary seats. And the Progressive Conservative share of 32.4 per cent in that election also produced a seat bonus (36.6 per cent) for that party.

As Duverger would also have observed, our SMP electoral system disadvantages third parties, but it does not necessarily eliminate them. Since 1921, Canada has had at least one significant third party in every election, but its share of parliamentary seats is generally much smaller than its share of the vote would warrant under other electoral arrangements. In 2021, for example, the NDP's 17.8 per cent share of the national vote produced twenty-five seats (7.4 per cent) and in 1965 the NDP share of the vote (17.9 per cent) yielded twenty-one seats (7.9 per cent). As the modern history of Canadian federal elections repeatedly demonstrates, the NDP is nearly always disadvantaged in federal election outcomes. It is truly still a third party in the system, despite the rise of other competitors in recent years. Only by briefly becoming the second party in 2011 was the NDP able to obtain parliamentary representation (33.4 per cent) commensurate with its vote share (30.6 per cent).

The electoral disadvantage produced by SMP however does not apply to third parties that are able to concentrate their votes regionally, and these have likewise been an important part of Canadian electoral politics since 1921. In that election, the Progressives won sixty-four seats, mainly in the West, to become the second largest party in parliament. Their vote total of approximately 23 per cent[8] yielded 27 per cent of the 235 seats in parliament at that time, while Arthur Meighen's Conservatives elected only forty-nine members (20.8 per cent) on 30 per cent of the total popular vote. The Progressives continued to be a significant factor in the federal politics of that time through the next several elections, largely because their votes were heavily concentrated in the Prairie provinces, even in 1926 when Mackenzie King won his first majority government. In the 1926 election, King's Liberals obtained 128 of 245 seats (52.2 per cent) on 46 per cent of the popular vote, while the Progressives won twenty seats (8.2 per cent) despite garnering only 4 per cent of the vote nationally[9]

These historic patterns of advantage and disadvantage conferred on particular parties by the strategic configuration of Canadian federal politics continue into the elections of today. In the 2021 election, the Bloc Québécois elected thirty-two members (9.5 per cent of the total 338) despite the fact that its percentage of the national vote was only 7.6 per cent. This, of course, occurred because its votes are obtained only in Quebec. Other minor parties, such as the Greens and People's Party of Canada are, like the NDP, disadvantaged because their votes are spread nationally across the country. The Green Party obtained 2.3 per cent of the vote in the 2021 election but elected only two members. And the PPC elected no members of the House of Commons despite tripling its vote in 2021 to 4.9 per cent – more than double that of the Greens.

Our characterization of the strategic configuration of Canadian electoral politics in 2021 extends to the behaviour of both the political parties and their voters operating within this framework, in addition to the institutions themselves. Through long experience, the parties have learned that their electoral coalitions are fragile creations that require constant renewal from one election campaign to the next. They frame policy discussions around issues on which there is broad agreement (valence issues) and focus their campaigns on the party leaders, promising better performance rather than clear policy alternatives. For the Liberals, a successful strategy for moving from the minority outcome of 2019 to a majority would have involved winning over some of those who voted for the Bloc in 2019 and persuading enough NDP voters to vote strategically for them, as well as appealing to new voters. For the Conservatives, success would have involved cutting into weak Liberal support in key areas, such as the 905 area code region of Greater Toronto and the Atlantic provinces. Given the inherent volatility of Canadian electoral politics, both strategies were feasible. But both failed.

Voters in turn have learned that the political parties cannot be expected to offer real choices among policy alternatives and that elections are a convenient way to express their discontents, with few consequences for future policy directions. Because under SMP they have only a single vote for a local candidate, they can be tempted to vote strategically for another party or can easily be moved by short-term factors, including feelings toward the leaders. As is suggested by the movement of the polls across the thirty-six-day campaign (see chapter 7), other outcomes in 2021 were entirely plausible. We know that, even in elections in which there appears to be considerable stability, there is always the potential for volatility both in vote choice and election outcomes. The temptation to conclude that this was an election in which nothing happened because of its similarity to the Liberal minority outcome of 2019 should be firmly resisted.

(STILL) A CHANGING ELECTORATE

As we have argued elsewhere, voting turnout in Canada has been in a long-term pattern of decline since 1993, driven mainly by the forces of generational replacement.[10] As new generations of voters enter the electorate, either at lower rates or later in life, gradually replacing older generations who had typically voted at much higher rates, turnout declines (see also chapter 13). This long-term pattern of declining turnout has persisted in every federal election up until 2015, with the one exception of a modest increase in 2006 when the Harper minority government came to power.

After reaching a new historic low of 59 per cent in 2008, as shown in Figure 15.2, there was some evidence that the turnout decline might be beginning to reverse. But the sudden jump upward in 2015 to 68 per cent provided mixed signals. On the one hand, the long-term evidence suggested that turnout was beginning to settle at a level just above 60 per cent, and that a gradual reversal of the decline might begin to take hold as the process of generational replacement slowed. However, the

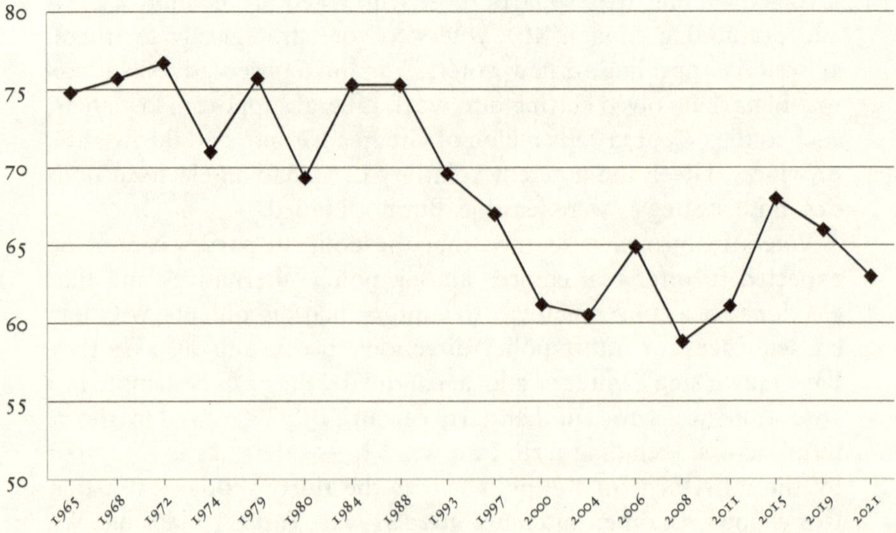

Figure 15.2 | Turnout (%) in Canadian federal elections, 1965–2021 (Source: Elections Canada)

unexpectedly large increase in 2015 further hinted that shorter term factors specifically associated with that election might also be at work. This was especially the case because the 2015 evidence suggested that higher voting rates among the youngest age cohorts accounted for a substantial amount of the increase in that election.[11]

Our analysis of turnout in the 2019 election indicated that both long-term and short-term factors were present. The decline in turnout to 66 per cent in that election suggested that the long-term patterns associated with the decline had not gone away. But the fact that much of the increase from 2015 remained in place indicated both that the long-term pattern of decline might be coming to an end and that the cohort of new voters who voted at higher rates in 2015 might subsequently remain in the electorate, perhaps developing a "habit of voting" that would carry through well into the future.[12]

The 2021 election provides some further evidence on both of these points. The overall decline from 66 per cent in 2019 to 63 per cent in 2021 strongly suggests that the long-term pattern of decline is not fully over. But as turnout in federal elections now appears to be settling into a range in the low 60s, there is clearly some evidence of

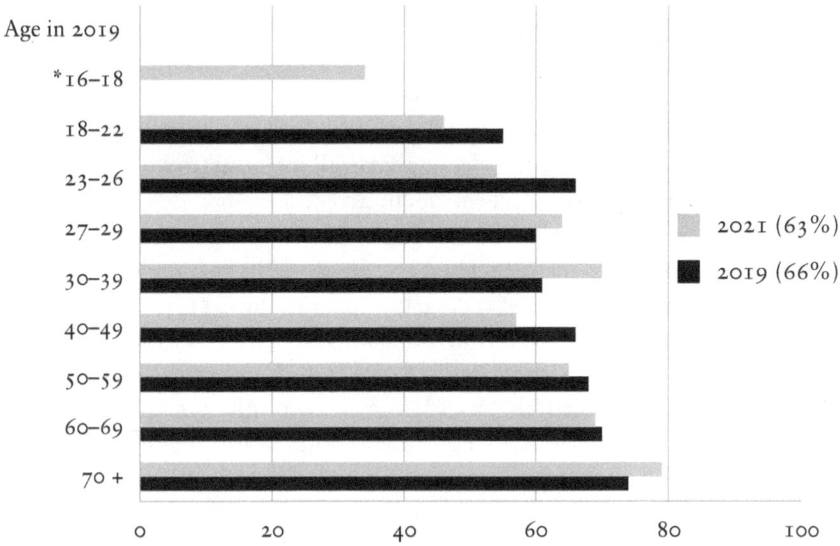

* Respondents aged 18 in 2019 but who reported that they were voting for the first time in 2021are included in this group.

Figure 15.3 | Estimated voting by age groups in the 2019 and 2021 federal elections (Source: Abacus Research Post-Election Surveys; data weighted by actual voting %: n [2019] = 1,517; [2021] = 2,000)

a bottoming process beginning to take hold. However, the 2021 data also indicate that not all of the voters who first entered the electorate in 2015 have remained active, although some have. Using data from Abacus post-election surveys conducted after the elections in both 2019 and 2021, it is possible to compare specific age groups from those two periods (Figure 15.3). To compare the cohorts, we lag the age groups by two years from 2019 to 2021, using age in 2019 as the basic measure. Those aged eighteen to twenty-two in 2019 are the cohort who voted for the first time in 2019, while the next older group (twenty-three to twenty-six) were also eligible to vote in 2015. For both of these groups, voting participation was lower in 2021 than in 2019, and the spread was widest for the twenty-three to twenty-six age group who had first been eligible to vote in the 2015 election that produced the Liberal majority.

Other patterns found in Figure 15.3 are more consistent with the longer-term generational interpretation. Voting rates among the two oldest age cohorts remain higher, as they have always been. And participation in the youngest group, eligible for the first time in 2021, appears to have been substantially lower.[13] Over time, patterns such as these will act to continue driving overall turnout lower unless other short-term factors intervene, as in 2015.

Some caution is warranted in both of these interpretations, largely because short-term factors are at work in most elections, and it is not always possible to clearly separate these from the longer-term trends. There were many reasons specifically associated with the 2021 election that might have acted to produce lower turnout. Beginning with the pandemic, it was always uncertain whether voters would decide to go to the polls in numbers comparable to previous elections. The pandemic also acted in some parts of the country, particularly urban areas, to reduce the number of available polling places, since many venues that had been used as polling locations in previous elections were deemed unsuitable in 2021 for public health reasons.

The timing of the election was also a factor. The 2021 election took place on 20 September, a date coincident with the beginning of the fall semester at most colleges and universities. Students moving to new residence locations often found the opportunity to vote in person severely constrained by this timing. Further, the short duration of the campaign meant that there was little time to arrange new polling locations. Shortly after the election call, Elections Canada announced that the Vote on Campus program, which in 2015 and 2019 had allowed students to vote on campus by special ballot directed to their home ridings would not be available in 2021.[14] These difficulties were however partially offset by advertising efforts designed to encourage voting at advance polls and by mail, and many voters both old and young took advantage of these arrangements. Slightly more than half of the Abacus respondents who voted reported that they voted in person on election day (53 per cent), while 38 per cent said that they voted in an advance poll. The remaining 9 per cent chose to vote by mail ballot. There was relatively little variation between the age groups with respect to the method of voting, although the older cohorts were somewhat more likely to have taken advantage of the advance polls. Surprisingly, given the challenges of organizing an election during a pandemic, 95 per cent of the respondents to the Abacus survey reported that the voting process went smoothly for them, and that they did not encounter problems.

(NOT) A NEW ELECTORAL MAP

It is certainly not unique to the Canadian federal election of 2021 that the regional distribution of party strength and voter support provide potential stumbling blocks to a political party seeking a majority government. We need only look back at the examples cited earlier in this chapter to observe the foundering of Liberal hopes in the West in 1965 and 2004–06, and the abortive Conservative plans for breakthroughs in Quebec in many elections, culminating in the fruitless quest for more seats in 2008. As noted earlier, the strategic configuration of Canadian party politics tends to encourage parties to concentrate on areas of regional strength and gives an electoral advantage to parties that are able to concentrate their votes. Thus, the Bloc has been successful in preserving its position in recent federal elections while parties such as the Greens have been unable to make a significant breakthrough.

The results of the federal election of 2019 brought with them a familiar pattern of seat distribution in the House of Commons. The Trudeau Liberals built their coalition from a base of seventy-nine of 121 seats in Ontario, thirty-five of seventy-eight in Quebec, and twenty-six of thrity-two in the Atlantic region. West of the Manitoba-Ontario border, the party only won fifteen seats, most of these in British Columbia. Party strategists looked at these results in comparison to those achieved in the victory of 2015 and saw that their support had dropped everywhere. In their earlier majority win, they had obtained not just most of the seats in the Atlantic region, but all of them. Their position in Quebec had weakened by 2019, largely because of the resurgence of the Bloc. The West, the leanest region for the Liberals in 2015, had been even weaker in 2019, with seat losses in Alberta, Saskatchewan, and BC. Even Ontario, the bedrock of previous Liberal support, had given them one seat less in 2019. Surely, they reasoned, there were places to pick up the seats needed, if not to equal the level of 2015, at least to regain majority status. The chapters in this book document the various ways in which the Liberals' majority quest failed, and why.

In many ways, this failure transcended Canadian regionalism. The overall Liberal plan, to appeal to public approval of the pandemic response, enhance social supports, and pledge to revive the economy, did not involve regional differentiation. But there was a regional dimension to the Canadian federal election of 2021, and that was the differential strength of the Liberal Party in the regions and the differential strength of the opposition parties that they faced in different parts of the country. The campaign in the Atlantic region was one where a relatively straightforward Liberal-Conservative battle could be fought. The election in Quebec, however, was quite different, as analysed in chapter 5 of this volume. In addition to some Conservative and NDP strength, the Liberals faced a strong opposition from the Bloc Québécois, and from the provincial government of the CAQ, determined to extract more commitments, financial and otherwise, for the province. And the more the Liberals agreed to such special Quebec benefits, the more difficult it became for the party to appeal to other regions as their benefactors as well. Gaining a few extra Quebec seats, a strategic element of the party's path to a 2021 majority, might come at a cost elsewhere.

The election in Ontario, another area where the Liberals hoped to pick up a few seats, took on a different complexion from the previous one. In 2019, the federal Liberals had based their campaign as an attack, not only against the federal Conservative Party led by Andrew Scheer, but also against the provincial Progressive Conservative Party led by Doug Ford, which had insisted on steering an unpopular rightist course following its election in 2018. During the pandemic, Ford had seized the opportunity to change course in several ways, abandoning some of his more controversial initiatives and concentrating on a strong pandemic response. He also virtually disappeared from public view during the election campaign and made no comments or endorsements of federal candidates.

The situation in Ontario had also changed from 2019 in another way. The new Conservative leader, Erin O'Toole, represented an Ontario constituency (Durham), marking a change in the image of the party. After its formation in 2003, the Conservative Party of Canada was led by two westerners, Stephen Harper and then Andrew Scheer. O'Toole differed from his predecessors in several ways. First, he was the first leader of the conservative parties taken broadly (including the Progressive Conservatives, Reform Party, and Canadian Alliance) to be an MP from Ontario since

George Drew, leader of the Progressive Conservatives from 1948 to 1956. In addition to being an Ontario MP, O'Toole, following his election as Conservative leader, adopted more moderate policy positions than his two immediate predecessors. As chapter 3 outlines, O'Toole had appeared to be more right wing during the party's leadership vote in order to win second choice support from supporters of the two social conservative opponents in the race. However, since the leadership win, O'Toole had taken pains to assert his support for same-sex marriage, gay rights, abortion, and other mainstream positions on social issues. He presided over the issuing of a new Conservative environmental policy which involved acceptance of carbon taxation. At the beginning of the campaign, Liberal attacks on O'Toole as being simply another version of Stephen Harper fell flat.

In contrast, the campaign in the West went slightly better for the Liberals in 2021, although not so well as to propel the party to majority victory by negating losses in other regions. In particular, the Liberals won two seats in Alberta, and went from eleven to fifteen in British Columbia, while retaining four seats in Manitoba. As a result of the election, the overall pattern of regional dispersion of seats in parliament actually looked slightly less regionalized than previously. The pattern of these victories shows that all of these seats came in the urban areas of Vancouver, Calgary, Edmonton, and Winnipeg. The urban nature of the Liberal appeal in the West is similar to the party's strength in other urban areas in the rest of the country, Toronto, and surrounding suburbs, Ottawa, Montreal, and Halifax. The Liberal concentration of support in the cities was enough in 2021 to win a minority but not a majority government. And of course, the ability of the Bloc to hold on to its seats in Quebec sealed their fate.

PERFORMANCE POLITICS

Despite the constraints presented by the regional concentrations of votes and the relatively low turnout, particularly among younger voters, the prospects of the Liberals in 2021 might have been better if the near-term performance of the minority Liberal government and its leader had been seen in a more positive light (see chapter 14). But, by the time of the 2021 election, feelings towards Justin Trudeau had turned more sharply negative than they were at the

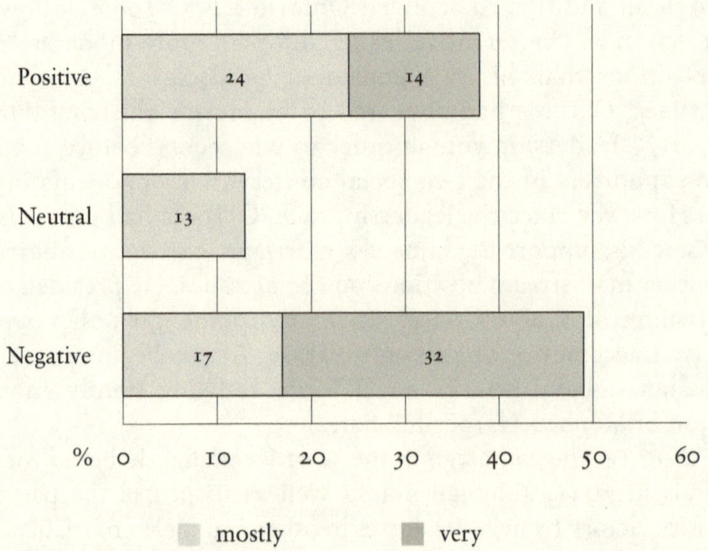

Figure 15.4 | Impressions of Justin Trudeau, 2021 (Source: Abacus Research 2021 Post-Election Survey; n=2000)

time of the 2019 election that produced the Liberal minority. As measured by the Abacus Research post-election survey, nearly a majority of respondents in 2021 held a negative overall impression of Justin Trudeau, with many of those reporting that their impressions were "very negative" (Figure 15.4). While there were still many who held a positive impression, a substantial number of these gave the more qualified response "mostly" positive. Few were neutral.

Campaign performance undoubtedly contributed to the ambivalence towards Trudeau felt by many Canadians going into the 2021 election. The stumbling start of the Liberal campaign and Trudeau's inability to explain the need for an election, together with weak and empty slogans ("Choosing Forward"), often made the Liberal campaign seem devoid of meaningful content. Events such as the leaders' debates gave the prime minister little chance to recover from these early missteps. The short duration of the campaign, which initially was thought to provide an advantage to the Liberals, had mostly the opposite effect. Attacks on the leader of the opposition failed

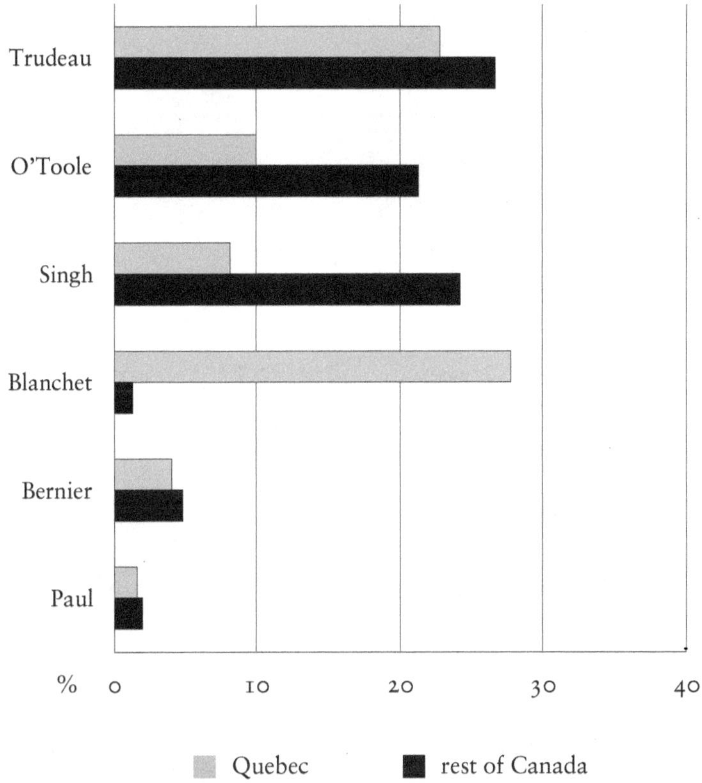

Figure 15.5 | Best performing leader in the election campaign (Source: Abacus Research 2021 Post-Election Survey; n=2,000. Includes non-response in percentages)

to resonate. While the prime minister retained a modest edge over his opponents in "campaign performance" (Figure 15.5), this proved insufficient in making up the lost ground. By the end of the campaign, Justin Trudeau's lead over Erin O'Toole as the leader "most preferred as the next prime minister" had diminished to only a few percentage points from the much wider spread recorded before the campaign began (Figure 15.6). As measured by this question, which is asked at regular intervals in the Nanos polls, it was almost entirely during the campaign period that Trudeau's early lead over his opponents diminished.

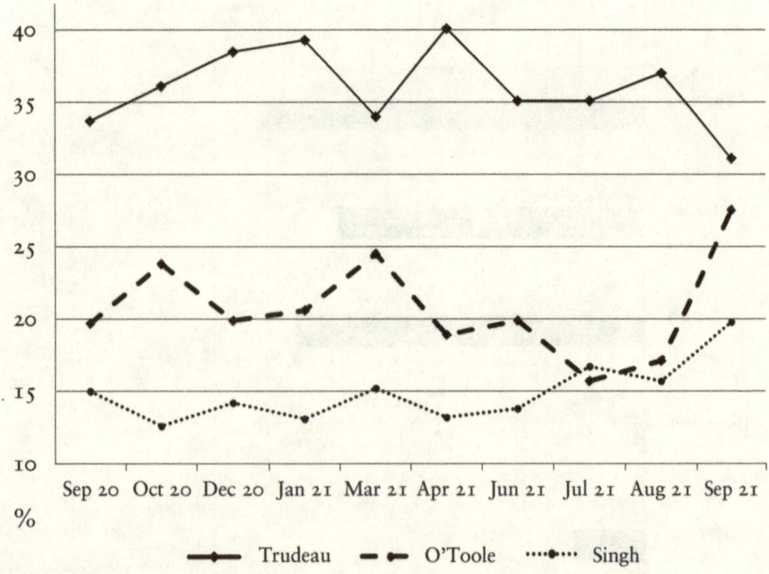

Figure 15.6 | Preferred prime minister (Source: Nanos Research)

It might be an overstatement to conclude that the 2021 election outcome was a referendum on Justin Trudeau. But, given the dominance of leaders in the world of Canadian federal politics, a conclusion along these lines is hard to avoid. A longer (and more substantial) campaign might have provided the opportunity to recover from the erosion of Trudeau's personal image over his six years in power. But if that opportunity was ever there, it was not seized. Historically, there are few political leaders who have been able to reverse a negative public image once it has become established. The weakness of the Liberal campaign, in which Justin Trudeau was entirely the central figure, produced only another minority. And, given the twists of the campaign, the Liberals may have been lucky to achieve even that.

THE FUTURE OF MINORITY GOVERNMENT

All during the 2021 election campaign, politicians, journalists, and many in the general public questioned whether the election was necessary. This strain of public comment only intensified after the inconclusive election result was in, to the point where some concluded that the election had not mattered at all.[15] We conclude, however, that the election was important. As we state in the first sentences of our book *Dynasties and Interludes*, "Elections are markers in a nation's political history. They provide occasions, both practical and symbolic, when a collective political decision is rendered by the citizenry."[16] This decision does not have to involve dramatic change, or even any change, to render it meaningful. The chapters in this book help us to unpack the meaning of the 2021 election.

Taking into account the consensus interpretation that the main goal of Justin Trudeau and his government in calling the election at this time was to obtain a majority of parliamentary seats (chapter 2), the collective decision means that there was insufficient support to produce this result. The narrow question was the degree to which voters approved of Trudeau and his party. The more general question is whether the factors which denied Trudeau a majority in 2021 are likely to inhibit the formation of any majority government in the foreseeable future, or whether a new political leader (or even one of the existing ones) could assemble enough votes in enough constituencies in the near future to produce a majority.

We have examined in this chapter three factors, aside from the personal qualities of the leaders themselves, which made the achievement of a Trudeau 2021 majority problematic. These were: the strategic configuration of the electoral and party systems; the vagaries of electoral turnout; and the impact of regionalism. Several of these factors regularly work together to make majority victories difficult to achieve. When the single-member plurality electoral system operates in combination with a multi-party system, in which party support is spread out among several parties competing for the support of the voter along a number of different issue dimensions, the ability of a single party to win a majority is difficult to engineer. In addition, the parties often have different degrees of regional strength; a party with a strong appeal in a region of limited size can make it difficult for a broad national party to pick up seats there, and a series of these situations can make it almost impossible. Finally, a low level of voting turnout will not usually provide the cadre of entrants to the voting mix (from both newly eligible and previous abstention) for a party to strongly boost its vote total and challenge for majority status.

All of these factors worked against the chances of the Trudeau Liberals forming a majority government in 2021. Turnout was down from 2019, a level which had already diminished from 2015, the last time a majority of seats went to a single party. In particular, a low turnout rate among the newly eligible eighteen- to twenty-year-old group illustrates that youthful enthusiasm for the Trudeau party was lacking. The regional results, while slightly less prominent than previously, showed that substantial gains were not available for the Liberals in the West and Quebec, two areas where they were counted on. The party system showed a new entrant into the multi-party mix, with the People's Party siphoning off voters from the Conservatives and from other parties as well. Of the factors working against Justin Trudeau, his own image was most important. Trudeau was simply not able to overcome a series of negatives which dampened enthusiasm, even among many of those who ended up voting Liberal.

What of the future, whenever a new election may come? It is not inconceivable that an elusive Trudeau majority could yet occur. This outcome would likely involve the Conservative Party falling victim to an opposition syndrome, whereby the leader is jettisoned and the party moves in the direction of extremists, in order to head off an evolving People's Party. It is possible that success in producing environmental policies to counter climate change, or action on issues such as reconciliation or inequality, which may have greater resonance for younger voters, could produce a more favourable public judgment on the governing record of the Liberals. Regional disparities in support might be overcome by an increasing urban-rural split in all areas. But it is equally plausible, if not more likely, that the majority will never come, and all of the factors mentioned above will simply accentuate division for the Liberals, and for the Conservatives as well. In each of the last six federal elections, the total popular vote for the winning party has been below 40 per cent. And, in 2021, the Liberal percentage (32.6 per cent) established a new historic low.

What seems particularly likely in any case is that the politics of discontent will continue, based on growing public disaffection with politicians of all stripes. This, as we have seen in many elections, is the product of the lack of ability of important issues to dominate elections so as to produce policy mandates for governments to move ahead with broad public support as manifested in patterns of voting behaviour. If environmental, health, and economic crises become more severe, and especially if they intersect with each other, there may be more unstable electoral times ahead. Or, alternatively, it may become necessary to abandon the quest for majority government entirely and either live with minority government or open the door to coalitions with the potential to offer both a broader base of public support and perhaps greater policy stability over the electoral cycle.[17]

NOTES

1 Lawrence LeDuc and Jon H. Pammett, *Dynasties and Interludes* (Toronto: Dundurn, 2016), 279.
2 Peter Russell and Lorne Sossin, eds., *Parliamentary Democracy in Crisis* (Toronto: University of Toronto Press, 2009).
3 Jon H. Pammett and Christopher Dornan, eds., *The Canadian Federal Election of 2011* (Toronto: Dundurn, 2011).
4 Special Committee on Electoral Reform, *Strengthening Democracy in Canada: Principles, Process and Public Engagement for Electoral Reform*, (Ottawa: House of Commons, 2016).
5 Harold D. Clarke, Jane Jenson, Lawrence LeDuc, and Jon H. Pammett, *Absent Mandate: Strategies and Choices in Canadian Elections* (Toronto: University of Toronto Press, 2019), chapter 1.
6 Alan Cairns, "The Electoral System and the Party System in Canada: 1921–65," *Canadian Journal of Political Science* 1 (1968): 55–80.
7 Maurice Duverger, *Political Parties* (London: Methuen, 1954).
8 Depending on how some independents and joint candidates are counted.
9 Again, these figures depend on how some joint candidacies (e.g., Liberal-Progressives) are tabulated.
10 Jon H. Pammett and Lawrence LeDuc, "Voting Turnout in 2019: The Long and the Short of It," in *The Canadian Federal Election of 2019*, eds. Jon H. Pammett and Christopher Dornan (Montreal: McGill-Queen's University Press, 2020), 246–64.
11 "Estimation of Voter Turnout by Age Group and Gender at the 2015 General Election," Elections Canada, last modified 27 August 2018, https://www.elections.ca/content.aspx?section=res&dir=rec/part/estim/42ge&document=p1&lang=e#a.
12 Jon H. Pammett and Lawrence LeDuc, "Voting Turnout in 2019: The Long and the Short of It," in *The Canadian Federal Election of 2019*, eds. Jon H. Pammett and Christopher Dornan (Montreal: McGill-Queen's University Press, 2020), 246–64.

13 Some caution is warranted in interpretation of the level of voting participation by this group in the 2021 election as the number of cases under age twenty at the time of the Abacus survey was smaller than that of other cohorts shown in Figure 15.3. However, it is clear from the patterns that voting participation was lower in 2021 among each of the three youngest age cohorts, indicating that participation by younger voters (including those who had previously voted in 2015) has not gone up.

14 "Vote on Campus Program," Elections Canada, last modified 9 December 2020, https://www.elections.ca/content.aspx?section=vot&dir=bkg&document=campu&lang=e.

15 Lori Turnbull, "What Election? Trudeau's Cabinet Shuffle Signals a Desire to Get Down to Business as Usual," *Globe and Mail*, 29 October 2021, A13.

16 Lawrence LeDuc and Jon H. Pammett, *Dynasties and Interludes* (Toronto: Dundurn, 2016), 279.

17 Peter Russell, *Two Cheers for Minority Government* (Toronto: Emond Montgomery, 2008).

APPENDIX

Results of the 2021 Canadian Federal Election

	Canada		*NL*		*PEI*		*NS*		*NB*		*QC*		*ON*		*MAN*		*SAS*		*ALB*		*BC*		*Terr*
	Seats	Votes	S	V	S	V	S	V	S	V	S	V	S	V	S	V	S	V	S	V	S	V	S
BQ	32	7.6									32	32.1											
CPC	119	33.7	1	32.5		31.6	3	29.5	4	33.6	10	18.7	37	34.9	7	39.2	14	59.1	30	55.4	13	33.1	
GPC	2	2.3				9.5		1.8		5.1		1.5	1	2.2		1.6		1.1		0.9	1	5.4	
LPC	160	32.6	6	47.8	4	46.2	8	42.4	6	42.5	35	33.7	78	39.3	4	28.0		10.6	2	15.4	15	26.9	2
NDP	25	17.8		17.3		9.2		22.1		11.9	1	9.8	6	17.9	3	23.0		21.1	2	19.1	13	29.3	1
PPC	0	4.9		2.4		3.3		4.0		6.1		2.7		5.4		7.6		6.6		7.3		4.9	
Oth		0.8				0.2		0.2		0.9		1.5		0.2		0.7		1.5		1.7		0.4	
Total	338	100%	7		4		11		10		78		121		14		14		34		42		3

(Source: Elections Canada Official Results)

Contributors

ANEURIN BOSLEY is an assistant professor in the School of Journalism and Communication at Carleton University in Ottawa, Canada. He joined Carleton after fourteen years as an editor at the *Toronto Star*. He has a Master of Journalism from Carleton and a Master of Arts in philosophy from the University of Ottawa. Before joining the *Toronto Star*, he was the editor of *The Internet Business Journal* and a technology columnist on CBC Radio One in Ottawa. He was also writer and co-producer for Paul Kane Interactive, a digital exhibit that was installed at the Royal Ontario Museum in Toronto. His recent published work examines innovation in Canadian media work.

HAROLD D. CLARKE, who died in January 2022, was Ashbel Smith Professor at the University of Texas at Dallas. He served as editor of *Electoral Studies* and *Political Research Quarterly* and as director of social and economic sciences at the National Science Foundation. He was a world recognized scholar on comparative elections, and published in virtually all of the well-known journals in political science. He was co-author of many books, including *Political Choice in Canada; Absent Mandate: Strategies and Choices in Canadian Elections; Brexit: Why Britain Voted to Leave the European Union;* and *Austerity and Political Choice in Britain.*

DAVID COLETTO is the founder and CEO of Canadian polling firm Abacus Data and an adjunct professor at the Arthur Kroeger College of Public Affairs at Carleton University. He has conducted public opinion research during seven Canadian federal elections, twenty-eight provincial elections, and eight municipal elections. He has also spent the last twelve years exploring the impact of generational and technological change on political behaviour, workplaces, and the consumer market. He earned his PhD in political science from the University of Calgary.

CHADWICK COWIE is a PhD candidate at the University of Alberta, a course lecturer at McGill University, and an incoming assistant professor at the University of Toronto Scarborough (UTSC). Chad is from the Michi Saagiig Nishnaabeg community of Pamitaashkodeyong (also referred to as Hiawatha First Nation). His areas of focus include Indigenous, Canadian, and comparative politics with interest in Indigenous governance, Indigenous participation in settler-electoral structures, elections and voting, federalism, Canadian and Indigenous relations, as well as provincial and Indigenous relations.

CHRISTOPHER DORNAN taught at Carleton University for thirty-three years, where he served for nine years as director of the School of Journalism and Communication and six years as director of the Arthur Kroeger College of Public Affairs. This is the eighth volume of the Canadian Federal Election series studies he has co-edited with Jon Pammett. His most recent work (for the Canadian Commission for UNESCO, the Canadian Committee for World Press Freedom, and the Public Policy Forum) addresses the state of the Canadian news media, disinformation, and the COVID pandemic.

NANA ABA DUNCAN is an associate professor and Carty Chair in Journalism, Diversity, and Inclusion at Carleton University's School of Journalism and Communication. Her research interests lie at the intersection of journalism, race, and leadership. She is currently pursuing a project that looks at the relationship between Black people in Canada and journalism. Previous to her role at Carleton, Nana aba was a host and producer at CBC Radio for fifteen years, where she was the founding co-chair of the corporation's employee resource group for racialized employees. Nana aba is also the cofounder of Media Girlfriends, a podcast production company that supports more perspectives in news media.

FARON ELLIS is an Alberta-based political scientist specializing in party politics, elections, and public opinion. His research into conservative politics includes *The Limits of Participation: Members and Leaders in Canada's Reform Party* (University of Calgary Press, 2005); various contributions to the *Crosscurrents: Contemporary Political Issues* series; contributions to the *Party Politics in Canada* series; and ten contributions to this book series. He earned his PhD and BA from the University of Calgary, and his MA from Carleton University.

SARAH EVERTS is the CTV Chair in Digital Science Journalism and an associate professor in the School of Journalism and Communication at Carleton University. Prior to joining Carleton's faculty in 2019, she spent over a decade in Berlin, Germany covering science and policy for a variety of media organizations, including Scientific American, New Scientist, Smithsonian, and Chemical and Engineering News. This is her second contribution to the Canadian Federal Election series.

ÉRIC GRENIER is a writer and political analyst who publishes the election-focused website TheWrit.ca. He was the Canadian Broadcasting Corporation's polls analyst and a member of the CBC's parliamentary bureau in Ottawa from 2014 to 2021. He has covered provincial and federal elections for over a decade with a focus on public opinion polling. He was the founder of ThreeHundredEight.com and before working at the CBC he wrote for *The Globe and Mail, The Huffington Post Canada, The Hill Times, Le Devoir* and *L'actualité*.

SUSAN HARADA is an associate professor with the School of Journalism and Communication at Carleton University. A former national parliamentary correspondent for the CBC, she has written about the Green Party of Canada for every edition of the Canadian Federal Election series since 2004. She profiled the Greens' then-leader Elizabeth May for The Walrus in 2012.

BROOKE JEFFREY is professor of political science at Concordia University, where she served for many years as director of the Graduate Program in Public Administration and Public Policy, and is currently president of the Canadian Association of Programs in Public Administration (CAPPA). A former senior Liberal adviser, she is the author of six books on Canadian politics including *Divided Loyalties: The Liberal Party of Canada 1984–2006* (2010) and *Road to Redemption: The Liberal Party of Canada 2006–2019* (2021), both published by University of Toronto Press.

LAWRENCE LEDUC is Professor Emeritus of Political Science at the University of Toronto. His publications include *Absent Mandate: Strategies and Choices in Canadian Elections* (with Harold D. Clarke, Jane Jenson, and Jon H. Pammett), *Comparing Democracies* (with Richard G. Niemi and Pippa Norris), *Dynasties and Interludes: Past and Present in Canadian Electoral Politics* (with Jon H. Pammett, Judith I. McKenzie, and André Turcotte), and *The Politics of Direct Democracy* as well as articles on voting, elections, and related topics in North American and European political science journals. In 2015, Professor LeDuc received the Mildred A. Schwartz lifetime achievement award from the Canadian politics section of the American Political Science Association.

ANDREW J.A. MATTAN is a doctoral candidate in the Department of Political Science at Carleton University. His research interests are parties, elections, and digital politics. He was the runner up in the Three Minute Thesis competition at the 2019 annual meeting of the Canadian Political Science Association. His work has been published in the *American Review of Canadian Studies* and the *Canadian Journal of Political Science*.

DAVID MCGRANE is currently professor of political studies at St Thomas More College at the University of Saskatchewan. His research interests include social democracy, political parties, political marketing, elections, and voter behaviour. He has published almost forty academic books, journal articles, and book chapters. His latest book is *The New NDP: Moderation, Modernization, and Political Marketing* (University of British Columbia Press, 2019), which won the Donald Smiley Prize awarded by the Canadian Political Science Association to the best book on Canadian government and politics.

LIAM MIDZAIN-GOBIN is an assistant professor in the Department of Political Science at Brock University. He is a settler scholar whose research focuses on the production and continual remaking of settler coloniality, and Indigenous governance practices, studying Indigenous-settler relationships as a form of international politics. His research has been published in *Millennium: Journal of*

International Studies, *Ethnic and Racial Studies*, *Critical Studies on Security*, and elsewhere.

ÉRIC MONTIGNY is a professor in the Department of Political Science at Université Laval. Director of master and doctoral programs, he teaches courses on Canadian and Quebec politics, nationalism and populism, governance, and political parties. He is Scientific Director of the Research Chair on Democracy and Parliamentary Institutions and a research associate of the Groupe de recherche en communication politique. He is also on the editorial board of the *International Journal of Comparative Politics*. His most recent work on data-driven campaigning was published in *Internet Policy Review* and his work on generational support for Quebec independence in *French Politics*. He has also co-edited a special issue of the journal *Politique et Sociétés* for the 50th anniversary of the Parti Québécois.

JON H. PAMMETT is Distinguished Research Professor in political science at Carleton University. His research has been concentrated in the fields of voting behaviour, political participation, and electronic voting. He is co-author of *Dynasties and Interludes: Past and Present in Canadian Electoral Politics* (Dundurn, 2016, with Lawrence LeDuc) and *Absent Mandate: Strategies and Choices in Canadian Elections* (University of Toronto Press, 2019, with Harold Clarke, Jane Jenson, and Lawrence LeDuc). He has co-edited and contributed to the Canadian Federal Election series since 1988.

BRETT POPPLEWELL is a journalist and journalism professor at Carleton University. His writing has appeared in *The Best American Sports Writing, Bloomberg Businessweek*, *Mother Jones*, *The Globe and Mail*, *Toronto Star*, *Maclean's*, *The Walrus*, *Toronto Life,* and more. He is co-author of *The Escapist: How One Man Cheated Death on the World's Highest Mountains* (HarperCollins 2016). His second book with HarperCollins is slated for publication in 2023.

THOMAS J. SCOTTO is professor of politics and dean of learning and teaching at the University of Glasgow. He publishes in the areas of voting behaviour and public opinion on matters of foreign policy. He co-authored *Making Political Choices: Canada and the United States* (University of Toronto Press, 2009) and co-edited *The Canadian Election Studies: Assessing Four Decades of*

Influence (University of British Columbia Press, 2012). His articles on Canadian politics and foreign policy attitudes appear in *The Australian Journal of International Affairs*, *PS: Political Science and Politics*, *Canadian Foreign Policy*, and *Electoral Studies*.

TAMARA A. SMALL is a leading expert in Canadian politics with a particular research focus on digital politics – the impact and use of digital technologies by Canadian political actors. She is the co-author of *Fighting for Votes: Parties, the Media and Voters in an Ontario Election* (University of British Columbia Press), the co-editor of *Digital Politics in Canada: Promises and Realities* (University of Toronto Press), *Political Communication in Canada: Meet the Press, Tweet the Rest* (University of British Columbia Press), and *Mind the Gaps: Canadian Perspectives on Gender and Politics* (Fernwood Press). She held a Fulbright Visiting Research Chair at Vanderbilt University (Nashville, Tennessee) in 2018. She is a full professor in the Department of Political Science at the University of Guelph.

MARIANNE C. STEWART is professor in the School of Economic, Political, and Policy Sciences at the University of Texas at Dallas. She has been editor of the *American Journal of Political Science*, and political science program director at the National Science Foundation. Her articles have been published in the *American Political Science Review, Political Analysis,* and many other journals. Her recent books (with colleagues) have included *Affluence, Austerity and Electoral Change in Britain*, and *Get Brexit Done! How Britain Left the European Union.*

ERIN TOLLEY is the Canada Research Chair in Gender, Race, and Inclusive Politics and associate professor of political science at Carleton University. She is an expert on the relationship between socio-demographic diversity and Canadian politics, with a specific interest in race, gender, and representation in political institutions. She is the author of the award-winning book, *Framed: Media and the Coverage of Race in Canadian Politics* (2016) and the co-editor of seven books, including *Women, Power, and Political Representation* (2021). She was previously a researcher and policy analyst in the Canadian civil service and a faculty member at the University of Toronto.

STEPHEN WHITE is associate professor of political science at Carleton University. His areas of teaching and research include public opinion and political behaviour, focusing mainly on the political engagement of foreign-born Canadians and Canadian attitudes toward immigration and diversity. His work has appeared in *Political Behavior*, *Political Research Quarterly*, *Publius: The Journal of Federalism*, and the *Canadian Journal of Political Science*. He is the co-editor of *Comparing Canada: Methods and Perspectives on Canadian Politics* (University of British Columbia Press, 2014).

www.ingramcontent.com/pod-product-compliance
Lightning Source LLC
LaVergne TN
LVHW041357090826
845264LV00023B/176
* 9 7 8 0 2 2 8 0 1 3 8 2 2 *